Heard on The Street:
Quantitative Questions from Wall Street Job Interviews

Heard on The Street:
Quantitative Questions from Wall Street Job Interviews

Timothy Falcon Crack

PhD (MIT), MCom, PGDipCom, BSc (HONS 1st Class), IMC

Published by:
Timothy Falcon Crack, P.O. Box 6385, Dunedin North, Dunedin 9059, New Zealand

First published 1995 (three editions). Revised 1997, 1998, 1999, 2000, 2002, 2004, 2007, 2008, 2009, 2009 (revised eBook edition), 2012, 2013, 2014, 2015, 2016, 2017, July 2018 (19th Edition), September 2018 (19th Edition, corrected), November 2018 (Kindle version of corrected 19th Edition), October 2019 (20th Edition), October 2019 (20th Edition Kindle version), August 2020 (21st Edition; 21st Edition Kindle version), August 2021 (22nd Edition; 22nd Edition Kindle version).

ISBN: 978-1-99-115541-2

Question: Is the ISBN of the hard copy previous 21st edition (i.e., $N = 9780995117341$) a prime number? What about the ISBN of the hard copy 20th edition (i.e., $N = 9780995117389$)? What is the quickest way, available at your fingertips right now, to answer these questions? How would you have answered these questions 50 years ago? What about 100 years ago? What characteristics will tell you immediately if N is not a prime number (e.g., $N > 2$ and N divisible by 2)? Look up "prime numbers" in the index to find several interview questions referring to them.

Typeset by the author.
www.InvestmentBankingJobInterviews.com
timcrack@alum.mit.edu

Contents

CONTENTS

Preface

THIS BOOK IS A MUST READ! It is the first and the original book of quantitative questions from finance job interviews. Painstakingly revised over 26 years and 22 editions, *Heard on The Street* has been shaped by feedback from hundreds of readers. With well over 60,000 copies in print, it is unmatched by any competing finance job interview book.

This revised 22nd edition contains 239 quantitative questions collected from actual job interviews in investment banking, investment management, and options trading. The interviewers use the same questions year-after-year, and here they are—with solutions! These questions come from all types of interviews (traditional corporate finance, sales and trading, quant research, etc.). The questions come from all levels of interviews (undergraduate, MBA, MS, PhD). This edition also includes 264 non-quantitative actual interview questions, giving a total of more than 500 actual finance job interview questions. There is also a section on interview technique—based on my experiences interviewing candidates for the world's largest institutional asset manager, and also based on feedback from interviewers worldwide.

This book bridges the considerable gap between the typical finance education and the knowledge required to successfully answer quantitative finance job interview questions. The considerable gap arises because Wall Street interviewers must separate the "wolves" from the "sheep." The sheep are confined by the boundaries of their education; the wolves are not. The interview questions reach beyond these boundaries in order to separate the two classes of interviewees. Hence the gap. Of course, most interviewers are wolves. Unfortunately, many interviewees are sheep. The butchering that takes place has been described to me as "horrific." That is why you need this book.

I bridge the above-mentioned gap by presenting quantitative questions from actual finance job interviews. My solutions and advice are carefully designed to sharpen your quantitative skills. My advice is based on my experiences as a frontline teaching assistant for MBA students at MIT, as a finance professor at Indiana University, and as the former head of a quant research team for the world's largest institutional asset manager.

My intended audience includes interviewees (wolves and sheep alike) seeking employment at Wall Street or other finance-related firms; their interviewers, who need to weed out the hapless sheep; university professors who want to "spice up" finance courses with Wall Street job interview questions (both for fun and to show the importance of the basic concepts on The Street); students of finance who want to fill in some gaps; and finally, doctoral students in need of entertainment during periods of downtime.

Many of the questions collected and presented here are "classics" that appear year-after-year without fail. However, this book is definitely not for people who just want "The Answers" to such questions. Such people are the archetypal sheep in wolves' clothing, and they are quickly identified as such in an interview. To benefit from this book, you must make a serious investment of your time.

I thank MIT students, MIT faculty, and practitioners who supplied me with information. I thank Olivier Ledoit, Cecily Lown, Bingjian Ni, Eva Porro, and Juan Tenorio for their constructive criticism. The first edition of this book was written and edited in 1995 while commuting to and from MIT on the subways and buses of the Massachusetts Bay Transit Authority ("Thank you for riding... ...the MBTA").

TFC/MIT/1995

I revised this book while working as a professor at Indiana University (IU). I now also thank Sean Curry and The MathWorks Inc for a free copy of MATLAB (used to check answers and draw figures), MBA Style Magazine (`www.mbastyle.com`) for horror stories, Andres Almazan, Tom Arnold, Mary Chris Bates, Klara Buff, Alex Butler, Victor W. Goodman, Tim Hoel, Taras Klymchuk, Victor H. Lin, Marianne Lown, Alan J. Marcus, David Maslen, Marc Rakotomalala, Jason Roth, Yi Shen, Valeri Smelyansky, Dahn Tamir, Paul Turner, and students (MBA and undergraduate) at each of MIT, UCLA, and IU.

TFC/IU/1996–2000

I updated this book while working as Head of Quantitative Active Equity Research (UK/Europe) at the world's largest institutional asset manager. I also thank Jinpeng Chang, Mark Rubinstein, Alex Vigodner, and Nick Vivian.

TFC/London/2001–2003

I updated this book as a Professor Emeritus of Finance in N.Z. I wish to give a special thank you to Paul Bilokon and the Thalesians (`www.thalesians.com`). I now also thank Giulio Agostini, David Alexander, Armen Anjargholi, Arta Babaee, Grahame Bennett, Todor Bonchev, Henri Bourdeau, Edward Boyce, HC, Adrien Brandejsky, Mark Cawston, Veeken Chaglassian, Yiannis Chardaloupas, Scott Chaput, Aidong Chen, Dongkyu Choi, Jun Chung, Nate Coehlo, Richard Corns, Malcolm A. Crack, Patrick de Man, Alessio Farhadi, Rachel Gillett, Robin Grieves, Joseph Guirguis, James Gwinnutt, Charles Hallion, Chris Hallquist, Chun Han, Eoin Healy, James Hirschorn, Alexander Joura, Philip Koop, NK, Josh Lavey, Mr. Lee, Steve Lee, Vince Moshkevich, Cedrick Ngalande, Thomas Oliveira, Stuart O'Neill, RBP, Ari Pakman, Katie Price, Wolfgang Prymas, Bryan Rasmussen, Adam Rej, CCS, Naoki Sato, Ashish Saxena, Tommaso Sechi, Torsten Schöneborn, Adam Schwartz, Avishalom Shalit, Yirong Shen, Ian Short, Craig Smith, Sudheer Naidu D, Olaf Torne, Mikhail Voropaev, Thomas C. Watson, Simon West, Jabran Zahid, and Li-fan Zeng.

TFC/N.Z./2004–2021

Tables

List of Figures

Introduction

This book first appeared in 1995 with questions collected from MIT students after interviews. Twenty-six years on, in 2021, the interviewers at top firms frequently send me their new questions directly! For example, one interviewer at a big-name New York investment bank sent me the bank's latest full written quantitative interview test with three dozen questions (and answers)! A European banking contact sent me 40 quantitative questions and 20 non-quantitative questions from a bulge-bracket bank's interviews. A top UK quant recently sent me 50 quant interview questions he uses, most with suggested answers, plus a handful of pointed non-quant questions.

Why do interviewers and other contacts at top firms give me their interview questions to put in a book to sell to their job candidates? It is because the job candidates who make a serious investment of time in studying the questions and answers are signaling that they deserve to be hired!

All of the quantitative questions are accompanied by detailed solutions. The questions are split into four categories: Purely Quantitative and Logic, Derivatives, Other Financial Economics, and Statistics (Chapters 1, 2, 3, and 4, respectively). The solutions appear in Appendices A, B, C, and D, respectively. Chapter 5 presents non-quantitative questions from actual interviews (with selected solutions in Appendix E). In the text, a name followed by a year (e.g., "Girsanov [1960]") refers to a work cited in the References (following the appendices).

Questions that appeared in, or are likely to appear in, **traditional corporate finance job** interviews are indicated with a bank (🏛) or half-bank (🏛) symbol in the margin, respectively (71 of the quant questions and 192 of the non-quant questions). This makes it easier for corporate finance interviewees to go directly to the questions most relevant to them. Most of these questions also appeared in capital markets interviews and quant interviews. So, the marked questions should *not* be skipped over by capital markets or quant candidates unless they are obviously irrelevant.

If you are interviewing for **options jobs** and you need a review book to complement the interview questions here, then you should buy my book *Basic Black-Scholes*, Crack (2021). See the advertisement at the end of this book for details, or go directly to www.BasicBlackScholes.com. *Basic Black-Scholes* started its life as an extended appendix to this book, but it was carved out as a book in its own right, and has been revised many times. Its original aim was to help interview candidates. So, the writing style should be well suited to your interview preparation.

Questions in This Book

The questions in this book were collected by me from interviewees, interviewers, and others. I have taken the liberty of rewording them for maximum clarity because, unlike in an interview, you have no immediate opportunity to ask me for clarification. Sometimes I give only part of a question that was asked; sometimes I combine related questions into a larger one. I remain faithful to the original problem statement wherever possible.

I sometimes add a footnote to a question. The footnote contains a slight variation on the question. Unless otherwise indicated, these "footnote questions" are made up by me and are not actual job interview questions. All other questions come from actual job interviews (even the "condom question").

Many of the questions require a serious investment of your time. Knowing the answer is not enough in and of itself. Interviewees should attempt as many of these questions as possible without peeking at the answers. Mastering the problem-solving process gets you the job. This may mean spending hours, or days, with a problem before you master it. Although my answers often provide guidance in technique, I think that the path of greatest resistance (i.e., not peeking at the answers) bears the highest rewards!

Interviewers can use these questions as they stand. However, I strongly encourage you to push candidates very hard for the underlying understanding. Ask them to explain the answer, not to simply solve the problem. This differentiates those who understand the problem from those who merely know the answer. The good ones meet the challenge; the bad ones do not. Many people can solve problems, but only the best genuinely understand what they are doing.

Will the questions in this book become obsolete or dated? The answer is no, for two reasons: First, many of the questions are "classics" that appear consistently year-after-year; and second, the body of quantitative skills required to solve these questions has remained unchanged for three decades. Even if some of the questions change, the skills required to solve them do not. It is these skills that my book promotes. For these reasons, it follows that these questions are genuinely timeless.[1]

Sometimes the classification of a question (and, therefore, the chapter it should be in) is by no means clear. For example, some of the financial economics questions look like statistics questions, and I have placed questions on stochastic calculus in the derivatives chapter instead of the statistics chapter.

Some questions have more than one solution technique. The "right answer" may be the wrong answer if you use a "brute-force" approach and completely miss an elegant alternative (I often give both techniques).

Some questions are more difficult than others. I have labeled difficult questions with two stars "(**)" and very difficult questions with three stars "(***)." By default, all other questions deserve one star. For the two-star or three-star questions, your approach, rather than your solution, may be of more importance. You should

---

[1]At first glance, some questions may seem dated (e.g., "Suppose that IBM is trading at $75 per share..."). However, I could easily have made it "Stock XYZ" (contrary to the original wording), and you would not have noticed. Where possible, I retain the original wording for authenticity.

be able to set up a general framework for a solution. If you can solve such questions on the spot, you are doing well.

Some of the questions are at a low level, and you may think it beneath your dignity to answer them. I have, however, interviewed people who claim to have degrees in finance, economics, statistics or mathematics, who cannot answer basic finance, economics, statistics, or mathematics questions, respectively. If you think the basic questions are beneath you, then prove it by walking through them like a hot knife through butter. If you cannot answer the basic questions, however, either because you are rusty on the basics, or simply never understood them, then why should anyone hire you? No one will want to put you in front of their team members, clients, or traders, all of whom will have basic questions for you.

If you are interviewing for a more quantitatively oriented job where knowledge of C (but probably not C++) is required for the interview (and C++ may be required for the job itself), I recommend Mongan, Suojanen and Giguère (2012) to you.

You must have already heard all the ordinary interview advice (cover letters, appearance, comments on previous employers, use of bad language, chewing gum, researching people who will interview you, researching the firm, knowing your strengths and weaknesses, and so on); if not, then see Fry (2016). To answer the type of questions in this book, however, you may need the *extraordinary* advice that follows.

Will They Ask me These Questions?

Yes; you must assume that they will. You can hope for the best, but you must prepare for the worst. Some firms use the first round of interviews to get to know you with soft and non-quantitative questions. In this case, a second round typically follows with quantitative questions. Other firms use a quantitative first round to screen applicants up front. However, some firms ask no quantitative questions. There is thus a chance that you will see no quantitative questions. In this unlikely event, my quantitative questions will have exercised your IQ, and my non-quantitative questions (Chapter 5) will have been of most assistance.

On the non-quantitative front, many interviewees have been asked, "Where did the Dow close yesterday?" or "Where did the Nikkei close?" or "Where is the 10-year bond?" In addition to current knowledge, you should also know how these (and other) basic economic variables have changed over the recent past, and where they are relative to all-time highs and lows—see Chapter 5 for more examples. Even if you are very busy interviewing with many firms, you must not be found ignorant on such basic market knowledge.

Interviewers care about the "four points of the compass": **skills**, **fit**, **effort**, and **acceptance**. The interviewer wants to know that you have the skills to do the job, that you fit into the culture of the firm, that you will make the effort needed if hired, and that you will accept the job if it is offered to you. If you fail to convince the interviewer on any one of these points, then you will not be shortlisted. Every job interview question, quantitative or otherwise, targets at least one of these four points. They are discussed further below, and on p. 311.

ATQ!

"ATQ" stands for "Answer The Question!" Let us suppose that I am the interviewer and that I have little patience. I am busy. Damn busy! I have a deadline for my boss on a project that is due tonight (he is in an earlier time zone). I walked away from the stack of work on my desk, and the spreadsheet (or code) I desperately need to finish just so that I can talk to you. Spending 30 minutes with you means I get home at 10:30PM instead of 8:00PM, because I have to finish my project, and I will miss the last direct train. I earn $250,000, $500,000, $1M, or more per annum. I got my job and kept it because I am efficient and I understand time management. I want to hire a good person, but if you waste my time then I will crucify you; perhaps not to your face, but to my colleagues, both at this firm, and at competing firms thinking of interviewing you.

I know from past experience that people with good resumes are not necessarily knowledgeable in their claimed area of expertise. If you have a degree in finance, or mathematics, or whatever, and cannot answer a basic question in that area, then how the heck can I let you answer the phone, or bring you to a meeting with a client, or let you talk to our traders, or take you to a meeting with the portfolio managers, or have you join me in a conference call with my boss? That is, how can I hire you if you cannot answer basic questions? I know that there will come a time in this interview or the next when I have to push you to answer some quantitative questions, so that I can see what you understand and what you do not. Some of the questions will be basic, and some of them will not be basic. I need to know the limits of your knowledge, and I cannot find them by asking soft wishy-washy questions about your resume.

If I ask you a question, then answer the damn question! If you know the answer, then tell me it. If you do not know the answer, but can work it out, then tell me that and outline the steps; I may be happy with that, and then not need to see the full derivation. If you have only a passing knowledge of the area, or no hope whatsoever of answering the question, then I need you to say so directly, and without wasting my time, so that I can ask you other questions. I need to know the boundaries of your abilities, and to find them I must ask you a mix of questions including ones that you cannot answer at all. Do not waste my time by floundering around and, in effect, drowning yourself in your own ignorance.

For example, suppose it is a bond trading job and I ask you whether the curvature in the plot of bond price versus yield to maturity is caused by changing Macaulay duration as yield changes. Let us suppose that you know the answer, but instead of giving it to me directly, you say:

"Well, that's an interesting question. We know that for a standard coupon-bearing bond with no embedded options, the plot of bond price versus yield to maturity is downward sloping and concave up. Let me draw that on the whiteboard here (draws picture). As yield rises, other things being equal, bond price falls, but the dollar rate at which the bond price falls actually decreases as yield to maturity rises. That is, the slope becomes less negative. Changing slope means that there is curvature, and sure enough the plot is concave up. Now, some people may think, naively, that the slope of the plot is just the Macaulay duration of

the bond. Now, it is well known that as yield to maturity rises, other things being equal, the Macaulay duration of a standard coupon-bearing bond with no embedded options falls. So, these people would deduce, naively and incorrectly, that as yield to maturity rises, the changing slope is simply a reflection of changing Macaulay duration. However, the simple fact that the Macaulay duration of a standard coupon-bearing bond with no embedded options is positive, and that the slope of our plot is negative, tells us that the slope is not the Macaulay duration. It is not the negative of the Macaulay duration either, and we can see that by looking at the case of a zero-coupon bond. Suppose we plot bond price versus yield to maturity for a ten-year zero with no embedded options. The plot is downward sloping and concave up, as before, with slope becoming less negative as yield to maturity rises, but the duration is 10 years regardless of the yield—because it is a zero. That is, where the slope is of large magnitude, the Macaulay duration is ten; where the slope is of intermediate magnitude, the Macaulay duration is ten; and, where the slope is of small magnitude, the Macaulay duration is ten. Thus, slope does not equal Macaulay duration, or negative Macaulay duration, and the curvature of the plot cannot simply be a reflection of changing Macaulay duration. Now, the slope of the plot of the price of the standard coupon-bearing bond versus its yield to maturity is a function of Macaulay duration, but it is also a function of bond price and yield to maturity. If we write down the slope explicitly, we see that it is $-\frac{D}{(1+r)}P$, where D is Macaulay duration, P is bond price, and r is yield. If we look at numerical examples, we can see however, that the duration does not change very much with changing yield. Indeed, as already mentioned, it does not change at all in the case of a zero, and low-coupon bonds are not that different from zeroes. Rather, it is the bond price that changes significantly with changing yield, and it is this that causes changes in the slope, thus producing curvature. Sure enough, in the case of a coupon-bearing bond, the changing Macaulay duration contributes to the change in slope, and thus to the curvature, but its contribution to curvature is much less important than the contribution of changing bond price. So, no, it is not changing Macaulay duration, but rather, changing price, that drives the change in slope, thus creating curvature."

Well, you just spent two and one-half minutes of my valuable time saying that. That is ten percent of your interview time. In your favor, you got to the correct answer, which is "no," but in so doing you gave me so many words that I ceased caring whether you knew the answer or not. I did figure out, however, that if you were working on my team, I could not take you to a presentation to clients because you would take *for bloody ever* to answer their questions. I also figured out that you really like hearing the sound of your own voice. You may well be someone who does not realize that time is money, that that money belongs to my clients, or to the firm, and that that money has a heck of a lot of zeroes on the end of it.

You should have just answered "No, changing bond price drives changing slope and creates curvature." You should then add that "Changing Macaulay duration contributes marginally to curvature for a coupon bearing bond, but not at all in the case of a zero." If the question has a "yes" or "no" answer, and you know the answer, then the first word out of your mouth should be "yes," or "no," respectively. Anything else means you are not getting to the point, and you are wasting my time and your golden opportunity! Obviously, you support your assertion immediately with more words, but answer the question first! ATQ!

I have had people talk a full ten minutes or more before coming anywhere near allowing me to detect whether they know the answer or not. After the first minute I have already decided that you are in the wrong building, and I am thinking about the stack of work on my desk. I stopped caring about your answer back in the first chapter of your saga. I am about to cancel the next person on your interview schedule because I value his or her time almost as much as I value my own. Unlike me, you get to go home early today.

To repeat, if the answer is "yes," and you know it, then say so! If the answer is "no," and you know it, then say so! You can add words after that, to support your answer, but for God's sake, get to the point! Suppose you are on a date with a person you find exceptionally attractive, and you are dancing, and this person says, "Do you want to kiss me?" Are you going to talk to them for ten minutes about how you arrive at your decision or are you going to get to the point? Similarly, you must have had a professor at college who when asked a question from the audience mid-lecture would take five minutes giving his answer. When he got to the end of it you did not know what the answer was he had given, and you just wished he would shut up and move on. He invariably followed it up with "Is that clear now?" and no one dared say "no," for fear he would talk more about it. The bottom line is, answer the question! Remember ATQ, or even *ATFQ!*, if it helps hammer it into your skull.

If you do not know the answer, but know enough to try to work it out, than say something like "Hmmm. I do not know, but I think I can work it out. I know that the slope is given by $-\frac{D}{(1+r)}P$, where D is duration, P is price, and r is yield. I am not sure how much of the change in slope is explained by changes in each of D and P, but I do know that a zero has fixed D, so I suspect that changing P is more important than changing D." That is fine. You told me you did not know, and then you tried to work it out. That differs from knowing, but failing to tell me until the end of a saga.

If a question is not clear, be sure to ask for clarification. For example, "Is it a straight bond with no embedded options?," "Are there coupons?," etc.

If the interviewer tells you that your answer is incorrect when you know it is correct, and if you are dead sure of your answer, then defend yourself to the hilt. Interviewers make mistakes, and you can earn their respect (and a job) by correcting them. Good people want you to do that in practice—though do it tactfully in front of their colleagues.

Other Advice

As an interviewer, I assume that you are at your best when I see you. You are wearing your best clothes and shoes, you have a great haircut, you are smiling, upbeat and positive, you are engaged in your best conversation, etc. You are, in all respects, on your best behavior. Nevertheless, I had a guy turn up to an interview wearing dirty clothes and smelling like he had not washed in six months. I watched in horror as another candidate made repeated flirtatious/inappropriate remarks about his married male interviewer's body during the interview. During a day of scheduled interviews, a candidate disappeared just after seeing my colleague, and just before he was supposed to see me. After five minutes of us wondering where he went, he turned up late and stinking of cigarette smoke. He obviously thought it was more important to step outside and grab a cigarette than it was to be on time with me. I listened to a female candidate who was so sleep deprived that she stumbled through an interview and was barely able to put two sentences together. I saw a candidate come to an interview with blood stains on his shirt collar; He said he had cut himself shaving that morning. (Always bring *two* shirts, cleaned and pressed, when you fly out to an interview!) On another occasion, a slow-talking European candidate with a deeply dull and depressing monotone voice spent an interminable amount of time during his phone interview describing the cold gray winter he was facing if he did not get a new job; I pictured him tying a noose while talking to us. I once interviewed a morbidly obese candidate who seemed depressed, moribund, and was barely able to communicate. After a five-minute bathroom break, however, he came back dancing like an excited ballerina and he could not stop talking or moving. What did he inhale? I once saw a guy turn up for a banking interview wearing a white jacket and white dress shoes. I could go on, and on. As an interviewer, I ask myself "If the candidate behaves this way during the job interview, then how will he/she behave on the job?" If this is you at your peak, and on your best behavior, then I have to assume that it is downhill from here.

Do not confuse the comments in the previous paragraph with a criticism of nervous behavior by candidates. We expect you to be a little bit nervous. As interviewers, we apply a discount rate for nervousness. What we will not put with, however, is lack of preparation, or a poor attitude, or stupid or bad behavior.

The finance community is small and interwoven, and corporate memory is long. If you interviewed at the firm before, your interviewer probably knows about it and will talk to the people you talked to, even if they have moved on. Indeed, if you worked/interviewed/studied anywhere in the world, the interviewer can find a former colleague, interviewer, adviser etc., of yours, who is known to them and who can assess you. Your resume may have circulated widely within the firm, both in its local offices and overseas, before you set foot in the building or pick up the phone. Indeed, your resume might have circulated so widely that no one informs HR, and no one even remembers where your resume came from; that can explain why you never got any response, not even a rejection.

I have never heard anyone else state it, but I cannot stress highly enough that you are not just interviewing for the job that was advertised. There are other openings at the firm that have not yet been advertised (and may never be advertised), and there are openings at other firms that your interviewer knows about because he or she knows people there. There will also be other openings at the interviewing firm in the future. If they like you and your CV, but do not think you are suited to that one job, then they may recommend you strongly to another team leader within their firm or even at another firm. (This backdoor network of contacts is used all the time in recruiting. If I pass your details on to someone at another firm today, they will pass their candidate's details to me next week. This *quid pro quo* is part of the equilibrium that helps equate supply and demand in the labor market; everybody benefits from it.) The implication of this is that if you discover quickly that you are not suited to the position advertised, or the firm, then you should steer the interview toward your strengths and ask the interviewer to keep you in mind for other positions. He or she may even tell you of another opening. (See also the first story on p. 40.) Of course, this phenomenon can work out badly for you too. If your interview is awful, the interviewer will happily pass that information to other people if they ask about you, at that firm and other firms. For a really bad performance, the interviewer will pass on information about you without even being asked.

I interviewed a guy who I was not sure about. I started the interview by saying that I thought he was not the right guy for the job. I was not trying to play some sort of psychological game; I was just expressing my doubts, assuming that he would turn around and tell me why he *was* the right guy. Instead, he amazed me by wilting on the spot. So, you should have a shortlist of several reasons prepared to counter any claim that you are not the right person for the job.

Your resume is often a starting point. Never, never inflate it. When a resume arrives on the desk of the interviewer, he or she looks at it and tries to figure out in advance some questions to ask. If you write on your resume that you took an option pricing class, and got an "A," then if the interviewer is an option pricing nut, you just guaranteed that the interview is going to get hot. If the area is a weakness for you, then do not make yourself a target. If you want to advertise that you took the class, then that is fine, but prepare yourself for incoming questions.

On 100% of CVs where the candidate lists "attention to detail" as a skill, I have found obvious errors caused by a lack of attention to detail! So, get your resume proofread by multiple people, including someone with English as a first language.

I received three cover letters that stand out in my mind. One from a young woman applying for a junior quant position who stated that she had "a lot of love to give," one from a graduate of Rutgers who seemed to think I was sufficiently stupid not to have heard of Rutgers and felt the need to describe the school in great detail, and one from someone saying that they had always wanted to work in investment banking (when I was working at that time for an asset management company). You have sent your CV and cover letter out to act as your ambassador in your absence. Remember, at every step of the interview process, your aim is to get to the next step of the process. So, a substandard effort here can kill your opportunity for an interview as surely as any ridiculous social media webpage or moronic email address can.

Do not smoke just before your interview. Get a stop smoking patch or something similar. The same goes for garlic for 24 hours before your interview. It stinks! Similarly, no one likes shaking hands with a limp dead fish. If your hands drip like a leaky faucet, then put your hand in your pocket (warm and dry), or palm down on your lap, or under your thigh if you are sitting, right up until the point at which you shake hands. It is simple but effective.

One in three males I have ever interviewed put his finger up his nose during the interview. I kid you not. They seem to be unaware of it. Perhaps it is nerves. They expect me to shake hands with them at the end of the interview, but I always find a way out of it. Keep your damn hands off your face during the interview!

Intelligent or genuinely humorous small talk is fine, but do not make a fool of yourself. For example, one guy came back a week later for a second round interview with me. I went to greet him in the foyer, and he looked at me blankly. Then he suddenly said "I remember you!" and "This is for the quant position, right?" Those were his first words! One of my co-authors said "You are better off being yourself . . . . . . but be your *best* self" (Butler and Crack, 2019, p. 4).

Cover letters go in the garbage can, and e-mails are deleted. Make sure your e-mail address and phone number are on your CV. Make sure you have reliable voicemail, and check it often. If HR cannot find you quickly, then someone else can interview for your job before you can—even if we ranked you higher.

Do not ask how many hours they work, or what they pay. You do not care how many hours it takes; You love working long days and nights. You do not care what the pay is; you just want to get your foot in the door.

Show me that you love the industry and the challenge. Even if the market is bad, and you are out of work, you must be upbeat. If you tell me a tale of woe, all I can think is that "99% of your life is what you make of it, and if your life sucks, you suck." Why would I want you sitting next to me at work all day? Be positive. People like people who like them.

Show passion; make it plain. The words "I want this job" should come out of your mouth plainly and clearly during the interview. Why? Well, surprisingly often (surprisingly often!), when you have gone, we interviewers sit down and discuss amongst ourselves whether you really wanted the job, and we conclude that you did not. We figured you for a "tourist," or someone seeking an offer to use as leverage with your current employer or some other employer, or someone whose heart was simply not in it. You failed to convince us on the *acceptance* point of the compass, and we are not going to waste a line on you (see the next paragraphs for further discussion of this). So, we are always amazed when we subsequently hear from some mutual contact that you were shattered not to get to the next stage. So many candidates interview with us for reasons other than getting a job that we have difficulty distinguishing between those who want a job and those who do not. Hell, you acted like you did not want the job! We are not psychic. If you want the job, then tell us you want the job!

Do not underestimate the importance of the last point of the compass: *acceptance*. From an interviewer's perspective, I am vigorously competing with other firms to hire out of the current pool of applicants. Making an offer to you uses up one "line" (think of them as fishing lines cast into the pool of applicants). I may have only one or two lines available. So, if I decide during the interview that you are unlikely to accept an offer, then I will not tie up one line with you (waiting for your answer, while my competitors pluck the best fish out of the pool). Even if you convinced me on *skills*, *fit* and *effort*, I would rather save that line for someone more likely to accept my offer. Indeed, one firm is famous for asking "If we offer you a job right now, will you say yes?" If you say "I have to think about it" or "I need to make a phone call" then you are out. Forget about it; why should I waste any further time on you?

Near the end of the interview, interviewers often ask "Do you have any questions for me?" If you have no question(s), then you fail on the *effort* and *fit* points of the compass. Having no question is like arrogantly slapping your interviewer in the face. What do you think will happen if you end the interview that way? Your question(s) must be one(s) whose answer(s) cannot be found online. For example, "Do you have any reservations about hiring me that we can discuss right now?," "What challenges will your division face over the next year?," or "Why did you join the company?," or "What do you find most satisfying about working here?" or "What is the best advice you can give me to achieve long-run success here?"

If you thought the interview was over when you walked out the door, then you misunderstood. At the very least, I expect to get a simple two-sentence follow-up email from you, almost immediately, thanking me for the interview. If you put a foot wrong during the interview, perhaps by giving a wrong answer to an interview question, then your follow-up email should say "Thank you for the interview. As soon as I walked out of the building I realized that in my nervousness I answered that question about [whatever it was] incorrectly. I should have said..." The interview is not over yet; I am sitting there waiting for your damn email! If I do not get that email, especially one that corrects a mistake, then your failure demonstrates a lack of effort, and that you did not really want the job in the first place. If I had any doubts previously, then I can now conclude for sure that you would not have accepted an offer from us, and so, I will not waste a line on you.

It's not over until it is over! If several weeks have passed since the interview, and you have heard nothing, but you are still interested, then I expect to get a follow-up email from you reiterating your interest, and reminding me that you exist. By this time I have already had second-round interviews with your competitors, and maybe they all failed, or failed to accept our offers. So, you may look very attractive now. If you are still interested, then I am expecting you to contact me again. If you do not contact me again, then I must conclude that you are not interested, either because you got a job already, or because you were never interested to begin with.

Finally, the ex-post probability that you get the job is either zero or one. If you prepare as though it is zero, then it will be. If you prepare as though it can be one, then you can make it so. I have every confidence in you.

Please feel free to send me e-mails with queries, corrections, alternative solutions, but especially with new interview questions. The errata (with corrections and comments) can be found at the website below.

www.InvestmentBankingJobInterviews.com
timcrack@alum.mit.edu

Chapter 1

Purely Quantitative & Logic Questions

With a few exceptions, the only prerequisites for answering the questions in this chapter are elementary quantitative skills and common sense. Some questions here have both an elegant technique and a brute-force technique. The technique you choose is revealing. Solutions for this chapter appear in Appendix A.

🏛 **Question** 1.1: You are given two glass jugs. Each contains the same volume, V, of liquid. One jug contains pure alcohol, and the other jug contains pure water. A modest quantity, Q, of water is poured from the water jug into the alcohol jug, which is then thoroughly mixed. The same modest quantity, Q, of (now diluted) alcohol is then poured back into the water jug to equalize the volumes of the jugs at their initial levels.

The initial concentration of alcohol in the alcohol jug equals the initial concentration of water in the water jug (at 100%). What is the relationship between the final concentrations of alcohol in the alcohol jug and water in the water jug?[1]

🏛 **Question** 1.2: Fischer and Myron just stepped side-by-side onto a moving escalator. They are climbing up the stairs, and counting steps as they climb. Myron is climbing more quickly than Fischer. Myron climbs three steps in the time it takes Fischer to climb only two steps. Neither of them skips any steps. Myron steps off at the top, having counted 25 steps. He waits at the top for the slower Fischer, who steps off having counted only 20 steps. How many steps are showing on the escalator at any instant?

🏛 **Question** 1.3: There are two bells. One rings five times per minute, and the other rings four times per minute. If they start at the same time, how long will it be until they next ring together?

---

[1]This is not a chemistry problem. Please ignore the fact that mixing a volume V_1 of water with a volume V_2 of alcohol results in a total volume less than $V_1 + V_2$. Follow-up question: Repeat the mixing, and ask the same question. Now do it again, and again, and ask the same question.

🏛 **Question 1.4:** What is the sum of the integers from 1 to 100?[2]

🏛 **Question 1.5:** An old style analog clock falls off the wall and the face breaks into three pieces. The numbers on each piece add to the same total. Describe the pieces.

🏛 **Question 1.6:** (**) You are given a set of scales and 12 marbles. The scales are of the old balance variety. That is, a small dish hangs from each end of a rod that is balanced in the middle (⚖). The device enables you to conclude either that the contents of the dishes weigh the same or that the dish that falls lower has heavier contents than the other.

The 12 marbles appear to be identical. In fact, 11 of them are identical, and one is of a different weight. Your task is to identify the unusual marble and discard it. You are allowed to use the scales three times if you wish, but no more. Note that the unusual marble may be heavier than the others, or it may be lighter; you do not know which. You are asked to both identify it and determine whether it is heavy or light.

🏛 **Question 1.7:** Suppose I inscribe a circle within a square so that the circle just touches the four sides of the square. Suppose there is exactly enough room to fit a rectangle of dimensions 5×10 into one corner of the square so that the rectangle just touches the circle. See Figure 1.1. What is the side length of the square?

🏛 **Question 1.8:** Interviewer: "You are a bug sitting in one corner of a *cubic* room. You wish to walk (no flying) to the extreme opposite corner (the one farthest from you). Describe the shortest path that you can walk. Be sure to mention direction, length, and so on."

🏛 **Question 1.9:** A mythical city contains 100,000 married couples but no children. Each family wishes to "continue the male line," but they do not wish to over-populate. So, each family has one baby per annum until the arrival of the first boy. For example, if (at some future date) a family has five children, then it must be either that they are all girls, and another child is planned, or that there are four girls and one boy, and no more children are planned. Assume that children are equally likely to be born male or female.

Let $p(t)$ be the percentage of *children* that are male at the end of year t. How is this percentage expected to evolve through time?

> **Story:** One candidate for a futures trading position in Chicago was asked: "Would you rather be beaten up, beat someone up, or run around the block naked?" The last response did not get him the job. My wife was horrified to hear this story. Welcome to Chicago!

---

[2]More generally, what is the sum of the integers from 1 to n?

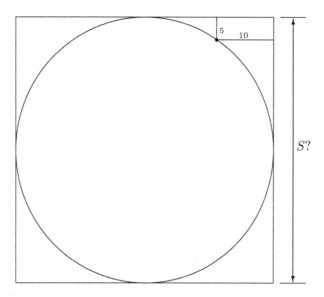

Figure 1.1: The Inscribed Circle Question

Note: A circle is inscribed within a square. A rectangle of dimensions 5×10 just fits in one corner. What is the side length S of the square?

Question 1.10: Picture a $10 \times 10 \times 10$ "macro-cube" floating in mid-air. The macro-cube is composed of $1 \times 1 \times 1$ "micro-cubes," all glued together. Weather damage causes the outermost layer of micro-cubes to become loose. This outermost layer falls to the ground. How many micro-cubes are on the ground?

Question 1.11: There are two cities, A and B, 1,000 miles apart. You have 3,000 apples at City A, and you want to deliver as many as possible of them to City B. The only delivery method available is a truck. There are, however, two problems. The truck can hold at most only 1,000 apples, and if there are any apples at all in the truck, the hungry dishonest driver will steal and eat one apple for every mile he drives. What is the maximum number of apples you can deliver from City A to City B? Note that you are welcome to stop part way, dump off some apples, and then come back and pick them up later.

Question 1.12: How many degrees (if any) are there in the angle between the hour and minute hands of a clock when the time is a quarter past three?

Question 1.13: What is the first time after 3PM when the hour and minute hands of a clock are exactly on top of each other?

Question 1.14: There are 100 light bulbs lined up in a row in a long room. Each bulb has its own switch and is currently switched off. The room has an entry door and an exit door. There are 100 stockbrokers lined up outside the entry door. Each bulb is numbered consecutively from 1 to 100. Each stockbroker is numbered consecutively from 1 to 100.

Broker number 1 enters the room, switches on *every* bulb, and exits. Broker number 2 enters and flips the switch on every *second* bulb (turning off bulbs 2, 4, 6, ...). Broker number 3 enters and flips the switch on every *third* bulb (changing the state on bulbs 3, 6, 9, ...). This continues until all 100 brokers have passed through the room.

What is the final state of bulb number 64? Is it illuminated or dark?

Question 1.15: Exactly the same set-up as Question 1.14, with a different final question: How many of the light bulbs are illuminated after the 100th person has passed through the room, and which light bulbs are they?

Question 1.16: Your bedroom sock drawer contains eight red socks and 11 blue socks that are otherwise identical. The light is broken in your bedroom, and you must select your socks in the dark. What is the minimum number of socks you need to take out of your drawer and carry into your (well-lit) living room to guarantee that you have with you at least a matching pair to choose from?

Question 1.17: Following on from the previous question, can you generalize your answer to otherwise-identical socks of N different colors? For example, suppose you have 50 socks of color 1, 50 socks of color 2, ..., and 50 socks of color N, how many socks must you pull from your sock drawer in the dark to guarantee that you have a matching pair?

Question 1.18: Following on from the previous two questions, your bedroom sock drawer contains 2 red, 4 yellow, 6 purple, 8 brown, 10 white, 12 green, 14 black, 16 blue, 18 gray, and 20 orange socks. It is dark, so you cannot distinguish between the colors of the otherwise-identical socks. How many socks do you need to take out of the drawer to guarantee that you have at least *three* pairs of socks of the same color?

> **Story:** One of my students was asked to "Describe the best boss you have ever had." Watch out for the opposite question: "Describe the worst boss you have ever had." Your answer may indicate disloyalty to a (former) employer.

Question 1.19: You and I are to play a competitive game. We shall take it in turns to call out integers. The first person to call out "50" wins. The rules are as follows:

1. The player who starts must call out an integer between one and 10, inclusive;

2. A new number called out must exceed the most recent number called by at least one and by no more than 10. For example, if the first player calls out "nine," then the range of valid numbers for the opponent is 10 to 19, inclusive.

Do you want to go first, and if so, what is your strategy?

Question 1.20: You are to open a safe without knowing the combination. Beginning with the dial set at zero, the dial must be turned counter-clockwise to the first combination number, (then clockwise back to zero), and clockwise to the second combination number, (then counter-clockwise back to zero), and counter-clockwise again to the third and final combination number, whereupon the door shall immediately spring open; there is no handle or key to turn. The dial has numbers from zero to 40, and the zero is not one of the combination numbers.

Without knowing the combination numbers, what is the maximum number of trials required to open the safe? One trial equals one attempt to dial a full three-number combination, and you must start again from zero for each trial.

> **Story:** 1. During the interview, an alarm clock went off from the candidate's briefcase. He took it out, shut it off, apologized, and said he had to leave for another interview. 2. An applicant came in wearing only one shoe. She explained that the other shoe was stolen off her foot in the bus.
>
> Interview Horror Stories from Recruiters
> Reprinted by kind permission of *MBA Style Magazine*
> ©1996–2021 MBA Style Magazine, www.mbastyle.com

Question 1.21: (**) You are given a set of scales and 90 coins (this question is similar to Question 1.6). The scales are of the old balance variety. That is, a small dish hangs from each end of a rod that is balanced in the middle. The device enables you to conclude either that the contents of the dishes weigh the same or that the dish that falls lower has heavier contents than the other. You must pay $100 every time you use the scales.

The 90 coins appear to be identical. In fact, 89 of them are identical, and one is of a different weight. Your task is to identify the unusual coin and to discard it while minimizing the maximum possible cost of weighing.[3] What is your algorithm to complete this task? What is the most it can cost to identify the unusual coin (assuming your strategy minimizes the maximum possible cost)?

Note that the unusual coin may be heavier than the others, or it may be lighter. You are asked to both identify it and determine whether it is heavy or light.[4]

Question 1.22: (***) Suppose that the function $f(z)$ is complex valued in the complex plane. Suppose also that $f(z)$ is both bounded and entire. Prove

---

[3]A slightly different task is to minimize the expected cost of weighing. Minimizing the expected cost of weighing does not necessarily minimize the maximum possible cost. This is a subtle distinction that you should not overlook.

[4]Does the answer change if you must identify the coin without saying whether it is heavy or light?

that $f(z)$ must be a constant.[5]

> **Story:** A student of mine was taken to a room and asked to choose a place to sit at a long oval-shaped table. He chose a place at random. Later the interviewer asked why he had chosen that spot. I think the intent was to see if he was a leader (sitting at the head) or a follower (sitting at the side).

🏛 **Question 1.23:**   I have dropped 10,000 ants randomly onto a ruler that is one meter (i.e., 100 centimeters) long and oriented to point north–south. The ants are of very small size and mass. Each ant walks at a steady pace of one centimeter per second in a straight line parallel to the long edge of the ruler. Their initial direction is randomly either north or south. The ants are all from the same colony and possess an inherited vision problem: they have peripheral vision only. This means that they can collide with each other if they meet head on (although very small, they are large enough to collide). If two ants do collide head on, however, then they each turn around instantly and head back the way they came at their steady pace. With so many ants in one small space, a single ant may experience multiple collisions before it walks off of the ruler. So, how long must you wait to be sure that all the ants have walked off of the ruler?

🏛 **Question 1.24:**   You start with a single lily pad sitting on an otherwise empty pond. You are told that the surface area of the lily pad doubles every day and that it will take 30 days for the single lily pad to cover the surface of the pond.[6]

If instead of one lily pad you start with eight lily pads (each identical in characteristics to the original single lily pad), how many days will it take for the surface of the pond to become covered?

🏛 **Question 1.25:**   Another lily pad problem. There are 27 lily pads on a pond. Each of the lily pads is one square foot in area. The pond is 6,000 square feet in area. Each lily pad doubles its size every day. How long until the pond is covered in lily pads?

🏛 **Question 1.26:**   Interviewer: "Alright, you're from MIT; you must be a quantitative type of person." Interviewee: (confidently, after a slight pause) "Yes indeed." Interviewer: "Give me the decimal equivalent of $\frac{13}{16}$ and of $\frac{9}{16}$."

🏛 **Question 1.27:**   A snail is climbing up a 10-foot pole. It climbs up by three feet every day. Each night it sleeps. While sleeping, it slides down by one foot. When does it reach the top of the pole?

---

[5]Recall that an "entire" function is a function that is analytic in the entire finite complex plane. Thus, $f(z)$ may be represented by an everywhere-convergent power series: $f(z) = \sum_{n=0}^{\infty} a_n z^n$ (Holland [1973, p. 5]).

[6]The student who was asked this question says that his interviewer used the number 30. However, he suggested that I use the number 3,000 to make it more complicated. What is wrong with saying that it takes 3,000 days for the lily pad to cover the pond?

🏛 **Question** 1.28: A windowless room contains three identical light fixtures, each containing an identical light bulb. Each light fixture is connected to one of three switches outside of the room. Each bulb is switched off at present. You are outside the room, and the door is closed. You may flip any of the external switches in any manner you choose. After this, you must take your hands off the switches and then you may go into the room and do as you please (but you will not be allowed to damage anything or touch the switches again). How can you tell which switch goes to which light?

🏛 **Question** 1.29: Inside of a dark closet are five hats: three blue and two red. Three smart men go into the closet, and each selects a hat in the dark and places it unseen upon his head. Each man knows both that the closet contains three blue hats and two red and that the other two men have the same knowledge.

Once outside the closet, no man can see his own hat. The first man looks at the other two, thinks, and says, "I cannot tell what color my hat is." The second man hears this, looks at the other two, and says, "I cannot tell what color my hat is either." The third man is blind. The blind man says, "Well, I know what color my hat is." What color is his hat, and how does he know?

Question 1.30: (**) Find the smallest positive integer that leaves a remainder of 1 when divided by 2, a remainder of 2 when divided by 3, a remainder of 3 when divided by 4, ... and a remainder of 9 when divided by 10.

🏛 **Question** 1.31: There are two motorcyclists on a single lane road. They are 25 miles apart. At a signal, they start moving toward each other with constant speeds. The first motorcyclist rides at 20 mph; the second rides at 30 mph. When the signal goes off, a fly on the helmet of the first motorcyclist is startled and starts flying toward the second motorcyclist at 40 mph. When the fly reaches the second motorcyclist (now moving toward the first), he immediately reverses course and flies back to the first motorcyclist. When the fly gets back to the first motorcyclist, he reverses course again. The fly continues to fly backwards and forwards between the two motorcyclists until they all collide. How many miles will the fly have traveled before his life is extinguished?

Question 1.32: Prove that the area of a triangle is given by

$$A = \sqrt{s(s-a)(s-b)(s-c)},$$

where a, b, and c are the side lengths, and $s \equiv \frac{a+b+c}{2}$ is the semi-perimeter.[7]

> **Story:** Instead of being asked her greatest weakness, one of my students was asked: "Why shouldn't we hire you?" It is pretty difficult to maneuver your way out of that one!

---

[7]Mark Rubinstein kindly pointed out to me that this is "Heron's Formula." Strogatz (2009, pp. 143–152, 160) refers to it as "Hero's Formula" and "Heron's Formula."

Question 1.33: A, B, C, D, E, F, G, H, and I, are the nine integers from one to nine (not necessarily in order). They satisfy the following constraints:

$$A + B + C + D = 20,$$
$$B + C + D + E + F = 20,$$
$$D + E + F + G + H = 20, \text{ and}$$
$$F + G + H + I = 20$$

What values are taken by each of A to I?

Question 1.34:   A very large number, N, of people arrive at a convention. There are exactly N single rooms in the hotel where the convention takes place. Each guest is given a numbered key for a specific room. Before they even go upstairs, they are all invited to a large party in the banquet hall. To gain admittance to the hall, they have to give up their keys to a doorman. At the end of the evening, the guests are not sober enough to recall their room numbers, so the doorman simply hands out the keys randomly. Each guest ends up spending the night in a random room. What is the probability that at least one guest ends up in the room to which he or she was originally assigned?

🏛 **Question** 1.35:   At another party, everybody shakes hands with everybody else. If there are 66 handshakes, how many people are at the party?

Question 1.36:   There are 25 people at a party. What is the expected number of *pairs* of people with the same birthday? For example, if John, Jon, Stephen, and Mark all have the same birthday, say, January 15, but nobody else at the party has a matching birthday, the count of pairs is six. (See also the next two questions.)

Question 1.37:   There are 25 people at another party. One person asks everybody to announce their birthday, and for anyone who has the same birthday as someone else to raise a hand. How many *hands* do you expect to see raised? For example, if John, Jon, Stephen, and Mark all have the same birthday, January 15, but nobody else at the party has a matching birthday, the count of hands is four.

Question 1.38:   A line is about to form outside the box office of a theater. You have inside information that the manager plans to announce that he will give a single free ticket to one person in line. To win the free ticket, it needs to be true that you are the first person in line who has someone ahead of you in line with same birthday as you. When (or where) do you join the line to maximize the probability of winning the free ticket?

🏛 **Question** 1.39:   A small boat is floating in a swimming pool. The boat contains a very small but very heavy rock. If the rock is tossed out of the boat into the pool, what happens to the water level in the pool?

Question 1.40: (**) In a certain matriarchal town, the women all believe in an old prophecy that says there will come a time when a stranger will visit the town and announce whether any of the men folk are cheating on their wives. The stranger will simply say "yes" or "no," without announcing the number of men implicated or their identities. If the stranger arrives and makes his announcement, the women know that they must follow a particular rule: If on any day following the stranger's announcement a women deduces that her husband is not faithful to her, she must kick him out into the street at 10AM the next day. This action is immediately observable by every resident in the town. It is well known that each wife is already observant enough to know whether any man (except her own husband) is cheating on his wife. However, no woman can reveal that information to any other. A cheating husband is also assumed to remain silent about his infidelity.

The time comes, and a stranger arrives. He announces that there are cheating men in the town. On the morning of the tenth day following the stranger's arrival, some unfaithful men are kicked out into the street for the first time. How many of them are there?

🏛 **Question 1.41:** In front of you are three poles. One pole is stacked with 64 rings ranging in weight from one ounce (at the top) to 64 ounces (at the bottom). Your task is to move all the rings to one of the other two poles so that they end up in the same order. The rules are that you can move only one ring at a time, you can move a ring only from one pole to another, and you cannot even temporarily place a ring on top of a lighter ring.

What is the minimum number of moves you need to make to achieve the task?

> **Story:** Here are some Fermi problems from Section 5.5: "How many McDonald's fast food outlets are there in the U.S.? How many gas stations are there in the U.S.? How many elevators are there in the U.S.?"

Question 1.42: Solve the following ordinary differential equation (ODE):

$$u'' + u' + u = 1$$

Question 1.43: Assume that the random variables X and Y are normally distributed: $X \sim N(\mu_X, \sigma_X^2)$, and $Y \sim N(\mu_Y, \sigma_Y^2)$. The correlation between X and Y is ρ. How can you choose constants a and b such that you minimize the variance of the random variable sum $S = aX + bY$ under the constraints that $a + b = 1$, $0 \le a \le 1$, and $0 \le b \le 1$?[8]

---

[8]Another version of this question asked in interviews is: "You are driving around with one wheel on the gravel and one wheel on the pavement. The variance of the gravel and pavement surfaces are described by σ_G^2 and σ_P^2. Whereabouts on the axle should you sit between $x = 0$ (right over the wheel on the gravel) and $x = 1$ (right over the wheel on the pavement) if you want the most comfortable ride?"

Question 1.44: Suppose there is a straight coastline and a lighthouse that is $L = 3$ miles away from the coast. The light revolves at one revolution per minute. How fast is the beam of light traveling along the coastline? When the beam is $3L$ away from the coastal point closest to the light, how fast is the light traveling along the coast?

Question 1.45: I have a 20×20 chessboard and a very large box of identical cubes. Each square on the chessboard is the same size as the face of any cube. I am going to arrange piles of cubes on the chessboard in a special pattern. I align one edge of the board so it is running north–south. I start at the northwest corner by placing one cube on that square. Whenever I step to the south or the east, I place a pile of cubes containing one more cube than in the previous square. This produces the pattern in Figure 1.2. How many cubes in total are there on the chessboard?

1	2	3	4	$\cdots$	19	20
2	3	4	5	$\cdots$	20	21
3	4	5	6	$\cdots$	21	22
4	5	6	7	$\cdots$	22	23
$\vdots$	$\vdots$	$\vdots$	$\vdots$	$\ddots$	$\vdots$	$\vdots$
19	20	21	22	$\cdots$	37	38
20	21	22	23	$\cdots$	38	39

Figure 1.2: Number of Cubes on Each Square of a 20×20 Chessboard (Q)

Question 1.46: You are standing at the center of a circular field of radius R. The field has a low wire fence around it. Attached to the wire fence (and restricted to running around the perimeter) is a large, sharp-fanged, hungry dog who likes to eat any humans he can catch. You can run at speed v. Unfortunately, the dog can run four times as fast, at $4v$. The dog will do his best to catch you if you try to escape the field. What is your running strategy to escape the field without feeding yourself to the dog?

Question 1.47: Please prove that the following relationship holds:

$$\int_{-\infty}^{+\infty} e^{-x^2} dx = \sqrt{\pi}$$

Question 1.48: What is $\int \sec\theta\, d\theta$ equal to?[9]

Question 1.49: As a follow-up to the previous question, now please integrate $\sec\theta$ from 0 to $\pi/6$.

Question 1.50: Does the infinite sum $\sum_{n=1}^{\infty} e^{-\sqrt{n}}$ converge?

🏛 **Question** 1.51: One analyst (John) is talking to another (Mary) while working on a deal book at 2AM. Mary learns that John's sister has three children. "How old are the children?" asks Mary. "Well," replies John, "the product of their ages is 36." Mary thinks for a while and says, "I need more information." "Hmmm, the sum of their ages is the same as this figure right here," says John pointing at the spreadsheet. "Still not enough information," says Mary after thinking for a minute. "The eldest is dyslexic," says John. How old are the children?

🏛 **Question** 1.52: You are given eight balls. They appear identical, but one is heavier than the rest. As in the previous ball questions, you have a pair of scales. How do you find the heavy ball?

Question 1.53: What are $\sum_{k=1}^{n} k^2$, and $\sum_{k=1}^{n} k^3$?

🏛 **Question** 1.54: We are to play a game on a table in the next room. We each have an infinite bag of identical quarters (i.e., American 25-cent pieces). We will take it in turns to put one quarter on the table. Quarters may not overlap on the table. When there is no room left on the table to put another quarter, the winner is the last person to put a quarter on the table. Let me tell you that there does exist a strategy for winning and that this strategy is independent of the size of the table.

1. What is the shape of the table?

2. Do you start?

3. What is your strategy for winning?

4. Is there any case where this does not work?

🏛 **Question** 1.55: You have a chessboard (8×8) plus a big box of dominoes (each 2×1). I use a marker pen to put an "X" in the squares at coordinates $(1,1)$ and $(8,8)$—a pair of diagonally opposing corners. Is it possible to cover the remaining 62 squares using the dominoes without any of them sticking out over the edge of the board and without any of them overlapping? You must not damage the board or the dominoes in the process or do anything weird like standing them on their ends—just answer the question.[10]

---

[9]Similarly, you could see questions on integrals (or derivatives) of $\sin\theta$, $\cos\theta$, $\tan\theta$, $\cot\theta$, and $\mathrm{cosec}\,\theta$.

[10]Naoki Sato has suggested a follow-up question. Place an "X" on two squares: one black, and one white. Can you cover the remaining squares with dominoes? See Answer 1.55 for the solution.

Question 1.56: (***) You have 52 playing cards (26 red, 26 black). You draw cards one by one. A red card pays you a dollar. A black one fines you a dollar. You can stop any time you want. Cards are not returned to the deck after being drawn. What is the optimal stopping rule in terms of maximizing expected payoff? Also, what is the expected payoff following this optimal rule?[11]

Question 1.57: One of my students interviewed with some folks who "wanted to get an idea of his comfort with formulae and with explaining things to clients." They asked why it is that if p is a prime number greater than 3, then $p^2 - 1$ is always divisible by 24 with no remainder.

Question 1.58: You are bidding B for a firm whose unknown true value is uniformly distributed between 0 and 1. Although you do not know the true value S of the firm, you do know that as soon as people learn that you have made a bid this news will cause the value to double to $2S$. Your bid, however, will be accepted only if it is at least as large as the original value of the firm. How do you bid so as to maximize your expected payoff?

Question 1.59: You have a string-like fuse that burns in exactly one minute. The fuse is inhomogeneous, and it may burn slowly at first, then quickly, then slowly, and so on. You have a match, and no watch. How do you measure exactly 30 seconds?

Question 1.60: You have two string-like fuses. Each burns in exactly one minute. The fuses are inhomogeneous, and may burn slowly at first, then quickly, then slowly, and so on. You have a match, and no watch. How do you measure exactly 45 seconds?

Question 1.61: How many places are there on the Earth where you can walk one mile south, one mile east, one mile north, and end up exactly where you started? Assume the Earth is a perfect sphere, that your compass bearing is constant on each leg of the walk, that all parts of the Earth are able to be walked upon, and that your feet are arbitrarily small.

Question 1.62: This is an absolute classic. A king demands a tax of 1,000 gold sovereigns from each of 10 regions of his nation. The tax collectors for each region bring him the requested bag of gold coins at year end. An informant tells the king that one tax collector is cheating and giving coins that are consistently 10% lighter than they should be, but he does not know which collector is cheating. The king knows that each coin should weigh exactly one ounce. How can the king identify the cheat by using a weighing device exactly once? (I have seen the same question asked with 10 pill bottles, nine of which have pills weighing 10g, but one of which has pills weighing 9g, and your task is to identify the bottle of light pills by using a weighing device exactly once.)

---

[11]Try the same question with four cards (two red, two black).

Question 1.63: How many consecutive zeroes are there at the end of 100! (100 factorial). For example, 12!=479,001,600 has two consecutive zeroes at the end.

Question 1.64: Again, an absolute classic. You hire a man to work in your yard for seven days. You wish to pay him in gold. You have one gold bar with seven parts—like a chocolate bar. You wish to pay him one gold part per day, but you may snap the bar in only two places. Where do you snap the bar so that you may pay him at the end of each day, and so that on successive days he may use what you paid him previously to make change?

Question 1.65: You have an array that contains 99 distinct integers from the set $\{1, 2, 3, \ldots, 100\}$. How would you write a program to figure out which integer is missing?

Question 1.66: Why are images in a mirror flipped horizontally and not vertically? For example, although I wear my wristwatch on my left wrist, and my reflection wears his on his right wrist, my reflection is not standing on his head.

Question 1.67: (**) I am told this is a genuine finance interview question. It had to be a trading interview, because no one but a trader would ask this in an interview. I considered transforming the question, but left it as is for authenticity. Avert your eyes if you are easily offended!

How can three men and one woman have mutually safe heterosexual intercourse with just two condoms? Assume that no condom can break or leak, and that you cannot wash a used one.[12]

Question 1.68: Consider a grid. You start at coordinate $(0, 0)$ and move one step at a time, eventually arriving at coordinate $(5, 5)$. With each step you may move only one step east or one step north but never diagonally. How many paths are there from $(0, 0)$ to $(5, 5)$?

Question 1.69: Six friends go out to lunch. The bill is $132.67. They decide to add a 20% tip and split the total six ways evenly. What does each person pay?

Question 1.70: You walk into a pizza shop. They sell three sizes of pizza: small, medium, and large. All are perfectly circular, have the same thickness, and have the same density of toppings. The price of a large pizza is equal to the price of a medium pizza plus the price of a small pizza: $P_L = P_M + P_S$. You see a group of your friends already sitting in the pizza store and they have just had one of each size pizza delivered to their table plus they have been given one empty box to take any leftovers home in. Each of their pizzas has been pre-cut into (perfect) sixths. Their box is a (perfect) square. You are looking

---

[12]With one man and three women, the answer is of similar type, but different. This question also appears in Derman (2004, p. 104), which is probably how it drifted to Wall Street.

at your friends' uneaten pizzas and are trying to choose between ordering one large pizza for yourself or ordering one medium plus one small for yourself. The cost is the same, but how can you determine which choice gives better value?[13]

Question 1.71: Find all of the roots to the equation $x^6 = 64$ (including the complex roots).

Question 1.72: A penny is dropped from the top of the Empire State Building. At what speed does it hit the ground, and how long does it take to get there?

Question 1.73: Please express the integral $f(x) = \int_{t=x}^{\infty} e^{-a\frac{t^2}{2}+bt}dt$ in terms of $N(x)$ (i.e., the cumulative standard normal).

Question 1.74: What is $\lim_{x\to\infty} \left(\sqrt{x^2 + x} - x\right)$?

Question 1.75: How do you differentiate x^x with respect to x?

Question 1.76: Following on from the previous question, what is the minimum of x^x? Please restrict your attention to $x > 0$.

Question 1.77: You are seated at a table that has 100 quarters on it. You are told that there are 10 heads and 90 tails turned up. Unfortunately, the room is pitch black (or you are blindfolded) and you cannot see the quarters. You also cannot tell by touch which way up they are. So, how can you divide them into two piles so that you have the same number of heads in each pile?

Question 1.78: How would you write a computer program to estimate π?

Question 1.79: There are 12 people sitting around a perfectly round table that is marked out to look like the dial of an analog clock. The host is sitting at 12 o'clock, and 11 guests are sitting at each hour from 1 o'clock to 11 o'clock, respectively. (In fact, the original question did not mention a clock, but I think it makes for a clear mental image.) The host holds a prize. He will pass the prize to someone seated next to him. Then that person will pass it to someone seated next to him, and so on. The host, or any guest, is equally likely to pass the prize clockwise or counter-clockwise. The last guest to touch the prize wins it. (That is, the 11th guest to lay hands upon the prize gets to keep it.) Which hour of the clock should you sit at to have the highest chance of winning the prize?

Question 1.80: What is a positive definite matrix?

Question 1.81: Following on from the previous question, in practice, how do you test whether a matrix is positive definite, without using any pre-canned routines?

---

[13]In the original question the pizza was not cut, there was no box, but you had a knife. I retained the spirit of the question but modified it because it was not, strictly speaking, able to be solved.

Question 1.82: Suppose that $f(x, y) = x^3 + y^3 - 2xy$. Does this function have a local maximum or a local minimum?

Question 1.83: Three random variables have equal pairwise correlation ρ. What is the possible range of ρ?

Question 1.84: What is an integral?

Question 1.85: How do you use a Monte-Carlo simulation to evaluate

$$E[g(X)] = \int_{x=-\infty}^{x=+\infty} g(x) f_X(x) dx,$$

where $g(x)$ is a real-valued polynomial and $X \sim N(\mu, \sigma^2)$?

Question 1.86: What is 29×29?

Question 1.87: What is 43×43?

Question 1.88: What is 21×19?

Question 1.89: There are three wooden barrels in the market. One contains apples only, one contains oranges only, and one contains both apples and oranges. Labels to this effect are pinned to the barrels, but the labels have been mixed up so that no label correctly identifies the contents of the barrel to which it is pinned. You can see the labels, but you cannot see inside, or feel inside, or smell inside, any barrel. You may ask for as many pieces of fruit as you want from any of the labeled barrels. What is the minimum number of pieces of fruit you can request, and from which barrel(s) should you request them, if your task is to re-pin the labels so that each label correctly identifies the contents of its barrel?[14]

Question 1.90: Is $11^{2.5}$ larger or smaller than 400? You must do this in your head. You are not allowed to use a calculator or pencil and paper.

Question 1.91: You are given that the lengths of two sides of a triangle are 5 and 6. What is the approximate length of the third side?

Question 1.92: You have two large blank-faced cubic dice and a marker pen. You are going to write a single-digit number on each face of each die so that you can display the two dice together on your desk to represent days of the month. You must use both dice. For example, $(0, 3)$ is the third of the month, $(1, 0)$ is the tenth of the month, $(1, 9)$ is the nineteenth of the month, and $(3, 1)$ is the thirty-first of the month. You can swap the order of the physical dice if you need to (e.g., maybe you only want a 0 on one die, so that you can use it first during the first nine days of the month, but use it second on the tenth day of the month). What numbers do you put on each die?

---

[14]I have also heard that this question was asked as a hot drink machine with three (mis)labels for "tea," "coffee," or "randomly tea or coffee."

Question 1.93:   I do not have a toaster, but I have a frying pan that can hold three slices of bread if I use it to make toast. It takes one minute to toast one side of the bread in my pan. Each side of the bread has to be toasted, so I can make at most three slices of toast in two minutes. (You may ignore any time required to flip the bread over.) How long will it take me to make *four* slices of toast?[15]

Question 1.94:   Consider a wire-frame 1×1 cube. Label one vertex as A and the opposing vertex as B, as in Figure 1.3. How many non-self-intersecting paths lead from A to B? (Non-self-intersecting means that a path may not touch a vertex more than once.)

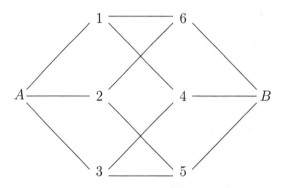

Figure 1.3: Graph of a Cube

Note: We are asked to count non-self-intersecting (i.e., touching any vertex no more than once) paths that lead from A to B.

Question 1.95:   Prove that there are infinitely many prime numbers.

Question 1.96:   Show that when given any positive integer n, there exists a sequence of n consecutive positive integers none of which is prime.

Question 1.97:   Finally, can the mean of two consecutive prime numbers (e.g., 7 and 11) ever be prime?

---

[15]It was not asked by the interviewer, but can you find a general formula $M(n)$ that describes the minutes, M, required to make n slices of toast using this pan? Assume $n \geq 2$.

Chapter 2

Derivatives Questions

A prerequisite for answering the questions in this chapter is knowledge of basic option pricing theory. I strongly recommend my book *Basic Black-Scholes: Option Pricing and Trading* (Crack [2021]) as the best resource. It provides a firm foundation in Black-Scholes option pricing, with practical advice about option trading. See the advertisement at the end of this book, or go directly to `www.BasicBlackScholes.com`. Solutions for this chapter appear in Appendix B.

Question 2.1: All Black-Scholes assumptions hold. Assume no dividends. The stock price is $100. The riskless interest rate is 5% per annum. Consider a one-year European call option struck at-the-money (i.e., strike equals current spot). If the volatility is zero (i.e., $\sigma = 0$), what is the call worth? After valuing the call, please tell me how to hedge the call (assuming you sold it).

Question 2.2: Two standard options have exactly the same features, except that one has long maturity, and the other has short maturity. Which one has the higher gamma?

Question 2.3: All Black-Scholes assumptions hold. Assume no dividends. Consider a standard European call and a standard European put on the same stock. Assume that each option has the same maturity, and is struck at-the-money (i.e., strike equals current spot). For the sake of simplicity, assume that the interest rate is zero. Draw the payoff diagrams for each option (i.e., terminal payoff to option versus level of underlying).

The put has limited upside potential and no downside; the call has unlimited upside potential and no downside. Given the random direction of the stock price movements between now and expiration, the disparity in potential payoffs seems to suggest that the call should be worth more than the put. However, put-call parity says that this is not so. Verify the put-call parity implications and reconcile them with the seemingly disparate potential payoffs.

Question 2.4: For a standard European call option, draw the graph of the "delta" as a function of current stock price, $S(t)$.

Question 2.5: Assume a Black-Scholes world without dividends. Consider a standard European call struck at-the-money (i.e., strike equals current spot) with one year to maturity. If the interest rate is $r = 0.06$, is the option's delta greater or less than 0.5? What does it depend on?

Question 2.6: Assume a Black-Scholes world with continuous dividends. Consider a standard European call struck at-the-money (i.e., strike equals current spot) with one year to maturity. If the interest rate is $r = 0.06$, and dividends are at rate $\rho = 0.03$, can you tell whether the option's delta is greater or less than 0.5? What does it depend on?

Question 2.7: You are long a call option on MITCO stock. You have delta hedged your position. You hear on the radio that the CEO of MITCO has just been arrested for running a massive Ponzi scheme. The stock price plunges $10. How do you adjust your hedge (qualitatively)? That is, do you borrow and buy stock or sell stock and lend? Explain carefully.

Question 2.8: How do you calculate an option's delta?[1]

Question 2.9: Explain very carefully the terms $N(d_1)$ and $N(d_2)$ that appear in the standard Black-Scholes European call option pricing formula without dividends.[2]

Question 2.10: Consider the European digital option (or "binary option") that pays a constant H if the stock price is above strike price X at expiration and zero otherwise. What is the price of this option, and how is it related to the price of the standard Black-Scholes European call option? Explain carefully.[3]

Question 2.11: Consider the European digital option (or "binary option") that pays H if the stock price is above strike price X at expiration and zero otherwise. How does the price of this option vary with volatility (that is, what is $\frac{\partial C}{\partial \sigma^2}$)? Intuitively? Rigorously? Explain carefully.

Question 2.12: Compare the "delta" of a standard European call option with the delta of a barrier option, for example a "down-and-out" call option.[4]

---

[1] Answer for a standard European call option (with and without dividends), and for an option with no closed-form solution (e.g., a plain vanilla American-style put or an exotic).

[2] Now use this explanation to deduce the standard Black-Scholes European put option pricing formula—if you can. Confirm that the pricing formulae verify the put-call parity relationship (with $D = 0$): $S(t) + p(t) = c(t) + Xe^{-r(T-t)} + D$.

[3] This is the "cash-or-nothing" digital option. You should also be able to answer this question for the "asset-or-nothing" digital option (which gives you the asset if $S(T) > X$ and nothing otherwise).

[4] Is the answer different for an up-and-out call? Explain carefully. Incidentally, who would buy an up-and-out call? Well, suppose you expect only limited upside on a security. If you wish to participate in this upside without paying for what you consider to be very unlikely further price appreciation, then an up-and-out-call could be just what you want (see Derman and Kani [1993, pp. 3–4]).

Question 2.13: (**) This is an applied theoretical option pricing problem taken from a telephone interview. You are given three time series of continuously compounded returns on an industry sector index: the ISI50. The time series are daily, weekly, and monthly over the same time period.[5] You are to price a standard European call option written on the level of the ISI50 with one month to expiration.

You decide to use the trusty Black-Scholes model. You observe all input variables except for the volatility term σ^2. Unsure of which of your three time series to use to estimate the volatility term, you calculate the sample volatility of each time series. You figure that the estimators $(\hat{\sigma}_d^2, \hat{\sigma}_w^2, \hat{\sigma}_m^2)$ should be related as $\hat{\sigma}_m^2 \approx 4\hat{\sigma}_w^2$, $\hat{\sigma}_m^2 \approx 20\hat{\sigma}_d^2$, and $\hat{\sigma}_w^2 \approx 5\hat{\sigma}_d^2$. You could thus get the monthly volatility either explicitly from the monthly estimate or implicitly from the weekly or daily estimates. You think the daily data are most reliable (they have the most observations).

You find, much to your horror, that $\hat{\sigma}_m^2 > 4\hat{\sigma}_w^2$, $\hat{\sigma}_m^2 > 20\hat{\sigma}_d^2$, and $\hat{\sigma}_w^2 > 5\hat{\sigma}_d^2$. Further investigation reveals that these differences are highly statistically significant. Your statistical observation is thus that the monthly volatility implicit in the daily and weekly time series is significantly smaller than the monthly volatility in the monthly time series.

How do you price the option? Explain your reasoning carefully.[6]

> **Story:** One of my students went to an interview with a big-name Wall Street firm in New York. He was interviewed by five quantitative guys in a row. Each interview was one hour, and there were absolutely no breaks. He had to work through multiple quantitative problems on their blackboard. They gave him no lunch. He was exhausted and starving by the end. He was swearing black and blue about the "&@!#@$%'s" when he got back. He said "The Russian" was the worst.

Question 2.14: Consider a plain vanilla American call option on a non-dividend-paying stock. The price of the call is $C(t)$ at time t. The "intrinsic value" of the call is $\max[S(t) - X, 0]$ (where $S(t)$ is stock price at time t, and X is exercise price). The excess of call value over intrinsic value is the "time value" of the option.[7]

Draw a graph of the time value, $C(t) - \max[S(t) - X, 0]$, versus $S(t)$. Explain carefully the different aspects of the plot.

---

[5] Feel free to assume that one week is exactly five days, one month is exactly 20 days, and that there are no missing observations or exchange holidays.

[6] Hint: Begin by explaining how and why your statistical observations could arise. What went wrong? Ask yourself whether Black-Scholes pricing is still applicable. If not, where do you turn?

[7] Perhaps a more natural definition of intrinsic value is $\max[S(t) - Xe^{-r(T-t)}, 0]$ (Merton [1973, p. 145]; Merton [1992, p. 260]; Smith [1976, p. 11]). What would the plot of time value versus $S(t)$ look like with this definition of intrinsic value?

Question 2.15: It is 10 months since you sold a one-year European call option to a customer. You have been delta-hedging your exposure to the written call since it was sold. The option is now well in-the-money, and the delta of your replicating portfolio is correspondingly high (at around 0.90, say).

Suppose that you watch the underlying stock price falling gently over the last two months of the life of the option. As the stock price falls over this time period, what happens to the delta of the replicating portfolio? That is, are you buying stocks or selling stocks as you watch the stock price fall? You may have to describe different possible scenarios—be clear on the assumptions you make.

Story: She threw up on my desk and immediately started asking questions about the job, like nothing had happened.

Interview Horror Stories from Recruiters
Reprinted by kind permission of *MBA Style Magazine*
©1996–2021 MBA Style Magazine, `www.mbastyle.com`

Question 2.16: What do you know about jump processes and jump diffusion processes? Explain when the pricing formula for a call option written on an asset whose price level follows a jump process can and cannot be derived using the Black-Scholes/Merton no-arbitrage technique.[8]

Question 2.17: This question concerns the standard European call option on a non-dividend-paying stock. You are asked to draw three closely related graphs as follows:

1. Please draw the graph of call price at maturity (time T) versus terminal stock price, $S(T)$.

2. Please draw the graph of call price at time t versus the futures price $F(t,T)$. The futures price $F(t,T)$ is observed at time t, prior to maturity. The futures contract and the option both mature at the same date T.[9]

3. Now draw the graph of call price versus stock price at time t, prior to maturity.

Explain carefully the relationships between the three graphs.

---

[8] Describe the form of the pricing formula for a European call option written on a stock whose price level follows a jump diffusion process (using Merton's notation): $\frac{dS}{S} = (\alpha - \lambda k)dt + \sigma dZ + dq$, where $dq = 0$ if the "Poisson event" (i.e., the jump) does not occur, $dq = (Y-1)$ if the jump does occur, $(Y-1)$ is a spike producing a finite jump in stock price from S to SY, α is the instantaneous expected rate of return on the stock, σ^2 is the instantaneous variance of returns assuming no jump occurs, dZ is a standard Wiener process, λ is the number of arrivals that you expect per unit time, $k \equiv E(Y-1)$ where E is the expectation operator over the random variable Y, and dZ is assumed independent of the Poisson process dq (see Merton [1992, p. 313]).

[9] Futures on single stocks have been traded in the U.S. since 2002. See `www.OneChicago.com` for details.

Question 2.18: Consider two European call options on the same underlying stock. The options have the same strike price. Assume constant interest rates. One option matures in one year; the other option matures in four years. Suppose that you put $\sigma = 15\%$ into the Black-Scholes formula to value the one-year option. What value of σ do you put into the Black-Scholes formula to value the four-year option? Assume that you set $T - t = 1$ in the Black-Scholes formula in both cases (i.e., one unit of time equals four years in the second case but only one year in the first case).

> **Story:** Some recent questions include "What do you think an investment banker does?" Not only that, but "Do you understand the hours investment bankers work and why?" Some of these folks look like Hell when you meet them. Are you sure about this career choice?

Question 2.19: (***) The Black-Scholes formula is derived assuming the stock price process $S(t)$ follows a geometric Brownian motion: $dS(t) = \mu S(t)dt + \sigma S(t)dw(t)$, where $w(t)$ is a standard Brownian motion. Suppose instead that a stock price process $\mathcal{S}(t)$ follows an arithmetic Brownian motion: $d\mathcal{S}(t) = \mu dt + \sigma_A dw(t)$. Derive the pricing formula for a call option on $\mathcal{S}(t)$. Please assume that the option is at-the-money [i.e., $\mathcal{S}(t) = \mathcal{X}$], that the riskless interest rate $r = 0$, and that the stock pays no dividends.

Question 2.20: Interviewer: "You are fully familiar with Black-Scholes pricing aren't you?" Interviewee: (confidently, after a slight pause) "Yes indeed." Interviewer: "What is the value of a three-month at-the-money (i.e., $S = X$) call option on a \$100 stock when the implied vol is 40? Please assume $r = 0$ (it is the least important ingredient anyway) and assume also that the stock pays no dividends. You have 10 seconds to perform the calculation in your head. Now tell me how your answer changes if it is instead a put."

Question 2.21: A customer calls up and wants a price on a European 100-day call option. You quote \$100. He calls back a minute later and wants a quote on the same option but with 200 days to maturity. How does the second price quote compare with the first price quote? Explain carefully.

Question 2.22: Assume a Black-Scholes world. You have a one-year European call option on a stock. There are no dividends, the interest rate is assumed to be zero, and the option is struck at-the-money (i.e., strike equals current spot). The current spot is \$100. The standard deviation of terminal stock price (conditional on current stock price) is \$10.[10] Is the call price closer to \$1, \$5, or \$10?[11]

---

[10]It follows that the standard deviation of continuously compounded returns is approximately 10% per annum.

[11]If the standard deviation is \$20 per annum, is the call price closer to \$5, \$10, or \$20?

Question 2.23: You hold a 100-day European call option on a stock with implied volatility 20. Suppose that you know right now that tomorrow the implied volatility will increase to 25, but that after that it will return to 20 for the remainder of its life. What extension to the life of the call would produce the same change in the present value of the call as the above-mentioned single-day increase in volatility (assuming a constant implied volatility at 20)? That is, other things being equal, what change in the term to maturity is equivalent to the quoted one-day change in the implied volatility? Explain carefully.

Question 2.24: You are long a straddle with a strike of $25. The underlying is at $25. The straddle costs you $5 to enter. What price movement are you looking for in the underlying?

Question 2.25: You are considering two contracts: a Eurodollar *futures* contract, with six months to maturity, selling at 5%, settled on three-month LIBOR, marked-to-market every day; and a Eurodollar *forward* contract, with six months to maturity, selling at 5%, settled on three-month LIBOR at maturity.[12]

1. Which contract do you prefer (or are you indifferent)?

2. Do you think there is a mis-pricing?

3. If you go long one and short the other, which one should be long, and which one should be short (or are you indifferent)?

Question 2.26: You are to value a call option using Monte-Carlo simulation. Is it better to simulate the geometric Brownian motion (GBM) process for the call itself, or the GBM process for the underlying?

Question 2.27: Suppose that you hold a long position in mortgage-backed securities. If you are expecting a bond market rally, would you be better off with positive convexity or negative convexity?

> **Story:** There is the old story of the candidate who flew to London for an interview. At the interview, the interviewer excused himself for a few minutes. However, before leaving he asked the interviewee to open a window. Once alone, the interviewee discovered that all the windows were sealed shut. Great! Michael Lewis (in his excellent book *Liar's Poker*) talks about this technique in use on Wall Street (Lewis, 1990, p. 27). He suggests that one desperate interviewee threw a chair through Lehman's 43rd floor window in Manhattan!

Question 2.28: What is wrong with the following strategy for hedging a short call option: buy one share if the stock price exceeds the strike, and sell the share if the stock price falls below the strike?

---

[12]Note: LIBOR is due to be retired after 2021 (Riquier, 2019), but an extension to mid-2023 is likely (Shaw, McCormick, Bolingbroke, and Torres, 2020).

Question 2.29: How fresh is your stochastic calculus? What can you tell me about $\int_0^T w(t)dt$, where $w(t)$ is a standard Brownian motion?

Question 2.30: What can you say about $\int_0^T w(t)dw(t)$, where $w(t)$ is a standard Brownian motion?

Question 2.31: Suppose that $w(t)$ is a standard Brownian motion. For which values of n is $w^n(t)$ a martingale?

Question 2.32: (**) Suppose that IBM is trading at \$75 per share. What does it cost to construct a derivative security that pays exactly one dollar when IBM hits \$100 for the first time? Explain carefully the construction of the security. You may ignore IBM's dividends, assume a riskless interest rate of zero, assume all assets are infinitely divisible, ignore any short sale restrictions, and ignore any taxes or transactions costs.

Story: "During his interview with me, a candidate bit his fingernails and proceeded to bleed onto his tie. When I asked him if he wanted a Band-Aid, he said that he chewed his nails all the time and that he'd be fine. He continued to chew away."

AUDREY W. HELLINGER
Chicago Office of Martin H. Bauman
Associates, New York

"Doomed Days: The Worst Mistakes Recruiters Have Ever Seen,"
The Wall Street Journal, February 25, 1995, pR4.
Reprinted by permission of *The Wall Street Journal*
©1995 Dow Jones and Company, Inc.
All Rights Reserved Worldwide.

Question 2.33: (**) The payoff to a European-style "power call" is given by $\max(S^\alpha - X, 0)$. Derive the price of a European power call option using Black-Scholes pricing.[13,14]

Story: "If we offer you a job right now, will you take it?" is often used by firms who will not make you an offer unless they know you will say yes.

Question 2.34: Why do you get a "smile" effect when you plot implied volatilities of options against their strike prices?

Question 2.35: Have you heard of a local volatility model? What is it?

---

[13]Try drawing the payoff diagrams for the cases $\alpha > 1$ and $\alpha < 1$. Add the current call value as a function of stock price to your diagrams.

[14]Jarrow and Turnbull (1996, p. 175) describe a "powered option" with payoff $[S(T) - X]^2$ if $S(T) \geq X$ and zero otherwise. I give the general result for the case $[S(T) - X]^\alpha$ in the solutions. Try to derive it before you peek at my solutions.

Question 2.36: Is the price of a double-barrier, knock-out option (i.e. one with both up-and-out and down-and-out barriers) just the price of an up-and-out plus the price of a down-and-out?

Question 2.37: Describe the analytical procedure for deriving (using calculus) the values of European digital asset-or-nothing and digital cash-or-nothing options.

Question 2.38: Consider an American-style double-barrier "out-in" call option. There is an out barrier above the current stock price (an "up barrier") and an in barrier below the current stock price (a "down barrier"). This option has a payoff only if all three of the following events happen: first, the stock price path includes a fall in price below the down barrier (i.e., the option is "knocked in"); second, the stock price path does not include a rise in price above the up barrier (i.e., the option is not "knocked out"); and third, the option is exercised when the stock price is above the strike (i.e., the option is in-the-money at exercise). This option is both path-dependent and American-style. Is there an easy technique for valuing the option?

Question 2.39: Suppose gold prices follow a Gaussian process.[15] The current price of gold is \$400. The riskless interest rate is zero. The volatility of gold in dollar terms is $\sigma = \$60$ per annum. What is the value today of a digital cash-or-nothing option that pays \$1 million in six months if the price of gold is at or above \$430?

> **Story:** Here is another Fermi problem from Section 5.5: "How many ping-pong balls can you fit in a jumbo jet (e.g., Boeing 747)?"

Question 2.40: (**) What is the value of a perpetual (i.e., potentially infinitely lived) American put option?

Question 2.41: Let "L" denote the three-month U.S. dollar LIBOR rate.[16] Consider an interest rate swap arrangement where Party A pays L to Party B, and Party B pays $24\% - 2 \times L$ to Party A. Can you reverse engineer this deal and express it in simpler terms?

Question 2.42: If an option is at-the-money, about how many shares of stock should you hold to hedge the option?

Question 2.43: Compare the price of an option on a stock if the stock price follows mean reversion versus if the stock price does not.

Question 2.44: When can hedging an options position make you take on more risk?

---

[15] This is an arithmetic Brownian motion. The future price of gold is thus assumed to be normally distributed (not lognormally as per Black-Scholes).

[16] Note: As mentioned already, LIBOR is due to be retired after 2021 (Riquier, 2019), but an extension to mid-2023 is likely (Shaw, McCormick, Bolingbroke, and Torres, 2020).

Question 2.45: How do you hedge a written put on a stock if you can neither short any stock nor use options on any stock?

Question 2.46: Another pizza question! You order a pizza for six people. The diameter of the pizza is 12 inches. What would the diameter have to be to feed eight people? Yes, this is a derivatives question.

Question 2.47: When do you want to be short a put option on IBM stock?

Question 2.48: You own two pieces of land—a huge field in Arizona and a tiny piece of beach in Florida. The field in Arizona is idle; you have no plans to develop the land in any way. The tiny beach in Florida is very popular. In fact, it is so popular that you charge a small entrance fee for beachgoers.

The government has offered to buy the Arizona field for \$1 million. Your neighbor has offered to buy the Florida beach for \$1 million as well. Other things being equal, which piece of land has the higher forward price?

Question 2.49: You have 30 days of "representative" stock price data. How do you calculate historical volatility $\hat{\sigma}^2$ to use in Black-Scholes?

Question 2.50: Suppose a "top issuer" (i.e., highest-rated financial institution used as a reference in setting the swap curve) issues a corporate bond for itself valued at 100. The issuer then re-prices this bond using the swap curve. What price do they get (100, above 100, or below 100)? To clarify, they fix the coupon rate of the bond so that it is priced at par, and then they try pricing this same bond by discounting those previously set coupons using the swap curve. Is the answer par, above par, or below par?

Question 2.51: Suppose I don't know any mathematics. How do you explain to me why you use the riskless rate instead of the required return on the stock to derive the Black-Scholes formula?

Question 2.52: Are you better off using implied standard deviation or historical standard deviation to forecast volatility?

Question 2.53: According to Black-Scholes, which is more valuable: a European call option that is 10% out-of-the-money, or a European put option that is 10% out-of-the-money?

Question 2.54: Why are theta and gamma of opposite signs? Are they always of opposite signs?

Question 2.55: Suppose that the riskless rate is zero. Suppose that a stock is at \$100, and one year from now will be at either \$130, or \$70, with probabilities 0.80 and 0.20 respectively. There are no dividends. What is the value of a one-year European call with strike \$110?

Question 2.56: (**) Find a formula for the European-style "product call" with payoff $\max(S_1 \times S_2 - X, 0)$, where S_1 and S_2 are the prices of assets following geometric Brownian motions with correlated random increments. All other Black-Scholes assumptions apply.

Question 2.57: Are Asian options cheaper or more expensive than plain vanilla European-style options?

> **Story:** One of my students was asked to "Describe the best party you have ever been to." She said this big-name Wall Street investment bank was looking for "fun loving" people.

Question 2.58: When can a plain vanilla American-style call be treated as a European-style one? When can a plain vanilla American-style put be treated as a European-style one?

Question 2.59: How many nodes are there in a recombining binomial tree with N time steps? How many nodes are there in a non-recombining binomial tree with N time steps?

Question 2.60: You have inside information that a foreign stock will rise for sure. You can legally trade in the foreign market without being subject to any insider trading rules. You can trade the stock, a forward on the stock, futures on the stock, or options on the stock. Assume interest rates are zero, there are no transactions costs, the exchange rate will not move, and there are no restrictions on trading the derivatives. What trade should you put on if you can only go long these instruments?

Question 2.61: (**) A call option is priced at c today. What is its expected price tomorrow?

Question 2.62: (**) If in Question 2.61 you answered that the expected call price tomorrow is higher than today's call price, then how do you reconcile your answer with time decay? That is, how do you reconcile a positive expected return with negative theta?

> **Story:** A friend in the City of London was interviewing a candidate for a position on a credit derivatives quant team. On asking the candidate why he moved out of theoretical physics, he replied: "Why does a bank robber rob a bank?" After asking him several probabilistic dice questions, the candidate replied: "I can't be bothered with this shit." On asking him why he left his previous job, he replied: "Because they were a bunch of @!&*#\$s." This is a true story!

Chapter 3

Other Financial Economics Questions

As a prerequisite to answering the questions in this chapter, it is expected that you have completed an introductory course in financial economics (or equivalent independent study). You also need a good deal of common sense. Solutions for this chapter appear in Appendix C.

Question 3.1: Consider the following game: a player tosses a fair coin until a head appears; if the head occurs on the kth toss, the player gets a payoff of $\$2^k$, and the game ends.[1]

1. What is the fair value of the game? That is, what is the expected payoff to a player?

2. A very important customer is on the line and wants you to quote him a bid-ask spread for exactly one play of the game. "Hurry up, I haven't got all day!" You have 15 seconds.

Question 3.2: If the standard deviation of continuously compounded annual stock returns is 10%, what is the standard deviation of continuously compounded four-year stock returns?

Question 3.3: From the term-structure of interest rates, you see that the five-year spot rate is 10% per annum and the 10-year spot rate is 15% per annum. What is the implied forward rate from year 5 to year 10?

Question 3.4: Explain carefully the difference between the "yield" on a bond and the "rate of return" on a bond.

Question 3.5: What is "chaos theory"? Can you use it to predict stock returns? If so, how?

---

[1]This game is over 250 years old and is known as the "St. Petersburg Game." It is quoted by Daniel Bernoulli ([Latin version 1738]; [English translation 1954]).

🏛 **Question 3.6:** Draw the graph of bond price versus yield-to-maturity. Why is the curve convex?[2]

Question 3.7: The Capital Asset Pricing Model (CAPM) says that the plot of $E(r)$ versus β is an upward sloping line through $(0, r_f)$ and $[1, E(r_M)]$ (i.e., the Security Market Line [SML]). Suppose, however, that when you plot average returns against estimated betas you find something else. Which of the following two scenarios is most likely?

1. An upward sloping curve beginning at $(0, r_f)$, wholly above the theoretical SML, initially more steep than the SML, but eventually roughly parallel to the SML

2. An upward sloping curve beginning at $(0, r_f)$, wholly below the theoretical SML, initially less steep than the SML, but eventually roughly parallel to the SML

Which CAPM assumptions (if any) are violated by the above two scenarios?

🏛 **Question 3.8:** From the term-structure of interest rates, you see that the two-year spot rate is 7.60% per annum, and the one-year spot rate is 7.15% per annum.

What is the implied forward rate for the second year?

Question 3.9: Consider a six-month forward contract on a 10-year riskless discount (zero-coupon) bond.

1. Is the bond selling at a forward premium or a forward discount?

2. Does your answer change if the bond is a riskless *coupon* bond (assume the coupon rate exceeds the current risk-free rate)?

Question 3.10: You believe that the yield curve is going to steepen very soon. It may be a fall in short-term rates, a rise in long-term rates, or some combination of these. What strategy should you pursue in the bond market to position yourself to profit from your beliefs?

🏛 **Question 3.11:** Define "duration" and "convexity." Describe their properties and uses.

Question 3.12: Describe briefly the GARCH(1,1) model in qualitative terms. Now write down the formal GARCH(1,1) model and explain each term carefully.[3]

🏛 **Question 3.13:** You have a long position in a $100 million 30-year bond. What can you do to limit your exposure to only $50 million?

---

[2]Can you give economic intuition for this convexity? What about mathematical intuition?

[3]Note that GARCH is an acronym for Generalized AutoRegressive Conditional Heteroskedasticity. How do you estimate the model? Why was it introduced?

Question 3.14: (**) You hold an 8% coupon, 30-year, $1,000 par, Mexican Brady bond. Interest rates in Mexico do not change. Interest rates in the U.S. increase by 1%. What is the change in the price of your bond? Make any necessary assumptions.

Question 3.15: You construct a yield curve for (coupon-bearing) treasuries. A particular five-year corporate zero-coupon bond has a default risk premium of 1% over the level of your treasuries yield curve at the five-year mark. You believe that the yield curve is going to flatten in such a way that the default risk premium of the five-year corporate zero remains constant (short-term rates rise, long-term rates fall, and the yield on the five-year coupon-bearing treasury and five-year corporate zero remain unchanged).

What strategy should you pursue using the five-year zero-coupon corporate bond and treasuries to position yourself to profit from your beliefs?

Question 3.16: The five-year interest rate is 10%, and the 10-year interest rate is 15%. You conclude that the forward rate from year 5 to year 10 is approximately 20%. Explain, *using plain English*, why the forward rate has to be *higher* than the 20% approximate value mentioned above.

Question 3.17: Here is a simple game. You get to toss a fair coin now. If it is heads, you get seven dollars 18 months from now. If it is tails, you lose two dollars immediately. The one-year interest rate is 12% per annum. The two-year interest rate is 18% per annum.

How much are you prepared to pay to play this game?

> **Story:** Many people are asked: "Are you married? What religion are you? Do you have children? What does your spouse do? How is your family? Where were you born? How old are you?" These are legal questions in the U.S., but discriminating on the basis of the answers is not legal. So, most employers avoid even the hint of possible discrimination. Nevertheless, you should be prepared to answer these questions.

Question 3.18: There are 20 traders in a room. They trade in 100 stocks. They trade for their own accounts and only amongst themselves—it is a "closed economy." Halfway through their morning trading session, a group of SEC officials arrives and announces that one of the traders has inside information on one stock and has been trading on it. The trader is not yet identified. The SEC officials seat themselves in the room to watch. What happens to trading volume after the SEC announcement? Explain carefully.

> **Story:** One of my students who got a job at a large mutual fund company described his firm's working environment as follows: "Dig a hole, fill the hole with water, fill the water with sharks, and promote anything that crawls out alive."

Question 3.19:   Two stocks have the same expected return. One has standard deviation of returns of 20%, and the other has standard deviation of returns of 30%. The correlation between their returns is 50%. How do I allocate money between these so as to minimize my risk.

Question 3.20:   The same question as Question 3.19 but with variance of returns 10% and 40%, respectively, and correlation 50%.

Story: Let me give some unorthodox advice.

1.   A colleague and I were interviewing a candidate for a quant equities job in London. After a few questions about his CV, we asked him a simple quant question. He was extremely uncomfortable. He declared it to be "not a proper interview," and to our amazement, he walked out the door! He made two fatal mistakes. First, walking out meant he was a quitter. Nobody likes quitters. Second, he should have attempted an answer because even if he was not suited to quant equities at my firm, we had vacancies in other areas and we knew of vacancies at other firms, and we would have passed his CV on if we thought he was talented—but not if we thought he was a quitter. It is in the interviewer's best interests to pass good CVs around the firm and to a network of contacts outside of it because the favor will be returned eventually. Remember, you are never interviewing for that one job only! If the interview is going badly, then be positive and focus on your strengths even if they are not strengths for that job!

2.   I was being interviewed for a practitioner job I really wanted. I was up to about the fifth person on my schedule for the day. From the moment this guy set eyes on me across the table I could tell he did not want to hire me. He was 100% negative and actually looked angry! I can read upside down, and, without him noticing, I quickly read the questions he had written on my CV across the table from me. I addressed his questions before he even asked them. That surprised him! I turned the conversation toward the markets and found some common ground. He became interested. I made a tasteful joke. He smiled. When our half-hour was up, he was 100% positive and I know he recommended that I be hired. There was nothing unethical about this manipulation of interview/interviewer: I love the markets, wanted the job, and thought the firm was a great fit for me.

3.   The two stories above are about losing and winning, respectively. I think a difference between these outcomes is mental preparation. I was given an inexpensive book called *The Dirty Dozen* written by Sergeant Major (Ret.) Lawrence A. Jordan. Sergeant Major Jordan served a 24-year Special Operations career with the U.S. Army Rangers and Special Forces. His book is about dirty fighting techniques, and Chapter 2, "The Winning Mind," is about mental preparation for life-or-death hand-to-hand combat in self defence. Although it is unorthodox of me to write this, I recommend that you read "The Winning Mind" chapter of *The Dirty Dozen* for interview preparation. If you can stomach it, it may give you just the edge you need.

Chapter 4

Statistics Questions

The only prerequisites for answering the statistics questions in this chapter are elementary statistical skills. Solutions for this chapter appear in Appendix D.

Question 4.1: A breakfast cereal company gives away a free toy in each box of cereal. There are four different toys. How many boxes do you expect to have to buy in order to get all four toys?

Question 4.2: Suppose we draw two random numbers X and Y each distributed uniform on the interval $[0, 1]$. If X and Y are independent, what is the probability that their product is greater than $1/2$?

Question 4.3: Suppose that $X \sim N(\mu, \sigma^2)$ (i.e., X is normally distributed with mean μ and variance σ^2). Please write down the pdf $f_X(x)$ of X. Where does the constant factor in the pdf come from?

Question 4.4: Suppose that $X \sim N(\mu, \sigma^2)$, as in the previous question. What is $E\left(X^2\right)$?[1]

Question 4.5: Suppose that X and Y are independent random variables each distributed standard normal: $X \sim N(0, 1)$, and $Y \sim N(0, 1)$. What are the variance and the standard deviation of $X - Y$.

🏛 **Question 4.6:** Consider the following game. The player tosses a die once only. The payoff is \$1 for each "dot" on the upturned face. Assuming a fair die, at what level should you set the ticket price for this game?

Question 4.7: I am going to toss four coins. You are going to toss five coins. You win if you get strictly more heads than I do. What is the probability that you win?

Question 4.8: I will roll a single die no more than three times. You can stop me immediately after the first roll, or immediately after the second, or you can wait for the third. I will pay you the same number of dollars as there are dots

---

[1]More generally, if $X \sim N(\mu, \sigma^2)$, can you give $E\left[(X - \mu)^n\right]$ and $E\left(X^n\right)$ for any n?

on the single upturned face on my last roll (roll number three unless you stop me sooner). What is your playing strategy?[2]

> **Story:** One of my MIT students was exceptionally well qualified. He was also one of the nicest guys I have ever met. He was quiet and soft-spoken. He was very understated (the kind of guy you might not notice). His starting salary at a big-name Wall Street firm was about four times the average MIT starting salary that year. The moral of the story: I don't care how hot you think you are—brains wins.

Question 4.9: The correlation between X and Y is ρ. What is the correlation between $X + 5$ and Y? What is the correlation between $5X$ and Y?

> **Story:** One interviewee told me that the interviewers aim to put you under as much pressure as possible, and that "you never know when they are going to bring out the guy in the chicken suit."

🏛 **Question 4.10:** (**) Two sealed envelopes are handed out. You get one and your competitor gets the other. You understand that one envelope contains m dollars, and the other contains $2m$ dollars (where m is unstated).[3]

1. *If* you peek into your envelope, you see \$X. However, you do not know whether your opponent has \$2X or \$$\frac{1}{2}X$. *Without peeking*, what is your expected benefit to switching envelopes? What is your opponent's expected benefit to switching envelopes (assuming your opponent sees \$Y)? Should you switch? If you do, do you do it again for the same reason (assuming neither of you peeked)?

2. Suppose that you both peek into your envelopes initially. What is the payoff to switching? Should you switch? If you do, do you do it again for the same reason?

Question 4.11: They call this the "World Series" problem in the U.S. Sports teams "A" and "B" are to play each other until one has four wins and is declared the series winner. You have \$100 to bet on Team A to win the series. You are, however, only allowed to bet on individual games, not the final outcome directly, and, you must bet a positive amount on each game. So, if Team A wins the series, you must walk away with \$200, but if Team A loses the series, you must walk away with zero, and you must do so having placed a non-zero bet on every game. Your best assessment is that Team A

---

[2]If you were running this game, how much would you charge players for repeated plays of the game? Suppose instead an amended game is played: I roll a single die three times without pause, and the payoff to the player is the maximum of the three rolls. What is the expected payoff to the player? Can you tell up front whether the original or amended game has the higher expected payoff?

[3]This problem is over 40 years old and is known as the "Exchange Paradox."

has a 70% chance of winning any game and Team B has a 30% chance. How do you place your bets?

Question 4.12: You have three children, but only one apple. You want to toss a fair coin to determine which child gets the apple. You want each child to be equally likely to get the apple. What is your strategy?[4]

Question 4.13: A follow-up question to Question 4.12: What is the expected number of tosses needed to complete this strategy?

Question 4.14: Another follow-up question to Question 4.12: You have a fair coin and you want to simulate an event that has probability $1/3$, and an event that has probability $2/3$. How do you do it?

Question 4.15: What is the expected number of tosses of an unfair coin needed to get two heads (HH) in a row (assume probability p of a head)? Same question with three heads (HHH) in a row.

Question 4.16: You are tossing a fair coin and writing down the outcomes. What is the probability that you will see the sequence HTH before you see the sequence HHT?

Question 4.17: You are tossing a fair coin and writing down the outcomes. What is the expected number of tosses needed to obtain the outcome HTH?

Question 4.18: You and I are to play a game. You roll a die until a number other than a one appears. When such a number appears for the first time, I pay you the same number of dollars as there are dots on the upturned face of the die, and the game ends. What is the expected payoff to this game?

Question 4.19: You are dealt exactly two playing cards from a well-shuffled standard 52-card deck. The standard deck contains exactly four Kings. What is the probability that both of your cards are Kings?

> **Story:** It is many years ago now, but I know of a well-qualified MIT student who got a job offer of \$X from a well-known firm (a good offer at that time). He declined, telling them that they had misjudged him. They called him back a couple of days later and offered him $\$X \times 1.67$ instead! Amazing! He took the job.

Question 4.20: (**) This is one version of the famous "Let's Make a Deal" or "Monty Hall" game show question. It is your turn to be on a weekly game show. There are three doors. You know that there is a prize behind one of them, and nothing behind the other two. The game show host tells you that you shall receive whatever is behind the door of your choice. However, before

---

[4]In similar vein, suppose you had two children, one apple, and a *biased* coin. How do you use the biased coin to fairly pick which child gets the apple?

you choose, he tells you that he knows the actual location of the prize, and he promises you that rather than immediately opening the door of your choice to reveal its contents, he will first open one of the other two doors to reveal that it is empty. He will then give you the option to change your mind and instead choose the remaining door that he did not open.

You may assume that whoever set up the doors and prizes placed the prize uniformly randomly behind a door (i.e., each door had an equal probability of being chosen as the prize location). You may assume that if you initially choose a door that has the prize, then the host is uniformly random in revealing one of the two remaining doors as empty. You may assume that the host must reveal an empty door.[5]

You choose Door 3. He opens Door 2 and reveals that it is empty. You now know that the prize lies behind either Door 3 or Door 1. Should you switch your choice to Door 1?

I strongly recommend that you not look at the answer until you have done your best.

Question 4.21: (**) Now we will ask you the same question as the previous one, except that when it comes time for the host to reveal an empty door, he instead selects someone from the audience who chooses randomly and by chance chooses a door that is revealed to be empty. Should you switch?

Note: There are two ways to interpret this question. You could assume that the game can be played repeatedly with an audience member always revealing a door to be empty, or you could assume a one-off game where the audience member (ignorant of the prize's location) just happens to have chosen an empty door. Try answering both.

> **Story:** A student interviewing with a top bulge bracket firm was asked how he would move Mount Fuji. One of my colleagues suggested the answer "Call Mohammed."

Question 4.22: You are presented with two empty jars and 100 marbles on a table. There are 50 white marbles and 50 black marbles. You are to put all 100 of the marbles into the two jars in any way you choose. I will then blindfold you. I will shake the jars up to ensure good mixing, and I will rearrange the placing of the jars on the table so that you do not know which one is which. You may then request either the "left-hand" or the "right-hand" jar. You get to choose exactly one jar, you are allowed to withdraw at most one marble from the jar, and you do not get a second chance if you are unhappy with your choice.

---

[5]You can imagine variations of the problem where the host is not required to open another door if doing so helps you, or where he does not open doors with equal likelihood. The solution may differ in those cases.

How many of each color marble should you place in each jar to maximize the probability that your blindfolded random draw obtains a white marble?[6]

Question 4.23:   (***) Your name is Mr. 10. You are standing in a field with two opponents: Mr. 30 and Mr. 60. Each of you has a gun and plenty of ammunition. Each of you is in clear sight of the others and well within firing range. The goal is to maximize the probability of survival. Unfortunately, you are not a very good shot. If you take a shot at one of your opponents, you have only a 10% chance of killing him. Mr. 30 is a better shot; he has a 30% chance of killing whomever he shoots at. Mr. 60 is even better; he has a 60% chance of killing his target. You take turns shooting in a pre-arranged order: first you, then Mr. 30, then Mr. 60, and then through this cycle again and again until only one person remains.

You get to shoot first. At whom, if anyone, do you shoot?[7]

Question 4.24:   Basketball! Your team is down two points, you are the best player, and you have the ball. There are only a few seconds left before the buzzer. You can take a shot from three-point land or move up and take one from two-point land. Historically, you have a 40% probability of getting the shot in from three-point land and a 70% probability of getting the shot in from two-point land.

Should you try for the three-point shot (a certain win if you make it), or should you try for the two-point shot? Note that a two-pointer produces a tie and puts you into overtime. We assume your team has a fifty-fifty chance of winning in overtime.

Question 4.25:   I will spin a fair roulette wheel with only five sections. Four of the five sections pay \$1; the fifth pays \$5.

1. If the cost is \$1.50 per spin, and you may play as often as you want, should you play the game?

2. If the cost is \$1.50 per spin, and you may play exactly once, should you play the game?

Question 4.26:   If you like gambling and you like betting on the outcome of sports matches, then you may like the "parlay card." A parlay card lets you bet on the outcomes of more than one match. In order to win a parlay bet, you must be correct on each of the matches you bet upon. Parlay cards offer big payoffs if you are right on every match (some even offer a payoff for "almost wins").

---

[6]Can you answer the same question except that you are to *minimize* the probability of a white marble? Does minimizing the probability of a white marble maximize the probability of a black one?

[7]Does the answer change if the order is first you, then Mr. 60, then Mr. 30, then you, and so on?

Suppose that your bookie will give you 10-to-1 odds for a parlay bet that covers four sports matches (with no almost wins). Should you take the bet?[8]

Question 4.27: What is the standard deviation of $(1, 2, 3, 4, 5)$?

🏛 **Question 4.28:** Welcome to your interview. Sit in this chair. Excuse me while I tie your arms and legs to the chair. Thank you. Now we are going to play "Russian roulette." I have a revolver with six empty chambers. Watch me as I load the weapon with two contiguous rounds (i.e., two bullets side-by-side in the cylindrical barrel). Watch me as I spin the barrel. I am putting the gun against your head. Close your eyes while I pull the trigger. Click! This is your lucky day: you are still alive! Our game differs from regular Russian roulette because I am not going to add any bullets to the barrel before we continue, and I am not going to give you the gun.

My question for you: I am going to shoot at you once more before we talk about your resume. Do you want me to spin the barrel once more, or should I just shoot?[9]

Question 4.29: You have a large jar containing 999 fair pennies and one two-headed penny. Suppose you pick one coin out of the jar and flip it 10 times and get all heads. What is the probability that the coin you chose is the two-headed one?

🏛 **Question 4.30:** Four cards are shuffled and placed face down in front of you. Their faces (hidden) display the four elements: water, earth, wind, and fire. You are to turn the cards over one at a time until you either win or lose. You win if you turn over water and earth. You lose if you turn over fire. What is the probability that you win?

Story: "In his first meeting with me, a candidate made himself a little too comfortable. Not only did he liberally pepper his conversation with profanities, he also pulled his chair right up to the edge of my desk and started examining papers and knickknacks."

NINA PROCT
Martin H. Bauman Associates, New York

"Doomed Days: The Worst Mistakes Recruiters Have Ever Seen,"
The Wall Street Journal, February 25, 1995, pR4.
Reprinted by permission of *The Wall Street Journal*
©1995 Dow Jones and Company, Inc.
All Rights Reserved Worldwide.

---

[8]Should you take the bet if the odds are 25-to-1?

[9]Edward O. Thorp, when discussing gambling roulette, mentions as an aside that when playing Russian roulette, the effect of gravity on the bullet(s) will influence the position of the revolver's cylinder (Thorp, 2017, p. 126–127). Please ignore this effect here.

Question 4.31: Two players A and B play a marble game. Each player has both a red and a blue marble. They present one marble to each other. If both present red, A wins \$3. If both present blue, A wins \$1. If the colors do not match, B wins \$2. The winnings come from an external source, not from the other player. Is it better to be A, or B, or does it not matter?

Question 4.32: A coin-making machine produces pennies. Each penny is manufactured to have a probability P of turning up heads. However, the machine draws P randomly from the uniform distribution on $[0, 1]$ so P can differ for each coin produced. A coin pops out of the machine. You flip it once, and it comes up heads. Given this information, what is the (conditional) distribution function $F_{P|H}(p)$ for the probability of a head for that coin (where "H" denotes conditioning on the head)?

What is the (conditional) distribution function for the probability of a head if you flip the coin 1,000 times and get 750 heads?

Question 4.33: Suppose that X is distributed normal with mean 0 and variance σ^2. What is $E(e^X)$?

Question 4.34: Two games are offered to you. In Game One, you roll a die once and you are paid \$1 million times the number of dots on the upturned face of the die. In Game Two, you roll a die one million times. For each roll you are paid \$1 times the number of dots on the upturned face of the die. You are risk averse. Which game do you prefer?

> **Story:** 1. Took a brush out of my purse, brushed his hair and left. 2. Pulled out a Polaroid camera and snapped a flash picture of me. Said he collected photos of everyone who interviewed him.
>
> Interview Horror Stories from Recruiters
> Reprinted by kind permission of *MBA Style Magazine*
> ©1996–2021 MBA Style Magazine, www.mbastyle.com

Question 4.35: In a survey of 1,000 people, 60% said they would vote for Candidate A for president (and 40% said they would vote for someone else). How can you calculate a margin of error on the 60% estimate?

Question 4.36: A disease occurs with probability 0.5% in the population. There is a test for the disease. If you have the disease, the test returns a positive for sure. If you do not have the disease, the test returns a false positive 7% of the time. A random stranger is given the test and it returns a positive. What is the probability that the stranger has the disease?

Question 4.37: How many different ways can you invest \$20,000 into five funds in increments of \$1,000? For example, one way to do it is

$$(\$0; \ \$4,000; \ \$1,000; \ \$2,000; \ \$13,000).$$

Question 4.38:   (**) You are making chocolate chip cookies. You add N chips randomly to the cookie dough, and you randomly split the dough into 100 equal cookies. How many chips should go into the dough to give a probability of at least 90% that every cookie has at least one chip?

Question 4.39:   You will roll a fair die until the game stops. The game stops when you get a 4, 5, or 6. For every number 1, 2, or 3 you have thrown your score increases by $+1$. If the game stops with a 4 or 5, you get paid the accumulated score. If the game stops with a 6 you get nothing. What is the expected payoff of this game?

Question 4.40:   Take a stick and break it randomly into three pieces (i.e., two randomly placed breaks on the stick). What is the probability you can form a triangle from the pieces?

Question 4.41:   (**) A variation on the previous question: What is the expected length of the longest piece?[10]

Question 4.42:   Consider four boxes in a row numbered 1, 2, 3, and 4. You start with a pebble in Box 1. We toss a fair coin. If it is heads you move the pebble forward one step to Box 2, but if it is tails you move the pebble forward two steps to Box 3. Then we toss the coin again. If it is heads, you move the pebble back to Box 1, but if it is tails you advance it to Box 4. If you reach Box 4 the game is over. If you are back in Box 1, however, then we toss again following the same rules. What is the expected number of coin tosses it will take to reach Box 4?

Question 4.43:   I tell you that I have two children and that at least one of them is a girl. What is the probability that I have two girls? Assume that boys and girls are equally likely to be born and that the gender of one child is independent of gender of another.

Question 4.44:   I tell you that I have two children and that one of them is a girl (I say nothing about the other). You knock on my front door and you are greeted by a girl who you correctly deduce to be my daughter. What is the probability that I have two girls? Compare and contrast your answer to the answer to the previous question. Assume that boys and girls are equally likely to be born and that the gender of one child is independent of gender of another.

Question 4.45:   You and I are to meet tomorrow under the big clock at the train station. We have agreed to meet somewhere between 1PM and 2PM. We have agreed that each of us will wait no more than 15 minutes for the other, and that neither of us will arrive before 1PM or remain after 2PM. What is the probability that we will actually meet?

---

[10]...and what about the expected length of the shortest piece? ...or the medium piece?

Question 4.46: A single fair coin is tossed until either three heads are seen or until three tails are seen. The three heads or three tails need not be consecutive. What is the expected number of tosses in the game?

Question 4.47: If the coin in Question 4.46 is biased, is the expected number of tosses to get "three of the same" going to be greater or less than it was with the unbiased coin?

Question 4.48: Let $L(N)$ be the length of the longest run of consecutive heads or tails in N tosses of a fair coin. So, for example, if $N = 7$, and the outcomes are HHTHHHT, then $L = 3$ in this case. What is $E[L(5)] - E[L(4)]$? Please give your answer to four decimal places, and you may not use a calculator.

Question 4.49: You are going to roll three fair dice. What is the probability that the difference between the highest and lowest numbers showing is exactly four? Please give the answer to three decimal places, without using a calculator.

Question 4.50: Let $P(N)$ be the population of some endangered species. Suppose that $P(0) = 100$, but that with each generation, either the population doubles, or the population is destroyed:

$$P(N+1) = \begin{cases} 2 \times P(N) & \text{with probability } 0.5 \\ 0 \times P(N) & \text{with probability } 0.5. \end{cases}$$

What is the expected number of generations until extinction?

Question 4.51: There are seven coins arranged in a circle. Every coin is heads-up. Your goal is to flip every coin so that it is heads-down. You may, however, only flip groups of three adjacent coins. You may flip any such group of three coins, and you may flip as many such groups as you choose, one group at a time. What is the minimum number of groups of three coins you can flip in order to flip every coin so that it is heads-down?[11]

Question 4.52: You are going to roll three dice. What is the probability that the highest of the three numbers will be exactly a 4? Please give your answer to three decimals without using a calculator.

Question 4.53: You are on vacation in a foreign country. You are sitting in a restaurant looking out the window. Your waiter tells you that the bus service stopping outside your restaurant window arrives as a Poisson process. As you eat your fishcakes, you pull out your stopwatch and you time two minutes between the arrival of the first and second bus that you see, and then 12 minutes between the second and third bus. Seven minutes passes after the arrival of the third bus, and the fourth bus is not yet in sight. Stop now and estimate the arrival rate λ of the Poisson process.

---

[11]I have also heard of this question asked with reference to a rotating circular chandelier, with seven illuminated light bulbs that you are trying to extinguish, and a switch that flips the state of the three nearest adjacent light bulbs. In practice, it is much easier to play with the problem at home using coins than using light bulbs.

Question 4.54: Your car has broken down in the desert. You call a friend who laughs and tells you that the probability of seeing a car (i.e., $N \geq 1$ cars) passing by during any hour is 36%. What is the probability that you will see a car drive by in the next half-hour?

Question 4.55: Italy is playing the U.S.A. in a football World Cup match. A successful pass is when a player on one team kicks the ball to a player on their team and it is not intercepted by the opposition. Is it possible for Italy to have a higher proportion of its passes be successful than the U.S. in both the first and second halves, and yet for the U.S. to have a higher proportion of its passes be successful over the game as a whole?

Question 4.56: We are going to play a game. You have a fair coin, and your opponent has a fair coin. You are going to toss your coins together. If the outcome is HH, you pay \$6. If the outcome is HT or TH, you receive \$5. If the outcome is TT, you pay \$4. If you play this game many times, will you win or lose money?

Question 4.57: Suppose that you can choose any probability p of a head for your coin in Question 4.56. However, your opponent will see your choice of p, and can choose his or her own probability of a head as p' in response. What p will you choose, and what will be the outcome of repeated play of the game?

Question 4.58: Write down the central limit theorem.

Question 4.59: Given two uncorrelated Gaussian random variables Z_1 and Z_2, how can you obtain two correlated Gaussian random variables X_1 and X_2, with correlation coefficient ρ?

Question 4.60: What is a p-value?

Chapter 5

Non-Quantitative Questions

Poor answers to non-quantitative questions can trip you up in an interview as surely as can poor answers to quantitative questions. If you are anything like me, you probably hate those invasive, wishy-washy, touchy-feely, namby-pamby, non-quantitative interview questions that you cannot solve using logic or mathematics. If you have prepared for the quantitative questions, but you are dreading those wishy-washy, non-quantitative ones, then you need to read this chapter.

My non-quantitative questions are broken into five categories: Questions About You, Questions About Your Job Awareness, Questions About the Markets or The Economy, Questions About Financial Management, and "Thinking Questions." In cases where I deem an answer necessary, the question is labeled with an "(A)," and its suggested answer appears in Appendix E.

Some of these questions have a single correct answer (great!). Others are roughly what you might expect in some sort of Freudian couch session after having been arrested for machine-gunning all the bag boys in your local supermarket. Some of the questions depend upon knowledge of financial management; others depend upon how many drinks you had at that last party you went to (and you might not get the job if you did not have any drinks at the last party or if you do not go to parties). Speaking of which, I saw a guy turn up to an interview wearing white shoes and a white jacket. He looked like he was arriving for 1970's disco.

5.1 Questions about You

Question 5.1.1: Describe yourself in one word. (I was tempted to say "concise!")

Question 5.1.2: Tell me about yourself.

Question 5.1.3: Walk me through your resume.

Question 5.1.4: Walk me through your resume/background, highlighting work experience, leadership activities, and outstanding extra-curricular achievements.

Question 5.1.5: Why is this important to you?

🏛 **Question** 5.1.6: What are your career goals? How will you achieve those goals?

🏛 **Question** 5.1.7: What do you see yourself doing in five years? Is this different from what you imagined when you entered the degree program at your college (if so, how so)?

🏛 **Question** 5.1.8: Describe your life experiences, explaining any major decisions you have made to date.

🏛 **Question** 5.1.9: What two or three accomplishments have given you particular satisfaction over your lifetime?

🏛 **Question** 5.1.10: Tell me in detail what you did while working for this company (that appears on your resume).

🏛 **Question** 5.1.11: (If you are currently employed and seeking to move...) How did you decide that it is time to leave your current job?

🏛 **Question** 5.1.12: What do you like about your current job? Be careful with this question. It is not about your current job, per se. Instead, it is about you and your preferences. Whatever you reveal should be part of your sales pitch to the interviewer. If I answer that "I like my corner office with the view" or "I like being able to close my office door so nobody can talk to me," then I make myself look bad.

🏛 **Question** 5.1.13: What is your primary motivation in seeking a new role?

🏛 **Question** 5.1.14: What do you dislike about your current job? Like the last question, be careful. This is not about your current job. If you say "My boss is an idiot" or "I have been treated unfairly," it makes you look bad.

🏛 **Question** 5.1.15: What are your expectations for this internship (or job)?

🏛 **Question** 5.1.16: What did you do, and what did you learn, at your investment banking internship?

🏛 **Question** 5.1.17: How would you value yourself in financial terms?

🏛 **Question** 5.1.18: How do you evaluate your success or the success of others?

🏛 **Question** 5.1.19: Which institutions have you already spoken to? Which departments/divisions did you speak with?

🏛 **Question** 5.1.20: How would you describe yourself? How would your friends describe you? How would a former supervisor describe you?

🏛 **Question** 5.1.21: What is your greatest strength?

🏛 **Question** 5.1.22: What is your greatest weakness?

🏛 **Question** 5.1.23: Describe a situation where you successfully sold your ideas.

Question 5.1.24:   Describe a situation in your life where you had to manage risk.

Question 5.1.25:   With reference to your trading, describe your biggest loss, and what you learned from it.

Question 5.1.26:   Tell me about a time when you had to sell a product and how you went about it.

Question 5.1.27:   What areas of your performance need improvement?

Question 5.1.28:   Why shouldn't we hire you? ...a tough spin on the traditional "What is your greatest weakness?" question.

Question 5.1.29:   Tell me something you tried but ended up quitting on.

Question 5.1.30:   What is the biggest risk you have taken in your life?

Question 5.1.31:   How do you handle stress?

Question 5.1.32:   Rate yourself on a scale of 1 to 10 on the type of risk taker you are. Tell me why and give examples to support your claims.

Question 5.1.33:   Tell me about a goal you set for yourself in the past that turned out to be either too easy or too hard to achieve. What did you learn from the situation?

Question 5.1.34:   What distinguishes you from other candidates we might hire?

Question 5.1.35:   What do you do for fun?

Question 5.1.36:   What sports do/did you play?

Question 5.1.37:   Describe the best party you have ever been to. What is your favorite bar/nightclub?

Question 5.1.38:   Have you ever made a mistake? What happened?

Question 5.1.39:   What is the biggest investment mistake you have ever made?

Question 5.1.40:   A student of mine was taken to a room and asked to choose a place to sit at a long oval-shaped table. He chose a place at random. Later the interviewer asked why he had chosen that spot. I think the intent was to see if he was a leader (sitting at the head) or a follower (sitting at the side).

Question 5.1.41:   What are the character traits of a follower? What about a leader? Are you a follower or a leader? How do you motivate others?

Question 5.1.42:   Tell me about a time when you had to deal with a highly ambiguous situation. What did you do? How did you deal with it?

Question 5.1.43:   Please describe an ethical dilemma you have faced at work, and tell me how you handled the situation.

Question 5.1.44: What is the most difficult decision you were ever faced with?

Question 5.1.45: How good are your writing skills? Please give me some convincing evidence.

Question 5.1.46: If you could go on a cross-country car trip with any three people, who would you choose?

Question 5.1.47: If you were holding a dinner party, and you could invite any three dead people (presumably resurrected), who would you choose? Please do not choose any relatives.

Question 5.1.48: Why did you decide to apply to your MBA college? Did you apply to other MBA programs (if so, which ones and why)?

Question 5.1.49: What do you do if the "picture-in-picture" does not work on your television? Yes, one of my students was asked this in a banking interview!

Question 5.1.50: How would you evaluate your experiences at your MBA college?

Question 5.1.51: What are the strengths and weaknesses of your MBA program?

Question 5.1.52: Describe a situation in which you had to make a decision based on very little information.

Question 5.1.53: Tell me about a situation when you were chosen as a leader by the members of your group.

Question 5.1.54: Would you rather meet a deadline and hand in low-quality work, or miss the deadline and hand in high-quality work?

Question 5.1.55: Repeat the conversation that you had with your team mates when things did not go well in your group.

Question 5.1.56: What have you enjoyed most about your experiences at your MBA college? What would you change?

Question 5.1.57: What is your GPA at your college? What about your GMAT score?

Question 5.1.58: Hong Kong or London? Which countries/regions would you consider working in? Do you hold the right to work in the EU? What about the U.S.?

Question 5.1.59: Which courses did you enjoy most at your MBA college (and why)?

Question 5.1.60: How has your course work at your MBA college helped you to develop skills relevant to this job?

🏛 **Question** 5.1.61: What has been most difficult for you at your MBA college, and how have you dealt with it?

🏛 **Question** 5.1.62: How much of your education did you personally fund?

🏛 **Question** 5.1.63: How do you spend your time outside of school and work? How do you balance your life?

🏛 **Question** 5.1.64: Describe your typical day.

🏛 **Question** 5.1.65: Are you innately intelligent, or do you have to work really hard? Do you work more or less than your peers who get the same grades?

🏛 **Question** 5.1.66: Describe a situation where you had to process information.

🏛 **Question** 5.1.67: From a candidate: "I was then taken to a more casual room where I met two of the young analysts and just had a chat that was 'off the record,' but it was quite reassuring and a good way to establish some rapport." Note that nothing is ever off the record during an interview.

🏛 **Question** 5.1.68: At interview end: "Is there anything important you have not had a chance to tell me?"

🏛 **Question** 5.1.69: At interview end: "You now have two minutes to add any further comments you may have." This is your time to address any misconceptions or mistakes, or to ask questions. It is not a time to remain silent (see my related comments on the next question).

Question 5.1.70: At interview end: "Do you have any questions you would like to ask me?" Candidates with no questions appear unmotivated/uninterested. Saying no is like slapping your interviewer in the face. Your questions must be ones whose answers cannot be found easily online. For example, "Do you have any reservations about hiring me that we can discuss right now?," "What challenges will your division face over the next year?," or "Why did you join the company?," or "What do you find most satisfying about working here?" or "What is the best advice you can give me to achieve long-run success here?"

5.2 Questions about Your Job Awareness

🏛 **Question** 5.2.1: What do you know about us? What makes us different that appeals to you?

🏛 **Question** 5.2.2: What makes us stand out to our peers?

🏛 **Question** 5.2.3: What do you think makes us stand out to a client?

🏛 **Question** 5.2.4: Please write a page or two about a recent news story that caught your eye, and how you feel that this story relates to our company.

🏛 **Question** 5.2.5: How does this position in this company fit into your career development plans? What other career options are you considering?

🏛 **Question** 5.2.6: Why do you want to work for this employer?

🏛 **Question** 5.2.7: Why investment banking?

🏛 **Question** 5.2.8: What is the main function of an investment bank?

🏛 **Question** 5.2.9: Sell yourself to me. Prove to me that you are someone I should seriously consider for our firm.

🏛 **Question** 5.2.10: Tell me the name of a person who you think has integrity. Make it someone I have heard of, and defend your position.

🏛 **Question** 5.2.11: **(A)** Why did we choose you to come to our final round interview?

🏛 **Question** 5.2.12: How (and how much) do you think this role impacts the company as a whole?

🏛 **Question** 5.2.13: What motivates you to put forth your best effort? What type of work environment brings out your best effort?

🏛 **Question** 5.2.14: What rewards do you seek from work? What rewards do you seek from this particular job (or company)?

🏛 **Question** 5.2.15: Tell me about a recent deal our company did.

🏛 **Question** 5.2.16: Descriptive: Walk me through the details of the deal. What parties were involved? Why did the deal take place? What were the proceeds (if any) used for? What numbers were involved, at least roughly?

🏛 **Question** 5.2.17: Process: What do you think the (our) team did when working on the deal? What process would their (our) team have undertaken?

🏛 **Question** 5.2.18: Contingencies: Were there stumbling blocks to getting the deal done? What is a problem with this deal? What's another problem? What's another problem? Why is this a problem? (They may push and push until you cannot go any further or until you get to the problem they want you to identify).

🏛 **Question** 5.2.19: Where do you think we make most of our money?

🏛 **Question** 5.2.20: Why are you not better matched with Firm X (our competitor)?

🏛 **Question** 5.2.21: Do you have any geographical preferences? What are your thoughts about travel or relocation?

🏛 **Question** 5.2.22: What aspect of our culture stands out the most to you?

🏛 **Question** 5.2.23:   What do you think are the core competencies for this role?

🏛 **Question** 5.2.24:   What do you see yourself contributing to our organization, both in the short term and in the long term?

🏛 **Question** 5.2.25:   What other companies are you interviewing with, and how do we compare?

🏛 **Question** 5.2.26:   **(A)** What do you think of our tombstone in today's *Wall Street Journal*?

Question 5.2.27:   Why fixed income rather than equities?

🏛 **Question** 5.2.28:   What do you think it takes to be successful in this position (or this organization)?

Question 5.2.29:   Why do you want to work as a trader?

Question 5.2.30:   What do you think traders do?

🏛 **Question** 5.2.31:   If you were in my position, interviewing candidates for this position, what qualities would you seek? How would you evaluate candidates?

🏛 **Question** 5.2.32:   Describe the best boss you have ever had. How would you define the qualities of a good manager?

🏛 **Question** 5.2.33:   What do you think an investment banker does?

🏛 **Question** 5.2.34:   How do you think we spend our day?

🏛 **Question** 5.2.35:   Do you understand the hours investment bankers work and why?

🏛 **Question** 5.2.36:   Describe how you build relationships in a new job.

🏛 **Question** 5.2.37:   Imagine you have received three job offers. How will you decide which one to accept?

🏛 **Question** 5.2.38:   If you were to get two other job offers in addition to one from us, from which firms would they most likely come, would you take them, and why?

🏛 **Question** 5.2.39:   Some people say investment banking is not value adding. How do you refute that?

🏛 **Question** 5.2.40:   If I give you a list of 5–10 tasks to be completed and then I walk out the door and you know you cannot contact me, how would you proceed? If I told you they need to be done by a particular deadline, but you cannot meet that deadline, what would you do?

🏛 **Question 5.2.41:** Similarly, if I give you a list of 5–10 tasks to be completed and then I walk out the door and you know you cannot contact me, and you cannot complete them by the end of the day, then what would you do?

🏛 **Question 5.2.42:** Imagine you are giving a presentation to a client and they tell you your numbers are wrong. What would you do?

🏛 **Question 5.2.43:** If we offer you a job right now, will you take it?

🏛 **Question 5.2.44:** **(A)** With your abilities, you seem to not fit in this position (or this firm). Perhaps you should consider a job in ...

5.3 Questions about the Markets or the Economy

🏛 **Question 5.3.1:** How will [insert recent economic event in the news] affect global markets or economies?

🏛 **Question 5.3.2:** What are three reasons house prices are so high in (San Francisco, London, Auckland, ...)?

🏛 **Question 5.3.3:** **(A)** Why had yields turned negative on the government bonds of a dozen countries by 2015? Why would any investor buy a government bond with negative yield?

🏛 **Question 5.3.4:** Name as many stocks as you can in the Dow Jones Industrial Average.

🏛 **Question 5.3.5:** What are the key differences between stocks and bonds?

🏛 **Question 5.3.6:** What is the "invisible hand" concept, and who introduced it?

🏛 **Question 5.3.7:** Name the chair of the Federal Reserve.

🏛 **Question 5.3.8:** How many financial market crises can you name? Can you explain the causes of each?

🏛 **Question 5.3.9:** How is a coupon-bond valued?

Question 5.3.10: Explain what an exchange-traded fund (ETF) is.

Question 5.3.11: What is a CDS? What is a repo? What is a hedge fund?

Question 5.3.12: What are the differences between a forward contract and a futures contract?

Question 5.3.13: Where is the DOW, or S&P500, or NIKKEI, or FTSE, or Hang Seng, or...? How does it compare now to where it has been over the last two years? Where do you see it two weeks from now (or six months from now)?

Question 5.3.14: Where is the JPY, or GBP, or CAD, or EUR, or...? How does it compare now with where it has been over the last two years? Where do you see it two weeks from now (or six months from now)?

Question 5.3.15: **(A)** What exact number will the S&P be at in a year? (From a sales and trading interview.)

🏛 **Question 5.3.16:** What does Company X (a well-known company) actually do?

Question 5.3.17: Do you trade? Do you own stock? What made you choose those stocks? How do you pick your stocks?

🏛 **Question 5.3.18:** Can you name two companies that you think should merge?

🏛 **Question 5.3.19:** What would you do if I gave you $10,000 to trade with? (Note that if you have never opened a brokerage account, you must not give lack of funds as an excuse. If you cannot generate $2,000 to open a brokerage account, then why should I hire you?)

Question 5.3.20: **(A)** Do you believe that markets are efficient?

🏛 **Question 5.3.21:** What is LIBOR, and what is today's LIBOR rate?[1,2]

Question 5.3.22: Why invest in a particular market (e.g., Korea, Russia, Germany)?

🏛 **Question 5.3.23:** Tell me how you keep up with the news.

🏛 **Question 5.3.24:** How would the following affect interest rates? A relative of Osama Bin Laden starts making trouble in the Middle East; another Asian currency crisis; Monica Lewinsky (alleged mistress of former U.S. president Clinton) is reported as the alleged mistress of the current U.S. president.

🏛 **Question 5.3.25:** **(A)** When inflationary fears arise, the government has two forms of macroeconomic policy to try to slow the economy down. Name these and explain them in a few words.

𝕀 **Question 5.3.26:** What stock do you recommend and why?

𝕀 **Question 5.3.27:** Tell me about a stock you like or hate and why.

Question 5.3.28: What sector should I be short? What sector should I be long?

---

[1]Note: As mentioned already, LIBOR is due to be retired after 2021 (Riquier, 2019), but an extension to mid-2023 is likely (Shaw, McCormick, Bolingbroke, and Torres, 2020).

[2]They probably mean the benchmark three- or six-month U.S. dollar LIBOR rates, but they might not say that. There are several different dimensions here: you should understand the distinction between USD LIBOR and GBP LIBOR, between three-month USD LIBOR and six-month USD LIBOR, between LIBOR (London InterBank Offered Rate) and EURIBOR (Euro Interbank Offered Rate), and between euro LIBOR and EURIBOR. If you do not, look in your favorite investments book, or use a search engine.

🏛 **Question 5.3.29:** What should be the (CAPM) beta for Intel Corp.?

🏛 **Question 5.3.30:** Where do you think the U.S. economy will go over the next year?

Question 5.3.31: **(A)** What are the "Dow Jones Dogs"?

🏛 **Question 5.3.32:** Tell me how the Dow Jones Industrial Average is calculated.

🏛 **Question 5.3.33:** Draw the yield curve showing 3M, 6M, 1YR, 2YR, 5YR, 10YR, 30YR rates.

Question 5.3.34: Do you think the stock market is efficient (in an EMH sense)? This is a very popular question for asset management.

Question 5.3.35: Suppose you are actively investing to beat the market. Are there more opportunities (i.e., inefficiencies) in the S&P500 or in the 500 largest stocks in Europe?

Question 5.3.36: What is a black swan? What do black swans mean for the use of VaR and other conventional statistical methods employed in quantitative finance? This obviously refers to the black swan concept in Nassim Taleb's books *Fooled by Randomness* and *The Black Swan*. A black swan is a surprise event with a major impact. After the fact we typically try to rationalize it as if it could have been anticipated.

5.4   Financial Management Questions

🏛 **Question 5.4.1:** How would you go about preparing a 2–3 page analyst report proposing to a client the acquisition of a waste management firm? How would you collect the information necessary for the valuation? What would be the key revenue drivers?

🏛 **Question 5.4.2:** How would you value a company? (This is a very popular question.) The main approaches include DCF methods, Comparables methods, and the LBO method (Crack, 2020b, Chapter 2).

🏛 **Question 5.4.3:** **(A)** How would you value a hot dog stand in Midtown Manhattan?

🏛 **Question 5.4.4:** Two companies have identical ratios except for one (e.g., P/E). Which company do you prefer?

🏛 **Question 5.4.5:** If using the P/E ratio to value a company, how would you determine if the stock price is undervalued or overvalued?

🏛 **Question 5.4.6:** Discuss two stocks affected by COVID-19 and how they are affected?

🏛 **Question 5.4.7:** If you could choose somewhere in [city of interview] to go for a beer, where would you go?

🏛 **Question 5.4.8:** **(A)** Which would have the greater impact on a firm's valuation: A 10% reduction in revenues or a 1% reduction in the discount rate? (I think they meant, for example, an absolute shift from 10% to 9%, rather than a relative shift from 10.0% to 9.9%.)

🏛 **Question 5.4.9:** Explain what a discount rate is, and how you calculate it for a publicly traded company. What is the WACC? How would you estimate a firm's beta? How would you calculate the required rate of return for equity holders for a company? What would you use for a market risk premium? How would you estimate the cost of debt for a company (assume that there is no publicly traded debt for that company outstanding)?

🏛 **Question 5.4.10:** What exactly is a beta and what does it measure? What is systematic risk and how does it differ from active risk?

🏛 **Question 5.4.11:** Compare the beta of an airport with the beta of a retailer.[3]

🏛 **Question 5.4.12:** If you were asked to put together a two-page analyst report on a company, what sort of information would you include? What specific ratios would you include?

🏛 **Question 5.4.13:** Suppose that the S&P500 index has a P/E ratio of 20. How would you value a manufacturing company with earnings of one million dollars?

🏛 **Question 5.4.14:** What key financial ratios do you look at when trying to determine a firm's financial health from its balance sheet?

🏛 **Question 5.4.15:** Why do pharmaceutical companies increase drug prices when they come off patent protection?

🏛 **Question 5.4.16:** Describe the CAPM.

🏛 **Question 5.4.17:** Can a company function without working capital?

🏛 **Question 5.4.18:** What happens to a company's balance sheet if the company buys an asset? Walk me through the steps.

🏛 **Question 5.4.19:** Two companies have the same ratios except for one (e.g., P/E ratio, or growth rate in EPS, etc.). Which company do you prefer and why?

🏛 **Question 5.4.20:** Two companies have the same price, but different ratios. What could be different? (For example, growth rate in EPS.)

---

[3] Mullins (1982) has a lovely table in it that lists betas by industry, ranging from Air Transport (1.80) down to Gold (0.35). The article pre-dates the Fama-French critique of the CAPM by 10 years (Fama and French [1992, 1993]) but gives excellent intuition for the CAPM. Watch out for the use of a riskless rate of 10% per annum and an expected return on the market of 19% per annum—which reflect the time period it was written in.

🏛 **Question** 5.4.21: **(A)** When is a motor vehicle that is owned by the company not recorded on the balance sheet as PPE ("physical plant and equipment" or "property plant and equipment")?

Question 5.4.22: How would you market this financial product (e.g., a structured note)?

🏛 **Question** 5.4.23: How do you use DCF to value a skyscraper in order to sell it? You need to come up with current revenue, costs, net income, estimates of future cash flows, and a discount rate.

🏛 **Question** 5.4.24: The late Kirk Kekorian attempted to force Chrysler to rid itself of what he called "excess cash"—through higher dividends and a stock buyback. What do you think of this sort of action?

🏛 **Question** 5.4.25: Give three reasons why house prices are so high.

🏛 **Question** 5.4.26: How would you market this company to our clients?

🏛 **Question** 5.4.27: Have you ever had to fire someone? If so, how did you handle this situation?

🏛 **Question** 5.4.28: Forecast the income statement for Duracell for this year.

🏛 **Question** 5.4.29: **(A)** In the calculation of free cash flow (i.e., FCF), does the level of long-term debt matter?

Question 5.4.30: How do you calculate VaR (i.e., Value at Risk)?

Question 5.4.31: Have you heard of LTCM? Tell me about it.

🏛 **Question** 5.4.32: What is the difference between default risk and prepayment risk?

Question 5.4.33: What is kurtosis?

Story: "During a lunch interview with me, a candidate ordered a bowl of French onion soup. When he started to eat the layer of cheese on top, it became stringy, and with his hands he tried to pull the strings of cheese apart. He pulled at those strings of cheese for a l–o–n–g time."

AUDREY W. HELLINGER
Chicago Office of Martin H. Bauman
Associates, New York

"Doomed Days: The Worst Mistakes Recruiters Have Ever Seen,"
The Wall Street Journal, February 25, 1995, pR4.
Reprinted by permission of *The Wall Street Journal*
©1995 Dow Jones and Company, Inc.
All Rights Reserved Worldwide.

5.5 Thinking Questions

Many of these questions have some sort of precise solution. If, however, you know exactly how many McDonald's outlets there are in the U.S., and you say so directly, then you have missed the point. The interviewer wants you to *work the answer out* and describe your reasoning (a Fermi problem, named after Enrico Fermi). Some of the questions have no quantitative answer, and require out-of-the-box thinking.

🏛 **Question 5.5.1:** Tell me a joke.

🏛 **Question 5.5.2:** The interviewee was told to memorize **10:32 green 9735** at the beginning of the interview. At the end of the interview he was asked to recall it.

🏛 **Question 5.5.3:** **(A)** You arrive at your desk, on the 50th floor of a 100-story building. Sitting on your desk is a ticking time bomb with a countdown timer that just ticked past 90 seconds. What do you do?

🏛 **Question 5.5.4:** You win a lottery and receive $10,000,000 after taxes. How will you invest the money?

🏛 **Question 5.5.5:** If I give you $10,000 to invest, on my behalf, how would you invest it? (You had better start by asking me about my wealth, my risk aversion, my investment horizon, etc.)

🏛 **Question 5.5.6:** Describe the evolution of the U.S. government yield curve since 1981. That is, tell me about the level and the shape, and how these have changed over time.

🏛 **Question 5.5.7:** If a cannonball is dropped in the deepest part of the Earth's oceans, how long will it take to reach the ocean floor?

🏛 **Question 5.5.8:** **(A)** How many ping-pong balls can you fit in a jumbo jet (e.g., Boeing 747)?

🏛 **Question 5.5.9:** **(A)** How many McDonald's outlets are there in the U.S.?

🏛 **Question 5.5.10:** How many windows are in this building?

🏛 **Question 5.5.11:** How many flight attendants does [name an airline] have?

🏛 **Question 5.5.12:** How many gas stations are there in the U.S. (or the UK)?

🏛 **Question 5.5.13:** How many lightbulbs are there in New York City, or London?

🏛 **Question 5.5.14:** How many photocopies were made in the U.S. last year?

🏛 **Question 5.5.15:** **(A)** What is your opinion of Adolf Hitler?

🏛 **Question 5.5.16:** **(A)** You are in a jail cell alone stripped of your possessions. It is Friday afternoon, and you desperately need a cigarette. How do you force the guard to give you one?

🏛 **Question 5.5.17:** How many elevators are there in the U.S.?

Question 5.5.18: How would you value an option on (famous basketball player) Michael Jordan [replace his name with any current star player]?

🏛 **Question 5.5.19:** **(A)** I toss a coin 100 times and get 100 heads in a row. What is the probability that the next outcome will be a head?

🏛 **Question 5.5.20:** How would you move Mount Fuji?

🏛 **Question 5.5.21:** **(A)** How do you weigh a jet airplane without using scales?

🏛 **Question 5.5.22:** You have a five-gallon jar and a three-gallon jar. You can have as much water as you want. How do you put exactly four gallons into the five-gallon container? This is too easy for me to supply an answer.

🏛 **Question 5.5.23:** Estimate the annual demand for car batteries.

🏛 **Question 5.5.24:** What would you estimate to be the size of the racquetball market in the U.S.?

🏛 **Question 5.5.25:** You are to build a plant for Coors to serve all beer customers in the state of Ohio. How large would you build it? That is, specifically how many cans do you anticipate being demanded for the year?

🏛 **Question 5.5.26:** Why do beer cans have tapered tops and bottoms?

🏛 **Question 5.5.27:** **(A)** Explain why airplanes can fly.

🏛 **Question 5.5.28:** How many fish are there in the Earth's oceans?

🏛 **Question 5.5.29:** How many barbers are there in Chicago?

🏛 **Question 5.5.30:** How many piano tuners are there in the U.S.?

🏛 **Question 5.5.31:** What is $\sqrt{204,000}$?

🏛 **Question 5.5.32:** What is 2.2^2?

🏛 **Question 5.5.33:** What is one percent of 1,000,000?

🏛 **Question 5.5.34:** **(A)** Finally, why are manhole covers round? According to Stone (2014), this was a favorite interview question for Jeff Bezos.

> **Story:** A student of mine interviewing at a top bulge bracket firm was asked to draw a picture of himself! They gave him pencil and paper, and he drew a picture (into his picture he also drew books, friends, and other goofy stuff to indicate that he was social and educated).

Appendix A

Purely Quantitative & Logic Answers

This appendix contains answers to the questions posed in Chapter 1.

Answer 1.1: This question has appeared over and over again. Although simple, it is rarely answered well. No calculation is required to determine the answer. If you used *any* algebra whatsoever, stop now, go back, reread the question, and try again.

When the quantity Q of water is poured into the alcohol jug, the concentration of alcohol in the alcohol jug becomes $\frac{V}{V+Q}$. After mixing and pouring some back, the concentration of alcohol in the alcohol jug does not change again (because no new water is added). However, when the diluted alcohol is poured back into the water jug, the concentration of water in the water jug changes from 100% to $\frac{V}{V+Q}$. That is, the final concentrations are identical.

How do you see that the final concentrations must be identical? Remember, you do not need any calculations at all. In fact, the only reason for any calculation is if you also want to find out what the final concentrations are (you were not asked this, but if you wish to work it out, your calculations need not go beyond those of the previous paragraph).

Here is how it works. At the end of the process, both jugs contain the same volume of fluid as they did at the start. The only way for the concentration of alcohol (for example) to have changed from 100% is if some alcohol was displaced by water. Similarly, the only way for the concentration of water to have changed from 100% is if some water was displaced by alcohol. Volume is conserved (both total volume and volume in each jug), so all that has happened is that identical quantities of water and alcohol have traded places (and these identical quantities are slightly less than Q). By symmetry, the concentrations of alcohol in the alcohol jug and water in the water jug must be identical. This final result is true no matter how many times you repeat the experiment.

If you are still stuck, here is another way of thinking about it. Imagine a black bucket with 1,000 black marbles in it and a white bucket with 1,000 white marbles in it. Suppose I take 100 black marbles out of the black bucket and put them in the white bucket and mix it up really well. Then I have 1,100 marbles in the white bucket, and the great majority of them are white. Suppose I then take 100 marbles from those 1,100 and use them to top the black bucket back up to 1,000 marbles. Then both buckets have 1,000 marbles again. Let us suppose that 91 (i.e., the great majority) of the 100 marbles used to top up the black bucket were white. That means I must have returned only 9 of the original 100 black marbles back to the black bucket when I topped it up. That means I must have left 91 black marbles behind in the white bucket—the same as the number of white marbles that migrated over to the black bucket. So, the proportions are identical!

Answer 1.2: I give three successively shorter solutions. The first is a hammer-and-tongs solution that lays everything out in detail. The second is more elegant, and the third is more elegant still. Each solution brings something slightly different to the table.

FIRST SOLUTION

Let D be the number of steps showing on the escalator at any moment (D for distance, counted in units of one step). Let e be the (assumed constant) speed of the escalator, in steps per second. Let v_M be Myron's relative speed of ascent up the escalator (which is the same whether the steps are moving or not). If $v_M = 0$, then Myron will climb zero steps under his own steam. If $v_M = \infty$, then Myron will climb D steps. So, it will be the relative differences in speed that let us identify D.

Myron's absolute speed up the incline holding the escalator is $e + v_M$. So, Myron must cover the distance D in time t_M, spent on the escalator, as given by Equation A.1.

$$t_M = D/(e + v_M) \tag{A.1}$$

How many steps does Myron climb in time t_M? Well, at speed v_M, we just need to multiply time taken by speed, as in Equation A.2.

$$\text{steps climbed (Myron)} = t_M \cdot v_M = Dv_M/(e + v_M) \tag{A.2}$$

We should double check that the RHS of Equation A.2 conforms to our intuition. If we plug $v_M = 0$ into Equation A.2 we get zero steps, as expected, for any $e > 0$. Similarly, if we take the limit of Equation A.2 as $v_M \to \infty$, we get D steps, for any $e \geq 0$.

Now let v_F denote Fischer's slower speed, where $2v_M = 3v_F$. Then, from Equation A.2 and the relative speeds, we have Equations A.3–A.5.

$$
\begin{aligned}
\text{steps climbed (Myron)} &= 25 &&= Dv_M/(e + v_M) & \text{(A.3)}\\
\text{steps climbed (Fischer)} &= 20 &&= Dv_F/(e + v_F) & \text{(A.4)}\\
2v_M &= 3v_F &&& \text{(A.5)}
\end{aligned}
$$

Now multiply Equation A.3 by the RHS denominator, and rewrite Equation A.5 as $v_M = 1.5v_F$, and plug it into the result. Then multiply Equation A.4 through by its RHS denominator and multiply the result by 1.25, to get the equations

$$D(1.5v_F) = 25e + 25(1.5v_F)$$
$$1.25Dv_F = 25e + 25v_F.$$

Now subtract the second equation from the first, and cancel out v_F to deduce that $D = 50$.

As an aside, note that Equations A.3–A.5 are three equations in four unknowns (D, e, v_M, and v_F). You will recall that if you have three linear equations in four unknowns, there can be no unique solution. In our case, however, the equations are *non-linear*, and there is a unique solution for D, as shown. We cannot, however, hope to solve for e, v_M, or v_F. Nor can we solve for time t_M or t_F spent on the escalator by Myron and Fischer, respectively. (We can see, however, from Equation A.1, that the faster is e or v, the lower is t, which makes sense.)

If, however, any one of e, v_M, v_F, t_M, or t_F is chosen, then we can immediately solve for all parameters. For example, can you confirm that $e = 1$ implies that $v_M = 1$, $v_F = 2/3$, $t_M = 25$, and $t_M = 30$? Similarly, can you show that $v_F = 1$ implies $e = 1\frac{1}{2}$, $v_M = 1\frac{1}{2}$, $t_M = 50/3$, and $t_F = 20$? What parameter values do you get if you assume $v_M = 3$? What parameter values do you get if you fix $t_M = 100$?

Can you confirm that for every proposed numerical example in the previous paragraph, it was also true that $e = v_M$ (i.e., the escalator speed is the same as the speed of the faster climber)? Must this be true for all numerical examples in the framework given? Could you have deduced this result before solving for $D = 50$, and used this fact to help solve the problem?

SECOND SOLUTION

Keeping all the notation from the first solution, note that Myron carries himself up 25 of the D steps, while the escalator carries him the other, say, x steps. Thus, $25 + x = D$. We will solve for x, and then for D.

Fischer walks more slowly than Myron. When Fischer has carried himself up only 20 steps, the escalator will have carried him up $k \cdot x$ steps, for some $k > 1$. Thus, $20 + (k \cdot x) = D$. That is, the escalator does more work on Fischer's behalf than it does on Myron's behalf, by a factor of k.

Now, because Myron and Fischer entered side-by-side and the escalator is moving at a constant speed, this means that when Myron reaches the top, the escalator has carried both of Myron and Fischer a total of x steps by that stage. Fischer, however, has climbed up only $\frac{2}{3}$ as many steps as Myron by then. That is, Fischer has climbed only $25 \cdot \frac{2}{3} = 16\frac{2}{3}$ of his eventual 20 steps by then. His full trip will take $\frac{20}{16\frac{2}{3}} = 1.20$ times as long as he has taken so far.

Given the constant speed of the escalator, this means that the escalator will end up carrying him an additional 20% of the x it has already carried him. That is, $k = 1.2$. Putting these together yields Equations A.6–A.8.

$$25 + x = D \qquad (A.6)$$
$$20 + (k \cdot x) = D \qquad (A.7)$$
$$k = 1.2 \qquad (A.8)$$

Plugging the third equation into the second, and subtracting the result from the first equation, yields $5 - 0.2x = 0$. So, $x = 25$, and $D = 50$, as before.

THIRD SOLUTION[1]

Alternatively, using the notation from the first two solutions, note that Fischer spent more time on the escalator than Myron. Myron travelled 25 steps at speed v_M, and Fischer travelled 20 steps at speed v_F. So, the ratio of time Fischer spent on the escalator to the time Myron spent on the escalator is

$$t_F/t_M = \frac{20}{v_F}\bigg/\frac{25}{v_M} = \frac{20}{25}\bigg/\frac{v_F}{v_M} = \frac{20}{25}\bigg/\frac{2}{3} = \frac{6}{5} = 1.2 = k, \text{ as above.}$$

In other words, $t_F = 1.2t_M$. Given that the escalator moves at a constant speed, and Myron was carried by it for x steps in time t_M, Fischer must have been carried by it for $1.2x$ steps in time $1.2t_M$. This yields Equations A.6–A.8, as before, thus yielding the solution $D = 50$.

Answer 1.3: If you answered 20 (i.e., 4×5) minutes, then go back to the question and think again. You need to be hardwired to ignore such "pickpocket answers" (see story on p. 250).

Although not stated, we should assume the bells ring at equal spaced intervals. If one bell rings five times per minute, then that is every 12 seconds. The other, at four times per minute, rings every 15 seconds. They will next ring together at the 60 second mark. The answer is one minute.

Story: "One cocky job candidate interviewed with several male managers at a major bank before being ushered into an interview with a female manager. He sat across from her, put his feet on her desk and said, 'Get me a Coke.' "

MICHAEL ZWELL
Michael Zwell & Associates, Chicago

"Doomed Days: The Worst Mistakes Recruiters Have Ever Seen,"
The Wall Street Journal, February 25, 1995, pR4.
Reprinted by permission of *The Wall Street Journal*
©1995 Dow Jones and Company, Inc.
All Rights Reserved Worldwide.

---

[1] I thank Malcolm A. Crack for suggesting this technique; any errors are mine.

Answer 1.4:   This is a very common question, and a very simple one. You need to figure out the sum: $1 + 2 + 3 + \cdots + 99 + 100$. There are several ways to do this.

FIRST SOLUTION

A simple technique is to note that the first and last terms add to 101. The second and second-to-last terms also add to 101. The same is true of the third and third-to-last terms. Continuing in this fashion, you soon find yourself with 50 pairs of numbers adding to 101; 50 times 101 is 5,050.

SECOND SOLUTION[2]

A simple technique you can picture easily is the following:

$$
\begin{array}{cccccc}
1 & 2 & 3 & \ldots & n-1 & n \\
\underline{n} & \underline{n-1} & \underline{n-2} & \ldots & \underline{2} & \underline{1} \\
n+1 & n+1 & n+1 & \ldots & n+1 & n+1
\end{array}
$$

There are n terms each equal to $n + 1$. The required sum is half the grand total: $\frac{n(n+1)}{2}$.

THIRD SOLUTION

I read somewhere many years ago that the high school drop-out Albert Einstein devised the following alternative solution technique at age 15. Think of each summand, i, in the sum $\sum_{i=1}^{100} i$ as a group of i marbles in a row from $i = 1$ to $i = 100$ (see the array following). Stacking each row of marbles on top of each previous row, you get the array including both the diagonal and the lower-triangular off-diagonal. Were the array full, it would contain $100 \times 100 = 100^2$ marbles. So, your answer must be roughly half this (roughly 50×100). This is not exact because although the array contains two triangular-shaped off-diagonals (upper and lower), there is only one diagonal. If you add another diagonal, and *then* split the total in two, you get the right answer. The diagonal contains 100 marbles, so the right answer must be $\frac{100^2+100}{2} = 5,000 + 50$, as before.

$$
\begin{pmatrix}
 & 1 & 2 & 3 & 4 & 5 & 6 & \cdots & 100 \\
1 & \bullet \\
2 & \bullet & \bullet \\
3 & \bullet & \bullet & \bullet \\
4 & \bullet & \bullet & \bullet & \bullet \\
5 & \bullet & \bullet & \bullet & \bullet & \bullet \\
6 & \bullet & \bullet & \bullet & \bullet & \bullet & \bullet \\
\vdots & \vdots & \vdots & \vdots & \vdots & \vdots & \vdots & \ddots \\
100 & \bullet & \bullet & \bullet & \bullet & \bullet & \bullet & \cdots & \bullet
\end{pmatrix}
$$

More generally, the sum from 1 to n may be written down as $\frac{n^2+n}{2} = \frac{n(n+1)}{2}$.

---

[2]I thank Tom Arnold for this solution technique; any errors are mine.

69

Just picture the square array of side length n, add another diagonal, and split the total in half.

To calculate $\frac{n(n+1)}{2}$ quickly in your head, note that one of n or $n+1$ must be even and thus divisible by two. You should divide the even number by two and multiply the odd number remaining by the result. In our case,

$$\frac{100 \times 101}{2} = \frac{100}{2} \times 101 = 50 \times 101 = 5,050.$$

Finally, note that four more solutions appear in the answers to Question 1.53, starting on p. 116; I particularly like the visual solution presented using grids.

Answer 1.5: The numbers on the dial add to 78 in total (recall that $\sum_{i=1}^{12} = \frac{12(12+1)}{2} = 6 \times 13$). So, each piece must have a total of 26 on it. My initial attempt was to find slices (like pizza slices) that satisfy the constraint. Walking around the dial looking for consecutive numbers that add to 26, you soon find that 5-6-7-8 adds to 26, and 11-12-1-2 adds to 26, but nothing else works. So, none of the pieces is pizza-slice shaped. They are 5-6-7-8, 11-12-1-2, and a band across the middle with 10-9-3-4.

Answer 1.6: This challenging question has been very popular. Sometimes it is balls, sometimes marbles, sometimes coins. I present two solutions.[3]

FIRST SOLUTION[4]

Let me write, say, 1H if marble 1 is heavy or potentially heavy (it should be clear by the context), but if it cannot be light. Similarly, let me write 1L if marble 1 is light or potentially light, but if it cannot be heavy. Using this notation, the 12 marbles yield 24 different possible outcomes, because each marble may be heavy or light, relative to its peers:

1H 2H 3H 4H 5H 6H 7H 8H 9H 10H 11H 12H

1L 2L 3L 4L 5L 6L 7L 8L 9L 10L 11L 12L.

Split the 12 marbles into three groups: Let these be, say, marbles 1–4, marbles 5–8, and marbles 9–12. Compare marbles {1 2 3 4} (in the first dish) with marbles {5 6 7 8} (in the second dish). There are three cases, as follows.

Case 1: The first dish is heavy. In this case, we have reduced the 24 possible outcomes to only eight possible outcomes, as indicated:

(1H 2H 3H 4H) 5H 6H 7H 8H 9H 10H 11H 12H

1L 2L 3L 4L (5L 6L 7L 8L) 9L 10L 11L 12L.

---

[3] One of my readers, who tried this at home, said that the methods given here, while successful in theory, would not work in practice. He said he would need to add the use of a marker pen to the problem statement to keep track of which marble was which when swapping marbles between the dishes on the balance.

[4] I thank Todor Bonchev and Jabran Zahid for this solution technique; any errors are mine.

The next step is to compare carefully chosen triplets.[5] Each triplet contains one possibly heavy marble and two possibly light marbles. Without loss of generality, let us compare

$$\{1H\ 5L\ 6L\}\ \text{with}\ \{2H\ 7L\ 8L\},$$

while holding out {3H 4H}.[6] There are three subcases, as follows.

- **Subcase 1:** The first dish is heavy. It must be that one of {1H 7L 8L} is true. So, just compare {7L} and {8L} to identify the odd marble from this triplet, and whether it is heavy or light.

- **Subcase 2:** The first dish is light. It must be that one of {5L 6L 2H} is true. So, just compare {5L} and {6L} to identify the odd marble from this triplet, and whether it is heavy or light.

- **Subcase 3:** The dishes are of equal weight. The odd marble was left out of the second weighing! So, one of {3H 4H} must be true. Now just compare {3H} and {4H} to identify the odd marble, which must be heavy.

Case 2: The second dish is heavy. Again, the 24 cases are reduced to only eight possible outcomes, as indicated:

1H 2H 3H 4H(5H 6H 7H 8H)9H 10H 11H 12H

(1L 2L 3L 4L)5L 6L 7L 8L 9L 10L 11L 12L.

This is perfectly analogous to Case 1. You get the same three subcases, but with "H" swapped with "L" in the arguments already given.

Case 3: The two dishes are of equal weight. Again, the 24 cases are reduced to only eight possible outcomes, as indicated:

1H 2H 3H 4H 5H 6H 7H 8H(9H 10H 11H 12H)

1L 2L 3L 4L 5L 6L 7L 8L(9L 10L 11L 12L.)

In this case, compare the suspect marbles {9 10 11} with three equal-weight marbles, say, {1 2 3}, while holding out suspect marble 12. There are three subcases, as follows.

- **Subcase 1:** The first dish is heavy. It must be that one of {9H 10H 11H} is true. So, just compare {9H} with {10H} to identify the odd marble from this triplet, which must be heavy.

- **Subcase 2:** The first dish is light. It must be that one of {9L 10L 11L} is true. So, just compare {9L} with {10L} to identify the odd marble from this triplet, which must be light.

---

[5]A slightly more complex solution in the 21st edition compares the quintuples {1H 2H 5L 6L 7L} and {9 10 11 12 8L} at this step.

[6]By symmetry, we could instead have compared, say, {5L 1H 2H} with {6L 3H 4H} at this step, while holding out {7L 8L}.

- **Subcase 3:** The dishes are of equal weight. So, suspect marble 12 must be guilty. Thus, either {12H} or {12L} is true. We can compare {12} with, say, equal-weight marble {1} to identify whether guilty marble {12} is heavy or light.

SECOND SOLUTION[7]

This solution uses triplets and singletons, and requires slightly different notation. Like the first solution technique, the first step is to split the 12 marbles into three groups of four. Each group of four has two subgroups, a singleton and a triplet: $\{\{1\}_A, \{3\}_A\}$, $\{\{1\}_B, \{3\}_B\}$, and $\{\{1\}_C, \{3\}_C\}$.

Compare $\{\{1\}_A, \{3\}_A\}$ with $\{\{1\}_B, \{3\}_B\}$. If they balance, then the odd ball is in group C. In this case, compare $\{3\}_C$ with $\{3\}_B$. If $\{3\}_C$ is heavier (or lighter), then comparing any two marbles from within $\{3\}_C$ immediately locates the odd one; if $\{3\}_C$ balances $\{3\}_B$, then compare $\{1\}_C$ with $\{1\}_B$ to see whether $\{1\}_C$ is heavier or lighter.

If the initial comparison is unbalanced, say $\{\{1\}_A, \{3\}_A\}$ is heavier than $\{\{1\}_B, \{3\}_B\}$, then rotate groups $\{3\}_A$, $\{3\}_B$, and $\{3\}_C$ and compare grouping $\{\{1\}_A, \{3\}_B\}$ with $\{\{1\}_B, \{3\}_C\}$ (while holding out $\{\{1\}_C, \{3\}_A\}$). If they balance, then a heavy marble is in $\{3\}_A$ and comparing any two marbles from within $\{3\}_A$ immediately locates the odd one. Suppose they do not balance. If $\{\{1\}_A, \{3\}_B\}$ is heavy, then either $\{1\}_A$ is heavy, or $\{1\}_B$ is light. Compare $\{1\}_A$ with $\{1\}_C$ to finish. If $\{\{1\}_A, \{3\}_B\}$ is light, then $\{3\}_B$ is light and comparing any two marbles within $\{3\}_B$ immediately locates the light one.

In each case, only three weighings are needed. This technique is generalized in Answer 1.21 (the "90-coin problem").

Answer 1.7: I have drawn a right-angle triangle on Figure A.1 using R, the radius of the circle. Once we solve for R, the side length is $S = 2R$.

From Figure A.1 we deduce that $R^2 = (R - 10)^2 + (R - 5)^2$ (via Pythagoras' Theorem).[8] Collecting terms, we quickly find that $R^2 - 30R + 125 = 0$. It follows (using the quadratic formula) that this polynomial has two roots R_1 and R_2 given by

$$R_1, R_2 = \frac{-B \pm \sqrt{B^2 - 4AC}}{2A} = \frac{30 \pm \sqrt{900 - 500}}{2} = 15 \pm 10 = 5, 25.$$

Only one of those, $R = 25$, has a sensible physical interpretation in our case.[9] It follows that $S = 2R = 50$.

---

[7]This solution combines independent contributions of Juan Tenorio, Bingjian Ni, Yi Shen, and Jinpeng Chang; any errors are mine.

[8]Recall Pythagoras' Theorem. Consider a triangle with side lengths X, Y, and Z. If the angle between the sides of length X and Y is $90°$, then it is a right-angle triangle. The side of length Z (the "hypotenuse") must be the longest side, and it must be that $X^2 + Y^2 = Z^2$.

[9]Note that the case $R = 5$ corresponds to $S = 10$, in which case the corner of the box touches the far side of the circle, not the near side. This is inconsistent with the diagram drawn by the interviewer.

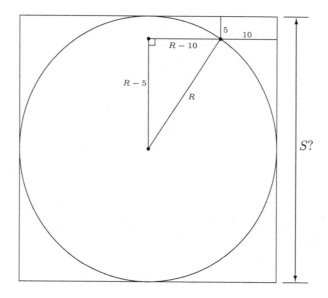

Figure A.1: The Inscribed Circle Answer

Note: A circle is inscribed within a square. A rectangle of dimensions 5×10 just fits in one corner. What is the side length S of the square? The radius satisfies $R = \frac{S}{2}$.

Answer 1.8: You (the bug) cannot fly; you have to walk. You must find the shortest path from corner to corner.

In any world, the shortest path between two points is called a "geodesic." On a spherical world (e.g., the Earth's surface), a geodesic is an arc of a "great circle." A great circle is a circle on the surface of the sphere with diameter equal to the diameter of the sphere. For example, airplanes typically follow great circles above the Earth (because it is the shortest path and, therefore, the most fuel-efficient path).

Like a spherical world, the cubic-room world has a two dimensional surface. However, the lack of curvature in the cubic-room world means that the shortest distance between two points must be a straight line rather than an arc of a great circle (in a world without curvature, geodesics are straight lines).

If the cubic room is opened up and flattened out it can be seen that the shortest path is a straight line from one corner to the other. In the un-flattened room, this straight line corresponds to two line segments that meet exactly halfway up one wall-floor or wall-wall boundary. Direct computation using Pythagoras' Theorem[10] reveals that the total path length is $\sqrt{5}$ units.

---

[10]In this case, the path is the hypotenuse of a triangle of side lengths 2 and 1 in the flattened-out room or two hypotenuses of triangles each of side lengths 1 and $\frac{1}{2}$ in the un-flattened room. In either case, the path is of total length $\sqrt{5}$.

Answer 1.9: People tend to overlook the brilliantly simple situation described. If you did any mathematics whatsoever, you probably missed the point.

No calculation is needed to see that at each stage an equal number of male babies and female babies are expected to be born. The proportions of male and female children are, therefore, expected to remain equal at 50%.

Still stuck? Here are the details (standing at $t = 0$ and looking at expected outcomes only): by the end of the first year, the 100,000 families have 50,000 boys and 50,000 girls. The proportion of male children stands at 50%. By the end of the second year, half of the 100,000 families (the ones without a son) have another child. This adds 25,000 boys and 25,000 girls. There are now 75,000 boys and 75,000 girls. The proportion of male children still stands at 50%. There are still 25,000 families without a son. They add another 12,500 boys and an equal number of girls, and so on.

Some people are tempted to suppose that because all large families have many daughters and a single son, there must be more girls than boys. However, there are not many large families.[11]

Answer 1.10: The 10×10 macro-cube question has been very popular. The most common mistake is for people to *count* the number of 1×1 micro-cubes on each face and add them up. Even if you do the mathematics correctly (and most people do not), you miss the whole point.

If you focus on the 1×1 micro-cubes on the faces and how to count them directly (e.g., How many faces? How many on each face? How many edges?), then you have been bumped by the pickpocket's accomplice (see story on p. 250). Go back now and figure out a better way. As I stated before, the path of greatest resistance bears the highest rewards, so read no further unless you did it a better way.

You must look for structure in a problem that leads you to a simple and speedy solution. The most structure here is to be found in the macro-cube you start with and the (now slightly smaller) macro-cube that remains. The difference between their volumes is how many micro-cubes fell.

The volume of a cube of side length n is n cubed; that is, n^3. The answer is, therefore, $10^3 - 8^3$.

How do you calculate this without a calculator? You should know that 10^k is a 1 with k zeroes attached, so $10^3 = 1,000$. You should know that $8 = 2^3$ and, therefore, that $8^3 = 2^{3 \times 3} = 2^9$. You should definitely know that 2^{10}

---

[11]In fact, the average number of children per family is only $\sum_{k=1}^{\infty} \frac{k}{2^k} = 2$. This formula is a special case of a more general series result: $\sum_{k=1}^{\infty} \frac{k}{x^k} = \frac{x}{(x-1)^2}$, for $|x| > 1$, derived as follows. Assume $|y| < 1$, then $\sum_{k=0}^{\infty} y^k = \frac{1}{1-y}$. Now differentiate both sides with respect to y, to find $\sum_{k=0}^{\infty} k \cdot y^k = \frac{y}{(1-y)^2}$. Now substitute in $y = 1/x$, for $|x| > 1$, and drop the null first term. Then, $\sum_{k=1}^{\infty} \frac{k}{x^k} = \frac{1/x}{(1-1/x)^2} = \frac{x}{(x-1)^2}$. I thank NK for pointing out this simple derivation; any errors are mine.

is 1,024. Thus, 2^9 is half of 2^{10} and, therefore, equal to 512. The answer is $1,000 - 512 = 488$. A common mistake is for people to think the answer is $10^3 - 9^3 = 271$, because only "one layer" fell off (you should of course know what 9^3 is also without having to work it out).

Answer 1.11: If not for the ability to stop and dump apples along the way, you could not deliver any apples at all.[12] So, the key is to make repeated trips where you dump apples in a pile at the side of the road and then you subsequently pick up and deliver apples from that apple dump. For example, suppose you made three trips where each time you left City A with 1,000 apples and dumped 500 uneaten apples at the 500-mile marker. You would then have accumulated 1,500 apples at the 500-mile marker and you could deliver 500 of those to City B (e.g., in one trip of 1,000 apples where 500 are delivered uneaten, and 500 are left to rot at 500-mile marker).

To find the optimal strategy, we must put some bounds on what is sensible. If you are driving away from City A, or away from an apple dump at the side of the road, then if there are 1,000 or more apples available, it would never make sense to leave with fewer than 1,000 apples on the truck. For example, suppose your very first move was to drive away from City A with only 900 apples. Well, no matter where you dump the uneaten balance, you missed out on giving an extra 100 apples a free ride to that spot, and that must be suboptimal. So, we should drive away from City A only three times, with 1,000 apples on board each time.

The next question is whether, for any one of these three departures from City A, we dump the uneaten apples at only one apple dump, or whether we dump them at more than one location. Suppose on one trip we dump 100 apples at the 100-mile marker, and then the uneaten balance at some later spot. That cannot be sensible, because again, no matter where you dump the uneaten balance, you missed out on giving an extra 100 apples a free ride to that spot. So, we must choose a single dump location for each run.

Could dump locations differ by run? Well, as long as we can get the dump contents to cumulate to a multiple of 1,000 (see below), they should all be dumped in the same place. Suppose instead that on the third run we dump apples beyond the location of the dump from the first two runs. Then driving that odd-lot of apples to a further location unnecessarily burns apples because it subsequently forces the truck to leave the earlier apple dump with fewer than 1,000 apples. So, not only must we dump the apples in only one location on any given trip, but we must dump them at the same location on each trip.

So, where do we dump the apples on the three departures from City A, before subsequently loading up from that combined dump and carrying them further on? Well, if we dump them at the k-mile marker, we will end up with a total

---

[12]Dumping apples part-way into the journey is akin to the "depoting" of food and supplies that took place during Antarctic journeys (Scott, 2008).

of $T = 3 \times (1000 - k)$ apples at the dump site. The arguments already given tell us that it makes no sense to drive away from the dump site with fewer than 1,000 apples on board (unless we have fewer than 1,000 apples available). So, we will carry the first 3,000 apples (spread over three trips) until we can dump them in a pile of 2,000 apples.

In general, starting with $N \times 1,000$ apples, we will carry them (spread over N trips) until we can dump $(N - 1) \times 1,000$ apples. If we dump the apples at the k-mile marker, it must be that $N \times (1,000 - k) = (N - 1) \times 1,000$. Solving for k yields $k = \frac{1,000}{N}$. So, to go from 3,000 apples down to 2,000 apples we dump them at the $\frac{1,000}{3}$-mile marker. Assuming we cannot slice apples up to get a continuous solution, let us dump them at the 333-mile marker. We will have $T = 2,001$ apples dumped there. Ignore one apple. Using the same argument again, we will drive the 2,000 apples in two trips, dumping them in two batches after another $\frac{1,000}{N} = \frac{1,000}{2} = 500$ miles. Then we will have 1,000 apples at the 833-mile marker. We can then drive them on the remaining 167 miles in one trip, delivering 833 apples.[13]

Extra notes: First, if we dump the apples at the 334-mile marker instead of the 333-mile marker, the final answer is unchanged. Second, we can think about the problem in terms of rate of apple consumption. When we leave City A, we are burning three apples per mile (one apple per mile per run). We would like to be running at this costly rate for the shortest distance possible. As soon as we get to the 333-mile marker, we can reduce this to two apples per mile (by dumping and then making two runs burning only one apple per mile per run). As soon as we have driven those 2,000 apples another 500 miles, we can cut the burn rate down to one apple per mile. You could argue that dumping 2,400 apples at the 200-mile marker would also let you cut the burn rate from three to two apples per mile. You would, however, leave 400 apples behind to rot. So, it is better to burn 399 of those 400 apples (over three runs) while carrying the other 2,001 apples an extra 133 miles closer to City B. Finally, this problem is isomorphic to one where we have $N \times 1,000$ apples and N trucks. After the N trucks drive the first $\frac{1,000}{N}$ miles, one truck can be decommissioned and it's uneaten load redistributed to top up the remaining $N - 1$ trucks. After another $\frac{1,000}{N-1}$ miles we decommission another truck and it's uneaten load is redistributed to top up the remaining $N - 2$ trucks, and so on.[14]

Answer 1.12: People have given me answers to this one ranging from 0° to 75° (and many answers in between). The big hand is on the three; the little hand

---

[13]If we could slice the apples up, the continuous solution would be to dump them first at the $333\frac{1}{3}$-mile marker, then again at the $833\frac{1}{3}$ mile marker, ultimately delivering $833\frac{1}{3}$ apples.

[14]If N is a very big number, and assuming a continuous solution, then using harmonic series and the Euler-Mascheroni result $\lim_{n \to \infty} \left[\sum_{j=1}^{n} \frac{1}{j} - \ln(n) \right] = \gamma$, where $\gamma \approx 0.5772156649$ is the Euler-Mascheroni constant, I was able to show that you end up delivering a proportion $\frac{1}{e}$ of your apples (roughly 36.8%). With $N = 3$ (3,000 apples), we deliver only 833 apples (27.8%), but this number rises steadily with N, converging to $\frac{1}{e}$.

is one-quarter of the way between the three and the four. The answer must be one-quarter of one-twelfth of 360°. That is, one-quarter of 30°. That is, 7.5° (or $\frac{\pi}{24}$ radians if you like measuring angles in radians).[15]

You should focus on what you know (the angle is non-zero, the big hand is on the three, one hour is one-twelfth of the full circle, and 15 minutes is one-quarter of one hour) and make sure that your answer accords with intuition. For example, if you get 75°, then something is wrong with your reasoning (or you have never owned an analog wristwatch).

Answer 1.13: I present three different solutions: first, an approximation that draws upon the answer to the previous question; second, an exact algebraic solution; and, third, an exact and slightly more elegant algebraic solution.

FIRST SOLUTION

An approximate answer is a great place to start.[16] There are 360° around the clock face. The minute hand therefore travels at 6° per minute. At 3:15 the minute hand is 7.5° behind the hour hand (from the previous answer). To travel that distance takes $7.5/6 = 1.25$ minutes. That is, one minute and 15 seconds, or 75 seconds. So, at 3:16:15 the minute hand will arrive where the hour hand was 75 seconds ago. Of course, the hour hand will have moved ever so slightly during that 75 seconds. So, maybe you need to wait another, say, five seconds until the two hands are perfectly coincident. That would be at 3:16:20. The exact solutions following are less than two seconds away from this approximate answer.

SECOND SOLUTION

The question asks the first time after 3PM when the hour and minute hands of a clock are coincident. More generally, we can ask the first time after nPM when the hour and minute hands are coincident, for $n = 1, 2, ..., 11$ (we miss out the 12 because the hands are not coincident after 12 and before 1).

Assume we start at nPM, for one of $n = 1, 2, ..., 11$. By the time the minute hand whips around to the n on the dial, the hour hand will have moved slowly on already. When the minute hand finally catches up with the hour hand, the hour hand will have moved by a total of $\theta(n)$ degrees past the n on the dial, say. The minute hand whips around the dial 12 times faster than the hour hand. So, while the hour hand covers $\theta(n)$ degrees, the minute hand covers $12 \cdot \theta(n)$ degrees.

We can also state that the minute hand must have covered $30n + \theta(n)$ degrees. That is $30n$ degrees to get around to the n on the dial, and another $\theta(n)$ degrees to finally catch the hour hand. So, we may write $30n + \theta(n) = 12 \cdot \theta(n)$, and thus, $\theta(n) = 30n/11$ degrees.[17]

---

[15]There are 2π radians in a full circle. Thus, $360° = 2\pi$ radians; $180° = \pi$ radians; $90° = \frac{\pi}{2}$ radians; and so on. It is just another way of measuring angles.

[16]I thank Eoin Healy for suggesting this approximation; any errors are mine.

[17]It also follows that $\theta(n) = n \cdot \theta(1)$ for $n = 1, 2, ..., 11$, where $\theta(1) = 30/11$ degrees.

So, the first time after 3PM that the hands are coincident is when the minute hand has traveled 15 minutes to get to the 3 on the dial and then another $\theta(3) = 90/11$ degrees past the 3 on the dial. One minute is six degrees. So, $90/11$ degrees is $\frac{90/11}{6} = \frac{90/11}{66/11} = \frac{90}{66} = 1\frac{24}{66} = 1\frac{4}{11}$ minutes. So, the hands are coincident at 16 and $\frac{4}{11}^{th}$'s of a minute after 3PM.

THIRD SOLUTION

At high noon, the hands are coincident. At midnight, the hands are coincident. The time between noon and midnight is cut into 11 equally-spaced time intervals of one-eleventh of 12 hours (1:05:27.27). At the end of each of these intervals, the hands are coincident. For the question at hand, the answer is three times one-eleventh of 12 hours: 3:16:21.82. The full set of "coincident times" are as follows:

$$\begin{pmatrix} 1:05:27.27 \\ 2:10:54.55 \\ 3:16:21.82 \\ 4:21:49.09 \\ 5:27:16.36 \\ 6:32:43.64 \\ 7:38:10.91 \\ 8:43:38.18 \\ 9:49:05.45 \\ 10:54:32.73 \\ 12:00:00.00 \end{pmatrix}$$

Answer 1.14: Well now, this looks pretty complicated the first time you see it. However, there is a simple way to figure it out. If you think about it, you see that the only brokers who touch the switch for light bulb number 64 are those whose numbers are divisors of 64.

That is, light bulb number 64 has its state of illumination changed by brokers whose numbers are factors of 64. That is, brokers 1, 2, 4, 8, 16, 32, and 64 flip the switch. Because light bulb 64 is originally *off*, it must be that after this odd number of switches it is *on*. See Answer 1.15 for a closely related but more general solution technique.

Answer 1.15: If you now know the answer to Question 1.14, you should be able to figure this one out swiftly. If you have not yet figured out Question 1.14, then read no further—solve that one first.

The only way for a light bulb to be illuminated after the 100th person has passed through is if its switch was flipped an odd number of times. The switch for light bulb number K gets flipped only by people whose numbers are factors of K. Thus, the only light bulbs illuminated at the conclusion are those with a number that has an odd number of factors.

However, factors for numbers go in pairs. For example, 32 has factors $(1, 32)$, $(2, 16)$, and $(4, 8)$. This means that 32 has an even number of factors, and bulb

32 is not illuminated at the conclusion. In fact, at first glance, all numbers have an even number of factors.

However, you do get an odd number of factors if two factors (one pair) are identical. For example, 64 has $(8, 8)$ as one pair. If one pair of factors are identical, then the original number must be a "perfect square." Therefore, the only numbers with an odd number of factors are the perfect squares.

There are exactly 10 perfect squares between 1 and 100, and they are 1, 4, 9, 16, 25, 36, 49, 64, 81, and 100 (i.e., 1^2, 2^2, 3^2, ... 10^2). These are the numbers of the 10 bulbs that are illuminated after the 100th person has passed through the room.

Answer 1.16: This is an old favorite. I have tried this out on people and have received almost all imaginable responses. The answer is three, and it cannot be anything else. Two socks can be different, but a third must match one of the first two—giving a matching pair.

Answer 1.17: With socks of N different colors, you must pull $(N + 1)$ socks from the drawer to be sure that you have a matching pair. The argument is the same as it was for the previous question; N socks can be different (the worst-case scenario), but the $(N + 1)^{st}$ sock must match one of the first N socks—giving a matching pair.

Answer 1.18: Like the answer to the previous question, ask yourself first what is the worst-case scenario? That is, what is the maximum number of socks you can select without obtaining the required three matching pairs? Recall that the counts/colors are 2 red, 4 yellow, 6 purple, 8 brown, 10 white, 12 green, 14 black, 16 blue, 18 gray, and 20 orange socks. You will never be able to get three-pair of the red or yellow socks because there are too few of them. There are only eight candidate colors remaining. Thus, the worst-case scenario is that you select 2 red, 4 yellow, and 5 of each of the remaining eight colors, giving a total of 46 socks. As soon as you select a 47th sock, however, its color must match the color of one of the previously selected quintuples in those eight colors. Thus, you need at least 47 socks to guarantee a matching pair.

Answer 1.19: You get the answer by working backwards. If I am your opponent, and I am able to call out "39," then you cannot reach 50, but I can after you say whatever you say. So, my goal is to call out "39." However, if I am able to call out "28," then you cannot get to 39, but I can after you say whatever you say. So, my goal is to call out "28." To get to 28, I need only to be able to call out "17," and to do this, I need only to be able to call out "6."

So, my strategy, as your opponent, is to get onto the series 6, 17, 28, 39, 50 at whichever point I can. If you get to go first, you should call out "6." As long as you know the winning numbers and stick to them, you cannot lose. If you start with anything other than 6, I cannot lose.

Answer 1.20: Safe-cracking in a finance interview? Yes indeed. The naive answer is that there are 40 possible numbers for the first combination, 40 for the second, and 40 for the third. It would then take at most 40^3 possible trials to get the safe open. That is 64,000 trials. There are two factors that reduce this number considerably. The first you should have figured out; the second you are excused.

The first factor is that although three numbers are required to open the safe, you need only find the first two of them. If you dial the first two numbers correctly, then you need only turn the dial until the safe pops open. You do not need to know the last number. This gives 40^2 possible combinations. That is only 1,600 trials. For extra safe-cracking advice along these lines see Gleick (1993, pp. 189–190).[18]

The interviewer in this case suggested a second factor, as follows (and I think it is a little unfair to any interviewee who is inexperienced in safe-cracking). The safe is a mechanical device designed with a particular tolerance for inaccuracy. If the first combination number is 14, then dialing either 13, 14, or 15 suffices. This tolerance for inaccuracy brings you down to roughly $\left(\frac{40}{3}\right)^2$ trials. This is fewer than 200 trials.

One reader suggested that because you need only find a sequence of numbers, different attempts could overlap with other attempts, to reduce the number of trials needed. If you need to start again at zero every time, however, then this approach fails. In practice, with real safes, you need to dial clockwise three times past zero to 75, counter-clockwise two times past zero to 50, clockwise once past zero to 25, or something like that. So, you need to start anew each time.

Answer 1.21: To minimize the maximum possible cost of weighing, your strategy must use the scales as few times as possible, wherever the location of the "bad" coin. From Answer 1.6, you know that you need three weighings to find a bad coin in a group of 12. You have 90 coins, so it must take at least four weighings. However, by the same argument, if you had 144 coins (12 groups of 12), you could identify a bad group of 12 in three weighings and then the bad coin in another three. So, (because 90 is less than 144) it should take no more than six weighings—either four, five, or six weighings.

In fact, it takes only five weighings (and at most $500) to both find the bad coin and identify it as heavy or light. I present two quite different solution techniques plus a third quasi-solution: the first is an ingenious "hammer-and-tongs" technique, the second is slightly more structured, and the third generalizes the second but applies only in special cases. In each case, it takes only five weighings to both find the bad coin and identify it as heavy or light.

---

[18]I went to a presentation at MIT at which Jim Gleick (pronounced "Glick") talked about his then soon-to-be-published book "Genius." He talked about genius in general and Richard P. Feynman in particular. Feynman was an interesting guy, and this is a good book about him.

FIRST SOLUTION[19]

The technique here is similar to the solution techniques in Question 1.6—be sure to answer that question before answering this one. The first move is to divide the 90 coins into three groups of 30. Weigh two of the groups of 30 coins. Either the scales balance, or they do not. If the scales balance, then you are left with one group of 30 containing the bad coin. You may "hold out" 10 of these 30 and compare the remaining 20—with 10 on each side. If the scales balance, you get one group of 10 containing the bad coin. If they do not balance, you have one group of 10 coins potentially heavy and one group of 10 coins potentially light. Stop here if you just wanted to know how to start the solution process. This should be enough for you to finish.

Return for a moment to the case in which the two groups of 30 do not balance. Set aside 10 potentially heavy coins and 10 potentially light coins. Take the remaining 20 potentially heavy and 20 potentially light coins and swap 10 of them from one side of the scales with 10 of them from the other side of the scales, keeping track of which were swapped and which stayed put. Whether they balance or not, you can immediately identify one group of 10 coins that is potentially heavy and one group of 10 coins that is potentially light—the other 40 are "good" coins.

Thus, after two weighings, the problem reduces either to one group of 10 coins containing the bad coin (no further information) or two groups of 10 coins (where one group potentially contains a heavy coin, and the other potentially contains a light one). I need only demonstrate the solution technique for each case.

Suppose you have 10 coins, and one of them is bad. You can find the bad one in three weighings simply by adding two good coins and following Answer 1.6 for the 12-ball case. This finds you the bad coin in a total of five weighings.

Suppose instead that you have the two groups of 10 coins (where one group potentially contains a heavy coin, and the other potentially contains a light one). Use the notation "3↑" to denote three potentially light coins, "3↓" to denote three potentially heavy coins, and "good" to denote one coin known to be neither heavy nor light. In this case, you begin at the end of the second weighing with {10↑} and {10↓} on the scales. Hold out 3↑ and 3↓ coins and place the following on the scales for weighing number three: {3↑,4↓} versus {3↓,4↑}.

Suppose the scales balance with {3↑,4↓} versus {3↓,4↑}. Then you have 3↑ and 3↓ coins left. Hold out 1↑ and 1↓ and weigh {1↑,1↓} versus {1↓,1↑}. If these balance, weigh the hold out 1↑ against one good coin to find the bad one; if they do not balance, you get 1↑ and 1↓ from the light and heavy sides, respectively; and you need only compare one of them with a good coin to find the bad one. This gives a total of five weighings in either case.

---

[19]I thank Eva Porro (then at the Universidad Complutense de Madrid) for this solution technique; any errors are mine.

Suppose the scales do not balance with {3↑,4↓} versus {3↓,4↑}. If the first group appears lighter, then you get 3↑ and 3↓ coins as in the previous paragraph and able to be solved in a total of five weighings. If the second group appears lighter, then you get 4↓ and 4↑ coins. This is just like the first weighing of two groups of four in the 12-ball problem in Question 1.6, and you know the bad coin can be identified in only two more weighings by rotating "triplets." In each case, the bad coin is both located and identified as heavy or light in only five weighings.

SECOND SOLUTION[20]

Begin by noting that if you have a group of 3^k coins that is known to contain a heavy coin, it takes only k weighings to identify it. You can see this as follows: split the group of 3^k coins into three subgroups each of size 3^{k-1}; now compare any two subgroups on the scales. Whether the scales balance or not, you know immediately which of the three subgroups contains the heavy coin. It thus takes only one weighing to go from a group of 3^k coins known to contain a heavy coin to a group of 3^{k-1} coins known to contain a heavy coin. Proceeding in this fashion, it takes k weighings to go from a group of 3^k coins known to contain a heavy coin to a single coin known to be heavy. The same result applies if the initial sample is known to contain a light coin.

Therefore, if you know that the bad coin in your sample is heavy (or if you know that it is light), Table A.1 gives the correspondence between sample size and number of weighings required to locate the bad coin. I now use Table A.1

Table A.1: Weighings Needed to Find Bad Coin

Sample Size	Weighings (if bad coin is known heavy)
3	1
9	2
27	3
81	4
243	5
⋮	⋮

Note: If you have a sample of coins and you know that there is a bad coin in your sample and that it is heavy (or if you know that it is light), then the table gives the number of weighings required to locate the bad coin.

to answer the question. Begin by splitting the sample into as few groups of form 3^k as possible.[21] In this case, $90 = 81 + 9$, so you choose one group of

---

[20]I thank Bingjian Ni for this solution technique; any errors are mine.

[21]Can you make a conjecture about the sample size, its ternary (i.e., base three) representation, and the number of weighings needed to find the bad coin/marble?

81 and one group of nine. Split the group of 81 into three subgroups of 27. Call these groups $\{27\}_A$, $\{27\}_B$, and $\{27\}_C$. Now use the scales to compare groups $\{27\}_A$ and $\{27\}_B$. Now use the scales again to compare groups $\{27\}_A$ and $\{27\}_C$. If the bad coin is in the group of 81, then these two weighings are sufficient to identify which subgroup of 27 the bad coin falls into and whether it is heavy or light. Consulting Table A.1, you can see that in this case it takes only three additional weighings to find the bad coin.

If both the initial weighings balance (i.e., $\{27\}_A$ versus $\{27\}_B$ and $\{27\}_A$ versus $\{27\}_C$ both balance), then the bad coin is in the group of nine. Compare the group of nine to nine good coins taken from the group of 81. This tells you whether the bad coin is heavy or light. Consulting Table A.1, you can see that in this case, it takes only two more weighings to find the bad coin. Alternatively, you could have split the group of nine into three groups of three and weighed two pairs of them. This identifies the group of three containing the bad coin and tells you whether it is heavy or light. Consulting Table A.1, you can see that in this case, it takes only one more weighing to find the bad coin. In each case, the bad coin is both located and identified as heavy or light in only five weighings (at a maximum cost of $500).

THIRD SOLUTION[22]
Suppose you are given $N = \frac{3^n - 3}{2}$ balls for some positive integer n. The balls appear identical, but one ball is odd—either heavy or light; you do not know which. Then it takes n weighings to both find the odd ball and identify it as heavy or light (see Table A.2).

Table A.2: Weighings Needed to Find Bad Coin

Balls Supplied $N = \frac{3^n - 3}{2}$	Weighings Needed n
3	2
12	3
39	4
120	5
363	6
$\vdots$	$\vdots$

Note: If you have a sample of coins and you know that there is a bad coin in your sample but not whether it is heavy or light, then the table gives the number of weighings required to locate the bad coin.

---

[22]I thank Yi Shen for this solution technique. I thank Yiannis Chardaloupas for improving upon it; any errors are mine.

It is no coincidence that the first column in Table A.2 is the partial sums of the first column in Table A.1—this technique generalizes the second. I prove the particular case $N = 120$ (i.e., $n = 5$), but the proof generalizes directly to any $N(n) = \frac{3^n - 3}{2}$.

Put the 120 balls into three groups of 40. Each group of 40 is a cohort of subgroups of size 3^k for $k = 0$ to $k = n - 2$: $\{\{1\}_A, \{3\}_A, \{9\}_A, \{27\}_A\}$; $\{\{1\}_B, \{3\}_B, \{9\}_B, \{27\}_B\}$; and $\{\{1\}_C, \{3\}_C, \{9\}_C, \{27\}_C\}$.

Compare cohorts A and B. If they balance, then you have 80 good balls, and cohort C contains the bad ball. In this case, compare $\{27\}_C$ to the good balls $\{27\}_A$. If $\{27\}_C$ contains the bad ball, then Table A.1 says you need three more weighings. If $\{27\}_C$ is good, then compare $\{9\}_C$ to the good balls $\{9\}_A$. If $\{9\}_C$ contains the bad ball, then Table A.1 says you need two more weighings. If $\{9\}_C$ is good, then compare $\{3\}_C$ to the good balls $\{3\}_A$. You need only one more weighing—either because $\{3\}_C$ is bad (see Table A.1), or because $\{3\}_C$ is good (thus $\{1\}_C$ is bad).

If the initial comparison of A and B does not balance, then rotate (like changing car tires) groups $\{27\}_A$, $\{27\}_B$, and $\{27\}_C$ and compare grouping $\{\{1\}_A, \{3\}_A, \{9\}_A, \{27\}_B\}$ to $\{\{1\}_B, \{3\}_B, \{9\}_B, \{27\}_C\}$ while holding out $\{\{1\}_C, \{3\}_C, \{9\}_C, \{27\}_A\}$.

There are three possible cases. First, if they balance, then $\{27\}_A$ contains the bad ball, and it is known to be heavy or light, and Table A.1 says three more weighings are needed. Second, if the scales tilt the same way as the initial comparison of A and B, then you can discard the $\{27\}$'s, rotate the $\{9\}$'s, and compare $\{\{1\}_A, \{3\}_A, \{9\}_B\}$ to $\{\{1\}_B, \{3\}_B, \{9\}_C\}$ while holding out $\{\{1\}_C, \{3\}_C, \{9\}_A\}$. You either find that $\{9\}_A$ is bad, known heavy or light, and apply Table A.1, or $\{9\}_B$ is bad, known heavy or light, and apply Table A.1, or you discard the $\{9\}$'s and rotate the $\{3\}$'s. Continue reducing the problem until convergence—in at most five weighings. Third, if the scales tilt the opposite way to the initial comparison of A and B, then $\{27_B\}$ contains the bad ball, and it is known to be heavy or light, and Table A.1 says three more weighings are needed.

One problem with this method is what to do if given only 90 balls (more than 39 but fewer than 120). I guess you ask for 30 extra ones and then follow the procedure for 120.

Answer 1.22: This question is unusually esoteric, but I like it. The result is known as Liouville's Theorem. It can be proved directly using Picard's Theorem,[23] or with very slightly more work, using a Cauchy integral.[24] I have

---

[23] Picard: A non-constant entire function assumes every complex value, with at most one possible exception. Thus, a bounded function must be a constant.

[24] Cauchy integral: let $C(z_0, r)$ be a circle or radius r about arbitrary $z_0 \in \mathbb{C}$, then $f'(z_0) = \frac{1}{2\pi i} \int_{C(z_0, r)} \frac{f(z)}{(z - z_0)^2} dz$ (a contour integral), so $|f'(z_0)| \leq \frac{1}{r} \sup_{z \in \mathbb{C}} |f(z)|$. Bounded f implies the RHS tends to zero as $r \to \infty$. Thus, $f'(z_0) \equiv 0$, for arbitrary $z_0 \in \mathbb{C}$, and f must be a constant.

chosen, however, to prove it from first principles.[25]

Begin by proving a lemma (a "helping theorem" to be used in a later proof). The lemma is used in the proof of a theorem that answers the interview question. If you have a mathematical background but cannot answer the question, you should read the statement of the lemma, and stop reading there. You should then try to complete the remainder of the proof on your own. This is more satisfying than seeing the full proof.

LEMMA: Maximum Modulus of Coefficients of a Power Series[26]
Suppose that $f(z)$ is analytic in the disc $|z| \leq r < \infty$. Let $M(r) \equiv \max\{|f(z)| : |z| \leq r\}$. Then the coefficients a_p in the power series expansion $f(z) = a_0 + a_1 z + \cdots + a_p z^p + \ldots$ satisfy the following bound:

$$|a_p| \leq \frac{M(r)}{r^p} \quad \text{for} \quad p = 1, 2, 3 \ldots$$

PROOF OF LEMMA
With $f(z) = a_0 + a_1 z + \cdots + a_p z^p + \ldots$ in $|z| \leq r < \infty$, divide by z^p to get

$$\frac{f(z)}{z^p} = a_0 z^{-p} + a_1 z^{-p+1} + \cdots + a_p + \ldots .$$

Now change to polar coordinates. Hold $r = |z|$ constant, and integrate $\frac{f(z)}{z^p}$ from $\phi = 0$ to $\phi = 2\pi$ [where $\phi \equiv arg(z)$]:

$$\int_0^{2\pi} \frac{f(z)}{z^p} d\phi = \int_0^{2\pi} a_0 z^{-p} d\phi + \cdots + \int_0^{2\pi} a_p d\phi + \ldots$$

The integral is convergent because, for fixed r and varying ϕ, the original series converges uniformly. Each term in the series expansion contributes an integral of form

$$a_{k+p} \int_0^{2\pi} z^k d\phi.$$

However, for $k \neq 0$ this integral contributes zero:

$$
\begin{aligned}
a_{k+p} \int_0^{2\pi} z^k d\phi &= a_{k+p} \int_0^{2\pi} r^k [\cos(k\phi) + i \, \sin(k\phi)] \, d\phi \\
&= a_{k+p} \, r^k \left[\frac{\sin(k\phi)}{k} - i \, \frac{\cos(k\phi)}{k} \right]_0^{2\pi} \\
&= 0
\end{aligned}
$$

---

[25] I thank Naoki Sato and Thomas C. Watson for suggesting the Picard Theorem and Cauchy integral approaches, respectively; any errors are mine.

[26] This lemma and its proof are adapted from Holland (1973, pp. 9–10), with copyright permission from Academic Press.

Thus, the only term that contributes anything to $\int_0^{2\pi} \frac{f(z)}{z^p} d\phi$ is $\int_0^{2\pi} a_p d\phi = 2\pi a_p$, (when $k = 0$). It follows that

$$a_p = \frac{1}{2\pi} \int_0^{2\pi} \frac{f(z)}{z^p} d\phi \quad \text{for} \quad p = 0, 1, 2, \ldots .$$

Now, with $M(r) = \max\{|f(z)| : |z| \leq r\}$, and $|z| = r$, it follows that for integer $p > 0$, you get

$$\begin{aligned}
|a_p| &\leq \frac{1}{2\pi} \int_0^{2\pi} \frac{|f(z)|}{|z|^p} d\phi \\
&= \frac{1}{2\pi r^p} \int_0^{2\pi} |f(z)| d\phi \\
&\leq \frac{1}{2\pi r^p} \int_0^{2\pi} M(r) d\phi \\
&= \frac{M(r)}{2\pi r^p} \int_0^{2\pi} d\phi \\
&= \frac{M(r)}{r^p} \quad \square
\end{aligned}$$

I now present the interview question as a theorem and use the previous lemma in its proof.

THEOREM: Bounded Entire Function[27]
If $f(z)$ is entire and bounded, then $f(z)$ is a constant.

PROOF OF THEOREM
Assuming that $f(z)$ is entire implies that $f(z)$ is analytic in the entire finite complex plane. Thus, the Taylor series $f(z) = \sum_{n=0}^{\infty} a_n z^n$ converges for all $|z| < \infty$. If the stated bound (of the theorem) is $|f(z)| \leq M$, say, then from the lemma it follows that

$$0 \leq |a_n| \leq \frac{M(r)}{r^n} \leq \frac{M}{r^n} \quad \text{for all } n > 0 \text{ and all } r.$$

If you let $r \to \infty$, then $0 \leq |a_n| \leq 0$ for all $n > 0$. Thus, $a_n = 0$ for all $n > 0$, and $f(z) = a_0$, a constant. $\square$

Answer 1.23: After 100 seconds you can be sure that the ants have all walked off the ruler. The answer is the same as if the ants had perfect vision. The key is that if two ants who collide, immediately about face and continue, then each member of any colliding pair effectively exchanges its exit route with the other; the ants are fungible. It is just as if one of the colliding pair crawled over the other and they both kept going without pause.

---

[27]This theorem and its proof are adapted from Holland (1973, p. 10), with copyright permission from Academic Press.

Answer 1.24:   If you can figure out the correct relationship between the eight lily pads and the single one, you get the answer. If you do not have it yet, or you think it is 3.75 days, then you should stop reading now, and go back and try again. I am serious; this is a nice question, and you lose a great deal by peeking at the answers to help you out.

The naive answer is that it takes $\frac{30}{8} = 3.75$ days. This is, of course, incorrect. The lily pads in the question all grow at the same rate. This means that you may think of the eight lily pads as being equivalent to one big lily pad. Indeed, when the single lily pad is three days old, it has the same area as the eight lily pads do at time zero. This means that you may think of the eight lily pads as a single lily pad that is three days old. It takes another 27 days for a three-day-old single lily pad to cover the pond, so it also takes 27 days for the eight lily pads to cover the pond.

The interviewee suggested that I use 3,000 days instead of 30 days as the time it takes for the single lily pad to cover the pond. The idea was to make the question more confusing. The problem with this is that, no matter how small the initial lily pad (assuming it is visible to the naked eye), it will cover the surface of the Earth within 100 days and the entire solar system not long after. Within 3,000 days, the universe will be blotted out—such is the power of compound growth.

Answer 1.25:   You use the same idea as in the previous lily pad question. Each pad needs to cover $\frac{6,000}{27}$ square feet to choke the pond. The size of each pad is 2^N after N days, so you need to solve: $\frac{6,000}{27} = 2^N$. The solution is $N = \frac{\log\left(\frac{2,000}{9}\right)}{\log(2)} \approx 7.8$ days.[28]

Without a calculator, you can still do it in your head. You calculate $\frac{6,000}{27}$ as approximately 200. You know that 2^8 is 256, which exceeds 200; whereas 2^7 is 128, which falls short, so eight days should do the trick.

Answer 1.26:   Decimal pricing was introduced on the New York Stock Exchange in 2001. I have left this question in because there are many people who lived with eighths and sixteenths for most of their working life, and they may be tempted to ask you about it. I am still seeing this question being asked every year.

Most people stumble a little. Do not memorize all the possible sixteenths before your interview—you have worse things to worry about (much worse). Add or subtract one-sixteenth to get the requested fraction into quarters or eighths and then compensate for your adjustment.

You should remember that $\frac{1}{8}$ is 0.1250 and deduce from that that $\frac{1}{16}$ is 0.0625 (you should be able to give *any* eighth in decimal form). The fraction $\frac{13}{16}$ is only one-sixteenth away from $\frac{12}{16}$ which is exactly three quarters (0.7500). You need

---

[28]An interesting aside here is that it does not matter which logarithm function you use. The result is the same regardless of the base.

only add 0.0625 to 0.7500 to get 0.8125. Similarly, $\frac{9}{16}$ is only one-sixteenth over one-half, and is, therefore, 0.5625.

Answer 1.27: This is a common question. The naive answer is that the snail climbs a net of two feet per day, so it reaches the 10-foot mark at the end of the fifth day. However, on the morning of the fifth day, the snail starts out at the eight-foot mark (having slid down from the nine-foot mark overnight). Two-thirds of the way through the fifth day, the snail reaches the 10-foot mark and stops because there is no pole left to climb.

> **Story:** One interviewee was asked, "If you are holding a dinner party, and you can invite any three dead people (presumably resurrected), who would you choose? Please do not choose any relatives." Give it some thought.

Answer 1.28: Here are two answers.[29]

1. Turn Switch #1 on. Wait a while. Then turn it off while simultaneously turning Switch #2 on. Go into the room. The illuminated light corresponds to Switch #2. The warm non-illuminated bulb corresponds to Switch #1. The cold non-illuminated bulb corresponds to Switch #3.

2. Guess. You have a one-in-six chance if they are random. However, light switches are not usually random. If you assume the switches are physically located in an order that relates to the physical placement of the bulbs (as they usually are), then you have a fifty-fifty chance!

Answer 1.29: The only way the first man can know the color of his own hat is if he sees the other two wearing red hats—of which there are only two. However, the first man does *not* know his hat color, so the other two must be wearing either both blue or one red and one blue. The second man, upon hearing the first, knows then that he and the third man are either both wearing blue hats, or one wears a red hat, and one a blue. If he still does not know what color hat he is wearing, it must be because the third man is wearing a blue hat. Why? Well, if the third man wears red, then that pinpoints his own hat as blue since this is the only option left from the choice of either both blue or one red and one blue. Since the second man does not know his hat color, then the third man must be wearing blue. The third man, upon hearing the first two, deduces that his own hat is blue via the same reasoning.

Answer 1.30: You may be looking to the solutions for a hint. My first hint is that, if you are using linear algebra (i.e., solving systems of equations by substitution) then stop that right now. There are nine equations in 10 unknowns, so this will get you nowhere. In fact, there are infinitely many integers that solve the problem statement; we are searching for the smallest such number. My second hint is that you might like to try drawing a picture.

---

[29]I thank Dahn Tamir for assistance on this question; any errors are mine.

FIRST SOLUTION

My first solution technique begins with the simultaneous equation approach and quickly abandons it. Let X denote the solution. Then I know there exist positive integers X_2, X_3, X_4, ..., X_{10}, such that

$$
\begin{aligned}
X &= 2 \times X_2 + 1, \\
X &= 3 \times X_3 + 2, \\
X &= 4 \times X_4 + 3, \\
X &= 5 \times X_5 + 4, \\
&\vdots \\
X &= 10 \times X_{10} + 9.
\end{aligned}
$$

Looking at the equations, it is clear that the coefficients on the right-hand side differ from the remainders by only one. If we simply add one to both sides of each equation, then the coefficients and the remainders will be identical, and we can collect terms to obtain the following:

$$
\begin{aligned}
X + 1 &= 2 \times X_2', \\
X + 1 &= 3 \times X_3', \\
X + 1 &= 4 \times X_4', \\
X + 1 &= 5 \times X_5', \\
&\vdots \\
X + 1 &= 10 \times X_{10}'
\end{aligned}
$$

Where $X_n' \equiv X_n + 1$ for each n between 2 and 10. With this simple restatement, the problem now requires that we find the smallest number X, such that $X + 1$ is perfectly divisible by 2, 3, 4, 5, 6, 7, 8, 9, and 10. That is, find a number X, such that $X + 1 = lcm(2, 3, 4, 5, 6, 7, 8, 9, 10)$, where $lcm(\cdot)$ is the lowest common multiple operator. Given various redundancies, we conclude that $X = lcm(6, 7, 8, 9, 10) - 1 = 2520 - 1 = 2519$ is the solution.

Looking at my restatement of the problem, it should be clear that if X solves $X + 1 = K \times lcm(6, 7, 8, 9, 10)$, for any positive integer K, then X is also a solution to the problem (but not the smallest unless $K = 1$). That is, $X = K \times lcm(6, 7, 8, 9, 10) - 1 = K \times 2520 - 1$ is also a solution for any positive integer K.

I think the interviewer would have been perfectly happy to hear that $X = lcm(6, 7, 8, 9, 10) - 1$, without your having to find the lcm. However, this does leave one question unanswered: What is the most efficient way to find the lowest common multiple of a group of numbers?[30]

---

[30]In this case, if you factor each of 6, 7, 8, 9, and 10, you get 2×3, 7, 2×4, 3×3, and 2×5. The lcm, when factorized, must include each of these expressions. Indeed, $2 \times 3 \times 3 \times 4 \times 5 \times 7 = 2,520$—the lcm.

SECOND SOLUTION

I did not discover the first solution by looking at the simultaneous equations and using algebra; I discovered it by drawing a picture. It is somewhat difficult to reproduce my picture, but here is an attempt using a sporting analogy (see Figure A.2).

I am searching for a number X with the divisor/remainder properties described. I have nine runners to help me: Mr. 2, Mr. 3, ..., Mr. 9, and Mr. 10. They are assembled at the start of an arbitrarily long, dead-straight, sand-covered, nine-lane racetrack that has distances measured in meters, beginning at "0" at the starting line (bear with me on this). Like many race tracks made for people, the people do not all start in the same place; their positions are staggered (which makes no sense for a straight track in the real world). Mr. 2 starts 1 meter from the zero line. Mr. 3 starts 2 meters from the zero line. Mr. 4 starts 3 meters from the zero line, ... and Mr. 10 starts 9 meters from the zero line.

The gun fires, and the race begins. Each Mr. n runs taking steps of length n meters (for n between 2 and 10). The runners each leave footprints in the sand on the track. Let them run for a very long time and then look at the footprints (we do not care who wins). Starting at the zero line, the divisor/remainder properties of X imply that the first time you find a row of nine footprints adjacent to each other must be after X meters.

The first time the footprints (the solid bullets in Figure A.2) are aligned vertically, is when they have reached the solution, X meters from the zero starting line. We can see that the number of meters they step out before beginning is one less than their step size when they run. If you look one pace backwards from the start line (back to position -1 on the race track), then it should be clear that the distance from the -1 position to X (i.e., $X + 1$) is just the *lcm* of the step sizes taken by the runners (how else could the footprints be adjacent?). It should also be clear that if you look beyond X, you will find another set of adjacent footprints after you travel another *lcm* meters. This solution is identical to the first.

Answer 1.31:   This is easier than it sounds. You do not need any infinite sums, and, if you used them, go back and try again before reading on. For every two miles covered by the first motorcyclist, the second covers three miles. Two plus three is five, and there are five multiples of five between them. This means they will meet after the first has traveled 10 miles and the second 15. We know that the fly moves at twice the speed of the first motorcyclist, so it must cover 20 miles before its miserable life ends.

Many other solutions exist. Here is one I liked.[31] The second motorcyclist is approaching the first at a *relative* speed of $20 + 30 = 50$ miles per hour. With 25 miles between them, they will collide after one-half of an hour. Meanwhile,

---

[31]I thank Adam Rej for suggesting this one; any errors are mine.

start

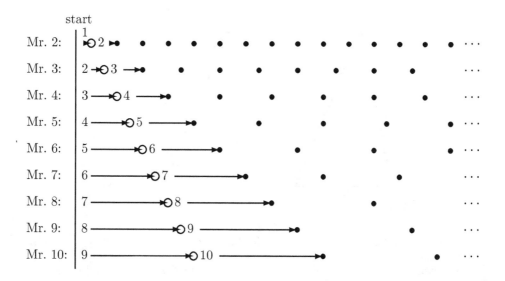

Figure A.2: A Road Race Analogy for the *lcm* Problem

Note: In the picture, the nine people run side by side. Mr. 2 steps out one meter to start (the hollow bullet) and then take steps of length two meters (his footsteps are solid bullets). Mr. 3 steps out two meters to start and then take steps of length three, and so on up until Mr. 10, who steps out nine meters to start and then takes steps of length 10.

the fly is travelling at 40 miles per hour. So, it must cover only 20 miles in that time.

Story: "Every morning I see job candidates who spend a day here. I talk to them, answer questions about our company, tell them whom they'll interview with, and send them off. At the end of the day, when they come back, I determine whom they'd most like to work for, brief them on employee benefits, and tell them what happens next. I went through the morning ritual recently with one young candidate and then told him I'd see him about 4P.M. 'I don't want to come back here,' he said, quite emphatically. 'I've already talked to a guy I know who has been here before, and he told me everything you're going to tell me.' "

ED GULICK
Recruiting Coordinator, Sandia National
Laboratory, Albuquerque, N.M.

"Doomed Days: The Worst Mistakes Recruiters Have Ever Seen,"
The Wall Street Journal, February 25, 1995, pR4.
Reprinted by permission of *The Wall Street Journal*
©1995 Dow Jones and Company, Inc.
All Rights Reserved Worldwide.

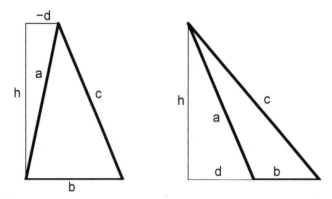

Figure A.3: Two Possible Triangle Configurations

Note: For both triangles configurations, the sides are a, b, and c, and the height is h. The variable d is defined so that $b+d$ measures the distance from the lower right corner to the point where a vertical dropped from the peak touches the base. It follows that $d < 0$ in the first case, and $d > 0$ in the second.

Answer 1.32: To derive Heron's (Hero's) formula, let A denote the area of a triangle of sides a, b, and c.[32] We may make several statements that apply to any triangle and which are clearly visible in Figure A.3:

1. The area A is given by $A = \frac{1}{2}bh$.

2. Pythagoras' Theorem implies that $a^2 = h^2 + d^2$ and $c^2 = h^2 + (b+d)^2$.

3. The first Pythagorean result implies $h^2 = a^2 - d^2$. When the second Pythagorean result is subtracted from the first, it yields $c^2 - a^2 = (b+d)^2 - d^2$, which implies that $d = \frac{c^2 - a^2 - b^2}{2b}$.

If we combine the above results, we get

$$
\begin{aligned}
A^2 &= \frac{1}{4}b^2h^2 = \frac{1}{4}b^2(a^2 - d^2) = \frac{1}{4}b^2 \left[a^2 - \frac{(c^2 - a^2 - b^2)^2}{4b^2} \right] \\
&= \frac{1}{4}b^2a^2 - \frac{1}{16}(c^2 - a^2 - b^2)^2 \\
&= \frac{1}{16}\left[(2ba)^2 - (c^2 - a^2 - b^2)^2 \right].
\end{aligned}
\tag{A.9}
$$

Equation A.9 stands out for several reasons. First, although expressed in terms of a, b, and c, it must, ultimately, be a polynomial in s, where $s = (a + b + c)/2$

---

[32]I thank Thomas C. Watson and Henri Bourdeau for comments and improvements on an earlier version of this proof; any errors are mine. I have since discovered that my proof is essentially the same as that in Raifaizen (1971), which I had not seen previously.

is the semi-perimeter.[33] Second, the $2ba$ term and the a^2 and b^2 terms look like parts of the squared term $(a+b)^2$. Third, Equation A.9 has the form $x^2 - y^2$ for $x = 2ba$ and $y = c^2 - a^2 - b^2$, and we know that $x^2 - y^2 = (x-y)(x+y)$. So, let us start again with Equation A.9, exploit the $x^2 - y^2$ form, collect terms, complete two squares, and then substitute in for s, as follows. (Look out for the two sign changes!)

$$
\begin{aligned}
A^2 &= \frac{1}{16}\left[(2ba)^2 - (c^2 - a^2 - b^2)^2\right] \\
&= \frac{1}{16}\left[2ba - (c^2 - a^2 - b^2)\right]\left[2ba + (c^2 - a^2 - b^2)\right] \\
&= -\frac{1}{16}\left[(c^2 - a^2 - b^2) - 2ba\right]\left[c^2 - (a^2 + b^2 - 2ab)\right] \\
&= -\frac{1}{16}\left[c^2 - (a+b)^2\right]\left[c^2 - (a-b)^2\right] \\
&= \frac{1}{16}\left[-(c-(a+b))(c+(a+b))\right]\left[(c-(a-b))(c+(a-b))\right] \\
&= \frac{1}{16}(a+b-c)(a+b+c)(b+c-a)(c+a-b) \\
&= \left(\frac{a+b+c}{2}\right)\left(\frac{b+c-a}{2}\right)\left(\frac{a+c-b}{2}\right)\left(\frac{a+b-c}{2}\right) \\
&= \left(\frac{a+b+c}{2}\right)\left(\frac{a+b+c-2a}{2}\right)\left(\frac{a+b+c-2b}{2}\right)\left(\frac{a+b+c-2c}{2}\right) \\
&= s(s-a)(s-b)(s-c),
\end{aligned}
$$

and thus $A(s) = \sqrt{s(s-a)(s-b)(s-c)}$, as required.[34]

A popular alternate proof of Heron's (Hero's) formula inscribes a circle in the triangle and then uses trigonometry (Strogatz, 2009, pp. 143–146). There is a related result (Brahmagupta's formula) for the area of a cyclic quadrilateral (i.e., one that may be inscribed in a circle): $A(s) = \sqrt{(s-a)(s-b)(s-c)(s-d)}$, where $s = (a+b+c+d)/2$ is the semi-perimeter, and a, b, c, and d are the side lengths (Strogatz, 2009, p. 160). Note that if we let $d \to 0$, we get Heron's formula, which makes sense.

---

[33] Every term in a polynomial involves positive integral powers of literal numbers (i.e., the letters that represent numbers) pre-multiplied by a factor that does not contain the literals. So, $2x^2y^2 + 5z^3 + 2$ is a polynomial, but $4\sqrt{y} + 2$ is not. The "degree" of a polynomial is the degree of the term having the highest degree and non-zero coefficient. The polynomial $2x^2y^2 + 5z^3 + 2$ is of degree four $(2 + 2 = 4)$. The polynomial $4x^2 + 2x + 1$ is of degree two. The Fundamental Theorem of Algebra says that every polynomial equation of form $f(x) = 0$ (i.e., only one literal) has at least one root (or "zero"). If the polynomial is of degree n, then it has n roots (or zeroes), where repeated roots are counted as often as their multiplicity. The Unique Factorization Theorem says that a factorization of the polynomial $f(x)$ into products of terms of form $(x - \text{root}_i)$ is unique up to trivial sign changes and ordering of terms. See Spiegel (1956) and Spiegel (1981) for more details—both part of the excellent Schaum Outline Series of books.

[34] Alternatively, without using the semi-perimeter s, you can stop half way through the above and get $A = \frac{1}{4}\sqrt{(a+b+c)(-a+b+c)(a-b+c)(a+b-c)}$, in terms of side lengths only.

> **Story:** The interviewer got up part way through the interview and walked to the door and opened it. The candidate said, "Are we out of time?" The interviewer replied, "No. Out of interest!"

Answer 1.33: Let me begin by repeating the constraints:[35]

$$
\begin{aligned}
A + B + C + D &= 20, \\
B + C + D + E + F &= 20, \\
D + E + F + G + H &= 20, \quad \text{and} \\
F + G + H + I &= 20
\end{aligned}
$$

We have four equations in nine unknowns. The additional information (A to I are some permutation of the integers 1 to 9) restricts the solution space, but there can be no unique solution.

If the first four (A to D) and the last four (F to I), each add to 20, then because $\sum_{i=1}^{i=9} i = 45$, it follows immediately that $E = 5$. If we subtract the second constraint from the first and use $E = 5$, we get $A = F + 5$. If we subtract the fourth constraint from the third, we get $I = D + 5$.

The derived restrictions $A = F + 5$, and $I = D + 5$ imply that F and D must be in the set $\{1, 2, 3, 4\}$. Once F and D are chosen, A and I are determined within the set $\{6, 7, 8, 9\}$. There are thus $4 \times 3 = 12$ possible permutations for F, D, A, and I (that is four choices for F followed by three choices for D; see example below). This leaves B, C, G, and H floating in the remaining four spaces. However, subtracting the second constraint from the third implies that $B + C = G + H$. There are four choices for B, but, once B is chosen, C is uniquely determined; see example below. There are thus $12 \times 4 \times 2 = 96$ different solutions.

For example, if $F = 3$ and $D = 4$, then $A = 8$ and $I = 9$ immediately. That leaves B, C, G, and H floating in the remaining four spaces: $\{1, 2, 6, 7\}$. If $B = 1$, then C must equal 7; there is no other choice for C that satisfies $B + C = G + H$. With B and C chosen, there are two ways to allocate G and H to the remaining two slots. In this example, it would either be $G = 2, H = 6$ or $G = 6, H = 2$.

Here are several solutions (reverse the orderings to get several more):[36]

$$
\begin{aligned}
&6\ 8\ 4\ 2\ 5\ 1\ 3\ 9\ 7, \\
&6\ 8\ 4\ 2\ 5\ 1\ 9\ 3\ 7, \\
&6\ 4\ 8\ 2\ 5\ 1\ 3\ 9\ 7, \\
&6\ 4\ 8\ 2\ 5\ 1\ 9\ 3\ 7.
\end{aligned}
$$

---

[35] I thank Dahn Tamir and James Hirschorn for contributions to this solution technique; any errors are mine.

[36] Note: The MATLAB commands **perms** and **unique** were useful in checking this answer.

Answer 1.34: I present two solution techniques: an elegant approach followed by a "hammer-and-tongs" brute-force approach. I think you should start with a rough guess; mine is about a half.

FIRST SOLUTION[37]

Simplify the problem by assuming that the "very large number" of people is almost an infinite number. In this case, it is as though each person is first in line to be allocated a key because the previous finite number of people are negligible compared to the almost infinite number of people waiting to receive keys. It follows that each person has the same probability, $\frac{1}{N}$, of being allocated his or her key. Let X be the number of people who end up sleeping in their own rooms, then

$$
\begin{aligned}
P(X \geq 1) = 1 - P(X = 0) \;\; &\overset{*}{=}\;\; 1 - \left(1 - \frac{1}{N}\right)^N \\
&= \;\; 1 - \left(1 + \frac{-1}{N}\right)^N \\
&\to \;\; 1 - e^{-1} = \frac{e-1}{e} \;\; \text{as} \;\; N \to \infty,
\end{aligned}
$$

where " * " is true for N infinitely large.

SECOND SOLUTION[38]

Consider first the simple cases in which there are two or three guests. It soon becomes clear that you need to consider many different overlapping events and that you need to account for intersections of events. That is, you need basic set theory.

Let A_k, for $k = 1$, ..., N, denote the event that the kth guest sleeps in the room to which he or she was originally assigned (i.e., his or her "own room"). What we need to find is the probability that *at least one* of the guests ends up in his or her own room. This event is the union of the individual events and occurs with probability: $P(\bigcup_{k=1}^{N} A_k)$.

If you draw the familiar case of three intersecting circles—each representing an event—it is relatively straightforward to deduce the following inclusion-exclusion formula:

$$
\begin{aligned}
P\left(\bigcup_{k=1}^{N} A_k\right) = &\sum_i P(A_i) \; - \sum_{1 \leq i < j \leq N} P(A_i \cap A_j) \\
&+ \sum_{1 \leq i < j < k \leq N} P(A_i \cap A_j \cap A_k) - \cdots \\
&+ (-1)^{N+1} P(A_1 \cap \cdots \cap A_N)
\end{aligned}
$$

All you are doing here is adding the original event probabilities, then taking out the intersections where you double counted, then adjusting for the fact

---

[37]I thank Jason Roth for supplying this technique; any errors are mine.
[38]I thank Taras Klymchuk for suggesting a very similar solution technique; any errors are mine.

that you over-compensated, and so on—all of which is very easily seen if you draw intersecting sets for the case $N = 3$. To figure this out, we need to find the probability of the intersection of any group of events. Given the symmetry here, we can, without loss of generality, look at the events in the following order: 1, 2, ..., N.

Given the random allocation of keys, each guest is equally likely to end up in his or her own room. That is, $P(A_i) = \frac{1}{N}$ for any $i \in \{1, 2, \ldots, N\}$. If guest 1 is given his own key, then guest 2 has a chance of only $P(A_2|A_1) = \frac{1}{N-1}$ of getting her own key back. So, $P(A_1 \cap A_2) = P(A_2|A_1)P(A_1) = \frac{1}{N(N-1)}$. In fact, this result is more general:

$$
\begin{aligned}
P\left(\bigcap_{k=1}^{m} A_i\right) &= \frac{1}{N(N-1)\cdots(N-m+1)} \\
&= \frac{(N-m)!}{N!} \\
&= \frac{1}{m!\binom{N}{m}}, \quad \text{for any } m \in 1, 2, \ldots, N.
\end{aligned}
$$

We may now plug this formula for probabilities of intersecting events back into the original inclusion-exclusion formula:

$$
\begin{aligned}
P\left(\bigcup_{k=1}^{N} A_k\right) &= \sum_{m=1}^{N} (-1)^{m+1} \binom{N}{m} P\left(\bigcap_{k=1}^{m} A_i\right) \\
&= \sum_{m=1}^{N} \frac{(-1)^{m+1}}{m!} \\
&= -1 \times \sum_{m=1}^{N} \frac{(-1)^m}{m!} \\
&= 1 - \sum_{m=0}^{N} \frac{(-1)^m}{m!} \\
&\to 1 - e^{-1} = \frac{e-1}{e} \quad \text{as } N \to \infty.
\end{aligned}
$$

The final result is about 63%, but a guess of $\frac{2}{3}$ is close enough.

Answer 1.35:   Assume there are N people at the party. Assume the first person starts the ball rolling by shaking hands with the $N-1$ other people. Then the second person has already shaken hands with the first person, and only needs to shake hands with $N-2$ people. Similarly, the third person only needs to shake hands with $N-3$ people. And so on. Eventually, the $(N-1)^{th}$ person shakes hands with the Nth person, and by this time, the Nth person has already shaken hands with everyone. So, the count of handshakes is $\sum_{i=1}^{N-1} i$. From Answer 1.4, we know this sum is $\sum_{i=1}^{N-1} i = N(N-1)/2$. We could set this equal to 66, and solve the quadratic, or we could just try a few values until we converge. The quadratic is $N^2 - N - 132 = 0$, with roots $N = \left(1 \pm \sqrt{529}\right)/2 = \{-11, 12\}$. Obviously, 12 is the answer.

In fact, I solved the problem slightly differently. I pictured N people standing in a row across the top of a chessboard-like empty matrix of squares, and the same N people standing down the side of the matrix. I put a mental dot into each square that corresponds to a handshake between someone on the vertical and someone on the horizontal. So doing marks out the upper-triangular part of the matrix, above the diagonal (or below it; you can choose). So, the total number of handshakes is the same as the number of elements above the diagonal in an $N \times N$ matrix. So, I take N^2 for the total count, subtract the diagonal count of N, and divide by two. That is, $(N^2 - N)/2 = N(N-1)/2$, as above. Then I guessed it must be 12 or 13, to get 66 off-diagonal dots.

Answer 1.36: Before tackling this problem (i.e., the expected number of pairs of people with a matching birthday in a group of 25), let us solve the more traditional birthday problem. In a group of N people, what is the probability $p(N)$ that there are at least two people with the same birthday? It is often easier to work out the complement. So, let us figure the probability that no people in a group of N people share a birthday.

Assume 365 days in a year, and all birthdays equally likely, and all birthdays independent across partygoers. Let $D(N)$ denote the event that all N persons have different birthdays. How does $D(N)$ happen? Well, without loss of generality, suppose the first person we pick has birthday January 1. Then, to have different birthdays, there are only 364 choices left for the second person. Without loss of generality, let us assume the second person's birthday is January 2. Then, to have different birthdays, there are only 363 choices left for the third person, and so on. The overall space of possible birthday $N-$tuples contains 365^N choices. So, the probability that all N persons' birthdays are different is given by Equation A.10, for $N = 1, \ldots, 365$.

$$P[D(N)] = \underbrace{\frac{365}{365} \cdot \frac{364}{365} \cdot \ldots \cdot \frac{(365 - N + 1)}{365}}_{N \text{ terms}}$$

$$= \frac{365!}{(365 - N)!365^N} = \binom{365}{N}\frac{N!}{365^N} \qquad (A.10)$$

Thus, the probability that there is at least one birthday match in the group of N partygoers is given by Equation A.11.

$$p(N) = 1 - p[D(N)] = \begin{cases} 1 - \binom{365}{N}\frac{N!}{365^N}, & \text{if } N = 1, \ldots, 365 \\ 1 & N \geq 366. \end{cases} \qquad (A.11)$$

For example, some values of $p(N)$ appear in Table A.3.

Table A.3: B'day Stats: P(No Match), P(Match), E(#B-Pairs), and E(#People)

N	$1 - p(N)$	$p(N)$	E(B-Pairs)	$E[H(N)]$	$E[H(N)]/N$
2	99.73%	0.27%	0.00	0.01	0.27%
5	97.29%	2.71%	0.03	0.05	1.09%
9	90.54%	9.46%	0.10	0.20	2.17%
10	88.31%	11.69%	0.12	0.24	2.44%
20	58.86%	41.14%	0.52	1.02	5.08%
23	49.27%	50.73%	0.69	1.35	5.86%
25	43.13%	56.87%	0.82	1.59	6.37%
50	2.96%	97.04%	3.36	6.29	12.58%
57	0.99%	99.01%	4.37	8.12	14.24%
83	0.00%	100.00%	9.32	16.72	20.15%
100	0.00%	100.00%	13.56	23.78	23.78%
254	0.00%	100.00%	88.03	127.12	50.05%
365	0.00%	100.00%	182.00	230.54	63.16%
366	0.00%	100.00%	183.00	231.54	63.26%
731	0.00%	100.00%	731.00	632.34	86.50%
1,000	0.00%	100.00%	1,368.49	935.48	93.55%
3,611	0.00%	100.00%	17,857.14	3,610.82	100.00%
5,000	0.00%	100.00%	34,239.73	4,999.99	100.00%
5,040	0.00%	100.00%	34,789.81	5,040.00	100.00%

Note: This table refers to Question 1.36 and Question 1.37. $p(N) = 1 - \binom{365}{N}\frac{N!}{365^N}$ is the probability that there exists at least one pair of people with matching birthdays in a random group of $1 \leq N \leq 365$ persons. The table shows $1 - P(N)$ (i.e., the probability of N people having different birthdays), as well as $p(N)$ (i.e., the probability of at least one match), to two decimal places. Only 23 people are required for $p(N) > 50\%$. E(B-Pairs) $= \binom{N}{2}\big/365$ is the expected number of pairs of people with a birthday match in a random group of size $N \geq 2$. For $N = 366$, we get E(B-Pairs) is exactly half N. If there are more than 731 people, then the expected number of pairs is greater than the number of people. For 5,000 people, more than 34,000 pairs are expected! $E[H(N)] = N\left(1 - \left(\frac{364}{365}\right)^{N-1}\right)$ is the expected number of hands raised to indicate a birthday match in a random group of size $N \geq 1$. The table shows $E[H(N)]$ to two decimal places, and also the expected proportion of hands raised in the group, as a percentage. Only 20 people are required for $E[H(N)] > 1$. Once we have 254 people, we expect 50% of the people to raise their hands to indicate a match. For $N \geq 3,611$, we expect 100.00% of the people to raise their hands (to two decimal places). For $N \geq 5,040$, we expect $N = E[H(N)]$ (to two decimal places).

Now let us turn to the problem of the expected number of *pairs* of people with the same birthday in a group of size N. Well, how many distinct pairs of people are there altogether, regardless of birthdays? In a group of size $N \geq 2$, there are $n = \binom{N}{2} = \frac{N(N-1)}{2}$ distinct pairs. For example, in a group of size $N = 4$, there are six pairs: $\{(1,2),(1,3),(1,4),(2,3),(2,4),(3,4)\}$. The pairs are not independent. For example, if pair $(1,2)$ have the same birthday, and pair $(2,3)$ have the same birthday, then what do we know about pair $(1,3)$? Surely, they have the same birthday too.

Now pick any pair. What is the likelihood that this particular pair have matching birthdays? It is just $p = 1/365$ (because given the birthday of the first person, there is one chance in 365 that the second person's birthday is a match).

With count of pairs of people $n = \binom{N}{2}$ regardless of birthdays, and probability of a match success $p = 1/365$, the expected number of birthday pairs is just given by $E(\text{B-Pairs}) = np = \binom{N}{2}/365$. Note that this is true even though the pairs are not independent (because it is just an expectation over the pairs).

For example, some values of $E(\text{B-Pairs})$ appear in Table A.3. In a group of size 25, we expect only 0.82 birthday pairs (slightly less than one pair). As the size of the party increases, the number of pairs raises at a quadratic rate.

Answer 1.37: Now let us turn to the expected number of *people* with a matching birthday in a group of 25. In the question, we said that we would ask the partygoers to raise a hand if someone else at the party had the same birthday. So, let us solve for $E[H(N)]$, where $H(N)$ is the number of hands raised, to indicate a birthday match, in a group of $N \geq 1$ people.

Let me number the people from 1 to N. Let me look at the first person. The probability that the first person does not have the same birthday as the second person is $364/365$. All birthdays are independent of each other. So, the probability that the first person does not have the same birthday as any of the other $N - 1$ people is $(364/365)^{N-1}$. So, the probability that the first person has the same birthday as at least one other person, and therefore raises a hand, is $1 - (364/365)^{N-1}$. This is true for each person. So, the expected number of hands raised to indicate a birthday match is

$$E[H(N)] = N \left(1 - \left(\frac{364}{365} \right)^{N-1} \right).$$

For example, some values of $E(H)$ appear in Table A.3. In a group of size 25, we expect only 1.59 hands to be raised. As the size of the party increases, the proportion of hands raised climbs slowly to 100%.

Answer 1.38: To maximize the probability that I win the free ticket, I will ask my twin brother to stand at position number one in line, and then I will stand right behind him. Failing that, let us assume that birthdays are uniformly distributed over the year, and that birthdays of people joining the line are independent of birthdays of other people joining the line, and that there are 365 days in a year (i.e., not a leap year).

Before doing any mathematics, we should give a gut instinct estimate, both to show the interviewer that we can give an estimate, and to give a benchmark with which we can compare our computed answer. Obviously you do not want to be first in line, and you do not want to be after position 366 (both discussed further below). You will recall also, from the traditional birthday problem discussed in Answer 1.37, that the likelihood of a birthday match ahead of you rises quickly with group size. So, if you stand at position 10, say, with 9 people ahead of you, there only a roughly 10% probability that there is a matching pair ahead of you, and you do not get the prize (see Table A.3). If you stand at position 24, say, with 23 people ahead of you, there is already a roughly 50% probability that there is a matching pair ahead of you, and you do not get the prize. If you stand at position 58, with 57 people ahead of you, there is a roughly 99% probability that there is a matching pair ahead of you, and you do not get the prize. You want a high probability that your birthday matches the birthday of someone ahead of you (which is true the further you stand from the box office), but a low probability that a matching pair is ahead of you (which is true the closer you stand to the box office). My guess is that I will not want to stand any further from the box office than position 25, and no closer than position 10.

Let $W(k)$ denote the event that the kth person in line $\underline{w}$ins the prize. Let $p(k) \equiv P[W(k)]$ be the probability of event $W(k)$. Let $D(k-1)$ be the event that the first $k-1$ people have $\underline{d}$ifferent birthdays. Let $S(k)$ be the event that the birthday of the kth person in line is the $\underline{s}$ame as the birthday of one of the first $k-1$ people.

Then, to win the ticket, it needs to be true both that all $k-1$ people ahead of me have different birthdays (i.e., event $D(k-1)$ happens), and that one of them has the same birthday as I do (i.e., event $S(k)$ happens). That is, Equation A.12 holds.

$$\begin{aligned} p(k) &= P[W(k)] \\ &= P[D(k-1) \cap S(k)] \\ &= P[D(k-1)] \cdot P[S(k)|D(k-1)] \end{aligned} \quad (A.12)$$

What about boundary conditions? From the structure of the problem, it must be that $p(1) = 0$, because there is nobody ahead of me. If I am second in line, then $P[D(1)] = 1$, and $P[S(2)|D(1)] = 1/365$. So, $p(2) = 1/365$. At the other end of the line, if I am at position 367 or higher, then $p(k) = 0$. (Absent leap years, two people among the first 366 must have the same birthday, so the prize can never go to someone after position 366.) So, $\bigcup_{k=2}^{366} W(k)$ is the entire sample space, and all the $W(k)$ events are mutually exclusive.[39] Thus,

[39]That is, $P\left[\bigcup_{k=2}^{366} W(k)\right] = 1$ and $P[W(i) \cap W(j)] = 0$ if $i \neq j$.

$p(k)$ for $2 \le k \le 366$ forms a valid probability mass function (pmf).

A simple argument, as given in Answer 1.37, now yields, without loss of generality, for $2 \le k \le 366$

$$P[D(k-1)] = \underbrace{\frac{365}{365} \cdot \frac{364}{365} \cdot \dots \cdot \frac{(365-k+2)}{365}}_{k-1 \text{ terms}},$$

$$= \frac{365!}{(365-k+1)!365^{k-1}}$$

$$P[S(k)|D(k-1)] = \frac{(k-1)}{365},$$

$$\text{and thus } p(k) = \frac{365!(k-1)}{(365-k+1)!365^k},$$

and $p(k) = 0$ otherwise.

Simple intuition tells us that $p(k)$ is at first increasing, because for very small k you want more people in front of you because $P[D(k-1)]$ does not change much with k at first, whereas $P[S(k)|D(k-1)]$ increases rapidly. For large k, however, $P[S(k)|D(k-1)]$ drops rapidly, outweighing the linear growth in $P[D(k-1)]$.

So, to find the peak in $p(k)$, we need to find where $p(k+1) - p(k) < 0$. That is, where the probability of winning at the next $(k+1)^{th}$ place in line is lower than it is at the kth place in line. Given the functional form of $p(k)$, working with differences is not going to reduce complexity. So, we should re-express this condition in ratios as

$$p(k+1) - p(k) < 0$$
$$\Rightarrow p(k+1) < p(k)$$
$$\Rightarrow \frac{p(k+1)}{p(k)} < 1$$
$$\Rightarrow \frac{\frac{365!k}{(365-k)!365^{k+1}}}{\frac{365!(k-1)}{(365-k+1)!365^k}} < 1$$
$$\Rightarrow \frac{(365-k+1)k}{365(k-1)} < 1$$
$$\Rightarrow (365-k+1)k < 365(k-1)$$
$$\Rightarrow -k^2 + k + 365 < 0$$
$$\Rightarrow k^2 - k - 365 > 0$$

To solve this, we set the LHS equal to zero, and use the quadratic formula: $k = (+1 \pm \sqrt{1 + 4 \cdot 365})/2 = (+1 \pm \sqrt{1461})/2$. The negative root is not meaningful in this context. The positive root is $(1 + \sqrt{1461})/2 \approx 19.61$, treating k as a real number. The closest we can come to a real-valued position of 19.61 in the line is position 20. Note that the single positive root does not guarantee a single peak in the pmf $p(\cdot)$—but calculation confirms it.

Sure enough, if you calculate $p(k)$ for $k = 2, \ldots, 366$, the pmf is a smooth (at least for a pmf) right-tailed uni-modal distribution with a peak at $p(20) \approx 0.032320$. Thus, your best bet is a roughly one-in-31 chance of winning if you stand in the 20th position.

As an aside, note that standing in the 54th position gives a roughly one-in-365 chance of winning (almost the same as when you stand in the second position). Beyond position 60, you have less than a one-in-1,000 chance of winning. Beyond position 63, you have less than a one-in-10,000 chance of winning. At position 100, you have a one-in-8,744,925 chance of winning. The odds drop dramatically from there, ending with $p(366) = 1/(6.87 \times 10^{156})$.

Answer 1.39: First of all, "very small" is classic physics slang for very, very small (i.e., so small that it is a pinpoint mass). If the rock is tossed overboard, the water level falls as though water equal in mass to the mass of the rock is being sucked out of the pool. The rock forces the boat to displace the rock's mass of water. After the rock is gone, the boat rises up, and the water level falls down (Archimedes' Principle).[40]

The next time you are washing dishes, try this experiment. With the sink half-full of water, float a drinking glass. Now drop a steel ball bearing gently into the glass. The glass sinks down, displacing a mass of water equal in mass to the mass of the ball bearing, and the water level rises. Now pluck the ball bearing from the glass, using a magnet. The reverse happens, the glass rises, and the water level falls as though water equal in mass to the mass of the ball bearing is being sucked out of the sink.

How does your answer change if the rock is replaced by a piece of pumice (i.e., floating volcanic glass), or by a 100lb ice cube, or by a tethered helium balloon (to be set free, tether and all)?

Answer 1.40: The answer involves both mathematical induction and game theoretic arguments. If there is *exactly one* cheating man in the town, Mr. C, say, then every wife except Mrs. C knows who he is. Not only that, but Mrs. C is unaware of any cheats—the stranger's announcement comes as a shock to her. Immediately after the stranger's announcement, Mrs. C asks: "Who can be cheating if I have seen no cheats?" The only possible answer is it is Mr. C. Come the next morning, his happy days are over, and out he goes.

Suppose instead that there are *exactly two* cheating men in town: Mr. C1 and Mr. C2. In this case, Mrs. C1 knows there is one cheat in town (Mr. C2), and Mrs. C2 knows there is one cheat in town (Mr. C1)—the stranger's announcement comes as no shock to either woman. Each thinks there is only one cheat

---

[40]Archimedes said simply that an object in a fluid experiences an upwards force equal to the weight of the fluid that is displaced by the object.

in town and fully expects him to be kicked out the next morning (each wife thinks the other poor woman is in the position of Mrs. C mentioned above). The first morning after the announcement comes, and the streets are bare. Mrs. C1 concludes that Mrs. C2 did not kick her husband out because she did not think he was a cheat. How could Mrs. C2 be so foolish? Mrs. C1 knows that Mrs. C2 believes the prophecy, so the only possible reason for Mrs. C2 not to have reacted is if Mrs. C2 saw a cheat herself. Mrs. C1 asks herself: "Who did Mrs. C2 see cheating, when the only cheat I can see is Mr. C2?" The only possible answer is that it is her own man, Mr. C1. Come the second morning after the announcement, Mr. C1 and Mr. C2 are both kicked out (the latter because Mrs. C2 went through the same thought process).

Suppose now that there are *exactly three* cheating men in town: Mr. C1, Mr. C2, and Mr. C3. In this case, each of Mrs. C1, Mrs. C2, and Mrs. C3 thinks that there are two cheats in town and believes in the innocence of her own man. However, come the second morning, they are each very surprised to find the streets empty. Had there been exactly two cheats, as each of the wives had surmised, then the cheats should have been kicked into the street two mornings after the announcement—as per the argument above. The empty street means that a third cheater exists—one previously assumed innocent! So, three mornings after the announcement, all three cheating men are bounced out into the street.

More generally, let me assert that if there are exactly n cheats, then they will all be kicked out into the street on the nth morning after the stranger's announcement. If my assertion is true for n cheats, and a wife sees n other cheats but finds the streets bare on the nth morning, then she is shocked to conclude that her own man must be unfaithful to her. She (and each of the other n wives) will kick her man out the next morning. That is, if there are $n + 1$ cheats, then they will be kicked out on the $(n + 1)^{st}$ morning. That is, if my assertion is true for n cheats, then it is also true for $n + 1$ cheats.

I proved my assertion to be true for n equal to each of one, two, and three. It follows my mathematical induction that it is true for all n (in fact, I needed only to prove it for $n = 1$ for the proof to go through).

It follows that if cheating men are kicked into the street for the first time on the tenth morning after the stranger's announcement, then there must be exactly 10 of them.

Answer 1.41: This is known as the Towers of Hanoi problem. If you are peeking here for a solution, then go back and think about mathematical induction.

Let $V(n)$ denote the minimum number of moves needed for n rings. I *assert* that $V(n) = 2^n - 1$, for all positive integers n (I will justify this shortly). The proof uses mathematical induction.

<u>Case $n = 1$:</u> With one ring, it certainly takes exactly one move. My assertion is thus true for the case $n = 1$.

Case $n = N$: Suppose that my assertion is true for $n = N$, and consider the case $n = N+1$. By assumption, it takes $V(N) = 2^N - 1$ moves to get the first N rings to pole #2. Use one additional move to get ring #$(N+1)$ to pole #3. Now use $V(N) = 2^N - 1$ moves to move the N rings on pole #2 to pole #3. The total number of moves used is $2V(N) + 1 = 2(2^N - 1) + 1 = 2^{(N+1)} - 1$. However, this is just $V(N+1)$. That is, if my assertion is true for $n = N$, it is also true for $n = (N+1)$.

The result follows, because I showed my assertion is true for $n = 1$, and I showed that if my assertion is true for $n = N$, then it is also true for $n = N+1$. In particular, because I showed the assertion to be true for $n = 1$, it follows that it must be true for $n = 2$. It then follows that because the assertion is true for $n = 2$, it is also true for $n = 3$, ... and so on, up to ∞.[41]

With $n = 64$ rings, it takes $V(64) = 2^{64} - 1 = 18,446,744,073,709,551,615$ moves. At one move per second, it would take you 584.5 billion (i.e., 584.5 thousand million) years to complete this task. The Earth will fall into the Sun in less than one-hundredth of this time period.

Answer 1.42: The ODE $u'' + u' + u = 1$ has a simple solution. This is a second-order linear ODE with constant coefficients, so we need only search for solutions to the homogeneous form $u'' + u' + u = 0$, and then tag on a solution to the specific nonhomogeneous equation given.

Solutions to a second-order linear homogeneous ODE of form $Au'' + Bu' + Cu = 0$ are of form[42]

$$u(x) = ae^{\lambda_1 x} + be^{\lambda_2 x},$$

where λ_1 and λ_2 are the roots of the characteristic equation:

$$A\lambda^2 + B\lambda + C = 0.$$

It follows (using the quadratic formula) that

$$\lambda_1, \lambda_2 = \frac{-B \pm \sqrt{B^2 - 4AC}}{2A} = \frac{-1 \pm \sqrt{1-4}}{2} = \frac{-1}{2} \pm \frac{\sqrt{3}}{2}i,$$

where $i \equiv \sqrt{-1}$. In our case, $u = 1$ is a solution to the specific nonhomogeneous ODE, so the general solution must be of form

$$u(x) = ae^{\left(\frac{-1}{2} + \frac{\sqrt{3}}{2}i\right)x} + be^{\left(\frac{-1}{2} - \frac{\sqrt{3}}{2}i\right)x} + 1,$$

for arbitrary constants a and b. To pinpoint a and b, you need two initial conditions (not supplied here) in addition to the ODE.

---

[41] A natural question to ask is how I guessed that $V(n) = 2^n - 1$ to begin with. I got this because I figured that $V(n+1) = 2V(n) + 1$ had to hold, and $V(1) = 1$ is obvious. These together are sufficient to deduce the functional form of $V(n)$.

[42] Unless $\lambda_1 = \lambda_2 = \lambda$, say (i.e., a repeated root), in which case solutions are of form $u(x) = axe^{\lambda x} + be^{\lambda x}$.

If you prefer a solution with real-valued functions (but with possible complex coefficients), then you may use $e^{(\lambda+\mu i)x} = e^{\lambda x}e^{\mu i x} = e^{\lambda x}[\cos(\mu x) + i\sin(\mu x)]$, and then add and subtract the two components of the general solution to get an equivalent solution (Boyce and DiPrima [1997, p. 148]):

$$u(x) = a'e^{-\frac{1}{2}x}\cos\left(\frac{\sqrt{3}}{2}x\right) + b'e^{-\frac{1}{2}x}\sin\left(\frac{\sqrt{3}}{2}x\right) + 1.$$

Answer 1.43: The obvious application is to proportions of a portfolio invested in risky assets (see Questions 3.19 and 3.20). Make the substitution $b = 1 - a$. Then the variance of the sum is

$$V(S) = a^2\sigma_X^2 + 2a(1-a)\rho\sigma_X\sigma_Y + (1-a)^2\sigma_Y^2.$$

The first-order condition is $\frac{\partial V(S)}{\partial a} = 0$. The partial derivative is:

$$\begin{aligned}
\frac{\partial V(S)}{\partial a} &= 2a\sigma_X^2 + 2\rho\sigma_X\sigma_Y - 4a\rho\sigma_X\sigma_Y + 2(1-a)(-1)\sigma_Y^2 \\
&= 2\left[a(\sigma_X^2 - 2\rho\sigma_X\sigma_Y + \sigma_Y^2) + \rho\sigma_X\sigma_Y - \sigma_Y^2\right].
\end{aligned}$$

Thus, the particular a that satisfies the first-order condition is

$$a^* = \frac{\sigma_Y^2 - \rho\sigma_X\sigma_Y}{(\sigma_X^2 - 2\rho\sigma_X\sigma_Y + \sigma_Y^2)}.$$

We should check the second-order condition

$$\left.\frac{\partial^2 V(S)}{\partial a^2}\right|_{a=a^*} > 0,$$

to make sure this is a minimum, not a maximum. This is straightforward:

$$\begin{aligned}
\frac{1}{2}\frac{\partial^2 V(S)}{\partial a^2} &= \sigma_X^2 - 2\rho\sigma_X\sigma_Y + \sigma_Y^2 \\
&\geq \sigma_X^2 - 2(+1)\sigma_X\sigma_Y + \sigma_Y^2 \\
&= (\sigma_X - \sigma_Y)^2 \\
&\geq 0,
\end{aligned}$$

and the first inequality is strict unless $\rho = +1$.

In fact, I have solved the unconstrained problem—ignoring the constraint $0 \leq a \leq 1$. If a^* breaches the constraints, the constrained solution for a is either 1 or 0, depending upon whether σ_X or σ_Y is the smaller respectively.[43]

---

[43]The a^* will breach the constraints if the correlation ρ is large enough or the standard deviations are disparate enough that either $\frac{\sigma_X}{\sigma_Y} < \rho$ or $\frac{\sigma_Y}{\sigma_X} < \rho$.

©2021 Timothy Falcon Crack   105   All Rights Reserved Worldwide

In the special case where $\rho = -1$ (perfect negative correlation), the solution for a^* is given by

$$
\begin{aligned}
a^* &= \frac{\sigma_Y^2 - \rho\sigma_X\sigma_Y}{(\sigma_X^2 - 2\rho\sigma_X\sigma_Y + \sigma_Y^2)} \\
&= \frac{\sigma_Y^2 + \sigma_X\sigma_Y}{(\sigma_X^2 + 2\sigma_X\sigma_Y + \sigma_Y^2)} \\
&= \frac{\sigma_Y(\sigma_X + \sigma_Y)}{(\sigma_X + \sigma_Y)^2} \\
&= \frac{\sigma_Y}{(\sigma_X + \sigma_Y)},
\end{aligned}
$$

and this particular a^* gives variance of $aX + bY$ equal to zero.

> **Story:** I recall reading in the WSJ about one young woman who was asked her greatest weakness (a common interview question). Without thinking, she blurted out the answer "chocolate!"

Answer 1.44: The lighthouse question is an old favorite.[44] The lighthouse is a distance L from the coast. The beam of light casts a "spot" a distance R across the sea from the lighthouse (see Figure A.4).

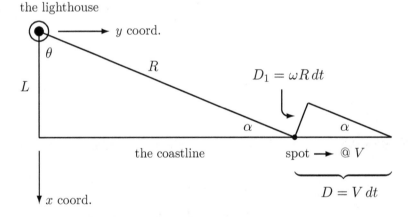

Figure A.4: The Lighthouse Problem

Note: Refer to this figure for both solutions to the lighthouse problem. The first solution uses the x-y coordinates and θ; the second solution uses α, D, and D_1; both solutions use L, R, and V.

---

[44]I thank Valeri Smelyansky for advice; any errors are mine.

FIRST SOLUTION

Using the coordinates in Figure A.4, the coastline is the line $x = L$. The spot hits the coastline at the coordinate pair $(x, y) = (L, L\tan(\theta))$, where θ is the angle between the beam and the x-axis. Suppose $\theta = 0$ when $t = 0$, then $\theta = \omega t = \frac{2\pi}{60}t$ where $\omega = \frac{2\pi}{60}$ is the angular velocity in radians per second (the beam makes one revolution per minute and t is measured in seconds). The speed V of the spot along the coastline is the partial derivative of $y = L\tan(\theta) = L\tan(\omega t)$ with respect to t:

$$V = \frac{\partial}{\partial t}[L\tan(\theta)] = \frac{\partial}{\partial t}[L\tan(\omega t)] = \omega L \sec^2(\omega t) = \frac{\omega L}{\cos^2(\omega t)}$$

From Figure A.4 we see that $\cos(\omega t) = \frac{L}{R}$, so we conclude that $V = \frac{\omega L}{(L/R)^2} = \frac{\omega R^2}{L}$. In our particular case, with $\omega = \frac{2\pi}{60}$ radians per second and $L = 3$, the speed of the beam is $\frac{\pi R^2}{90}$ miles per second. When the beam is $3L = 9$ miles down the coastline, $R^2 = 10L^2 = 90$, and the speed is just π miles per second.

More than once, people have suggested to me that the velocity V is a constant (i.e., V is the same regardless of how far along the coast the spot is cast)—this is clearly incorrect.

SECOND SOLUTION

Follow the beam's course for a small time interval dt. In Figure A.4, we see that the beam's spot covers a distance $D = V dt$ along the coast, while the beam's "perpendicular motion" covers a distance $D_1 = \omega R dt$ (where V is the spot's speed along the coast, and $\omega = \frac{2\pi}{60}$ radians per second is the beam's angular velocity). For small dt, the distance triangle is a right-angle triangle, so $\sin(\alpha) = \frac{D_1}{D} = \frac{\omega R dt}{V dt} = \frac{\omega R}{V}$. Looking at the larger triangle, we see $\sin(\alpha) = \frac{L}{R}$. Thus, $V = \frac{\omega R^2}{L}$, as before.

Answer 1.45: I present an elegant approach followed by three algebraic approaches. Please see Figure A.5 for reference.

FIRST SOLUTION

Imagine the 20×20 chessboard in front of you, with the stacks of cubes on it as in Figure A.5. Now slice through the cubes horizontally at height 20 units. The cubes above the slice all lie in the southeast lower-triangular section below the non-leading diagonal. Now flip the above-the-slice cubes across the diagonal from southeast to northwest. They will fill the lower stacks to a height of 20 units. You now have a solid cube, and the total number of cubes must be $n^3 = 20^3 = 8,000$.

SECOND SOLUTION[45]

Think of each row as being like successive images of a moving ticker tape containing the numbers 1 to 39. We view the tape through a window, and we see only 20 numbers at a time. The tape is moving to the left, one step at a

---

[45]I thank Sudheer Naidu D for this approach; any errors are mine.

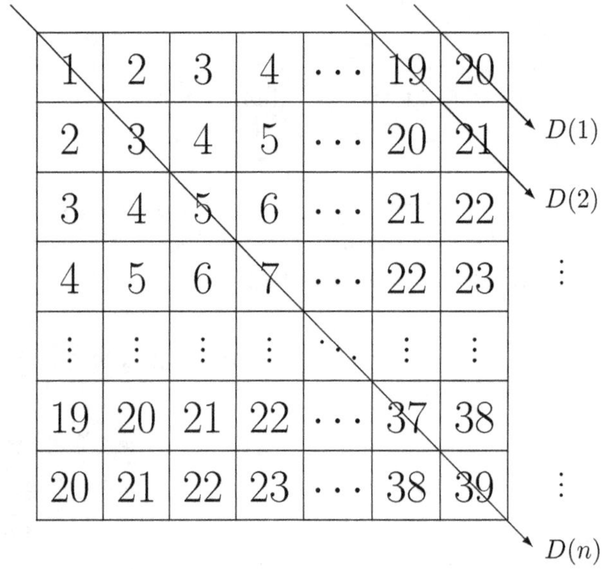

1	2	3	4	$\cdots$	19	20
2	3	4	5	$\cdots$	20	21
3	4	5	6	$\cdots$	21	22
4	5	6	7	$\cdots$	22	23
$\vdots$	$\vdots$	$\vdots$	$\vdots$	$\ddots$	$\vdots$	$\vdots$
19	20	21	22	$\cdots$	37	38
20	21	22	23	$\cdots$	38	39

$D(1)$
$D(2)$
$\vdots$
$D(n)$

Figure A.5: Number of Cubes on Each Square of a 20×20 Chessboard (A)

Note: The figure shows the number of cubes on each square of a chessboard, starting with one in the northwest corner and stepping up one each time you step south or east.

time. As we move from Row 1 to Row 2, the 1 drops off the screen, but the 21 appears, adding a net of 20 to the total. As we move from Row 2 to Row 3, the 2 drops off the screen, but the 22 appears, again adding a net of 20 to the total. This pattern happens all the way down to the 20th row.

Let us express the sums using n instead of 20. So, the first row contains $S = \sum_{i=1}^{n} i = \frac{n(n+1)}{2}$ cubes. The second row contains $S + n$ cubes. The third row contains $S + 2n$ cubes, and so on. Finally, the nth row contains $S + (n-1)n$ cubes. So, the total sum is

$$
\begin{aligned}
nS + \left(\sum_{i=0}^{n-1} i\right) n &= n\left(S + \sum_{i=1}^{n-1} i\right) \\
&= n\left(\frac{n(n+1)}{2} + \frac{(n-1)n}{2}\right) \\
&= \frac{n^2}{2}[(n+1) + (n-1)] = n^3.
\end{aligned}
$$

THIRD SOLUTION[46]

Let $D(i)$ be a sum on a diagonal (see Figure A.5). Take the top-right square as the first diagonal. So, $D(1) = n = 20$. The second diagonal contains 19 and 20 cubes. Thus, $D(2) = 2 \cdot n = 40$. Indeed, we have $D(i) = i \cdot n$ all the

---

[46]I thank Sudheer Naidu D for this approach; any errors are mine.

way up to the longest diagonal with $D(20) = D(n) = n \cdot n = 400$. Then the lower diagonals repeat $D(1)$ through $D(n-1)$ again, in reverse order.

Imagine inserting an extra copy of the nth diagonal, containing $D(n) = n^2$ cubes, so that it appears twice. Then all the diagonals will appear twice. So, the total sum (unwinding our insertion) will be

$$
\begin{aligned}
\left(2\sum_{i=1}^{n} D(i)\right) - D(n) &= \left(2\sum_{i=1}^{n} i \cdot n\right) - n^2 \\
&= \left[2\left(\sum_{i=1}^{n} i\right) \cdot n\right] - n^2 \\
&= 2\left[\frac{n(n+1)}{2}\right]n - n^2 \\
&= n^2(n+1) - n^2 = n^3.
\end{aligned}
$$

FOURTH SOLUTION

Identify the squares using horizontal and vertical indices, counting from the northwest corner. Let i count down and j count across. Then it is readily seen that the square with coordinates (i, j) has $(i + j - 1)$ cubes on it. It follows that[47], in the general case of an $n \times n$ chessboard), the total number of cubes is given by

$$
\begin{aligned}
\sum_{i=1}^{n}\sum_{j=1}^{n}(i+j-1) &= \sum_{i=1}^{n}\sum_{j=1}^{n}[(i-1)+j] \\
&= \sum_{i=1}^{n}\left[n(i-1) + \frac{n(n+1)}{2}\right] \\
&= \left[n\left(\frac{n(n+1)}{2} - n\right) + n\left(\frac{n(n+1)}{2}\right)\right] \\
&= n\left(\frac{n^2 + n - 2n + n^2 + n}{2}\right) = n^3.
\end{aligned}
$$

Answer 1.46: The naive strategy is to run directly away from the dog toward the edge of the field. However, at speed v, it takes you $\frac{R}{v}$ units of time to get to the perimeter, while it takes the dog only $\frac{1}{2}\frac{2\pi R}{4v} = \frac{\pi R}{4v} \approx \frac{3}{4} \times \frac{R}{v}$ units of time to get there—so he will meet you and eat you. You somehow need to get further from him and closer to the fence before you make a run for it.

Suppose you behave somewhat like the dog. Step away from the center of the circle until you are at a radius of $\frac{R}{4}$. Now constrain yourself to running circuits around that radius. It takes you $\frac{\pi R}{4v}$ units of time to run half-way around this circle. The dog can also run half-way around the field in the same time. That is, at this radius, you and the dog are perfectly matched in your abilities to run around in circles.

---

[47]I make use of the property that $\sum_{j=1}^{n} j = \frac{n(n+1)}{2}$ (see Answer 1.4).

Now suppose you step slightly closer to the center of the circle. Let us say you now start running around in circles of radius $\frac{R}{4} - \epsilon$, for some small ϵ. In this case, you have a slight advantage over the dog: you can run around your circle in slightly less time than he can run around his. As you run, the dog tries to track you. However, you are gaining a little on the dog with every circuit. Eventually, you will be at the "top" of your circle, when he is at the "bottom" of his. Now it is time to make a run for it. You only have to travel a distance of $R - \left(\frac{R}{4} - \epsilon\right) = \frac{3}{4}R + \epsilon$. The dog has to travel a distance πR to meet you. You can outrun him as long as the time it takes you at speed v is less than the time it takes him at $4v$, that is

$$\frac{\frac{3}{4}R + \epsilon}{v} < \frac{\pi R}{4v}$$

$$\Leftrightarrow \quad \frac{3}{4}R + \epsilon < \frac{\pi R}{4}$$

$$\Leftrightarrow 3R + 4\epsilon < \pi R$$

$$\Leftrightarrow \quad \epsilon < \frac{(\pi - 3)R}{4}.$$

It follows that if you choose an ϵ such that $0 < \epsilon < \frac{(\pi-3)R}{4}$, then you can run in a circle of radius $\frac{R}{4} - \epsilon$ until you are as far from the dog as possible and then you can escape by running away from him.

Answer 1.47: There are two methods. The first method assumes a known probability result (this may be sufficient for you); the second method subsumes the first by proving the aforementioned probability result before proceeding.

FIRST SOLUTION

The integral is immediately recognized as a simple transformation of an integral over the entire domain of a normally distributed random variable.

The standard normal distribution has probability density function $f(u) \equiv \frac{1}{\sqrt{2\pi}}e^{-\frac{1}{2}u^2}$, for $-\infty < u < +\infty$. Integrating over the entire domain must produce total probability mass of unity:

$$\int_{-\infty}^{+\infty} f(u)du = \int_{-\infty}^{+\infty} \frac{1}{\sqrt{2\pi}}e^{-\frac{1}{2}u^2}du = 1$$

If we substitute in $x = \frac{1}{\sqrt{2}}u$ (to make the integral look like the one we seek), then $dx = \frac{1}{\sqrt{2}}du$, and we get

$$\int_{-\infty}^{+\infty} \frac{1}{\sqrt{\pi}}e^{-x^2}dx = 1.$$

Multiply both sides by $\sqrt{\pi}$, and the result follows immediately.

SECOND SOLUTION

Let $I = \int_{-\infty}^{+\infty} e^{-x^2}dx$. Then squaring gives the following:

$$
\begin{aligned}
I^2 &= \left(\int_{-\infty}^{+\infty} e^{-x^2}dx\right) \cdot \left(\int_{-\infty}^{+\infty} e^{-y^2}dy\right) \\
&= \int_{x=-\infty}^{+\infty}\int_{y=-\infty}^{+\infty} e^{-(x^2+y^2)}dydx \\
&\stackrel{\text{see below}}{=} \int_{\theta=0}^{2\pi}\int_{r=0}^{+\infty} e^{-r^2}rdrd\theta \\
&= \int_{\theta=0}^{2\pi} \left.-\frac{1}{2}e^{-r^2}\right]_{r=0}^{\infty} d\theta \\
&= \frac{1}{2}\int_{\theta=0}^{2\pi} d\theta = \pi.
\end{aligned}
$$

Thus, $I = \sqrt{\pi}$, as required.

The above basis change from Cartesian coordinates to polar coordinates uses the transformation $x = r\cos\theta$, and $y = r\sin\theta$. This implies that $x^2 + y^2 = r^2$. However, there is more to it than this. You also need to know the general result

$$
\int_x\int_y f(x,y)dxdy = \int_\theta\int_r f(x(r,\theta), y(r,\theta))rdrd\theta.
$$

The "r" in the integrand on the right-hand side is the "Jacobian" of the transformation from Cartesian to polar coordinates. The Jacobian, J, is just the determinant of the matrix of partial derivatives of the transformation. That is

$$
\int_x\int_y f(x,y)dxdy = \int_\theta\int_r f(x(r,\theta), y(r,\theta))Jdrd\theta, \quad \text{where}
$$

$$
\begin{aligned}
J \equiv \frac{\partial(x,y)}{\partial(r,\theta)} &\equiv \begin{vmatrix} \frac{\partial x}{\partial r} & \frac{\partial x}{\partial \theta} \\ \frac{\partial y}{\partial r} & \frac{\partial y}{\partial \theta} \end{vmatrix} \\
&= \begin{vmatrix} \frac{\partial[r\cos\theta]}{\partial r} & \frac{\partial[r\cos\theta]}{\partial \theta} \\ \frac{\partial[r\sin\theta]}{\partial r} & \frac{\partial[r\sin\theta]}{\partial \theta} \end{vmatrix} \\
&= \begin{vmatrix} \cos\theta & -r\sin\theta \\ \sin\theta & r\cos\theta \end{vmatrix} \\
&= r\cos^2\theta + r\sin^2\theta \\
&= r(\cos^2\theta + \sin^2\theta) = r.
\end{aligned}
$$

For more on Jacobians, determinants, and transformations, consult DeGroot (1989, pp. 162–166) and Anton (1988, pp. 1068–1069).

Answer 1.48:   Of all the simple trigonometric functions that you might be asked to integrate, $\int \sec\theta d\theta$ has arguably the most complicated answer. I get reports of that being asked often.

Perhaps it is useful to review quickly the definitions of these trigonometry functions. Consider a right-angle triangle (see Table A.4). Let θ be one of the acute angles (i.e., one of the two angles of less than 90 degrees). Let the lengths of the sides of the triangle be denoted by "A" (the side adjacent to the angle θ), "O" (the side opposite to the angle θ), and "H" (the hypotenuse—opposite the right angle), then the elementary trigonometric functions may be defined as in Table A.4.[48]

Table A.4: Trigonometric Functions: Definitions

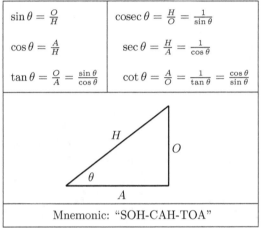

$\sin\theta = \frac{O}{H}$	$\operatorname{cosec}\theta = \frac{H}{O} = \frac{1}{\sin\theta}$
$\cos\theta = \frac{A}{H}$	$\sec\theta = \frac{H}{A} = \frac{1}{\cos\theta}$
$\tan\theta = \frac{O}{A} = \frac{\sin\theta}{\cos\theta}$	$\cot\theta = \frac{A}{O} = \frac{1}{\tan\theta} = \frac{\cos\theta}{\sin\theta}$

Mnemonic: "SOH-CAH-TOA"

Note: These definitions are for the triangle illustrated. The sides are of length A (a̲djacent to the angle θ), O (o̲pposite to the angle θ), and H (the h̲ypotenuse).

For the particular problem given, $\int \sec\theta d\theta$, we see in Table A.5 that the answer is $\ln|\sec\theta + \tan\theta|$ (up to an arbitrary constant of integration), which is readily verified via differentiation.

Answer 1.49: Using Table A.5, we get that

$$\int_0^{\frac{\pi}{6}} \sec\theta = \ln|\sec\theta + \tan\theta|\Big|_0^{\frac{\pi}{6}}$$

$$= \ln\left|\sec\frac{\pi}{6} + \tan\frac{\pi}{6}\right| - \ln|\sec 0 + \tan 0|.$$

From Table A.4, we have that $\sec\theta = \frac{1}{\cos\theta}$ and $\tan\theta = \frac{\sin\theta}{\cos\theta}$. Looking at the limits, we need $\sin 0 = 0$, $\cos 0 = 1$, $\sin\frac{\pi}{6} = \frac{1}{2}$, and $\cos\frac{\pi}{6} = \frac{\sqrt{3}}{2}$, which are standard results. Plugging these in, and using $ln1 = 0$, yields $\int_0^{\frac{\pi}{6}} \sec\theta = \ln\sqrt{3}$.

---

[48]The trigonometric functions' names are short for sine, cosine, tangent, cotangent, secant, and cosecant.

Table A.5: Trigonometric Functions: Calculus

$\int f(x)dx$	$f(x)$	$f'(x)$
$-\cos\theta$	$\sin\theta$	$\cos\theta$
$\sin\theta$	$\cos\theta$	$-\sin\theta$
$\ln|\sec\theta|$	$\tan\theta$	$\sec^2\theta$
$\ln|\sin\theta|$	$\cot\theta$	$-\operatorname{cosec}^2\theta$
$\ln|\sec\theta+\tan\theta|$	$\sec\theta$	$\sec\theta\tan\theta$
$\ln|\tan\frac{1}{2}\theta|$	$\operatorname{cosec}\theta$	$-\operatorname{cosec}\theta\cot\theta$

Note: The middle column gives a trigonometric function. The columns to the left and right give the integral of the function (ignoring arbitrary constant), and the derivative of the function, respectively.

Answer 1.50: The sum $\sum_{n=1}^{\infty} e^{-\sqrt{n}}$ takes the form $\sum_{n=1}^{\infty} a_n$, where $a_n \equiv e^{-\sqrt{n}}$. There is a whole host of tests for the convergence of such sums. Before we look at these, a short review of the terminology is in order.

A "sequence" is a set of numbers a_1, a_2, a_3, ... indexed in a particular order corresponding to the natural numbers. We may denote the sequence as "$\{a_n\}$." Each number, a_n, in the sequence is a "term." The "limit of a sequence" exists and is equal to $l < \infty$ if the numbers a_n get closer and closer to l as n gets larger. That is, $\lim_{n\to\infty} a_n = l$. If such a limit exists, then the sequence is said to "converge" to that limit, and the limit is unique. If a sequence does not converge, then it "diverges." There is no mention of additivity here: A sequence is a succession, not a sum.

A "series" is formed from a sequence via partial sums. Let $S_1 = a_1$, $S_2 = a_1 + a_2$, $S_3 = a_1 + a_2 + a_3$, and so on, so that $S_n = \sum_{i=1}^{n} a_i$ is the nth "partial sum" of the sequence $\{a_n\}$. Then the sum $\sum_{n=1}^{\infty} a_n$ is referred to as an "infinite series." The infinite series $\sum_{n=1}^{\infty} a_n$ is said to be "convergent" if the sequence of its partial sums $\{S_n\}$ is convergent.

A necessary (but not sufficient) condition for convergence of an infinite series $\{a_n\}$ is that $a_n \to 0$ as $n \to \infty$. In our case, $a_n = e^{-\sqrt{n}} \to 0$, so we cannot reject convergence.

The first (of several) formal tests that comes to mind is **The Ratio Test** (for series with positive terms only):

$$\lim_{n \to \infty} \frac{a_{n+1}}{a_n} \begin{cases} < 1, & \Rightarrow \sum a_n \text{ converges,} \\ > 1, & \Rightarrow \sum a_n \text{ diverges,} \\ = 1, & \Rightarrow \text{ the test fails.} \end{cases}$$

In our case, the test fails because

$$\lim_{n \to \infty} \frac{a_{n+1}}{a_n} = \lim_{n \to \infty} \frac{e^{\sqrt{n}}}{e^{\sqrt{n+1}}} = 1.$$

The next formal test for convergence that comes to mind is **The nth Root Test** (for series with positive terms only):

$$\lim_{n \to \infty} \sqrt[n]{a_n} \begin{cases} < 1, & \Rightarrow \sum a_n \text{ converges,} \\ > 1, & \Rightarrow \sum a_n \text{ diverges,} \\ = 1, & \Rightarrow \text{ the test fails.} \end{cases}$$

In our case, the test fails because

$$
\begin{aligned}
\lim_{n \to \infty} \sqrt[n]{a_n} &= \lim_{n \to \infty} \left(e^{-\sqrt{n}} \right)^{\frac{1}{n}} \\
&= \lim_{n \to \infty} e^{-n^{\frac{1}{2}} \times n^{-1}} \\
&= \lim_{n \to \infty} e^{-n^{-\frac{1}{2}}} \\
&= \lim_{n \to \infty} \frac{1}{e^{\frac{1}{\sqrt{n}}}} \\
&= 1.
\end{aligned}
$$

When the two tests above fail, we head for **Raabe's Test** (for series with positive terms only):

$$\lim_{n \to \infty} \left[n \left(1 - \frac{a_{n+1}}{a_n} \right) \right] \begin{cases} > 1, & \Rightarrow \sum a_n \text{ converges,} \\ < 1, & \Rightarrow \sum a_n \text{ diverges,} \\ = 1, & \Rightarrow \text{ the test fails.} \end{cases}$$

In our case, the test indicates convergence because

$$\lim_{n \to \infty} \left[n \left(1 - \frac{a_{n+1}}{a_n} \right) \right] = \lim_{n \to \infty} \left[n \left(1 - e^{\sqrt{n} - \sqrt{n+1}} \right) \right] > 1.$$

However, the algebraic proof that that last limit exceeds one is by no means elegant. Instead of proving it, I present another test of convergence that is both elegant and conclusive.

The **Integral Test** applies to a series $\sum a_n$ of positive terms. Let $A(x)$ denote the function of x obtained by replacing n in a_n by x. Then if $A(x)$ is decreasing and continuous for $x \geq 1$,

$$\sum_{n=1}^{\infty} a_n \quad \text{and} \quad \int_{x=1}^{+\infty} A(x)dx$$

either both converge, or both diverge (Anton [1988, p. 623]).

In our case, $a_n = e^{-\sqrt{n}}$. To test for convergence of $\sum_{n=1}^{\infty} a_n$, we may look at convergence of $\int_{x=1}^{+\infty} A(x)$, where $A(x) \equiv e^{-\sqrt{x}}$ is seen to be both decreasing and continuous for $x \geq 1$.

We need $\int e^{-\sqrt{x}}dx$. My first guess for this integral is

$$\int e^{-\sqrt{x}}dx = e^{-\sqrt{x}} + x^{\frac{1}{2}}e^{-\sqrt{x}} = (1 + \sqrt{x})e^{-\sqrt{x}}.$$

However, differentiation shows that I am out by a factor of -2. If you cannot guess this directly, you need some practice with integration by parts. We get the following integral:

$$
\begin{aligned}
\int_{x=1}^{+\infty} e^{-\sqrt{x}}dx &= \left. -2(1 + \sqrt{x})e^{-\sqrt{x}} \right|_1^{\infty} \\
&= \left. 2(1 + \sqrt{x})e^{-\sqrt{x}} \right|_{\infty}^{1} \\
&= \left. 2(1 + \sqrt{x})e^{-\sqrt{x}} \right|_1 - \left. 2(1 + \sqrt{x})e^{-\sqrt{x}} \right|_{\infty} \\
&= \frac{4}{e} - 2 \lim_{x \to \infty} \frac{(1 + \sqrt{x})}{e^{\sqrt{x}}} \\
&= \frac{4}{e} - 2 \lim_{u \to \infty} \frac{(1 + u)}{e^u} = \frac{4}{e},
\end{aligned}
$$

because $\sqrt{x} \to \infty$ if and only if $x \to \infty$, and $\lim_{u \to \infty} \frac{(1+u)}{e^u} = 0$ is well known. It follows that the series is convergent! Incidentally, the limit of the series $\sum_{n=1}^{+\infty} e^{-\sqrt{n}}$ is only slightly below $\frac{4}{e}$.

The **Comparison Test** says that if there exists $N < \infty$ such that $0 \leq a_n \leq b_n$ for $n \geq N$, and if $\sum_{n=1}^{+\infty} b_n$ is convergent, then so too is $\sum_{n=1}^{+\infty} a_n$. This also works in reverse: If $\sum_{n=1}^{+\infty} a_n$ is divergent, so too is $\sum_{n=1}^{+\infty} b_n$. This test requires that you construct b_n. In our case, if $n \geq 75$, then $a_n = e^{-\sqrt{n}} < \frac{1}{n^2} = b_n$, and $\sum_{n=1}^{+\infty} \frac{1}{n^2}$ is known to converge! In fact, $\sum_{n=1}^{+\infty} \frac{1}{n^2} = \frac{\pi^2}{6}$ (Spiegel [1968, p. 108]).

It is worth noting that if $\sum |a_n|$ converges, then $\sum a_n$ converges also. The former is referred to as "absolute convergence." Thus, absolute convergence of an infinite series is sufficient for convergence. Absolute convergence is not, however, a necessary condition for convergence. A series that is convergent, but not absolutely convergent, is said to be "conditionally convergent."

A final convergence test we might have tried is **Gauss' Test** (for series with positive terms only): If $\frac{a_{n+1}}{a_n} = 1 - \frac{\mathcal{L}}{n} + \frac{b_n}{n^2}$, where there exists an $M > 0$, and an N such that $|b_n| < M$ for all $n > N$, then the series $\sum_{n=1}^{\infty} a_n$ is

1. convergent if $\mathcal{L} > 1$, and

2. divergent or conditionally convergent if $\mathcal{L} \leq 1$.

For more information on tests of convergence of series, look to your favorite calculus book. Most of the above-mentioned tests should appear if the book is worthwhile.

Answer 1.51: The numbers used and the situation described may differ from question to question, but the general solution technique is always the same. Factor the product into all possible triplets: (1,2,18), (1,3,12), (1,4,9), (1,6,6), (2,2,9), (2,3,6), and (3,3,4). Which one is it? Well, Mary knows the sum, and these potential triplets sum to 21,16,14,13,13,11, and 10, respectively. Knowing the sum was not sufficient for Mary to pin down the triplet, so it must be a triplet with a non-unique sum: 13 in this case. This cuts down the candidates to (1,6,6) and (2,2,9). John says the eldest is dyslexic, so there must be an eldest (ignoring rubbish answers like one twin is 20 minutes older than the other). That just leaves (2,2,9).

Answer 1.52: You know one of the eight balls is heavy. Compare one group of three to another group of three. You need only one more weighing—for a total of two weighings.

Answer 1.53: The sums in Table A.6 are well known (the first is discussed extensively in the answer to Question 1.4).[49] You should certainly know the first sum by heart, and you should note that the third is the first squared.

Table A.6: Sums of k, k^2, and k^3

$\sum_{k=1}^{n} k$	$\frac{n(n+1)}{2}$
$\sum_{k=1}^{n} k^2$	$\frac{n(n+1)(2n+1)}{6}$
$\sum_{k=1}^{n} k^3$	$\frac{n^2(n+1)^2}{4}$

I give four quite different solutions. My first solution uses what I have named a "visual staircase" technique, and almost no algebra. My second solution uses the binomial theorem and Pascal's triangle.[50] My third solution uses a sensible guess plus induction. My fourth solution is similar, but requires that you notice, or already know, a special result.

---

[49]The fourth-order result is not well known: $\sum_{k=1}^{n} k^4 = \frac{n(n+1)(2n+1)(3n^2+3n-1)}{30}$ (Spiegel [1968, p. 108]).

[50]Pascal's triangle has the following rows: [1], [1 1],[1 2 1], [1 3 3 1], [1 4 6 4 1], and so on. Apart from the 1's, each item is the sum of the two items above when stacked like a pyramid. The $(n+1)^{st}$ row gives the coefficients in the polynomial expansion of $(a+b)^n$.

FIRST SOLUTION[51]

Case 1: The following grids and staircases have been marked out to aid in the derivation of $\sum_{k=1}^{n} k$. I use $n = 5$, but the result is stated for any n.

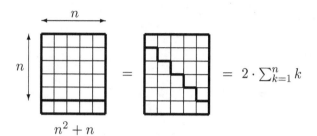

It follows from symmetry of the diagram that $\sum_{k=1}^{n} k = \frac{n^2+n}{2} = \frac{n(n+1)}{2}$.

Case 2: Again we double up what we are solving for, this time drawing pairs of squares, each of area k^2 for $k = 1, \ldots, n$ (but we show only the case $n = 5$). We aim to express $\sum_{k=1}^{n} k^2$ in terms of $\sum_{k=1}^{n} k$.

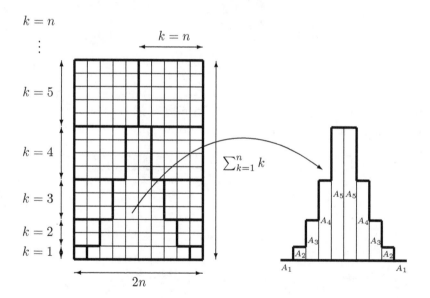

The large rectangle on the left has area $2n \cdot \sum_{k=1}^{n} k$, and is built from pairs of squares of total area $2 \cdot \sum_{k=1}^{n} k^2$ plus the central double-staircase (copied over to the right) of total area $2 \cdot \sum_{k=1}^{n} A_k$. For each $k \geq 2$, however, $2 \cdot A_k = 2 \cdot \sum_{i=1}^{k-1} i = (k-1)k = k^2 - k$, using the result for Case 1. Trivially, we also

[51]I thank Grahame Bennett, formerly a professor at Indiana University, for the elegant proof used in Case 3. This, in turn, inspired the proofs used in Cases 1 and 2.

have $A_1 = 1^2 - 1 = 0$. So, it follows that

$$2n \cdot \sum_{k=1}^{n} k = 2 \cdot \sum_{k=1}^{n} k^2 + \sum_{k=1}^{n} (k^2 - k)$$

$$\Rightarrow (2n+1) \cdot \sum_{k=1}^{n} k = 3 \cdot \sum_{k=1}^{n} k^2$$

$$\Rightarrow \sum_{k=1}^{n} k^2 = \left(\sum_{k=1}^{n} k \right) \cdot (2n+1) \Big/ 3$$

$$\Rightarrow \sum_{k=1}^{n} k^2 = n(n+1)(2n+1)/6 \, ,$$

using the result from Case 1, as required.

Case 3: Following on from the previous cases, let us draw a grid for general k, aiming to express $\sum_{k=1}^{n} k^3$ in terms of $\sum_{k=1}^{n} k$.

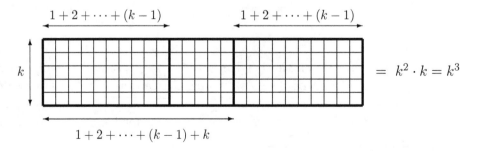

It follows from the diagram that the square of area k^2 is composed of a row of length k and two staircases, each of area $1 + 2 + \cdots + (k-1)$. Let us reshape this square of area k^2 into a corresponding single row, as follows.

$$\boxed{} = k^2$$

$$\underbrace{1 + 2 + \cdots + (k-1)}_{} \quad \underbrace{k}_{} \quad \underbrace{1 + 2 + \cdots + (k-1)}_{}$$

Now stack k copies of this row on top of each other, giving a strip of area $k^2 \cdot k = k^3$, as follows.

$$\overbrace{1 + 2 + \cdots + (k-1)} \qquad \overbrace{1 + 2 + \cdots + (k-1)}$$

$$= k^2 \cdot k = k^3$$

$$\underbrace{1 + 2 + \cdots + (k-1) + k}$$

Now reshape this strip of area k^3 into an L-shape, still of area k^3, as follows.

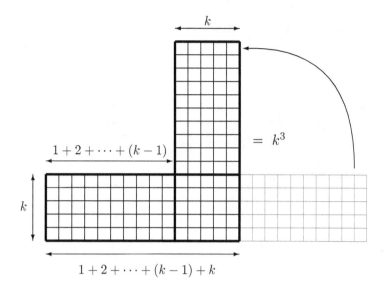

Now take L-shaped blocks for consecutive k, each of area k^3, and tile them in a consecutive nested fashion as follows.

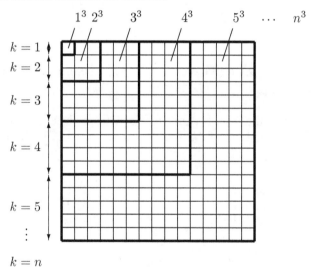

If we continue tiling until $k = n$, then it should be clear that the border of the square has length $\sum_{k=1}^{n} k$ while the square itself has total area $\sum_{k=1}^{n} k^3$. This total area must also be the border length squared. If we combine this result with the result from Case 1, it follows that

$$\sum_{k=1}^{n} k^3 = \left(\sum_{k=1}^{n} k\right)^2 = \left[\frac{n(n+1)}{2}\right]^2, \text{ as required.}$$

SECOND SOLUTION[52]
Let $S_i = \sum_{k=1}^{n} k^i$ for $i = 1, 2, 3$ be the three sums we are interested in.

---

[52]I thank Yiannis Chardaloupas, for suggesting this technique; any errors are mine.

Case $i = 1$: We want to derive $S_i = \sum_{k=1}^{n} k^i$ for $i = 1$. Write down the series of binomial expansions of $(k+1)^{i+1}$ for $k = 1, \ldots, n$ in Equations A.13 for $\underline{i = 1}$.

$$
\begin{aligned}
2^2 &= (1+1)^2 &= 1^2 &+ 2\cdot 1 &+ 1 \\
3^2 &= (2+1)^2 &= 2^2 &+ 2\cdot 2 &+ 1 \\
4^2 &= (3+1)^2 &= 3^2 &+ 2\cdot 3 &+ 1 \\
&\ \ \vdots \\
(k+1)^2 &= (k+1)^2 &= k^2 &+ 2\cdot k &+ 1 \\
&\ \ \vdots \\
n^2 &= [(n-1)+1]^2 &= (n-1)^2 &+ 2\cdot(n-1) &+ 1 \\
(n+1)^2 &= (n+1)^2 &= n^2 &+ 2\cdot n &+ 1
\end{aligned}
\tag{A.13}
$$

Now add all the Equations A.13 vertically, but cancel from both sides the summation $2^2 + 3^2 + \cdots + n^2$. This yields Equation A.14.

$$
(n+1)^2 \ = \ \Sigma \ = \ 1 \ + \ 2\cdot S_1 \ + \ n, \tag{A.14}
$$

where I just put a Σ in place of the superfluous middle summation. It follows immediately that $S_1 = \frac{(n+1)^2 - (n+1)}{2} = \frac{n(n+1)}{2}$.

Case $i = 2$: Let me now repeat the derivation, but this time using the series of binomial expansions of $(k+1)^{i+1}$ for $k = 1, \ldots, n$ in Equations A.15 for $\underline{i = 2}$.

$$
\begin{aligned}
2^3 &= (1+1)^3 &= 1^3 &+ 3\cdot 1^2 &+ 3\cdot 1 &+ 1 \\
3^3 &= (2+1)^3 &= 2^3 &+ 3\cdot 2^2 &+ 3\cdot 2 &+ 1 \\
4^3 &= (3+1)^3 &= 3^3 &+ 3\cdot 3^2 &+ 3\cdot 3 &+ 1 \\
&\ \ \vdots \\
(k+1)^3 &= (k+1)^3 &= k^3 &+ 3\cdot k^2 &+ 3\cdot k &+ 1 \\
&\ \ \vdots \\
n^3 &= [(n-1)+1]^3 &= (n-1)^3 &+ 3\cdot(n-1)^2 &+ 3\cdot(n-1) &+ 1 \\
(n+1)^3 &= (n+1)^3 &= n^3 &+ 3\cdot n^2 &+ 3\cdot n &+ 1
\end{aligned}
\tag{A.15}
$$

Now add all the Equations A.15 vertically, but cancel from both sides the summation $2^3 + 3^3 + \cdots + n^3$. This yields Equation A.16.

$$
(n+1)^3 \ = \ \Sigma \ = \ 1 \ + \ 3\cdot S_2 \ + \ 3\cdot S_1 \ + \ n, \tag{A.16}
$$

where I again put a Σ in place of the superfluous middle summation.

If we collect terms, plug $S_1 = n(n+1)/2$ into Equation A.16, and multiply through by $2/(n+1)$, we get

$$(n+1)^3 = (n+1) + 3 \cdot S_2 + 3\frac{n(n+1)}{2}$$

$$(n+1)^2 = 1 + \frac{3 \cdot S_2}{(n+1)} + 3\frac{n}{2}$$

$$2(n+1)^2 = 2 + \frac{6 \cdot S_2}{(n+1)} + 3n$$

$$2(n+1)^2 - 2 - 3n = \frac{6 \cdot S_2}{(n+1)}$$

$$2n^2 + n = \frac{6 \cdot S_2}{(n+1)},$$

from which it follows immediately that $S_2 = \frac{n(n+1)(2n+1)}{6}$.

Case $i = 3$: Continuing with the Pascal's triangle theme in Equations A.14 and A.16, if we repeat the exercise but this time using the series of binomial expansions of $(k+1)^{i+1}$ for $k = 2, \ldots, n$ for case $i = 3$, I hope you can see that we will get Equation A.17.

$$(n+1)^4 = 1 + 4 \cdot S_3 + 6 \cdot S_2 + 4 \cdot S_1 + n \qquad \text{(A.17)}$$

If we collect terms, plug in expressions for S_1 and S_2, and divide by $(n+1)$, Equation A.17 yields

$$(n+1)^4 = (n+1) + 4 \cdot S_3 + (2n+1)(n+1)n + 2n(n+1)$$

$$(n+1)^3 = 1 + \frac{4 \cdot S_3}{(n+1)} + (2n+1)n + 2n$$

$$= \frac{4 \cdot S_3}{(n+1)} + (2n+1)(n+1)$$

$$\frac{4 \cdot S_3}{(n+1)} = (n+1)[(n+1)^2 - (2n+1)]$$

$$= (n+1)n^2,$$

from which it follows immediately that $S_3 = \left[\frac{n(n+1)}{2}\right]^2$.

THIRD SOLUTION[53]

Given $\sum_{k=1}^{n} k = n(n+1)/2$, let us assume $\sum_{k=1}^{n} k^i$ equals an $(i+1)^{th}$-order polynomial $f^{(i)}(n)$. In the case $i = 2$ (i.e., trying to find $\sum_{k=1}^{n} k^2$), let this polynomial be $f^{(2)}(n) = an^3 + bn^2 + cn + d$. We can calculate $f^{(2)}(n)$ for $n = 1$–4, and set up the system of Equations A.18.

$$\begin{array}{rcrcrcrcrcr}
f^{(2)}(1) &=& a &+& b &+& c &+& d &=& 1 \\
f^{(2)}(2) &=& 8a &+& 4b &+& 2c &+& d &=& 5 \\
f^{(2)}(3) &=& 27a &+& 9b &+& 3c &+& d &=& 14 \\
f^{(2)}(4) &=& 64a &+& 16b &+& 4c &+& d &=& 30
\end{array} \qquad \text{(A.18)}$$

---

[53] I thank Vince Moshkevich for suggesting this technique; any errors are mine.

Standard row-reduction techniques soon yield $a = 1/3$, $b = 1/2$, $c = 1/6$, and $d = 0$. Thus, $f^{(2)}(n) = \frac{2n^3+3n^2+n}{6} = \frac{n(n+1)(2n+1)}{6}$. Having obtained a formula that works for $n = 1\text{--}4$, we must now prove, by induction, that if it works for n, then it works for $n+1$. That is, we show that $f(n) + (n+1)^2 = f(n+1)$:

$$
\begin{aligned}
f(n) + (n+1)^2 &= \frac{2n^3 + 3n^2 + n}{6} + (n^2 + 2n + 1) \\
&= \frac{2n^3 + 9n^2 + 13n + 6}{6} \\
&= \frac{(n+1)(n+2)(2n+3)}{6} \\
&= \frac{[(n+1)][(n+1)+1][2(n+1)+1]}{6} \\
&= f(n+1), \text{ as required.} \qquad \text{(A.19)}
\end{aligned}
$$

The case $f^{(3)}(n) = \sum_{k=1}^{n} k^3$ may be proved in exactly the same fashion, and I leave it as an exercise.

FOURTH SOLUTION

If you notice that $\sum_{k=1}^{n} 1 = n$ and $\sum_{k=1}^{n} k = n(n+1)/2$, you might deduce the following pattern:[54]

$$
\begin{aligned}
\sum_{k=1}^{n} 1 &= n \\
\sum_{k=1}^{n} k &= \frac{n(n+1)}{2} \\
\sum_{k=1}^{n} k(k+1) &= \frac{n(n+1)(n+2)}{3} \\
\sum_{k=1}^{n} k(k+1)(k+2) &= \frac{n(n+1)(n+2)(n+3)}{4} \\
&\vdots
\end{aligned}
$$

These can each be proved easily using mathematical induction. For example, the third equality immediately above is easily proved true when $n = 1$ (both sides equal 2). To prove this third equality in general, we now need only show that increasing n by one on each side of the equality has the same incremental effect on both sides. That is, we need only show that the right-hand side evaluated at $n = (N + 1)$ less the right-hand side evaluated at $n = N$ gives

---

[54] I thank David Maslen for suggesting this technique; any errors are mine.

what would be the $(N+1)^{st}$ term in the summation on the left-hand side:

$$
\begin{aligned}
&\frac{(N+1)(N+2)(N+3)}{3} - \frac{N(N+1)(N+2)}{3} \\
&= \frac{(N+1)(N+2)}{3}((N+3) - N) \\
&= \frac{(N+1)(N+2)}{3}(3) \\
&= (N+1)(N+2) \\
&= \left. k(k+1) \right|_{k=N+1} \quad \text{QED.}
\end{aligned}
$$

The results we are interested in follow quite easily now because, for example, $\sum_{k=1}^{n} k^2 = \sum_{k=1}^{n} k(k+1) - \sum_{k=1}^{n} k$, and we have expressions for both the latter summations.

Answer 1.54: You win if you can place the last coin on the table and leave no space for me to place a further coin. A necessary condition is that the table be radially symmetric. That is, there must exist a central point on the table (at its center of mass if the table is of uniform density and thickness) such that any line drawn upon the table passing through this central point is evenly bisected at this central point. Simple examples are a square, an ellipse, a rectangle, a circular disc, etc.

You should play first and place your first quarter at the center of the table. You should make subsequent moves by imitating me: Place your quarter in the mirror image of my position when viewed looking through the central point. This ensures victory because if I can still place a coin on the table, then so can you.[55]

Although radial symmetry is necessary, it is not sufficient. The strategy does not necessarily work if the table is a regular shape but not a simply-connected one; for example, an annulus.[56] If the table is an annulus and the hole in the middle is bigger than a quarter, then the only change to your winning strategy is that you should let me go first.

> **Story:** A student of mine was asked "How would you value yourself?" That is, put a dollar figure on your value using discounted cash flow analysis.

Answer 1.55: No, you definitely cannot tile the 62 squares with the dominoes. If you cannot see why, then go back and think again before reading on.

---

[55] I thank Tim Hoel and Victor H. Lin for this elegant solution technique.

[56] An "annulus" is a disc with a hole in the center—like a musical compact disc, for example. An annulus is path connected (any two points may be joined by a line), and is therefore connected (it cannot be split into two non-empty non-intersecting open sets), but it is not simply connected (which requires path-connectivity and that any loop may be shrunk continuously within the set).

Each domino covers two squares that are side-by-side on the board. Each of these pairs of squares consists of a black and a white. As you place the dominoes, you cover the same number of black squares as white ones. However, the two squares that are off limits are the same color (opposing corners on a chessboard must be the same color). Thus, the number of white squares to be covered is not the same as the number of black, and the dominoes cannot cover them all.[57]

Naoki Sato has supplied an answer to his follow-up question. Imagine a closed path on the chessboard that passes through every square exactly once (moving horizontally and vertically, eventually returning to the original square). The two "X"s, unless adjacent, divide this path into two sections. Since one "X" is on black, and one is on white, the two sections each cover an even number of squares. They may thus be tiled using the dominoes. If the two "X"s are adjacent, the solution is obvious.

Answer 1.56: Deciphering the optimal strategy is analogous to locating an optimal stock price exercise boundary for an American-style option. Calculating the expected payoff to the game, assuming the optimal strategy, is analogous to valuing an American-style option. Like valuing an American option, you have to work backward through a decision tree, calculating the expected payoffs to proceeding versus stopping at each node. For two, four, six, and eight cards, the expected payoff to the game is $\$\frac{1}{2}$, $\$\frac{2}{3}$, $\$\frac{17}{20}$, and $\$1$, respectively, when following the optimal strategy. The two-card game decision tree is a sub-tree of the four-card game decision tree, so later results can be appended to earlier ones. Stop reading here and try to replicate these numbers.

Let R and B denote the number of red and black cards, respectively, when you begin play ($R = B = 26$ in our case). Let r and b denote the number of red and black cards remaining in the deck at some intermediate stage of the game when you are trying to decide whether to take another card. You get $+1$ for each red card drawn and -1 for each black card drawn, so your current accumulated score is the number of reds drawn so far less the number of blacks drawn so far: $(R - r) - (B - b)$. The expected value of the game $V(r, b)$ is the current accumulated score plus the additional expected value, if any, remaining in the deck, assuming optimal play. With r and b cards remaining, denote this additional expected value as $E(r, b)$. Thus, the value of the game is $V(r, b) = (R - r) - (B - b) + E(r, b)$. Simple logic dictates that

---

[57]An alternative solution has been suggested to me by Aidong Chen. Let each square on the board be described by its coordinates (x, y) for $1 \leq x, y \leq 8$. Any domino covers two adjacent squares, either (x, y) and $(x, y + 1)$, or (x, y) and $(x + 1, y)$. If we add those coordinates up, we get $2x + 2y + 1$ in either case. To tile the 62 remaining squares requires 31 dominoes. If we add up 31 coordinate sums, each of form $2x + 2y + 1$, we must get an odd number. If we add up the coordinate sums of the 62 remaining squares, however, we must get an even number (because the sum of the coordinate sums of all 64 squares is even by symmetry, and the two corners to subtract, (1,1) and (8,8), have even sums). So, it cannot be done.

$E(r, b)$ is defined recursively as follows:[58]

$$E(r,b) = \begin{cases} 0, & \text{if } r = 0 \\ r, & \text{if } b = 0 \\ \max\left\{0, \frac{r}{r+b}[1 + E(r-1, b)] + \frac{b}{r+b}[-1 + E(r, b-1)]\right\}, \\ & \text{otherwise.} \end{cases}$$

Table A.7 gives all the necessary information for you to solve the easier game in which there are four cards of each color. It is worth noting that the recursive definition of $E(r, b)$, when seen in action in Table A.7, produces a complicated Pascal's triangle type of calculation when working from the lower right to the upper left. That is, $E(r, b)$ in each cell depends on $E(r, b)$ in the cells immediately to the right and below. As mentioned previously, in the two-, four-, six-, and eight-card games, the expected payoffs are $\$\frac{1}{2}$, $\$\frac{2}{3}$, $\$\frac{17}{20}$, and $\$1$, respectively, and these are visible on the leading diagonal in Table A.7.

If the additional remaining value in the deck when playing optimally is zero [i.e., $E(r, b) = 0$], you are not indifferent about continuing. Rather, you want to quit immediately because in every case except one, $E(r, b) = 0$ implies $\frac{r}{r+b}[1 + E(r-1, b)] + \frac{b}{r+b}[-1 + E(r, b-1)]$ is negative, and that the "max" function is being used in the recursive definition of $E(r, b)$. The only exception is when $(r, b) = (1, 2)$, and even then $\frac{r}{r+b}[1 + E(r-1, b)] + \frac{b}{r+b}[-1 + E(r, b-1)]$ is zero and a risk-averse player would quit. When playing optimally, the last card drawn is always red. That is, you never pick a black card and then quit. The optimal score to quit at cannot be negative because you always have the safety net of a zero payoff for sure if you draw every card. The optimal score to quit at is a non-increasing step function of the number of black cards drawn (drawing red cards has no effect on the optimal score to quit at). Drawing black cards can lower the optimal score to quit at. In the eight-card game, the optimal stopping rule is: If you have turned over zero or one black card, then quit if you can get to a score of 2 without seeing another black card; if you have turned over two or three black cards, then quit if you can get to a score of 1 without seeing another black card; if you have turned over four black cards, then the best you can do is draw every card and get a payoff of 0. In the $2n$ card game with n red cards and n black cards, the expected payoffs are shown in Table A.8.[59]

Answer 1.57:   A prime number has no factors other than itself and 1. Thus, 4 is not prime because it has factors: (1,4), and (2,2). Drawing a number line might be a good way to explain this to an interviewer. I will just use words.

1. A prime p bigger than 2 cannot be an integer multiple of 2, else it would not be prime. Thus, a prime bigger than 2 must be odd. Thus, $p - 1$ is even. Thus, $p - 1 = 2n$ for some positive integer n. Thus, $p = 2n + 1$.

---

[58]I thank Paul Turner for solving this problem when it was posted as a challenge question on my web site; any errors are mine.

[59]I thank David Maslen for the final ratio in the table; any errors are mine.

Table A.7: The Red/Black Card Game

0 (4,4) 1 $\left(\frac{4}{8},\frac{4}{8}\right)$ 1 Y	1 (3,4) $\frac{12}{35}$ $\left(\frac{3}{7},\frac{4}{7}\right)$ $1\frac{12}{35}$ Y	2 (2,4) 0 $\left(\frac{2}{6},\frac{4}{6}\right)$ 2 N	3 (1,4) 0 $\left(\frac{1}{5},\frac{4}{5}\right)$ 3 NN	4 (0,4) 0 $\left(\frac{0}{4},\frac{4}{4}\right)$ 4 NN
-1 (4,3) $1\frac{23}{35}$ $\left(\frac{4}{7},\frac{3}{7}\right)$ $\frac{23}{35}$ Y	0 (3,3) $\frac{17}{20}$ $\left(\frac{3}{6},\frac{3}{6}\right)$ $\frac{17}{20}$ Y	1 (2,3) $\frac{1}{5}$ $\left(\frac{2}{5},\frac{3}{5}\right)$ $\frac{6}{5}$ Y	2 (1,3) 0 $\left(\frac{1}{4},\frac{3}{4}\right)$ 2 N	3 (0,3) 0 $\left(\frac{0}{3},\frac{3}{3}\right)$ 3 NN
-2 (4,2) $2\frac{2}{5}$ $\left(\frac{4}{6},\frac{2}{6}\right)$ $\frac{2}{5}$ Y	-1 (3,2) $1\frac{1}{2}$ $\left(\frac{3}{5},\frac{2}{5}\right)$ $\frac{1}{2}$ Y	0 (2,2) $\frac{2}{3}$ $\left(\frac{2}{4},\frac{2}{4}\right)$ $\frac{2}{3}$ Y	1 (1,2) 0 $\left(\frac{1}{3},\frac{2}{3}\right)$ 1 N	2 (0,2) 0 $\left(\frac{0}{2},\frac{2}{2}\right)$ 2 NN
-3 (4,1) $3\frac{1}{5}$ $\left(\frac{4}{5},\frac{1}{5}\right)$ $\frac{1}{5}$ Y	-2 (3,1) $2\frac{1}{4}$ $\left(\frac{3}{4},\frac{1}{4}\right)$ $\frac{1}{4}$ Y	-1 (2,1) $1\frac{1}{3}$ $\left(\frac{2}{3},\frac{1}{3}\right)$ $\frac{1}{3}$ Y	0 (1,1) $\frac{1}{2}$ $\left(\frac{1}{2},\frac{1}{2}\right)$ $\frac{1}{2}$ Y	1 (0,1) 0 $\left(\frac{0}{1},\frac{1}{1}\right)$ 1 N
-4 (4,0) 4 $\left(\frac{4}{4},\frac{0}{4}\right)$ 0 Y	-3 (3,0) 3 $\left(\frac{3}{3},\frac{0}{3}\right)$ 0 Y	-2 (2,0) 2 $\left(\frac{2}{2},\frac{0}{2}\right)$ 0 Y	-1 (1,0) 1 $\left(\frac{1}{1},\frac{0}{1}\right)$ 0 Y	0 (0,0) 0 (0,0) 0 N

Note: Each cell is laid out as

Accum. Score	(r,b)
$E(r,b)$	(p_{red}, p_{black})
$V(r,b)$	$Y, N,$ or NN

, where r and b are the number of red and black cards remaining in the deck, "Accum. Score" is the accumulated score so far (i.e., $(R-r)-(B-b)$, where $R=B=4$ in this case); p_{red} and p_{black} are the probabilities that the next card drawn will be red or black, respectively; $E(r,b)$ is the expected additional value remaining in the deck assuming optimal play; $V(r,b)$ is the expected payoff of the game, assuming you start in the top left cell (it is the sum of the two items above it); "Y" means *yes* you should continue playing; "N" means *no* you should halt (the cells are shaded to pick out the boundary), and "NN" means *no* you should halt, but you should also note that it is *not* possible to get to this cell if you start with an even number of each color card and play optimally.

2. A prime p bigger than 3 cannot be an integer multiple of 3, else it would not be prime. However, draw a number line and it must be that either $p-1$ or $p+1$ (but not both) is a multiple of 3. That is, p is 1 away from a multiple of 3, but we do not know in which direction. Thus, $p\pm 1 = 3m$ for some positive integer m, where $\pm$ means exactly one of $+$ or $-$, but not both. Thus, $p = 3m \pm 1$.

3. The question asks about $p^2 - 1$. From #1 we see that $p^2 - 1 = 4n^2 + 4n = 4n(n+1)$. One of n or $n+1$ must be even, and with that 4 there, we see that $p^2 - 1$ contains a factor of 8 (i.e., $2 \times 2 \times 2$).

4. From #2, we see that $p^2 - 1 = 9m^2 \pm 6m = 3m(m \pm 2)$. Thus, $p^2 - 1$ contains 3 as a factor.

5. If we picture $p^2 - 1$ factored out into all possible numbers of smallest

Table A.8: E(Payoff) in Red/Black Card Games ($2n$ cards, n red, n black)

$2n$	$r = b = n$	$V(r,b)$ (ratio)	$V(r,b)$ (decimal)
2	1	$\frac{1}{2}$	0.500000000000
4	2	$\frac{2}{3}$	0.666666666667
6	3	$\frac{17}{20}$	0.850000000000
8	4	$\frac{1}{1}$	1.000000000000
10	5	$\frac{47}{42}$	1.119047619048
12	6	$\frac{284}{231}$	1.229437229437
14	7	$\frac{4,583}{3,432}$	1.335372960373
$\vdots$	$\vdots$	$\vdots$	$\vdots$
52	26	$\frac{41,984,711,742,427}{15,997,372,030,584}$	2.624475548994

Note: These expected payoffs are derived using the same rules used in the eight-card game. I have included the ratio form of the expected payoff in case anyone spots a simple pattern.

possible size, then the results from #3 and #4 cannot overlap. That is, $p^2 - 1$ contains factors of $2 \times 2 \times 2$ and 3; thus, $p^2 - 1$ is an integer multiple of 24.

Answer 1.58: Let B be your bid. Let S be the true value of the firm. The density function of S equals unity for $0 \le S \le 1$, and zero otherwise. Your payoff P is

$$P(S) = \begin{cases} 2S - B, & \text{if } B > S \\ 0, & \text{otherwise.} \end{cases}$$

The maximum post-bid firm value is 2, so you should bid no more than 2. You want to maximize $E[P(S)]$ with respect to choice of B in the interval $[0, 2]$. Your expected payoff is

$$\begin{aligned} E[P(S)] &= \int_{S=0}^{S=1} P(S) \cdot 1 \cdot dS \\ &= \int_{S=0}^{S=\min(B,1)} (2S - B) dS \\ &= (S^2 - BS)\Big|_{S=0}^{S=\min(B,1)} \\ &= \begin{cases} 0, & \text{if } B \le 1 \\ 1 - B, & \text{if } B > 1, \end{cases} \end{aligned}$$

so you should bid less than or equal to 1 and expect to break even.

Answer 1.59:   What is going to happen if you light both ends simultaneously? The two fizzing sparking flames are going to burn toward each other and meet. When they meet 60 seconds worth of fuse has been burnt in two sections that each took the same amount of time. How much time? It has to be exactly 30 seconds because they both took the same time, and these times add to 60 seconds. Of course, you have to bend the fuse so that you can light both ends simultaneously and when they meet it probably won't be in the center of the fuse.

Answer 1.60:   Light Fuse 1 at both ends and simultaneously light Fuse 2 at one end. As soon as Fuse 1 is burned out (i.e., after 30 seconds), light the other end of Fuse 2.

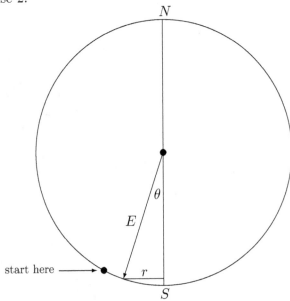

Figure A.6: S-E-N Problem: The Earth

Note: The Earth is a perfect sphere with radius E. You start your trek one mile north of a line of latitude having circumference $1/n$ miles, and radius r miles (so $2\pi r = 1/n$). You must start a distance of $1 + E \cdot \arcsin \frac{1}{2\pi n E}$ miles from the south pole—see Answer 1.61.

Answer 1.61:   If your answer is "none" or "one," then go back and think again. There are, in fact, an uncountably infinite number of starting points that solve this problem.

First of all, you could start at the north pole. On the middle leg of your walk you would always be one mile south of the north pole, so the final leg would put you back where you started. Second, if you start at a point close to the south pole but one mile north of a line of latitude having circumference one mile, then the middle leg of your walk begins and ends in the same spot; the final leg takes you back to your starting point. There are infinitely many such starting points on the line of latitude that is one mile north of the line of latitude having circumference one mile.

Similarly, if you start slightly further south, at a point one mile north of a line of latitude having circumference one-half mile, then the middle leg of your walk begins and ends in the same spot, and the final leg returns you to your starting point.

More generally, if you begin on a line of latitude one mile north of a line of latitude having circumference $1/n$ miles, then you will walk one mile south, circle the line of latitude n times, and return to your starting point.

In the latter case, how far is your starting point from the south pole? Well, assume the Earth is perfectly spherical, and let E be its radius. Let r be the radius of the line of latitude having circumference $1/n$ miles, so, $2\pi r = 1/n$. A simple sketch shows that the angle θ between the axis of the Earth, and a line drawn from the center of the Earth to any point on the line of latitude having circumference $1/n$ miles, satisfies $\sin\theta = r/E$ (see Figure A.6 and the trig' review on p. 112). Thus, the arc length from the pole to this line of latitude is the fraction $\frac{\arcsin\frac{r}{E}}{2\pi}$ of the circumference of the Earth, $2\pi E$. That is, the arc length is $E \cdot \arcsin\frac{1}{2\pi nE}$ (using $r = 1/(2\pi n)$). You start one mile north of this, at a distance of $1 + E \cdot \arcsin\frac{1}{2\pi nE}$ miles from the south pole.

Answer 1.62: The king should take one coin from bag one, two coins from bag two, three coins from bag three, and so on, finishing with ten coins from bag ten. Place this collection on the weighing device, and look for the discrepancy from $\sum_{i=1}^{10} i$ ounces. If the actual weight is 0.40 ounces short, for example, then bag four is light, and collector four is the cheat.

Answer 1.63: $100!=100 \times 99 \times 98 \times \cdots \times 3 \times 2 \times 1$. Factor each number and count how many supply a 5. Combine the 5's with all the 2's going spare to get the 10's that give 0's at the end of 100!. The following supply a 5 (or two fives, as indicated): 5, 10, 15, 20, 25(2), 30, 35, 40, 45, 50(2), 55, 60, 65, 70, 75(2), 80, 85, 90, 95, 100(2). This gives the 24 zeroes at the end of 100!:[60]

```
              933 26215
44394 41526 81699 23885 62667
00490 71596 82643 81621 46859
29638 95217 59999 32299 15608
94146 39761 56518 28625 36979
20827 22375 82511 85210 91686
40000 00000 00000 00000 00000
```

---

[60]Type `vpa factorial(100)` 158 in MATLAB; vpa is variable precision arithmetic.

Story: He took off his right shoe and sock, removed a medicated foot powder and dusted it on the foot and in the shoe. While he was putting back the shoe and sock, he mentioned that he had to use the powder four times a day, and this was the time.

Interview Horror Stories from Recruiters
Reprinted by kind permission of *MBA Style Magazine*
©1996–2021 MBA Style Magazine, www.mbastyle.com

Answer 1.64: Snap the bar into pieces that are one, two, and four parts long, respectively. On day one, give him one part. On day two, exchange your two parts for his one. On day three, give him back the one part. On day four, exchange four parts for his three. On day five, give him one more part. On day six, exchange your two parts for his one. On day seven, give him back the one part.

You may have missed it on first reading, but the lengths of the pieces are 2^0, 2^1, and 2^2 parts, respectively. So, we are counting in binary.[61] More generally, if we have a gold bar that is $(2^N) - 1$ parts long, we can generate any integer payment from zero parts up to $(2^N) - 1$ parts by breaking the bar into N pieces, with lengths 2^i parts, for $i = 0, 1, \ldots, 2^{N-1}$.

Answer 1.65: We know the sum $\sum_{i=1}^{100} i = \left. \frac{n(n+1)}{2} \right|_{n=100} = 5,050$. So, add up all the integers in the array and subtract them from 5,050 to find the missing number.

Answer 1.66: Let us attack the mirror problem in stages.

Your Perspective, No Rotations: Put your wristwatch on your left wrist and stand facing a mirror with your arms held out as though you are being crucified (it is a tough interview remember). Your reflected self's wristwatch-bearing arm is pointing the *same* direction as yours. Your wristwatch is to the left of your head, and your reflected self's wristwatch is also to *your* left of his or her head. *There has been no flipping of left for right.* Similarly, if your head is pointing up, then your reflected self's head is also pointing up, and *there has been no flipping of up for down.*

Perhaps this is clearer if you write a sentence on a transparent plastic sheet, and hold the sheet in front of your body, as though there is no mirror at all and you are simply reading what you have just written. Now look in the mirror. The reflection of your sheet in the mirror is *not* reversed. That is, the left-most word is still left most, the right-most word is still right most, and you can still read the reflected image from left to right.

Viewed from your perspective, everything about you that is left, right, up, or down is still left, right, up, or down, respectively, in your reflected image. There is thus *no* flipping of left for right or up for down. What *has* flipped

---

[61] I thank Mark Cawston for discussions regarding this answer; any errors are mine.

is that if you are facing east, then your reflection is facing west. It does not matter for the sentence written on the transparent sheet, because it has no depth. It does matter for you, because your reflected nose is facing the opposite direction.

Your Perspective, Rotation of Yourself: If your interviewer suggests that there really is a flipping left for right of your reflected self, but not up for down, then this requires an implicit additional rotation of your perspective about a vertical axis. In other words, suppose we can somehow physically flip you left for right, without changing the direction in which you are facing (ouch!). Then, yes, both you and your reflection will be wearing your wristwatches on your right hands. You and your reflection will, however, be facing in opposite directions. So, to get a one-to-one mapping, we still need an additional rotation of your body 180° about a vertical axis. (Equivalently, we could rotate you about the vertical axis first, and then flip you left for right).

Note that had we somehow physically flipped you up for down (without changing the direction in which you are facing), then, yes, both you and your reflection will be wearing your wristwatches on your right hands. Like the previous case, however, you and your reflection will still be facing in opposite directions. So, to get a one-to-one mapping, we still need an additional rotation of your body 180° about a horizontal axis. (Equivalently, we could rotate you about the horizontal axis first, and then flip you up for down).

The fact that neither a flipping left for right nor a flipping up for down (and neither a rotation about a horizontal axis nor a rotation about a vertical axis) alone suffices to provide a one-to-one mapping into the imagined boots of your reflected self confirms my earlier assertion: There is not a flipping of left for right, nor up for down, but rather, a flipping in the direction of the depth.

If your interviewer firmly believes that a mirror does flip left for right, then he or she is predisposed toward rotation about a vertical axis (something many of us do every day), and has not thought through the consequences of the attempted one-to-one mapping.

Answer 1.67: Yes, it can be done, in theory if not in practice. If you are stuck and looking for a hint, think about inverting a condom and covering it with another.

Let us label the condoms $C1$, and $C2$, and the men $M1$, $M2$, and $M3$. $M1$ wears $C1$ with $C2$ placed over it. $M2$ then uses $C2$, which is still clean inside. $M3$ then wears $C1$ inverted ($C1$'s outside, you will recall, was kept clean by $C2$), and places the twice-used $C2$ over it. Don't try this at home.

Answer 1.68: You will take a total of ten steps. Five of these steps will be east; five will be north. You only need to choose which five of the ten steps are east. There are $\binom{10}{5} = \frac{10!}{5!(10-5)!} = \frac{10\cdot9\cdot8\cdot7\cdot6}{5\cdot4\cdot3\cdot2\cdot1} = \frac{30,240}{120} = 252$ ways to make this choice.

Answer 1.69: Easier than it looks! If the bill is X, then with the tip it is $1.2X$

and $\frac{1.2}{6}$ is just one fifth (i.e., 0.20). So, all you have to do is multiply the quoted bill by 2 and move the decimal place! The bill was 132.67, so times 2 gives 265.34 and move the decimal place to get \$26.534 (you should be able to do that in your head). The key here is that $\frac{1.2}{6}$ multiplied by 132.67 has much more structure than dividing the multiple of 1.2 and 136.67 by 6.

Answer 1.70: We need to figure out whether the area of the large pizza is greater or smaller than the sum of the areas of the medium and small pizzas. The area of a circle is proportional to the square of the diameter. So, let L, M, and S be the diameters of the three pizzas, respectively. We need only take half of each pizza and lay the three halves on the table so that the corners touch and the three diameters form a triangle. If the angle in the corner where the small and medium pizzas touch is a right angle (check it using one corner of the pizza box!), then $L^2 = M^2 + S^2$ holds by Pythagoras' Theorem and the two orders are equally attractive. If the angle is larger than a right angle, then $L^2 > M^2 + S^2$ and the large pizza is the better deal. If the angle is smaller than a right angle, then $L^2 < M^2 + S^2$ and the small pizza plus medium pizza is the better deal. We could alternatively use a single slice from each pizza (with side length equal to the radius of the circle) and form a triangle of side lengths.

Answer 1.71: A sixth order polynomial has six roots. From complex analysis you may recall that the roots to this sort of equation are distributed evenly on a circle in the complex plane of radius equal to the positive real root. So, the roots are $z_k = 2\,e^{\frac{k2\pi i}{6}}$ for $k = 0, 1, 2, 3, 4, 5$. Note that $e^{\pi i} = -1$, so $2e^{\pi i} = -2$, which makes sense.

Answer 1.72: Let us use the standard high school physics equations for linear motion with constant acceleration. There are, however, two good reasons for having a sensible guess before doing any math. First, if our calculations give an answer that is wildly different from our guess, then we have some baseline figure for suspecting we may have made an error in the math. Second, if you start with a guess, it may be that your interviewer will hold up a hand and say "OK, fine, let's move to the next question." He or she may just have wanted to get an estimate out of you to see if you can estimate anything. They may not be interested at all in whether you remember simple equations of motion. So, I would say "Well, I can estimate it using equations for linear motion with constant acceleration, but first let me guess that it is something like ...five seconds and 100 miles per hour" (or whatever *your* guess is).

Now, if we have to go on to the math, I would tell the interviewer that these equations of motion ignore air resistance, and any updraft caused by wind hitting the building. The penny may in fact reach "terminal velocity" (i.e., when drag from the air resistance produces an upward force that perfectly counters the force of gravity, and the penny stops accelerating). Even if it does not reach terminal velocity, my estimate of speed will be an upper bound only because the air resistance and updraft will slow the penny down.

Now, to do the math, we need to know how high the Empire State Building is. From memory it is about 100 floors. Looking at the building I am sitting in, I guess that each floor is probably about four meters, so let us assume it is 400 meters high.

Now, let v be final velocity, u be initial velocity (i.e., zero), D be the 400m traveled, and t be the time taken. We can use $v^2 = u^2 + 2 \cdot g \cdot D$, where $g = 9.8 m/s^2 \approx 10 m/s^2$ is the acceleration due to gravity. Then $v^2 \approx 2 \cdot 10 \cdot 400 = 8,000 m^2/s^2$, so $v \approx 90 m/s$ (because $9^2 = 81$, so $90^2 = 8,100$). I keep track of units so that I can do a "dimensional analysis" (i.e., so that I can quickly confirm that the units of the RHS match the units of the LHS).

Then we can use $v = u + g \cdot t$ to deduce that $90 \approx 0 + 10 \cdot t$, so $t \approx 9s$. So, it takes nine seconds, and it is traveling at 90 m/s when it hits the ground. What is this in miles per hour (mph)? Well, we need to multiply by 60 and then again by 60 to get meters per hour, then divide by 1,609m/mile to get miles per hour. I don't even need the back of an envelope to get $90 \times 60 \times 60/1,609 = 324,000/1,609$, but that's very close to $320,000/1,600$ which is just 200. So, it takes nine seconds and hits the ground at 200 miles per hour. That's not wildly different from my initial guess, so I have no reason to suspect any mathematics error. This is an upper bound on speed, and a lower bound on time taken, but given air resistance and updraft, I would be tempted to halve the calculated speed and double the time taken.

For comparison, a bullet leaves the muzzle of a gun at something like 2,000 feet/s. With roughly three feet to a meter, that is just over 600 m/s. So, our penny's upper bound on speed is roughly one-seventh of the speed of a bullet.

> **Story:** 1. She wore a Walkman and said she could listen to me and the music at the same time. 2. Balding candidate abruptly excused himself. Returned to office a few minutes later, wearing a hairpiece.
>
> Interview Horror Stories from Recruiters
> Reprinted by kind permission of *MBA Style Magazine*
> ©1996–2021 MBA Style Magazine, www.mbastyle.com

Answer 1.73: You are asked to express the integral $f(x) = \int_{t=x}^{\infty} e^{-a\frac{t^2}{2}+bt} dt$ in terms of $N(x)$. If you take that literally, then you will get stuck because that cannot be done for general x. Rather, we will aim to express the integral as a function of $N(g(x))$ for some $g(\cdot)$.

We are aiming for the integrand to take the functional form of the pdf of the standard normal: $n(u) \equiv \frac{1}{\sqrt{2\pi}} e^{-\frac{1}{2}u^2}$. So, we need to "complete the square" in the exponent, change variables, and be sure to remember the $\sqrt{2\pi}$ multiplier. Let us focus on completing the square in the exponent first; we need the minus one-half multiplier, so we can pull that out and then add and subtract half the square of the coefficient of the linear term as follows:

$$
\begin{aligned}
-a\frac{t^2}{2} + bt &= -\frac{1}{2}\left(at^2 - 2bt\right) \\
&= -\frac{1}{2}\left[a\left(t^2 - 2\frac{b}{a}t\right)\right] \\
&= -\frac{1}{2}\left[a\left(t^2 - 2\frac{b}{a}t + \left(\frac{b}{a}\right)^2 - \left(\frac{b}{a}\right)^2\right)\right] \\
&= -\frac{1}{2}\left[a\left(\left(t - \frac{b}{a}\right)^2 - \left(\frac{b}{a}\right)^2\right)\right] \\
&= -\frac{1}{2}a\left(t - \frac{b}{a}\right)^2 + \frac{b^2}{2a}
\end{aligned}
$$

Now for the change of variables. Let $u = \sqrt{a}\left(t - \frac{b}{a}\right)$. Then $du = \sqrt{a}\,dt$, and $t = x \Rightarrow u = \sqrt{a}\left(x - \frac{b}{a}\right)$. So, making the change of variables and collecting terms, we get

$$
\begin{aligned}
f(x) &= \int_{t=x}^{\infty} e^{-a\frac{t^2}{2}+bt}\,dt \\
&= \frac{1}{\sqrt{a}}\int_{u=\sqrt{a}\left(x-\frac{b}{a}\right)}^{\infty} e^{-\frac{1}{2}u^2+\frac{b^2}{2a}}\,du \\
&= e^{\frac{b^2}{2a}}\sqrt{\frac{2\pi}{a}}\left[\frac{1}{\sqrt{2\pi}}\int_{u=\sqrt{a}\left(x-\frac{b}{a}\right)}^{\infty} e^{-\frac{1}{2}u^2}\,du\right]
\end{aligned}
$$

We may rewrite this as follows:

$$
\begin{aligned}
f(x) &= e^{\frac{b^2}{2a}}\sqrt{\frac{2\pi}{a}}\left[\frac{1}{\sqrt{2\pi}}\int_{u=\sqrt{a}\left(x-\frac{b}{a}\right)}^{\infty} e^{-\frac{1}{2}u^2}\,du\right] \\
&= e^{\frac{b^2}{2a}}\sqrt{\frac{2\pi}{a}}\left[1 - N\left(\sqrt{a}\left(x - \frac{b}{a}\right)\right)\right] \\
&= e^{\frac{b^2}{2a}}\sqrt{\frac{2\pi}{a}}N\left(-\sqrt{a}\left(x - \frac{b}{a}\right)\right),
\end{aligned}
$$

where I used the property $[1 - N(z)] = N(-z)$. The skills required to answer this question are very similar to the skills required to manipulate pdfs when deriving option pricing formulae in a Black-Scholes world.

Answer 1.74: Well, if the answer were zero they wouldn't be asking it. Just multiply by the ratio of its conjugate to itself and divide numerator and denominator by x:

$$\lim_{x \to \infty} \left(\sqrt{x^2 + x} - x \right) = \lim_{x \to \infty} \left[\left(\sqrt{x^2 + x} - x \right) \cdot \left(\frac{\sqrt{x^2 + x} + x}{\sqrt{x^2 + x} + x} \right) \right]$$

$$= \lim_{x \to \infty} \left[\frac{x^2 + x - x^2}{\sqrt{x^2 + x} + x} \right]$$

$$= \lim_{x \to \infty} \left[\frac{x}{\sqrt{x^2 + x} + x} \right]$$

$$= \lim_{x \to \infty} \left[\frac{1}{\sqrt{1 + \frac{1}{x}} + 1} \right]$$

$$= \frac{1}{2}$$

Answer 1.75: Let $y = x^x$, then take logs, differentiate implicitly, use the product rule, and then use the definition of y to recover the answer:

$$\ln(y) = x \ln(x)$$

$$\frac{1}{y} \frac{dy}{dx} = \ln(x) + 1$$

$$\frac{dy}{dx} = x^x (1 + \ln(x)).$$

Answer 1.76: Following on from the previous question, $y = x^x$ implies that $\frac{dy}{dx} = x^x (1 + \ln(x))$. Solving the first-order condition $\frac{dy}{dx} = 0$, restricted to $x > 0$, yields immediately $\ln(x) = -1$, and thus that $x = e^{-1} = 1/e$ at the minimum. Plugging this x back into $y = x^x$ yields $y = (1/e)^{1/e} = e^{-1/e}$ at its lowest point.

We should check the second-order condition to confirm that this is a minimum. We can use the product rule and our first derivative result.

$$\frac{dy}{dx} = x^x (1 + \ln(x))$$

$$\implies \frac{d^2 y}{dx^2} = (x^x)^2 (1 + \ln(x)) + x^x \cdot \frac{1}{x}$$

$$= \left(x^{2x} \right) (1 + \ln(x)) + x^{x-1}$$

Plugging in our argmin, $x = 1/e$, yields $\left. \frac{d^2 y}{dx^2} \right|_{x=1/e} = e^{1-1/e} = e^{(e-1)/e} > 0$. So, we have found the minimum.

Note that when $x < 0$, $y = x^x$ is not continuously real valued (nor is it a uniquely-valued function; see Meyerson [1996]). There are, however, some negative x values where $y = x^x$ is unambiguously real valued. For example,

135

at $x = -1$, $y = -1^{-1} = -1$, which is lower than the minimum $e^{-1/e} \approx 0.6922$ that we found above.[62]

Answer 1.77:   If you ask, your interviewer will confirm that he or she expects an exact solution and not some estimate, that you are allowed to flip any coin if you wish, and that the two piles need not have the same number of coins in each. Now go back and try again before peeking any further.

You know the total number of heads in the 100 coins is equal to 10. So, suppose you form one pile of N coins, and one pile of $100 - N$ coins. Let us assume that there are H heads and $N - H$ tails in the first pile (but you do not know H).

Thus there are $10 - H$ heads in the second pile and $90 - (N - H)$ tails in the second pile. How can you get the number of heads in each pile to be the same? Well, you cannot balance H and $10 - H$ because you don't (and can't) know what H is.

What do you know? You know you can flip any coin. What if you flipped every coin in one pile? There is, after all, some sort of constrained symmetry going on here. Let's say you flip every coin in the first pile. Then you have $N - H$ heads in the first pile. Can you choose N so that the number of heads in each pile is the same in that case, that is, $N - H = 10 - H$? Yes, clearly choosing $N = 10$ does the job.

So, all you have to do is split the coins into a pile of 10 coins and a pile of 90 coins, and then flip every coin in the pile of 10 coins. If you had chosen instead to flip every coin in the second pile (i.e., the pile of $100 - N$ coins), the algebra would have yielded exactly the same solution (you should check that).

If you get mixed up in the interview, just plug some numbers in. For example, suppose you start off with 3 heads and 7 tails, say, in the pile of 10 coins, then you must have 7 heads and 83 tails in the pile of 90 coins. You can see immediately that flipping every coin in the pile of 10 coins will give 7 heads in each pile.

In practice, of course, you don't know how many heads are in each pile, just that they are the same number. You might even end up with zero heads in each pile if you happened to initially move all 10 heads into the pile of 10 coins.

If the interviewer had asked instead for the same number of tails in each pile, you would form a pile of 10 coins and a pile of 90 coins, and flip every coin in

---

[62]Meyerson (1996) argues that $x^x = e^{x \log(x)}$ takes the values $e^{x \mathrm{Log}|x| + i\pi n x}$ where $\mathrm{Log}(\cdot)$ is the real-valued logarithm, $\log(x)$ is the complex multiple-valued logarithm, n is even if $x > 0$, n is odd if $x < 0$, and each n corresponds to a "thread" around a spindle-shaped three-dimensional plot (i.e., an Argand plane of complex-valued $z = x^x$ perpendicular to real-valued x, where $-\infty < x < \infty$). I used MATLAB to draw this three-dimensional plot for $-4 \leq x \leq 2$ with $n = -9, -7, -5, -3, -1, 0, 2, 4, 6, 8, 10$ (i.e., 11 threads); it looks cool when rotated in three dimensions. This interview question deals only with the special case $x > 0$ when $n = 0$.

the pile of 90 coins. You can do the same algebra to confirm that. You can even do this from the safety of your home.

Answer 1.78: I will give two different approaches to estimate π. The first approach uses a simple Monte-Carlo simulation. The second uses the Leibniz formula. Other techniques exist.

FIRST SOLUTION

Simulate pairs of random variables (x, y), each distributed uniform on the unit interval $[0, 1]$. These pairs, when plotted in two dimensions, populate a unit square. A circle with unit diameter may be inscribed within the unit square. I just need to count what proportion of points (x, y) satisfy $x^2 + y^2 \leq 1$. The area of the circle dividend by the area of the unit square is $\pi \cdot r^2 / 1 = \pi \cdot \left(\frac{1}{2}\right)^2 / 1 = \pi/4$. So, just multiply the relative proportion of points within the circle by four. Even with sample size only 1,000,000, the answer is generally accurate to within a tenth of a percentage point (i.e., first two decimal places correct).

SECOND SOLUTION

The famous Leibniz formula for π is given in Equation A.20.[63]

$$\frac{\pi}{4} = \sum_{n=0}^{\infty} \frac{(-1)^n}{2n+1} \tag{A.20}$$

Cutting off Equation A.20 at $n = 10,000$ yields an approximation accurate to three decimal places (i.e., 3.14169264359053). Cutting it off at $n = 10,000,000$ is accurate to six decimal places (i.e., 3.14159275358978). Convergence is a little slow.

Note, however, that the partial sums in Leibniz's approximation (like many numerical techniques for pricing options) bounces up and down as n increases, alternately overestimating and then underestimating $\pi/4$. Like acceleration techniques for pricing options, using the average of two successive estimates will therefore improve accuracy (Crack, 2021). So, let $B(N) = 4 \cdot \sum_{n=0}^{N} \frac{(-1)^n}{2n+1}$. Then with $N = 10,000$, $[B(N) + B(N-1)]/2 = 3.14159264859028$, which is accurate to seven decimal places, or eight if you round. With $N = 10,000,000$, $[B(N) + B(N-1)]/2 = 3.14159265358979$, which is accurate to 14 decimal places.

Answer 1.79: The short answer is that sitting in any position from 1 o'clock to 11 o'clock is equally likely to win the prize, with probability $p = 1/11$ for each seat. If you are peeking here for hints, go back now and think again.

---

[63]Note that $\arctan(z) = \sum_{k=0}^{\infty} \frac{(-1)^k z^{2k+1}}{2k+1}$ for $|z| \leq 1$ and $z \neq -1$ (Abramowitz and Stegun, 1972, p. 81). Plug in $z = 1$ to get the Leibniz formula.

The setup of this problem is known as a "random walk on a circle." The solution overlaps with the "gambler's ruin" problem. So, I will describe how someone seated at the table can win, in terms of the random walk on a circle, and then I will remind you of the gambler's ruin problem, and use its solution to solve our problem.

Assume you are seated at the ith hour of the clock-table, for some $1 \leq i \leq 11$. Now imagine an arc painted on the outer edge of the clock-table, where the arc records who has been visited by the prize as it is passed around. This arc begins as a single blob of paint at the 12 o'clock position, but grows in clockwise or counter-clockwise jumps as the prize is passed around. In order for you, seated at the ith hour, to win the prize, every other guest has to touch it before you. In order for this to happen, two specific events must happen.

First, the arc that records who has touched the prize so far must jump to a person sitting next to you at either the $(i-1)^{th}$ or $(i+1)^{th}$ hour. (Note that we are counting modulo-12 here, with no zero. So, in the case $i = 1$, $i - 1 = 12$ and the arc is already touching the $(i-1)^{th}$ hour.) Indeed, the game cannot conclude unless a person next to you touches the prize; this happens with probability unity. Given the symmetry of the argument that is about to follow, we can, without loss of generality, assume that the arc reaches the $(i+1)^{th}$ hour before it reaches the $(i-1)^{th}$ hour.

Second, if the arc has reached the $(i+1)^{th}$ hour before it reaches the $(i-1)^{th}$ hour (e.g., you are sitting at four o'clock, and the prize arrives at five o'clock, not yet having arrived at three o'clock), then in order for you to win the prize, the prize must walk right around the clock again, and reach the $(i-1)^{th}$ hour (three o'clock in my example) without landing in your hands in the interim. No matter what happens next, you know that you have won the game if the prize walks its way a net of 10 seats clockwise from the $(i+1)^{th}$ hour without ever backtracking far enough to land in your hands. Another way to say this is that if we count the net clockwise progress of the prize from the $(i+1)^{th}$ hour, this net balance must reach 10 hours *before* it reaches -1 hours (note that reaching -1 hours is not needed for the game to conclude). We can now use a gambler's ruin argument to find the probability of this event.

Suppose that you are a gambler with \$10 in your hand. Your opponent has \$1 in his hand. A fair coin is tossed repeatedly. If it is heads, you gain a dollar from your opponent, and if it is tails you lose a dollar to your opponent. If your wealth reaches \$11 (i.e., your net balance increases by \$1 and your opponent is ruined), then the game stops and you win. If, however, your wealth reaches \$0 (i.e., your net balance drops by \$10 and you are ruined), then the game stops and your opponent wins.

The probability that you are ruined in this gamble is the same as the probability that your opponent's wealth steps up by a net change of \$10, never having reached a net change of $-\$1$. Given that the advance-decline probabilities are the same in both games (i.e., 50-50), the probability of your ruin is the same as the probability of the prize walking a net of 10 hours clockwise, never having walked a net of -1 hours. So, if we can find the probability of your gambling ruin, we have the answer to our clock-table game.

Consider a more general gambler's ruin problem. You have $\$n$ in your pocket (in our case, $\$n = 10$). Your opponent has $\$m$ in his pocket (in our case, $\$m = 1$). A fair coin is tossed repeatedly. If it is heads, you gain a dollar from your opponent, and if it is tails you lose a dollar to your opponent. The game continues until one of the players is ruined. Let $P(i)$ be the probability that a player with $\$i$ in his hand is ultimately ruined playing exactly this game, for $0 \leq i \leq n+m$.

Now consider some intermediary balance $\$i$ where $1 \leq i \leq n+m-1$. There is half a chance that the next coin toss is favorable, and there is half a chance that the next coin toss is unfavorable. So, by the total probability theorem, we have Equation A.21.[64]

$$\begin{aligned} P(i) &= P(\text{ruin}|\text{favorable coin toss}) \cdot P(\text{favorable coin toss}) + \\ &\qquad P(\text{ruin}|\text{unfavorable coin toss}) \cdot P(\text{unfavorable coin toss}) \\ &= P(i+1) \cdot \frac{1}{2} + P(i-1) \cdot \frac{1}{2} \end{aligned} \tag{A.21}$$

Multiplying Equation A.21 through by 2 and rearranging, we get the second-order recurrence in Equation A.22.

$$P(i+1) - 2P(i) + P(i-1) = 0, \text{ for } 1 \leq i \leq n+m-1 \tag{A.22}$$

To solve a second-order recurrence, we need two boundary conditions. In our case, $P(0) = 1$ (you are already ruined), and $P(n+m) = 0$ (you already won).

The (homogeneous) characteristic equation for the recurrence in Equation A.22 is given by Equation A.23.

$$\lambda^2 - 2\lambda + 1 = 0 \tag{A.23}$$

This quadratic equation has repeated characteristic roots at $\lambda_0 = 1$. So, we are looking for solutions of the form given in Equation A.24.[65]

$$P(i) = A \cdot 1^i + B \cdot i \cdot 1^i = A + B \cdot i \tag{A.24}$$

Plugging the boundary conditions into Equation A.24, we quickly deduce that $A = 1$ and $B = -1/(n+m)$. It follows that the probability of ruin is given by Equation A.25.

$$P(i) = \frac{n+m-i}{n+m} \tag{A.25}$$

[64]The total probability theorem is just the familiar result that for mutually exclusive events $A_i, 1 \leq i \leq n$, such that $\sum_{i=1}^{n} P(A_i) = 1$, $P(B) = \sum_{i=1}^{n} P(B|A_i)P(A_i)$.

[65]If the two roots were distinct, say λ_1 and λ_2, we would seek general solution $P(i) = A \cdot \lambda_1^i + B \cdot \lambda_2^i$. With repeated roots λ_0, we seek general solution $P(i) = A \cdot \lambda_0^i + B \cdot i \cdot \lambda_0^i$.

Back to our clock-table game, we plug $i = 10$, $n = 10$ and $m = 1$ into Equation A.25 to find that the probability of ruin (and of winning the clock-table game) is given by $p = 1/11$, as expected. More generally, for g guests seated around a circular table, the probability that any guest wins the prize is equally likely and given by $p = 1/g$.

Answer 1.80: A symmetric $n \times n$ real-valued matrix A is said to be positive definite if for all non-zero $n \times 1$ real-valued vectors $\vec{z}$, we have that $\vec{z}' A \vec{z} > 0$, where $\vec{z}'$ is the transpose of $\vec{z}$ (Ayers, 1962). Similarly, A is negative definite, positive semi-definite, or negative semi-definite, if under the same conditions $\vec{z}' A \vec{z} < 0$, $\vec{z}' A \vec{z} \geq 0$, or $\vec{z}' A \vec{z} \leq 0$, respectively. Matrices that are none of the above are called indefinite.

These definitions can also be given in terms of eigenvalues. A symmetric $n \times n$ real-valued matrix A is positive definite, negative definite, positive semi-definite, or negative semi-definite, respectively, if and only if all of the eigenvalues of A are positive, negative, non-negative, or non-positive, respectively. Indefinite matrices have both positive and negative eigenvalues.

A more general definition of a positive definite matrix allows that A and $\vec{z}'$ be complex valued. In that case, an $n \times n$ Hermitian matrix A (i.e., one that is equal to its complex conjugate transpose) is positive definite if for all complex-valued $n \times 1$ vectors $\vec{z}$, the real part of $\vec{z}^* A \vec{z} > 0$, where $\vec{z}^*$ is the complex conjugate of the transpose of $\vec{z}$.

All the above assumes that the matrix be symmetric (if real-valued) or Hermitian (if complex valued). The definition of a positive definite matrix can, however, be generalized to non-symmetric and non-Hermitian matrices (`mathworld.wolfram.com`). In that case, the definition is applied only to the symmetric part or Hermition part of the matrix, respectively.[66]

What about portfolio theory applications, theoretical and otherwise? In practice, portfolio optimization tools often assume that the VCV matrix is positive definite (Kwan, 2010). For example, to obtain the standard Markowitz frontier assuming short selling, you need that the variance-covariance (VCV) matrix be invertible (Crack, 2020b). A positive definite matrix is invertible, but a positive semi-definite matrix might have a zero eigenvalue, and therefore be non-invertible.

Suppose that $\vec{R}$ is an $n \times 1$ vector of future random returns to financial assets. Let V be the population VCV matrix with $\sigma_{ij} = \mathrm{cov}(R_i, R_j)$ in the ij^{th} position. Then, V is positive semi-definite, because for any real-valued $n \times 1$ vector $\vec{z}$,

$$\vec{z}' V \vec{z} = \mathrm{var}\left(\vec{z}' \vec{R}\right) \geq 0. \tag{A.26}$$

---

[66] A square matrix A may be written as $A = A_S + A_A$, where $A_S = \frac{1}{2}(A + A')$ is the symmetric part of A, and $A_A = \frac{1}{2}(A - A')$ is the anti-symmetric part of A. An analogous result holds for Hermition matrices, using the complex conjugate transpose.

If none of the eigenvalues is zero, then V is also positive definite, and therefore invertible. If $\vec{z}$ in Equation A.26 is a sensible vector of portfolio weights, then $\vec{z}'\vec{R}$ is the future return to that portfolio. Note, however, that Equation A.26 does not require that $\vec{z}$ be a sensible vector of portfolio weights.

Note that in the simple theoretical classroom example with only two assets, an assumption of perfect negative correlation between their future returns allows a zero-risk portfolio to be constructed (see Answer 3.20). In this case, the population VCV matrix must be positive semi-definite, but not positive definite (because weights can be chosen to create a zero-variance portfolio). Thus, the population VCV matrix is non-invertible in this case (it must have determinant zero, and a zero eigenvalue). What happens if the returns to the two assets are assumed to be perfectly *positively* correlated?

Finally, in the case of the standard sample VCV matrix, $\hat{V}$, if you have fewer time series observations than you have financial assets in the cross section (e.g., one year of daily observations on the S&P 500 stocks), then $\hat{V}$ will be non-invertible, with at least one eigenvalue equal to zero. Note that numerical issues with finite precision mean that in some cases, a sample VCV matrix may even be negative definite.

Answer 1.81:   In practice, how do you test whether a square matrix is positive definite? You cannot possibly test whether $\vec{z}'A\vec{z} > 0$, for all non-zero $\vec{z}'$. So, let us look at several techniques. Then we will discuss which one is computationally easiest without using pre-canned routines.

First, I would like to use Sylvester's criterion, but we need to review some terms. A sub-matrix obtained by deleting the ith row and the jth column of an $n \times n$ matrix is an $(n-1) \times (n-1)$ matrix. The determinant of this sub-matrix is called a minor (or, more fully, a minor determinant of order $n-1$), and is sometimes denoted $M_{i,j}$. If any two rows $\{i_1, i_2\}$ and any two columns $\{j_1, j_2\}$ are deleted, then the determinant of the resulting sub-matrix is a minor of order $n-2$, denoted M_{i_1, i_2, j_1, j_2}, and so on. If the numbering of the deleted row(s) is *identical* to the numbering of the deleted column(s), then the determinant of the resulting sub-matrix is a *principal* minor (of order k, where $n-k$ rows and the same $n-k$ columns have been deleted). The determinants of the *upper-left* sub-matrices, in particular, are known as the "leading principal minors" (Ayers, 1962).

So, for example, for a 5×5 matrix, deleting the first row and the fifth column produces a sub-matrix whose determinant, $M_{1,5}$, is a minor. It is not, however, a principal minor, leading or otherwise. Deleting the second row and the second column of the original matrix produces a sub-matrix whose determinant, $M_{2,2}$, is a principal minor, but it is not a leading principal minor. Finally, deleting rows $k:5$ and columns $k:5$, for any $k \in \{2, 3, 4, 5\}$ produces a sub-matrix whose determinant, $M_{k:5, k:5}$, is a leading principal minor. (Note that deleting no rows and no columns of the original matrix produces, trivially, a sub-matrix whose determinant is a minor, a principal minor, and a leading principal minor.)

Now, **Sylvester's criterion** says that a symmetric real-valued matrix A is positive definite if and only if the determinants of all $m \times m$ upper-left sub-matrices (i.e., all leading principal minors) are positive (Gilbert, 1991). Similarly, but slightly more taxing, a symmetric real valued matrix is positive semi-definite if and only if *all* principal minors, leading or otherwise, are non-negative (Swamy, 1973). So, in that case, the determinants of all sub-matrices obtained by deleting any group of identically numbered rows and columns must be non-negative.

For example, the matrix

$$A = \begin{pmatrix} 1 & 2 & 3 \\ 2 & 5 & 6 \\ 3 & 6 & 9 \end{pmatrix} \tag{A.27}$$

has upper-left sub-matrices

$$(1), \quad \begin{pmatrix} 1 & 2 \\ 2 & 5 \end{pmatrix}, \quad \text{and} \quad \begin{pmatrix} 1 & 2 & 3 \\ 2 & 5 & 6 \\ 3 & 6 & 9 \end{pmatrix}.$$

The determinants of these three matrices (i.e., the leading principal minors) are

$$M_{2:3,2:3} = A_{11} = 1,$$

$$M_{3,3} = A_{11}A_{22} - A_{21}A_{12} = 1 \cdot 5 - 2 \cdot 2 = 1, \text{ and}$$

$$+A_{11}(A_{22}A_{33} - A_{23}A_{32}) - A_{12}(A_{21}A_{33} - A_{23}A_{31}) + A_{13}(A_{21}A_{32} - A_{22}A_{31}) =$$
$$+1(5 \cdot 9 - 6 \cdot 6) - 2(2 \cdot 9 - 6 \cdot 3) + 3(2 \cdot 6 - 5 \cdot 3) = 0.$$

In this case, the third leading principal minor is non-positive. So, by Sylvester's criterion, the matrix A is not positive definite. Also, of course, in this case, the overall determinant is zero, which implies that at least one of the eigenvalues is zero (because the determinant of a matrix is the product of its eigenvalues). So, the matrix A cannot be positive definite because not all of its eigenvalues are positive.

Consider, however, the matrix B, differing in only one element from A:

$$B = \begin{pmatrix} 1 & 2 & 3 \\ 2 & 5 & 6 \\ 3 & 6 & 10 \end{pmatrix}. \tag{A.28}$$

The matrix B has leading principal minors 1, 1, and 1, all positive (I leave you to check that). So, by Sylvester's criterion, B is positive definite.

Second, in theory, you can calculate all eigenvalues of a matrix and check whether they are positive. For matrices of small dimensions, this is relatively straightforward. Given square matrix A, the eigenvalues λ solve $A\vec{z} = \lambda\vec{z}$, for any non-zero $\vec{z}$ (Ayers, 1962). Rewriting yields $(\lambda I - A)\vec{z} = 0$ for any non-zero $\vec{z}$ and conformal identity matrix I. This, in turn, requires that the determinant of $(\lambda I - A)$ equals zero.

For example, in the case of matrix A in Equation A.27, solving $\det(\lambda I - A) = 0$ yields the characteristic equation (i.e., the characteristic polynomial equated to zero)

$$f(\lambda) = +\lambda^3 - 15\lambda^2 + 10\lambda = 0. \tag{A.29}$$

Equation A.29 can be factored as $f(\lambda) = \lambda(\lambda^2 - 15\lambda + 10) = 0$, with eigenvalue roots 0, $(15 + \sqrt{185})\big/2$, $(15 - \sqrt{185})\big/2$. The eigenvalues are non-negative, but one is zero. So, A is positive semi-definite, but not positive definite.

In contrast, in the case of matrix B in Equation A.28, solving $\det(\lambda I - B) = 0$ yields the characteristic equation

$$f(\lambda) = +\lambda^3 - 16\lambda^2 + 16\lambda - 1 = 0. \tag{A.30}$$

Equation A.30 can be factored as $f(\lambda) = (\lambda - 1)(\lambda^2 - 15\lambda + 1) = 0$, with eigenvalue roots 1, $(15 + \sqrt{221})\big/2$, $(15 - \sqrt{221})\big/2$. We can see that the eigenvalues are all positive. So, the matrix B is positive definite.

Let me add some notes here. As an exercise, can you confirm, for each of matrices A and B, that the product of the eigenvalues equals the determinant, and the sum of the eigenvalues equals the trace? Note also that the diagonal elements of a real-valued symmetric positive definite matrix must be positive (just take $\vec{z}$ to be the unit vector with a 1 in the ith position to see that diagonal terms $A_{ii} = \vec{z}'A\vec{z} > 0$ for each i). Can you confirm also that the characteristic polynomial is monic (i.e., the coefficient of λ^n is one), the coefficient of λ^{n-1} is $-1 \cdot$ trace, where trace is the trace of the matrix, and the constant is $(-1)^n \cdot$ determinant, where determinant is the determinant of the matrix?

Third, we may be able to use Descartes' rule of signs without actually solving for all eigenvalues. For example, Looking at Equation A.30, we see that there are three sign changes in the coefficients. The number of positive roots of the characteristic polynomial (counting multiple roots separately) is either equal to the number of sign changes between consecutive non-zero coefficients, or it is less than that by an even number (Spiegel, 1956). In the case of Equation A.30, there must be either three or one positive root. Conversely, if we look at $f(-\lambda)$, we see that there are no sign changes in the coefficients. So, the count of negative roots equals zero. Clearly $\lambda = 0$ is not a root of Equation A.30, so we deduce that there must be exactly three positive roots, without actually having to factor the polynomial.

Fourth, you can use a Cholesky factorization (or decomposition) of the matrix. Suppose that A is a symmetric positive definite real-valued matrix. Then A may be factored, or decomposed, as $A = U'U$ where U is a unique upper-triangular matrix (or, equivalently, as $A = LL'$, where $L = U'$

is a unique lower-triangular matrix) with real positive diagonal entries (Press et al., 1996, p. 96–97; Bronshtein et el., 2004, p. 890).[67] This decomposition is sometimes referred to as taking the square root of the matrix (Press et al., 1996, p. 96). Then, for real-valued $\vec{z}$, $\vec{z}'A\vec{z} = \vec{z}'(U'U)\vec{z} = (U\vec{z})'(U\vec{z}) = \vec{y}'\vec{y} = \|\vec{y}\|_2^2 = \sum_{i=1}^{n} y_i^2 \geq 0$, for the $n \times 1$ vector $\vec{y} \equiv U\vec{z}$.[68] If $\vec{z} \neq 0$, the latter inequality is strict.

Matrix A must be positive definite, given the above decomposition, because if U, in the Cholesky decomposition, has positive real diagonal entries, then U is invertible.[69] It follows that $U\vec{z} = 0$ if and only if $\vec{z} = 0$ (just multiply through by U^{-1}). It follows that $\vec{z}'A\vec{z} = 0$ if and only if $\vec{z} = 0$, and thus that A is positive definite.

So, how in practice do we obtain the matrix U in the Cholesky decomposition? Consider our matrix A in Equation A.27. Rewrite it as in Equation A.31

$$A = \begin{pmatrix} 1 & 2 & 3 \\ 2 & 5 & 6 \\ 3 & 6 & 9 \end{pmatrix} = \begin{pmatrix} A_{11} & A'_{2:3,1} \\ A_{2:3,1} & A_{2:3,2:3} \end{pmatrix}, \tag{A.31}$$

where

$$A_{11} = 1, \quad A_{2:3,1} = \begin{pmatrix} 2 \\ 3 \end{pmatrix}, \quad \text{and } A_{2:3,2:3} = \begin{pmatrix} 5 & 6 \\ 6 & 10 \end{pmatrix}.$$

Then, if there exists upper-triangular U such that $A = U'U$, we must have that

$$A = \begin{pmatrix} A_{11} & A'_{2:n,1} \\ A_{2:n,1} & A_{2:n,2:n} \end{pmatrix} = U'U$$

$$= \begin{pmatrix} U_{11} & 0 \\ U'_{1,2:n} & U'_{2:n,2:n} \end{pmatrix} \cdot \begin{pmatrix} U_{11} & U_{1,2:n} \\ 0 & U_{2:n,2:n} \end{pmatrix}$$

$$= \begin{pmatrix} U_{11}^2 & U_{11}U_{1,2:n} \\ U_{11}U'_{1,2:n} & U'_{1,2:n}U_{1,2:n} + U'_{2:n,2:n}U_{2:n,2:n} \end{pmatrix},$$

where 0 is a conformal row or column vector of zeroes, as appropriate.

---

[67]Note that Cholesky decomposition also generalizes to a positive definite Hermitian matrix $A = U^*U$, where U^* is the complex conjugate of the transpose of U. I will restrict attention to the real-valued case only.

[68]I used the standard L^p norm $\|\vec{y}\|_p = (|y_1|^p + |y_2|^p + \cdots + |y_n|^p)^{\frac{1}{p}}$.

[69]For example, $\begin{pmatrix} a & b & c \\ 0 & d & e \\ 0 & 0 & f \end{pmatrix} \begin{pmatrix} 1/a & -b/(ad) & (be-cd)/(afd) \\ 0 & 1/d & -e/(fd) \\ 0 & 0 & 1/f \end{pmatrix} = \begin{pmatrix} 1 & 0 & 0 \\ 0 & 1 & 0 \\ 0 & 0 & 1 \end{pmatrix}$.

Similarly, $\begin{pmatrix} a & 0 & 0 \\ b & c & 0 \\ d & e & f \end{pmatrix} \begin{pmatrix} 1/a & 0 & 0 \\ -b/(ac) & 1/c & 0 \\ (be-cd)/(acf) & -e/(cf) & 1/f \end{pmatrix} = \begin{pmatrix} 1 & 0 & 0 \\ 0 & 1 & 0 \\ 0 & 0 & 1 \end{pmatrix}$.

By comparing terms, we can deduce that

$$U_{11} = \sqrt{A_{11}} \qquad (A.32)$$

$$U_{1,2:n} = \frac{1}{\sqrt{A_{11}}} A'_{2:n,1} \qquad (A.33)$$

$$U_{2:n,1} = 0 \ (\text{conformal}) \qquad (A.34)$$

$$A_{2:n,2:n} - U'_{1,2:n} U_{1,2:n} = U'_{2:n,2:n} U_{2:n,2:n}, \qquad (A.35)$$

where Equation A.32, A.33, and A.34 enable us to solve for the first row and the first column of U, and Equation A.35 may be rewritten as Equation A.36

$$S = U'_{2:n,2:n} U_{2:n,2:n}, \qquad (A.36)$$

where

$$
\begin{aligned}
S &= A_{2:n,2:n} - U'_{1,2:n} U_{1,2:n} \\
&= A_{2:n,2:n} - \frac{1}{A_{11}} A_{2:n,1} A'_{2:n,1}
\end{aligned}
$$

is the Schur complement of A_{11} (Haynsworth, 1968).[70] The $(n-1) \times (n-1)$ matrix S can easily be shown to be positive definite if A is positive definite.[71] That is, we have reduced the problem by one dimension, having identified the first row and first column of U. Next, we repeat the process, applied to $S = U'_{2:n,2:n} U_{2:n,2:n}$ to identify the first row and first column of $U_{2:n,2:n}$. After having calculated the Schur complement matrix $n-1$ times, we will have solved for all rows (and columns) of U. That fact that the lower-right sub-matrices of U are all upper-triangular and positive definite guarantees that the process converges (assuming, of course, that the original matrix A is positive definite).

For example, for matrices A and B from Equations A.27 and Equation A.28, I get

$$A = \begin{pmatrix} 1 & 2 & 3 \\ 2 & 5 & 6 \\ 3 & 6 & 9 \end{pmatrix} = U'_A U_A = \begin{pmatrix} 1 & 0 & 0 \\ 2 & 1 & 0 \\ 3 & 0 & 0 \end{pmatrix} \begin{pmatrix} 1 & 2 & 3 \\ 0 & 1 & 0 \\ 0 & 0 & 0 \end{pmatrix}, \text{ and}$$

$$B = \begin{pmatrix} 1 & 2 & 3 \\ 2 & 5 & 6 \\ 3 & 6 & 10 \end{pmatrix} = U'_B U_B = \begin{pmatrix} 1 & 0 & 0 \\ 2 & 1 & 0 \\ 3 & 0 & 1 \end{pmatrix} \begin{pmatrix} 1 & 2 & 3 \\ 0 & 1 & 0 \\ 0 & 0 & 1 \end{pmatrix}.$$

---

[70] More generally, if H is an $n \times n$ Hermitian matrix, and we have, without loss of generality, permuted the matrix to put a non-singular matrix H_{11} into the principal sub-matrix position, so that $H = \begin{pmatrix} H_{11} & H_{12} \\ H_{12}^* & H_{22} \end{pmatrix}$, where H_{12}^* is the complex conjugate transpose of H_{12}, then $K_{22} = H_{22} - H_{12}^* H_{11}^{-1} H_{12}$ is the Schur complement of H_{11}, and $\det(H) = \det(H_{11})\det(K_{22})$ (Haynsworth, 1968).

[71] Given any $n \times 1$ vector $\vec{y} \neq 0$, let $x = - A'_{2:n,1} \cdot \vec{y}/A_{11}$, then because A is positive definite, we must have that $\vec{y}' S \vec{y} = \begin{pmatrix} x \\ \vec{y} \end{pmatrix}' A \begin{pmatrix} x \\ \vec{y} \end{pmatrix} = \begin{pmatrix} x \\ \vec{y} \end{pmatrix}' \begin{pmatrix} A_{11} & A'_{2:n,1} \\ A_{2:n,1} & A_{2:n,2:n} \end{pmatrix} \begin{pmatrix} x \\ \vec{y} \end{pmatrix} > 0$. Thus, S is positive definite.

We can see that the elements of the leading diagonal of U_B are all positive, and thus that B is positive definite. The elements of the leading diagonal of U_A are not all positive, however, and thus A is not positive definite.

Note, however, that in some cases, where the original matrix is not positive definite, the Cholesky decomposition process halts before completion, failing to identify U, and indicating that the original matrix is not positive definite. For example, if $A_{11} = -1$, then the decomposition will fail to identify U.

In summary, for a small matrix, Sylvester's criterion and the Cholesky decomposition appear roughly equally easy to program from scratch and would consume essentially no computing time. Solving for all eigenvalues is easy enough for matrices no larger than 4×4, but Descartes' rule of signs might fail to be specific enough to conclude whether a matrix is positive definite. For a large matrix, if you cannot use any pre-canned routines, the outcome of the Cholesky decomposition is likely to be the most efficient means of determining whether a matrix is positive definite.

Answer 1.82: To identify local extrema of a function of two variables, we need to conduct the second (partial) derivative test (Abramowitz and Stegun, 1972, p. 14; Spiegel, 1981, p. 164). Let me review the test procedure, and then we can apply the test to the case $f(x, y) = x^3 + y^3 - 2xy$.

Suppose that $f(x, y)$ is a function of two variables whose second partial derivatives exist. Then Equation A.37 gives the Hessian matrix of $f(x, y)$.

$$H(x, y) = \begin{pmatrix} \frac{\partial^2 f(x,y)}{\partial x^2} & \frac{\partial^2 f(x,y)}{\partial x \partial y} \\ \frac{\partial^2 f(x,y)}{\partial y \partial x} & \frac{\partial^2 f(x,y)}{\partial y^2} \end{pmatrix} = \begin{pmatrix} f_{xx}(x, y) & f_{xy}(x, y) \\ f_{yx}(x, y) & f_{yy}(x, y) \end{pmatrix} \qquad (A.37)$$

Let $D(x, y)$ be the determinant of H. Then $D(x, y)$ is called the discriminant of the second derivative test, and is given in Equation A.38.

$$\begin{aligned} D(x, y) = \det[H(x, y)] &= f_{xx}(x, y) f_{yy}(x, y) - f_{xy}(x, y) f_{yx}(x, y) \\ &= f_{xx}(x, y) f_{yy}(x, y) - [f_{xy}(x, y)]^2 \qquad (A.38) \end{aligned}$$

Suppose now that (x_c, y_c) is a critical point of the function $f(x, y)$. That is, $f_x(x_c, y_c) = 0$ and $f_y(x_c, y_c) = 0$. Then, we have the following rules.

- If $D(x_c, y_c) > 0$ and $f_{xx}(x_c, y_c) > 0$, then (x_c, y_c) is a **local minimum** of the function $f(x, y)$.

- If $D(x_c, y_c) > 0$ and $f_{xx}(x_c, y_c) < 0$, then (x_c, y_c) is a **local maximum** of the function $f(x, y)$.

- If $D(x_c, y_c) < 0$, then (x_c, y_c) is a **saddle point** of the function $f(x, y)$.

- If $D(x_c, y_c) = 0$, then the test is **inconclusive**, and (x_c, y_c) could be any of a local maximum, local minimum, or saddle point of the function $f(x, y)$.

There are several notes to add to this.

- If f is a function of three or more variables, then the determinant of H does not carry enough information for us to discriminate between cases. Instead, we need to look at whether H is positive definite (local minimum), negative definite (local maximum), indefinite (saddle point), or either positive semi-definite or negative semi-definite (inconclusive).

- Note that the first two rules in the list use the sign of $f_{xx}(x, y)$ to distinguish between a local minimum and a local maximum. For the two-variable case, let λ_1 and λ_2 be the eigenvalues of H. Recall, as discussed on p. 143, that the product of the eigenvalues equals the determinant, and the sum of the eigenvalues equals the trace. That is,

$$\begin{aligned} \text{trace}(H) &= f_{xx}(x, y) + f_{yy}(x, y) = \lambda_1 + \lambda_2 \\ \det(H) &= f_{xx}(x, y) f_{yy}(x, y) - [f_{xy}(x, y)]^2 = \lambda_1 \cdot \lambda_2. \end{aligned}$$

  From our discussion in Answer 1.80, however, we know that H is positive definite if and only if $\lambda_1, \lambda_2 > 0$. This condition is equivalent to having $\lambda_1 \cdot \lambda_2 > 0$ and $\lambda_1 > 0$, or $\lambda_1 \cdot \lambda_2 > 0$ and $\lambda_1 + \lambda_2 > 0$, or $\lambda_1 \cdot \lambda_2 > 0$ and $\lambda_2 > 0$. So, the first rule, "If $D(x_c, y_c) > 0$ and $f_{xx}(x_c, y_c) > 0$, then (x_c, y_c) is a local minimum of the function $f(x, y)$" can, in fact, be re-stated using either $f_{xx}(x, y) > 0$, or $f_{yy}(x, y) > 0$, or $\text{trace}(H) = f_{xx}(x, y) + f_{yy}(x, y) > 0$. You should confirm that the second, third, and fourth rules refer directly to the signs of the eigenvalues needed to ensure that H is negative definite, indefinite, or semi-definite, respectively.

- Note that $D(x, y)$ and $f_{xx}(x, y)$ are the leading principal minors of $H(x, y)$ (see Answer 1.81 for discussion of Sylvester's criterion). So, for example, confirming that these are both positive confirms that H is positive definite.

- In the case that the second derivative test is inconclusive, further analysis is required. You may need to look at behavior of higher-order derivatives at the critical point, or you may need to think geometrically. For example, consider the simple function $f(x, y) = x^2 + y^2$. Although this is a very simple case, the function is so flat at the origin that we have $D(0, 0) = 0$, and the second derivative test is inconclusive (try plotting $f(x, y) = x^{2n} + y^{2n}$ for any small positive integer n to see this flatness accentuated; the test in inconclusive in these cases too). Direct inspection, however, tells us that $f(x, y) = x^2 + y^2$ is cup-shaped with a global minimum at $(0, 0)$ (in fact, it is an elliptic paraboloid).

Now to our function $f(x, y) = x^3 + y^3 - 2xy$. We begin with the first order conditions as shown in Equation A.39 and Equation A.40.

$$\begin{aligned} f_x(x, y) &= 3x^2 - 2y = 0 & \text{(A.39)} \\ f_y(x, y) &= 3y^2 - 2x = 0 & \text{(A.40)} \end{aligned}$$

Solving Equation A.39 for y yields Equation A.41.

$$y = \frac{3}{2}x^2 \tag{A.41}$$

Plugging Equation A.41 into Equation A.40 in place of y, yields

$$3\left(\frac{3}{2}x^2\right)^2 - 2x = 0$$

$$\Rightarrow \frac{27}{4}x^4 - 2x = 0$$

$$\Rightarrow x\left(\frac{27}{4}x^3 - 2\right),$$

which implies either that $x = 0$ or that $x = \frac{2}{3}$. Plugging these solutions for x back into Equation A.41 yields $y = 0$ and $y = \frac{2}{3}$, respectively (given the symmetry in $f(x, y)$ we had to get symmetry in the critical point co-ordinates). Thus, the two critical points are $(x, y) = (0, 0)$ and $(x, y) = \left(\frac{2}{3}, \frac{2}{3}\right)$.

Now we calculate the Hessian matrix as shown in Equation A.42.

$$H(x, y) = \begin{pmatrix} f_{xx}(x, y) & f_{xy}(x, y) \\ f_{yx}(x, y) & f_{yy}(x, y) \end{pmatrix} = \begin{pmatrix} 6x & -2 \\ -2 & 6y \end{pmatrix} \tag{A.42}$$

So, the discriminant is $D(x, y) = \det[H(x, y)] = 36xy - 4$. At $(x, y) = (0, 0)$ we get $D(0, 0) = -4 < 0$, so $(x, y) = (0, 0)$ is a saddle point. At $(x, y) = \left(\frac{2}{3}, \frac{2}{3}\right)$, we get $D\left(\frac{2}{3}, \frac{2}{3}\right) = 12 > 0$. We have $f_{xx}\left(\frac{2}{3}, \frac{2}{3}\right) = 4 > 0$, so $\left(\frac{2}{3}, \frac{2}{3}\right)$ is a local minimum.

Answer 1.83:   At first glance, this sounds like a statistics question. I put it in this chapter, however, because it follows naturally from the previous two questions about matrices and their properties. I discuss two solution techniques. The first uses Sylvester's criterion, and the second uses eigenvalues.

FIRST SOLUTION

We have that the correlation matrix, C, of the three random variables, is given by Equation A.43.

$$C = \begin{pmatrix} 1 & \rho & \rho \\ \rho & 1 & \rho \\ \rho & \rho & 1 \end{pmatrix} \tag{A.43}$$

Before hitting this problem over the head with any deep analysis, ask yourself what values of ρ are possible in Equation A.43. Well, $\rho = 0$ is perfectly feasible, because that is what we would get if the three random variables were statistically independent of each other. Also, $\rho = 1$ is perfectly feasible, because that is what we would get if each random variable were perfectly correlated with each other. For example, if the three random variables are

$$X_1 = aY + d$$
$$X_2 = bY + e$$
$$X_3 = cY + f,$$

where $a, b, c > 0$, for some common random variable Y, then we would have $\rho = 1$ (adding a constant or multiplying by a positive constant has no effect on correlation; see also Question 4.9 and its answer).

What about $\rho = -1$. Well it is perfectly feasible for X_1 and X_2 to be perfectly negatively correlated, and for X_2 and X_3 to be perfectly negatively correlated, but then X_1 and X_3 would be perfectly positively correlated. So, $\rho = -1$ is not possible. So, at first glance, it looks like positive correlations ρ are feasible, but we cannot step too far into negative territory.

Now, given any correlation matrix, C, for three random variables X_1, X_2, X_3, C is also the VCV matrix for the random variables Z_1, Z_2, Z_3, where $Z_i \equiv (X_i - \mu_i)/\sigma_i$, for $i = 1, 2, 3$ (via simple reasoning from first principals as mentioned when referring to Question 4.9, above). That is, any correlation matrix is also a VCV matrix for the standardized variables.

We know, however, from Answer 1.80, that any population VCV matrix must be positive semi-definite (see the discussion on p. 140, just before Equation A.26).

We know, from Sylvester's criterion, that a matrix is positive semi-definite if and only if all principal minors are non-negative (see discussion on p. 142). That is, the determinants of all sub-matrices obtained by deleting same-numbered rows and columns in C are non-negative. There are seven such sub-matrices, but only three unique ones, as shown in Equation A.44.

$$(1),\quad \begin{pmatrix} 1 & \rho \\ \rho & 1 \end{pmatrix},\quad \begin{pmatrix} 1 & \rho & \rho \\ \rho & 1 & \rho \\ \rho & \rho & 1 \end{pmatrix} \tag{A.44}$$

These matrices produce three principal minors, set here to be non-negative.

$$
\begin{aligned}
1 &\geq 0 \\
1 - \rho^2 &\geq 0 \\
2\rho^3 - 3\rho^2 + 1 &\geq 0
\end{aligned}
$$

The first two are trivially true for all $\rho \in [-1 \;\; 1]$. The last may be rewritten as Equation A.45.

$$\det(C) = 2\left(\rho + \frac{1}{2}\right)(\rho - 1)^2 \geq 0 \tag{A.45}$$

Simple inspection of Equation A.45 shows that C is positive semi-definite if and only if $\rho \in [-\frac{1}{2} \;\; 1]$, in accordance with our initial intuition. Note also that, by Sylvester's criterion, C is positive definite if and only if $\rho \in (-\frac{1}{2} \;\; 1)$.

SECOND SOLUTION
In theory, we can solve for the eigenvalues of C in Equation A.43, and figure which values of ρ ensure that these eigenvalues are non-negative, so that

C is positive semi-definite. If we write down the characteristic polynomial for $\det[\lambda I - C] = 0$, we get Equation A.46, factored as Equation A.47, and rewritten as Equation A.48 (see the discussion of the coefficients on p. 143).

$$
\begin{aligned}
f(\lambda) &= \lambda^3 - 3\lambda^2 + 3\left(1 - \rho^2\right)\lambda - \left(2\rho^3 - 3\rho^2 + 1\right) & \text{(A.46)}\\
&= \lambda^3 - 3\lambda^2 + 3(1-\rho)(1+\rho)\lambda - 2\left(\rho + \frac{1}{2}\right)(\rho - 1)^2 = 0 & \text{(A.47)}\\
&= (+1)\lambda^3 - \operatorname{trace}(C)\lambda^2 + 3(1-\rho)(1+\rho)\lambda + (-1)^n \det(C) & \text{(A.48)}
\end{aligned}
$$

The roots of Equations A.46–A.48 are the eigenvalues of C, as a function of ρ. In practice, solving Equation A.47 for the roots for general ρ requires the formula for the roots of a cubic polynomial, and this is much messier than the first solution I presented using Sylvester's criterion.

We can, however, easily find the roots for some special cases by looking at Equation A.47:

- The case $\rho = 1$ yields characteristic equation $f(\lambda) = \lambda^3 - 3\lambda^2 = \lambda^2(\lambda - 3) = 0$, with roots $\lambda = 0$ (twice) and $\lambda = 3$. In this case, C is positive semi-definite, but not positive definite, as found previously.

- The case $\rho = +\frac{1}{2}$ yields characteristic equation $\lambda^3 - 3\lambda^2 + 3\left(\frac{1}{2}\right)\left(1\frac{1}{2}\right)\lambda - 2(1)\left(\frac{1}{4}\right) = \lambda^3 - 3\lambda^2 + \frac{9}{4}\lambda - \frac{1}{2} = (\lambda - 2)\left(\lambda - \frac{1}{2}\right)^2 = 0$, with roots $\lambda = \frac{1}{2}$ (twice) and $\lambda = 2$. In this case, C is positive semi-definite, and positive definite.

- The case $\rho = 0$ yields characteristic equation $f(\lambda) = \lambda^3 - 3\lambda^2 + 3\lambda - 1 = (\lambda - 1)^3 = 0$, with root $\lambda = 1$ (thrice). In this case, C is positive semi-definite, and positive definite, as found previously.

- The case $\rho = -\frac{1}{2}$ yields characteristic equation $\lambda^3 - 3\lambda^2 + 3\left(1\frac{1}{2}\right)\left(\frac{1}{2}\right)\lambda = \lambda\left(\lambda - \frac{3}{2}\right)^2 = 0$, with roots $\lambda = 0$ and $\lambda = \frac{3}{2}$ (twice). In this case, C is positive semi-definite, but not positive definite, as found previously.

- The case $\rho = -1$ yields characteristic equation $\lambda^3 - 3\lambda^2 - 2\left(-\frac{1}{2}\right)(4) = \lambda^3 - 3\lambda^2 + 4 = (\lambda + 1)(\lambda - 2)^2$, with roots $\lambda = -1$ and $\lambda = 2$ (twice). In this case, C is indefinite, and although C is perfectly valid as a mathematical entity (an indefinite matrix), it cannot represent a valid VCV matrix or correlation matrix.

Given the smooth functions involved, inspection of this handful of results is strongly suggestive of the same solution we found previously. That is, C is positive semi-definite if and only if $\rho \in [-\frac{1}{2} \ \ 1]$.

Answer 1.84:   The point of this question is not for you to give a formal definition of an integral, or a rundown of different types of integrals, but rather to provide an opportunity for you to demonstrate simple/deep intuition.

There are many different types of integrals (Riemann, Lebesgue, Itô, etc.). There are many different applications (pure calculus, probabilistic applications, stochastic calculus, etc.). I think the best answer is to give some simple examples and counter examples. Although the following is a relatively low-level explanation, I have spoken with a surprising number of mathematics majors who had never seen this basic intuition.

Example 1: Consider the integral in Equation A.49.

$$\int_{x=3}^{x=4} x^2 dx \tag{A.49}$$

Equation A.49 is a particular case of the more general integral in Equation A.50.

$$\int_{x=a}^{x=b} f(x) dx \tag{A.50}$$

I am confident that most people reading this book can drive a numerical answer to Equation A.49 in 30 seconds or less. That is unimpressive. Can you, however, read Equation A.49 or Equation A.50 (or much more complicated integrals) as fluently as you can read this sentence?

When I see the integral in Equation A.49, I read it on two levels. First, I read it at the simple mechanical level that an advanced high school student reads it, and can calculate it. Second, I read it like reading a sentence. Please see Figure A.7, Equation A.51, and the discussion following for details.

Regarding Figure A.7 and Equation A.51, note that the Latin letter "S", the Greek capital letter sigma, "Σ", and the integral sign "$\int$", have in common that they denote the first letter in the word "summation." My understanding is that when mathematicians needed a symbol for summation in a continuous setting they were running out of choices. So, they took a standard letter "S" and grabbed the top and the bottom and stretched it out to get the integral sign in Equation A.51.

I read Equations A.49, A.50, or A.51, like a sentence. Each is the limiting value of a summation of the products of height times width, where the limit is taken as the width of the slices tends to zero (or the count of the slices between given limits tends to infinity). In my head, I picture the summation for any particular choice of the value of w_i, and I imagine that sum tending to the integral in the limit, yielding the area between the curve and the x-axis. My fourth example, below, gives, however, a counter example.

For any given finite step length w_i, the finite summation is an approximation to the integral (you can see the approximation at the top of the shaded region in Figure A.7). As the width of the narrow slices tends to zero, the approximation becomes more accurate, yielding exactly the integral in the limit as $w_i \to 0$. We are free to read the integral sign in Equation A.51 as "sum" or "summation" as long as we understand it is so only in the limiting sense as the width w_i goes to zero.

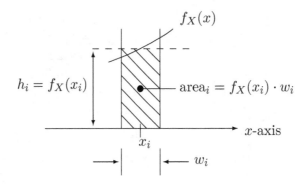

Figure A.7: Integral: Zoomed View of ith Narrow Slice

Note: Please compare this figure with Equation A.51. I assume a discretization of the x-axis into small steps numbered using i, x_i sits at the center of the ith small step, $h_i = f_X(x_i)$ is the height of the function f_X at x_i, w_i is the width of the ith small step centered on x_i, and $area_i$ is the area of the ith narrow slice centered on x_i. Note, of course, that $f_X(x_i)$ could be negative, giving a negative $area_i$.

$$
\begin{array}{ccc}
\displaystyle\int & f_X(x) & dx \\
\uparrow & \uparrow & \uparrow \\
\lim_{w_i \to 0} \quad \text{sum}_i & f_X(x_i) \cdot & w_i \\
\uparrow & \uparrow & \uparrow \\
\lim_{w_i \to 0} \quad \text{sum}_i & h_i \quad \cdot & w_i \\
\lim_{w_i \to 0} \quad \sum_i & \underbrace{}_{area_i}
\end{array}
\tag{A.51}
$$

Story: "We had narrowed our search for a senior-level executive at a major financial institution to three candidates and felt that one in particular was the best choice in terms of experience and background. We prepped all three for their interviews with the company's general counsel, but we really spent time prepping the top candidate. When he got into the interview, it suddenly seemed he'd come from another planet. He asked about his office furniture, his expense-account allowances and health-care plan. He asked nothing whatsoever about the functions of the job and his qualifications for it. I sat there in horror."

ARNOLD M. HUBERMAN
Arnold Huberman Associates, New York

"Doomed Days: The Worst Mistakes Recruiters Have Ever Seen,"
The Wall Street Journal, February 25, 1995, pR4.
Reprinted by permission of *The Wall Street Journal*
©1995 Dow Jones and Company, Inc.
All Rights Reserved Worldwide.

Example 2: Consider again the integral in Equation A.49, but this time, calculate it algebraically. Let us begin with a guess, work it out analytically, using the rules we learned in high school, and then work it out algebraically (which is where the rules we learned come from anyway).

The function $f(x) = x^2$ for $x \in [3 \ 4]$ ranges from 9 to 16. We can guess that the area under the curve between these limits is roughly height (i.e., approximately $\frac{16+9}{2}$) times base (i.e., 1). This yields the estimate 12.5.

If we perform the integration using standard rules for polynomials, we get $\int_3^4 x^2 dx = \frac{1}{3}x^3\Big|_3^4 = \frac{4^3-3^3}{3} = \frac{64-27}{3} = 12\frac{1}{3}$. This is close to our estimate.

To both demonstrate the definition of the integral as a limiting sum, and to illustrate numerical integration by using algebra to perform calculus, let me cut the interval $[3 \ 4]$ into n small steps, each of length $1/n$. Then we get

$$
\begin{aligned}
\int_a^b x^2 dx &= \lim_{n\to\infty} \sum_{i=1}^n \underbrace{f\left(a + i \cdot \frac{(b-a)}{n}\right)}_{\text{height}} \cdot \underbrace{\frac{(b-a)}{n}}_{\text{width}}, \text{for general } f(x),\ a, \text{ and } b \\
&= \lim_{n\to\infty} \sum_{i=1}^n f\left(3 + i\frac{(4-3)}{n}\right)\frac{1}{n}, \text{ for our } a = 3,\ b = 4 \\
&= \lim_{n\to\infty} \sum_{i=1}^n \left[\left(9 + \frac{6i}{n} + \frac{i^2}{n^2}\right) \cdot \frac{1}{n}\right], \text{ for our } f(x) = x^2 \\
&= \lim_{n\to\infty} \sum_{i=1}^n \left[\frac{9}{n} + \frac{6i}{n^2} + \frac{i^2}{n^3}\right] \\
&= \lim_{n\to\infty} \left[\frac{9\sum 1}{n} + \frac{6\sum i}{n^2} + \frac{\sum i^2}{n^3}\right] \\
&= \lim_{n\to\infty} \left[\frac{9n}{n} + \frac{6\frac{n(n+1)}{2}}{n^2} + \frac{\frac{n(n+1)(2n+1)}{6}}{n^3}\right], \qquad (*) \\
&= \lim_{n\to\infty} \left[9 \cdot 1 + 3 \cdot \left(\frac{n(n+1)}{n^2}\right) + \frac{1}{3} \cdot \left(\frac{n(n+1)(n+\frac{1}{2})}{n^3}\right)\right] \\
&= 9 + 3 + \frac{1}{3} \\
&= 12\frac{1}{3},
\end{aligned}
$$

where at Step-($*$) I used the results $\sum_{i=1}^n i = \frac{n(n+1)}{2}$, $\sum_{i=1}^n i^2 = \frac{n(n+1)(2n+1)}{6}$, and $\sum_{i=1}^n i^3 = \frac{n^2(n+1)^2}{4}$; note that the third result is the first squared (see Question 1.53).

Like numeric differentiation, in theory, this algebraic integration can be executed for any integrable function. In practice, it can get algebraically messy—but a computer can easily perform this sort of numeric integration using mindless CPU cycles.

Example 3: When dealing with probability, the intuitive approach to integrals in Example 1 needs to be modified. If X has pdf $f_X(x)$, then the expected value of X (i.e., the mean of X) is denoted $E(X)$ and is given by Equation A.52.

$$E(X) = \int x f_X(x) dx. \tag{A.52}$$

Do we have simple intuition for the integral in Equation A.52? Well, suppose we were to follow the intuition from Example 1, above. Then, we could define $g(x) \equiv x \cdot f_X(x)$, and we could think of $E(X) = \int g(x) dx$ as the limiting value of $\sum_i \text{area}_i$, where $\text{area}_i = g(x_i) \cdot \text{width}_i = h_i \cdot w_i$, as before. Although correct, this is definitely not the most intuitive way to look at an expected value. This approach ignores the special properties of the pdf $f_X(x)$.

Instead, recall first that if X_d is a discrete random variable, taking values x_i with probability p_i, then $E(X_d) = \sum_{i=1}^{i=n} x_i \cdot p_i$. The continuous case in Equation A.52 is, in fact, perfectly analogous to this simple discrete case. That is, if we now look back at Figure A.7, and consider the special case where the function $f(x)$ is a pdf given by $f_X(x)$, then the area under $f_X(x)$, be it exact or approximated, is a lump of probability mass. So, the term $f_X(x) \cdot dx$ appearing under the integral sign in Equation A.52 is just an infinitesimal lump of probability mass. That is, $f_X(x) \cdot dx$ is the area of an (infinitesimally thin) small vertical slice taken under the pdf of X (with height $f_X(x)$ and infinitesimal width dx). The sum of all such areas is equal to one by definition of a pdf (i.e., $\int f_X(x) dx = 1$). So, with this intuition, we may use Figure A.7 to rewrite Equation A.52 for expected value as Equation A.53—all perfectly analogous to the simple discrete case.

$$
\begin{aligned}
E(X) &= \int \quad x \quad \underbrace{\underbrace{f_X(x)}_{h_i} \underbrace{dx}_{w_i}}_{\substack{\text{area}_i \\ \uparrow \\ p_i}} \\
&= \lim_{w_i \to 0} \quad \text{sum}_i \quad x_i \quad \cdot \quad p_i \\
&= \lim_{w_i \to 0} \sum_i x_i \cdot p_i
\end{aligned}
\tag{A.53}
$$

So, in this probabilistic case, we can read the integral $E(X) = \int x f_X(x) dx$ as the limiting value of a discrete sum, where this sum is a probability-weighted average of values of x, just as in the discrete case, and the limit is taken as the width of the slices of probability mass goes to zero.

Example 4: Finally, in each of the above three examples, I defined the integral as the limiting value of a discrete summation, with the limit taken as the width of small steps in the discretization of the x-axis tends to zero. Embedded within this intuition is the notion of convergence. For example, no matter how we define the discretization of the x-axis when calculating $E(X)$ for a normally distributed random variable X, the integral converges to the same limiting value as the widths of the discrete probability masses goes to zero. This, however, is not always the case.

For example, the standard Cauchy distribution is defined as the ratio of independent standard normals. The standard Cauchy is also known as the Lorentz or Breit-Wigner distribution. Although, to the untrained eye, the standard Cauchy distribution looks quite "normal," the standard Cauchy distribution has such fat tails relative to a standard normal distribution that different discretizations can yield different answers for the limiting value of the probability-weighted values of the random variable. That is, the integral $E(C)$ is not convergent when C follows a standard Cauchy distribution.

The standard Cauchy distribution is the same thing as a t-distribution with one degree of freedom (Crack, 2020b). This can be seen because, by definition, a t-distribution with one degree of freedom is the ratio of a standard normal to the square root of a statistically independent chi-squared distribution with one degree of freedom sitting on its degrees of freedom, $t_1 \sim Z \big/ \sqrt{\chi_1^2/1}$. By definition, a chi-squared distribution with one degree of freedom is, however, just a standard normal distribution squared. Combining all these, we see that $t_1 \sim Z_1/Z_2 \sim C$, where C is standard Cauchy. (Note that whether the denominator is the unsigned $\sqrt{\chi_1^2/1}$ or the signed Z_2 is irrelevant; each yields a standard Cauchy.)

The t-distribution may be thought of as bridging the gap between the standard Cauchy distribution and the standard normal distribution. That is, as the degrees of freedom increase from $\nu = 1$ to $\nu = \infty$, the Student-t with ν degrees of freedom deforms continuously from the ill-behaved standard Cauchy distribution to the well-behaved standard normal distribution

The very fat tails of the standard Cauchy distribution are attributable to the probability mass near zero in the denominator of the ratio $C = Z_1/Z_2$. Very small values of the denominator amplify the numerator so significantly that the convergence of the integral we discussed in Figure A.7 and Equation A.53 fails.[72] That is, depending upon how we calculate the limit as the widths of the slices of probability mass in the integral go to zero, we can get different answers. The convergence fails so badly that no central moments exist for the standard Cauchy distribution. To be precise, the odd raw moments (including the mean) do not exist at all, the even raw moments do exist but are infinite, and because the central moments (e.g., the variance) require the mean, no central moments exist.

---

[72]This amplification effect is ameliorated somewhat in the case of the t-distribution with degrees of freedom $\nu > 1$, because there is less probability mass near zero in the denominator in that case. Nevertheless, the Student-t with $\nu = 2$ still has infinite variance—but at least the variance is defined in that case. The fat tails at low degrees of freedom mean that the Student-t distribution requires $\nu \geq 3$ to get finite variance, $\nu \geq 4$ to get finite skewness (which is equal to zero), and $\nu \geq 5$ to get finite kurtosis.

The bottom line is that our intuition for what an integral is must also include ill-behaved cases where the integral is not convergent.

Answer 1.85: Following on from our previous answer about integrals, $E[g(X)]$ may be interpreted as a probability-weighted average of values of $g(X)$, where $X \sim N(\mu, \sigma^2)$. A Monte-Carlo simulation does not discretize the domain of the pdf (though that would work too), but rather it relies upon the strong law of large numbers.

Khinchine's Strong Law of Large Numbers (SLLN) says that if the sample $Y_1, Y_2, \ldots, Y_N, \ldots$ are IID with $E(Y_i) = \mu_Y$ (a finite number) for each i, then, with probability one,

$$\bar{Y}_n \equiv \frac{1}{N} \sum_{i=1}^{N} Y_i \to \mu_Y, \text{ as } n \to \infty.$$

That is, in plain English, the sample mean approaches the true mean as the sample size increases.

So, all we have to do is sample N values x_i from $N(\mu, \sigma^2)$ via computer program, and calculate

$$\widehat{E[g(X)]} = \frac{1}{N} \sum_{i=1}^{N} g(x_i).$$

Convergence is guaranteed because the $g(x_i)$ are IID with expected values $E[g(X)]$.

Typical values of N are of the order of 10,000 or 20,000. Standard central limit theorem results allow us to put a confidence interval about our estimator. Large sample sizes give narrower confidence intervals.

Answer 1.86: When I saw 29×29, I immediately noticed that 29 is only 1 less than 30. I know that $30 \times 30 = 900$, so all I have to do is add 29 and 30 (to get 59) and then subtract that from 900 to get 841. Let me explain...

You likely already know that $a^2 - b^2 = (a+b)(a-b)$. In the case that $a = b+1$, this reduces to $a^2 - b^2 = a + b$. The fact that 29 is one less than 30, and that $30^2 = 900$ is easy to figure in your head, suggests to me that they want you to find the answer as $30^2 - 29^2 = 30 + 29 = 59$. So, 29^2 is 59 less than 900, which is 841.

Alternatively, just multiply it out and add the parts:

$$
\begin{aligned}
9 \times 9 &= 81 \\
20 \times 9 &= 180 \\
9 \times 20 &= 180 \\
20 \times 20 &= 400,
\end{aligned}
$$

and 400+360+81=841.

Answer 1.87:   Unlike the previous question, when I saw 43×43, I immediately thought I should just multiply it out and add the parts:

$$
\begin{aligned}
3 \times 3 &= 9 \\
3 \times 40 &= 120 \\
40 \times 3 &= 120 \\
40 \times 40 &= 1,600,
\end{aligned}
$$

and 1,600+240+9=1849.

Answer 1.88:   When I heard 21×19, it jumped out at me as $(n+1) \times (n-1)$, for $n = 20$. We know that $(n+1) \times (n-1) = n^2 - 1$, and that $20^2 = 400$, so we get 399 immediately.

Answer 1.89:   You need only ask for a single piece of fruit to deduce the correct labeling. If you are peeking here for a hint, then go back and ask yourself how it can be done with only a single piece of fruit.

Given the symmetry of the problem, my initial instinct was that asking for fruit from the barrel labeled "Apples," or the one labeled "Oranges," was not going to solve the problem.

If you ask for a single piece of fruit from the barrel labeled "Apples and Oranges," then, given the mis-labeling, you know that every other piece of fruit in that barrel is the same as the piece you requested. So, suppose you are handed an apple from this barrel. Then, you have located the true "Apples" barrel, currently labeled "Apples and Oranges." Given that you now know where the true "Apples" barrel is, then you now know that the barrel labeled "Oranges" cannot be the true "Apples" barrel. By construction, however, the barrel labeled "Oranges" also cannot be the true "Oranges" barrel (because every barrel is mis-labeled). Therefore, the barrel labeled "Oranges" must be the true "Apples and Oranges" barrel (there is no other choice remaining). Thus, we deduce that the remaining barrel, labeled "Apples," must be the true "Oranges" barrel.

Another way to think about the problem is that once you have identified that the barrel labeled "Apples and Oranges" contains only apples, then you can unpin the "Apples" label from its barrel, remove the "Apples and Oranges" label, and pin the "Apples" label in its correct place. This leaves you with a correctly labeled "Apples" barrel, an unlabeled barrel, an incorrectly labeled "Oranges" barrel, and the "Apples and Oranges" label in your hand. You know that the "Oranges" label has to move, and that the unlabeled barrel is the only place to pin it. So, having done that, you can then pin the "Apples and Oranges" label on the remaining barrel.

Of course, if at the initial step you are instead handed an orange from the barrel labeled "Apples and Oranges," then the argument is analogous (i.e., the

"Apples and Oranges" barrel holds only oranges, and the "Apples" barrel can then be neither oranges nor apples, etc.).

Note that if you instead request the initial piece of fruit from the barrel labeled "Apples" or the barrel labeled "Oranges," then the only-a-single-piece-of-fruit-is-needed argument fails.

Answer 1.90: To compare $11^{2.5}$ with 400, I am going to square both sides and ask how 11^5 compares with 400^2. I can quickly figure that 400^2 is a 16 with four zeroes after it. So, I will be looking at the leading digits of 11^5 to see how they compare with 16.

The number 11 has nice properties. For example, I know that $11^2 = 121$. In fact, any number made just of ones, when squared, gives what I will call a "podium" number. For example, $1,111^2 = 1,234,321$.

I have also memorized that $11^3 = 1,331$. So, to get 11^5, I need to multiple 1,331 and 121 in my head. I can picture that (and I don't know about you, but I have to close my eyes for this one) I am going to have to add 133,100, 26,620, and 1,331. Subtracting 100,000 from the first term and dropping any thing smaller than 1,000, leaves me with 33,000, 26,000, and 1,000 which add to give 60,000. So, adding back in the numbers I dropped, which I am not going to actually bother doing, brings the grand sum to just over 160,000. Thus, $11^{2.5}$ is a little bit bigger than 400.

Answer 1.91: The interviewer told you that the lengths of two sides of a triangle are 5 and 6, and asked you for the length of the third side. Let the two sides have angle θ between them, then for $0° < \theta < 180°$, the third side has length $1 < L < 11$, respectively. You get equality only in the degenerate case of a triangle with no area (i.e., when $\theta = 0°, 180°$).

If the interviewer meant that it is a right-angle triangle (i.e., $\theta = 90°$), then we can use Pythagoras' Theorem to find $L^2 = 5^2 + 6^2 = 61$, and thus $L = \sqrt{61}$. With no calculator, I noted that $8 = \sqrt{64}$, and with 61 just below 64, I figured maybe $L \approx 7\frac{3}{4}$. My guess is out by less than 1%: $L = \sqrt{61} \approx 7.81$.

Answer 1.92: Let me try a step-by-step approach. I know that the doubles $(1, 1)$ and $(2, 2)$ are needed. So, each die needs a 1 and a 2. I need a 0 somewhere. So, let me start with $\{0, 1, 2\}$ and $\{1, 2\}$. I tried adding 3, 4, 5, and 6 to the second die to have $\{0, 1, 2\}$ and $\{1, 2, 3, 4, 5, 6\}$, and then 7, 8, 9 to the first die to get $\{0, 1, 2, 7, 8, 9\}$ and $\{1, 2, 3, 4, 5, 6\}$. Then I discovered that I could not get $(0, 7)$ or $(0, 8)$. I could, however, get $(0, 9)$ by inverting the 6. Using that logic, let us drop the 6 and replace it with a 0: $\{0, 1, 2, 7, 8, 9\}$ and $\{0, 1, 2, 3, 4, 5\}$. I can see other equally-good choices obtained by any shuffling of the 3, 4, 5, 7, 8, and 9.

Answer 1.93: Like so many of the simpler quantitative interview questions, there is a naive answer that is near at hand: If you think it takes four minutes to make four slices of toast, then stop reading here, go back and think again.

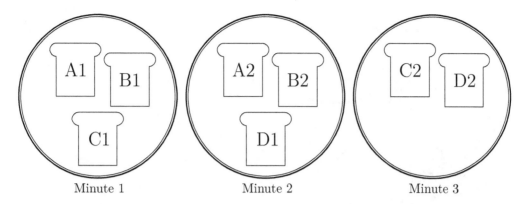

| Minute 1 | Minute 2 | Minute 3 |

Figure A.8: Making Toast

Note: The frying pan holds three slices of bread. It takes one minute to toast each side. Place slices A, B and C in the pan for one minute; then flip over slices A and B, while holding out slice C and introducing slice D (taking a second minute); finally, finish off slices C and D (taking a third minute).

Let us think in terms of *sides* of bread. In one minute, the pan can toast three (or fewer) sides of toast simultaneously. Four pieces of bread possess only *eight* sides, so it seems reasonable to expect that if we take three minutes and use the pan three times (i.e., enough to toast nine sides), we should be able to do the job. In fact, in three minutes, we should be able to toast all four slices of bread on both sides, and also toast half of one more slice. It is just a matter of figuring out how to do so, subject to the constraint that we cannot toast both sides of any one slice simultaneously.

Let us label the four slices of bread as A, B, C, and D, and their sides as 1 and 2. Figure A.8 illustrates the process.

Beyond the question posed, can you find a general formula $M(n)$ that describes the minutes, M, required to make n slices of toast using this pan, for $n \geq 2$?

Well, n slices of bread possess $2n$ sides to be toasted. You can fit only three sides in the pan at a time. So, if you round $2n/3$ up to the nearest whole number, this is how many minutes M it takes to toast the n slices. That is,

$$M(n) = \text{ceil}\left(\frac{2n}{3}\right),$$

for $n \geq 2$, where ceil($\cdot$) rounds up to the nearest whole number.

Answer 1.94: Let me label the vertices closest to A as 1, 2, and 3, and the vertices closest to B as 4, 5, and 6, as shown again in Figure A.9. Note that every path that leaves A must first hit one of 1, 2, or 3. Each of these paths has two possible next choices. This gives us six beginnings of paths. At this point, the path then either jumps to B in one step (with no choice), or to B

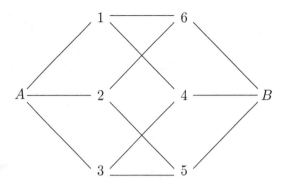

Figure A.9: Graph of a Cube

Note: We are asked to count non-self-intersecting (i.e., touching any vertex no more than once) paths that lead from A to B.

in three steps (with no choice), or to B in five steps (with no choice, having traversed all eight vertices). So, there are $6 \times 3 = 18$ possible paths. These 18 paths, ending in one step, three steps, and five steps, respectively, are listed below.

$A - 1 - 6 - B$	$A - 1 - 6 - 2 - 5 - B$	$A - 1 - 6 - 2 - 5 - 3 - 4 - B$
$A - 1 - 4 - B$	$A - 1 - 4 - 3 - 5 - B$	$A - 1 - 4 - 3 - 5 - 2 - 6 - B$
$A - 2 - 6 - B$	$A - 2 - 6 - 1 - 4 - B$	$A - 2 - 6 - 1 - 4 - 3 - 5 - B$
$A - 2 - 5 - B$	$A - 2 - 5 - 3 - 4 - B$	$A - 2 - 5 - 3 - 4 - 1 - 6 - B$
$A - 3 - 4 - B$	$A - 3 - 4 - 1 - 6 - B$	$A - 3 - 4 - 1 - 6 - 2 - 5 - B$
$A - 3 - 5 - B$	$A - 3 - 5 - 2 - 6 - B$	$A - 3 - 5 - 2 - 6 - 1 - 4 - B$

Answer 1.95: I give two related proofs that infinitely many prime numbers exist.

FIRST SOLUTION

Euclid gives a proof in about 300BC (Euclid, 2008, Book 9, Proposition 20). Given a finite list of prime numbers $p_1, p_2, \ldots, p_N$, let $\Pi = p_1 \cdot p_2 \cdots p_N$ be their product. Consider $(\Pi + 1)$; either $(\Pi + 1)$ is a prime number or it is not. If $(\Pi + 1)$ is a prime number, then our finite list of prime numbers was incomplete, for $(\Pi + 1)$ is yet another. If $(\Pi + 1)$ is not a prime number, then it is a composite number (i.e., a non-prime number). All composite numbers are divisible by a prime number (Euclid, 2008, Book 7, Proposition 31). Let this prime divisor be p. Then p cannot be one of $p_1, p_2, \ldots, p_N$. For, if it were, say, $p = p_i$, then $(\Pi + 1)$ would be divisible by p_i, but Π (by its very definition) is also divisible by p_i. In this case, it follows that $1 = (\Pi + 1) - \Pi$ is also divisible by p_i, which is absurd. Thus our finite list of prime numbers was incomplete, for p is yet another.

In other words, given any finite list of prime numbers, yet another prime number can be found. So, there must be infinitely many prime numbers.

SECOND SOLUTION

Suppose you are given some positive integer $n > 2$. Consider $n! = n \cdot (n - 1) \cdots 2 \cdot 1$. Without loss of generality, $n!$ is divisible by each of 2, 3, ..., n. (So, $n!$ is not prime.) Now consider $(n! + 1)$. Either $(n! + 1)$ is prime, or it is not prime. For example, $(11! + 1) = 39,916,801$ is prime, but $(12! + 1) = 479,001,601$ is not prime.

If $(n! + 1)$ is prime, then we have discovered a prime number larger than the given n. If $(n! + 1)$ is not prime, then it is a composite number, and is therefore divisible by a prime number. We know, however, that $(n! + 1)$ is not divisible by any of 2, 3, ..., n (because it has remainder 1 when divided by any of these numbers, by construction). So, $(n! + 1)$ must be divisible by a prime number larger than n. Again, we have discovered a prime number larger than the given n.

It follows that given any positive integer $n > 2$, we can find a prime number larger than n. So, there must be infinitely many prime numbers.

Answer 1.96: Following on from the answer to the previous question, let us use factorials to construct a sequence of n consecutive positive integers none of which is prime.[73] Given positive integer n, without loss of generality, consider the following n successive numbers:

$$[(n + 1)! + 2], [(n + 1)! + 3], [(n + 1)! + 4], \ldots, [(n + 1)! + (n + 1)].$$

The first number is divisible by 2, the second number is divisible by 3, and so on, up until the nth number which is divisible by $(n + 1)$. It follows that none of these n consecutive numbers is prime, which was to be shown.

Note that the *first* number at which a run of n successive composite numbers begins may be much lower than $[(n + 1)! + 2]$. For example, when $n = 3$, sure enough $[(3 + 1)! + 2] = (4! + 2) = 26$, and 26, 27, 28 are consecutive composite numbers, but so too are 8, 9, 10.

Answer 1.97: Can the mean of two consecutive prime numbers be prime? No, of course not. Replace the word "prime" with any other word, and the answer is still no. If they are consecutive, then by definition there are none of them in between!

---

[73]I thank Paul Bilokon for this proof; any errors are mine.

Appendix B

Derivatives Answers

This appendix contains answers to the questions posed in Chapter 2.

Answer 2.1: Most people incorrectly deduce that the call option is worthless. If this is your conclusion, then you have been bumped by the pickpocket's accomplice again (see story on p. 250). You missed the point. So, stop looking at the answers and go back and think again.

Many people think that zero volatility means the stock price is going nowhere. However, volatility of returns is, by definition, the average deviation from expected returns. It follows that zero volatility means the stock price drifts up at the expected return on the stock with no deviations from this path.

With no volatility, the stock is riskless. In the absence of arbitrage opportunities, the stock must offer an expected return equal to the riskless rate. This is true in both the real world and the theoretical risk-neutral world. This result (expected return equals r) is very strange in the real world—stocks normally offer higher returns. Do note, however, that *all* stocks in the risk-neutral world have expected return equal to the riskless rate. Although I discuss option pricing in the risk-neutral world, the same arguments apply in the real world in the no-volatility case.[1]

The required rate of return on the stock is the riskless interest rate. It follows that with no volatility, the stock price rises to about \$105 for sure.[2] That is, the option finishes in-the-money for sure and is thus riskless. The discounted expected payoff is thus roughly $\frac{(\$105-\$100)}{1.05} = \frac{5}{1.05}$. At 5%, you lose about five cents on every dollar when you discount over a year. The discounted expected payoff is, therefore, about \$4.75, and this is the call value.

---

[1]If option pricing is done using real world probabilities rather than risk-neutral ones, then the discount rate on the option is a path-dependent random variable that changes as the stock price changes (Arnold and Crack [2004]; Arnold, Crack and Schwartz [2009, 2010]). Such a model allows inference of real world probabilities of a real option project being successful, a financial option finishing in-the-money, or a corporate bond defaulting.

[2]If the interest rate is an effective (i.e., simple) rate, then this is exact; if it is continuously compounded, this is an approximation.

This is a good place to mention an often overlooked connection between options and forwards. Suppose that $S(t)$ is the price today of a stock that pays no dividends. Let r denote the continuously compounded interest rate per annum. Then a fair price for delivery of the stock at time T is: $F = S(t)e^{r(T-t)}$. In the absence of volatility, the expected time-T stock price is just the forward price. Once volatility is introduced into the picture, the distribution of terminal stock price $S(T)$ becomes spread out. However, the mean of the (risk-neutral) distribution of $S(T)$ is unchanged, and this mean equals the forward price, which is also unchanged: $S(t)e^{r(T-t)}$. That is, the expected time-T stock price in the risk-neutral world is just the forward price.

Back to our option: With no volatility, the value of the option at time t is just the discounted expected time-T payoff in a risk-neutral world:

$$\begin{aligned} c(t) &= e^{-r(T-t)} \max(S(T) - X, 0) \\ &= e^{-r(T-t)} \max(S(t)e^{r(T-t)} - X, 0) \\ &= e^{-r(T-t)} \max(F - X, 0), \end{aligned}$$

where $F = S(t)e^{r(T-t)}$ is the forward price for the stock, and X is the strike price. If follows that the option has value if and only if the forward price exceeds the option's strike.

How do you hedge this? If $F > X$, the option will finish in-the-money for sure, so you need a delta of $+1$. If $F \leq X$, the option will die worthless for sure, so you need a delta of 0 (who would buy the option in this case anyway?).

Answer 2.2:   The gamma of an option is the rate of change of its delta, Δ, with respect to stock price—denoted Γ. Option gamma is also called "curvature," or "convexity." Gamma is non-negative for standard puts and calls (their deltas rise with increasing S). Put-call parity tells us that the gamma of a European call is the same as the gamma of a European put.

Option value "decays" toward kinked final payoff as expiration approaches (see Figure B.1—first panel). This time decay is called "theta." We usually think about theta as being negative for plain vanilla options, but there are two clear exceptions. A deep in-the-money European-style call can have positive theta if the dividend yield is high enough—because high dividends can push price down below intrinsic value and the option then has to "decay upward" in value as expiration approaches. Similarly, a deep in-the-money European put decays upward in value—because life does not get much better than a deep-in-the-money American put, but the European put cannot be exercised immediately and hence the discount. Crack (2021) discusses this in more detail.

Theta is large and negative for at-the-money options, and it increases in magnitude as maturity approaches. Theta and gamma are typically of opposing signs (the positive theta cases mentioned above are exceptions), so large negative theta typically goes hand-in-hand with large positive gamma. That is, shortening maturity accelerates at-the-money option prices towards the kink and also gives more curvature (i.e., gamma) in the plot of option value as a function of stock price (see Figure B.1—third panel).

The maturity/gamma relationship is reversed away from the strike price. If a call is deep in-the-money, then $\Delta \to 1$, as expiration approaches (for a deep in-the-money *put*, $\Delta \to -1$ as expiration approaches). Thus, short maturity calls or puts that are deep in-the-money have deltas that do not vary much as S changes. With little variation in delta, the gamma is close to zero. If an option is instead deep *out*-of-the-money, then its gamma is also close to zero because its delta is close to zero with little variation across S. It follows that for away-from-the-money standard options, shorter maturity implies lower gamma for both puts and calls (see Figure B.1—third panel).

The gamma (i.e., convexity) for a standard European call on a stock that pays a continuous dividend at rate ρ is given as follows:

$$\Gamma(t) \equiv \frac{\partial^2 c(t)}{\partial S(t)^2} = \frac{e^{-\rho(T-t)-\frac{1}{2}d_1^2}}{S(t)\sigma\sqrt{2\pi(T-t)}},$$

where

$$d_1 = \frac{\ln\left(\frac{S(t)}{X}\right) + (r - \rho + \frac{1}{2}\sigma^2)(T-t)}{\sigma\sqrt{T-t}}$$

With $(T-t) > 0$, the formula for Γ shows that as $S(t) \to \infty$, the numerator goes to zero (because $d_1 \to \infty$), and the denominator goes to infinity. Both limits have the same effect on Γ, pushing it to zero. Similarly, if $(T-t) > 0$, then as $S(t) \to 0$, $d_1^2 \to \infty$ so the numerator goes to zero again. However, having S in the denominator pushes Γ in the opposite direction as $S \to 0$. The exponentiation of d_1^2 in the numerator is much more powerful than the linearity of S in the denominator, so the ratio, Γ, is forced to zero as $S \to 0$.

If the option is exactly at-the-money [i.e., $S(t) = X$], then as maturity approaches, you have a knife-edge singularity. You get $d_1 \to 0$, so the numerator of Γ goes to **1**. However, the denominator tends to zero, so the ratio, Γ, blows up. That is, you get "infinite gamma" at the kink as maturity approaches.

Infinite gamma means the sensitivity of delta to small changes in price of the underlying is infinite. This means that the delta can jump from one-half up to one, or down to zero with just a hair's breadth move in the stock price. In this knife-edge scenario, any delta-hedge that you establish is extremely sensitive to a move in the underlying—you are not hedged.

If you try gamma-hedging (adding traded options to your delta-hedge to replicate the convexity of the derivative), you will need many traded options in your hedge portfolio, and it may become difficult to manage the position.[3] Your

---

[3]In practice, even with a day left to maturity, although the gamma can be quite large, you might need only 10 three-month calls to replicate the convexity of a standard call with one day to maturity—we are not talking infinity here.

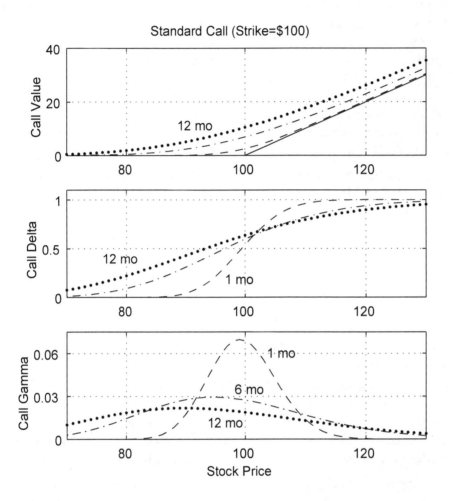

Figure B.1: Standard Call: Price, Delta, and Gamma.

Note: For maturities of 12 months "·····", six months "·—·—", and one month "————", the call price, delta, and gamma are plotted as a function of price of underlying (see Answer 2.2). One of the spreadsheets that accompanies my book *Basic Black-Scholes*, Crack (2021) allows you to interactively plot these and other Greeks. Go to www.BasicBlackScholes.com and follow the instructions to download the EXCEL spreadsheet Greeks tool. The password is marylebone.

problems are similar (but much worse) if hedging barrier options (i.e., "knock-outs") as the price of the underlying approaches the knock-out barrier. The problem is worse near a knock-out's barrier than near a standard call's kink. This is because the knock-out's delta can jump from one to zero whereas the standard call's delta jumps only from one-half to zero, or one-half to one.

For most American-style options (and for the more complicated Europeans), there is no closed-form formulae. You will probably have to calculate Γ using numerical techniques.

Answer 2.3:   The key here is the shape of the risk-neutral distribution of final stock price, $S(T)$, conditional on current stock price, $S(t)$. Many people mistakenly assume the distribution of final stock price to be both symmetric and normal. The distribution is in fact lognormal.

The lognormal distribution is "right skewed," which is also known as "positively skewed." It looks as though its top has been shoved from the right while keeping its base fixed. So, it has a right tail.

If we start with $S(t) = X$, and $r = 0$, then the skewness in the distribution of $S(T)$ means that the final stock price is more likely to end up below the strike than above it.[4]   The call has bigger potential payoffs than the put but (because of skewness) lower probabilities of achieving them.   The put has smaller potential payoffs than the call but (because of skewness) higher probabilities of achieving them. The bigger payoffs and lower probabilities for the call exactly match the smaller payoffs and higher probabilities for the put. It follows that the put and call have the same risk-neutral expected payoff and, therefore, have the same value. It is straightforward to confirm this equality of values using put-call parity.

Answer 2.4:   This is a common question. Stock price, $S(t)$, ranges from \$0 to \$$\infty$; the "delta" varies from 0 to +1. When $S(t)$ is very low (well out-of-the-money), delta is close to zero; when $S(t)$ is very high (well in-the-money), delta is close to one; when $S(t) = X$ (at-the-money), delta is very slightly higher than one-half (assuming no dividends). The curve is smooth and looks very much like a cdf (cumulative distribution function). This is not surprising, given that delta $= N(d_1) = N(d_1(S))$, and $N(\cdot)$ is a cdf, and $d_1(S)$ is an increasing function of S. The delta is illustrated in the second panel in Figure B.1.

How about the intuition? The delta is how many units of stock you need to hold to hedge a short call option. If your call option is deep in-the-money, you need one unit of stock because the option will be exercised and the stock will be called; if your option is deep out-of-the-money, you need no stock because the option will expire worthless and the stock will not be called; if your option

---

[4]With $r = 0$, the median of the risk-neutral distribution of $S(T)$ conditional on $S(t)$ is $S(t)\, e^{(r-\frac{1}{2}\sigma^2)(T-t)} = S(t)\, e^{-\frac{1}{2}\sigma^2(T-t)} < S(t)$. The option is struck at-the-money [i.e., $S(t) = X$], so the median is below the strike.

is at-the-money, you are not too sure, and you have about one-half a unit of stock just in case.

Answer 2.5: Without dividends, the standard Black and Scholes (1973) pricing formula for the European call option is given by

$$c(t) = S(t)N(d_1) - e^{-r(T-t)}XN(d_2), \quad \text{where}$$

$$d_1 = \frac{\ln\left(\frac{S(t)}{X}\right) + (r + \frac{1}{2}\sigma^2)(T-t)}{\sigma\sqrt{T-t}}, \quad \text{and}$$

$$d_2 = d_1 - \sigma\sqrt{T-t}.$$

The option's "delta" is given by $\frac{\partial c(t)}{\partial S(t)} = N(d_1)$. With the option struck at-the-money, $S(t) = X$, and thus, $\ln\left(\frac{S(t)}{X}\right) = 0$ [remember that $\ln(1) = 0$]. All other terms in d_1 are positive. Therefore, $d_1 > 0$, and $N(d_1) > 0.5$ (remember that $N(0) = 0.5$ and $N(\cdot)$ is an increasing function of its argument). Thus, an at-the-money option on a non-dividend-paying stock always has a delta slightly greater than one-half.

Answer 2.6: With continuous dividends at rate ρ, the standard Black-Scholes pricing formula for the European call option is given by[5]

$$c(t) = S(t)e^{-\rho(T-t)}N(d_1) - e^{-r(T-t)}XN(d_2), \quad \text{where}$$

$$d_1 = \frac{\ln\left(\frac{S(t)}{X}\right) + (r - \rho + \frac{1}{2}\sigma^2)(T-t)}{\sigma\sqrt{T-t}}, \quad \text{and}$$

$$d_2 = d_1 - \sigma\sqrt{T-t}.$$

The option's "delta" is given by $\frac{\partial c(t)}{\partial S(t)} = e^{-\rho(T-t)}N(d_1)$. With the option struck at-the-money, $S(t) = X$, and thus, $\ln\left(\frac{S(t)}{X}\right) = 0$ [remember that $\ln(1) = 0$]. This, combined with $r > \rho$ yields $d_1 > 0$, and thus $N(d_1) > 0.5$. The naive answer is that $N(d_1) > 0.5$ and that this is the delta—forgetting that $e^{-\rho(T-t)}$ pre-multiplies $N(d_1)$ in the continuous-dividend case. In general, you cannot tell whether the delta, $e^{-\rho(T-t)}N(d_1)$, is larger or smaller than 0.5: it depends upon the size of σ^2. However, in this particular case, $\rho = 0.03$ is so small that $\Delta > 0.5$ for any σ.

Answer 2.7: Almost every person I have asked has got the answer to this one backwards at first. This is unfortunate, because it is a commonly asked question. Think it through carefully before answering, and do not get caught out. The delta is the number of units of stock in the replicating portfolio. Other things being equal, the delta falls with a fall in stock price. However, you are long the call and short the replicating portfolio. This means that the number

---

[5]This extension of Black-Scholes is due originally to Merton (1973, Footnote 62). Note, however, that his original formula has an obvious typo in it (he omits the dependence of d_1 and d_2 on ρ).

of units of stock you are short has to fall. So, you must borrow more money and buy back some stock.

If you got it wrong, think about it as follows. Ask yourself how the replicating portfolio changes (e.g., delta falls, so less stock is needed in the replicating portfolio). Then ask yourself whether you are long or short the replicating portfolio (you are short here). If you are short, be sure to reverse the implications (less stock shorted means you must borrow to buy some back).

Answer 2.8: With the standard European call, you have a simple closed-form expression for the option's delta. For example, (under the Black and Scholes [1973] assumptions) the delta of a standard European call on a non-dividend-paying asset is equal to $N(d_1)$ where

$$d_1 = \frac{\ln\left(\frac{S(t)}{X}\right) + (r + \frac{1}{2}\sigma^2)(T - t)}{\sigma\sqrt{T - t}}.$$

See Answer 2.6 for the delta in the case where there are continuous dividends at rate ρ.

Unfortunately, only a few known options have closed-form pricing formulae. For exotic options with no closed-form pricing formula, you need a pricing algorithm. This may be a Monte-Carlo simulation,[6] a binomial tree, a numerical PDE solution routine, or perhaps an ODE approximation to a PDE. By varying the input value of the current level of underlying, you can use the pricing algorithm to calculate a numerical derivative of price with respect to level of underlying; i.e., the delta. All you are doing is using the computer rather than the calculus to tell you how the option price changes with a change in stock price.

Answer 2.9: The pricing formula for the standard Black-Scholes European call option on a non-dividend-paying stock is:

$$c(t) = S(t)N(d_1) - e^{-r(T-t)}XN(d_2),$$

where d_1 and d_2 are as previously defined. $N(d_1)$ is the option's "delta," sometimes denoted "Δ." $\Delta = N(d_1)$ is the same thing as the partial derivative

---

[6] As an introduction to exotic options and Monte-Carlo techniques, I recommend the Monte-Carlo chapter of my book *Basic Black-Scholes* (Crack [2021]). The earliest Monte-Carlo reference I know of in option pricing is Boyle (1977). Boyle also gives techniques for accelerating the convergence of Monte-Carlo estimation and some references to the mathematics literature (see Hull [1997, pp. 365–368] for other techniques). For background information on the development of exotics and the players in the market, see Fraser (1993); for a slightly higher-level than Hunter and Stowe (1992), see Ritchken, Sankarasubramanian, and Vijh (1993) or Hull (1997); at a slightly higher level still, see Goldman, Sosin, and Gatto (1979) or Conze and Viswanathan (1991). Note that the value of a look-back option to buy at the minimum or sell at the maximum might arguably be considered an upper bound on the value of market timing skills—see Goldman, Sosin, and Shepp (1979) for more details.

of call price with respect to underlying: $\frac{\partial c(t)}{\partial S(t)}$. It measures how the call price changes per unit change in the price of the underlying.

Another interpretation of the terms involves a replicating portfolio. $\Delta = N(d_1)$ is the number of units of stock you must hold in a continuously rebalanced portfolio that replicates the payoff to the call. The term $e^{-r(T-t)}XN(d_2)$ is the value of the borrowing (or a short position in bonds) required in a continuously rebalanced portfolio that replicates the payoff to the call. The value of the borrowing in the replicating portfolio is always less than or equal to the value of the replicating portfolio's long position in the stock. This is equivalent to stating that the call has non-negative value.

Another interpretation of the terms involves expected benefits and expected costs to owning the call. The term $S(t)N(d_1)$ is the discounted value of the expected *benefit* of owning the option (expectations taken under a risk-neutral probability measure). Why is the $N(d_1)$ there? Well, $N(\cdot)$ is a cumulative distribution function, so it must be that $N(d_1) \leq 1$. This in turn implies that $S(t)N(d_1) \leq S(t)$. This is because the future benefit of owning the option is $S(T)$ if the option finishes in-the-money and zero if it finishes out-of-the-money (or "under water"). This benefit is strictly dominated by a long position in the stock (a position that returns $S(T)$ regardless of whether the option is in- or out-of-the-money and costs $S(t)$ now). It follows that you value the benefit from the call at less than the long position in the stock, $S(t)N(d_1) \leq S(t)$. It is for this reason that the $N(d_1)$ term multiplies the $S(t)$ term.[7]

The term $e^{-r(T-t)}XN(d_2)$ is the discounted value of the expected *cost* of owning the option (with expectations taken under a risk-neutral probability measure). You can see all the components of the discounted expected value as follows: $N(d_2)$ is the (risk-neutral) probability that the call option finishes in-the-money (see extended discussion in Crack [2021]); X is your cost if it does; and $e^{-r(T-t)}$ is the discounting factor.

Here is a summary of the foregoing paragraphs (where "$P(in)$" denotes the risk-neutral probability that the call finishes in-the-money):

$$c(t) = \overbrace{S(t)\underbrace{N(d_1)}_{\Delta}}^{\text{stock position \& benefit}} \underbrace{-e^{-r(T-t)}X\overbrace{N(d_2)}^{\text{bond position}}}_{\text{borrowing \& cost}}{}_{P(in)}$$

The value of the standard European put on a non-dividend-paying stock may now be deduced. The present value of the *benefit* of owning the put is

---

[7]The first term is $S(t)N(d_1) = e^{-r(T-t)}E^*[S(T)\mathcal{I}_{S(T)>X}|S(t)]$, where E^* denotes expectation taken with respect to the risk-neutral probability measure, and $\mathcal{I}_{S(T)>X}$ is as given in Equation B.1.

$$\mathcal{I}_{S(T)>X} = \begin{cases} 1 \text{ if } S(T) > X, \\ 0 \text{ if } S(T) \leq X. \end{cases} \tag{B.1}$$

$e^{-r(T-t)}X[1 - N(d_2)]$, where $[1 - N(d_2)]$ is the (risk-neutral) probability that the put option finishes in-the-money (i.e., the call finishes out-of-the-money), X is your payoff if it does, and $e^{-r(T-t)}$ is the discounting factor.

The present value of the *cost* of owning the put option is $S(t)[1 - N(d_1)]$. There are two probabilistic interpretations of $N(d_1)$, each under a competing martingale measure (see Crack [2021]).

Using the property that $[1 - N(z)] = N(-z)$, the value of the put option must be

$$p(t) = e^{-r(T-t)}XN(-d_2) - S(t)N(-d_1),$$

where d_1 and d_2 are as already defined for the call.

Put-call parity says that

$$S(t) + p(t) = c(t) + Xe^{-r(T-t)} + D.$$

If you plug in $c(t) = S(t)N(d_1) - e^{-r(T-t)}XN(d_2)$, and $D = 0$, you do indeed get that $p(t) = e^{-r(T-t)}XN(-d_2) - S(t)N(-d_1)$, as deduced above.

See Crack (2021, Chapter 8) for extensive discussion of Black-Scholes interpretations and intuition.[8]

Answer 2.10: Questions about a "digital option" or "binary option" are quite common. The digital "cash-or-nothing" option that pays H if $S(T) > X$ has a value of $He^{-r(T-t)}N(d_2)$. This is simply the discounted (risk-neutral) expected payoff to the option: $N(d_2)$ is the (risk-neutral) probability that the option finishes in-the-money; H is the payoff if it does; and $e^{-r(T-t)}$ is the discounting factor. H is sometimes called the "bet." If H is chosen to equal the strike of the standard Black-Scholes option, then the cash-or-nothing option has the same value as the second term in the Black-Scholes formula: $e^{-r(T-t)}XN(d_2)$.

The first term in the Black-Scholes formula, $S(t)N(d_1)$, is the value of a long position in a digital "asset-or-nothing" option. A long position in the asset-or-nothing option, combined with a short position in the cash-or-nothing option, replicates the payoff to the European call—and, therefore, has the same value (you should draw the payoff diagrams to verify this).[9]

Be sure to see Question 2.11 and Answer 2.11 for more details on the binary option.

Answer 2.11: I look at this intuitively first and then more rigorously. Intuitively, if the digital "cash-or-nothing" option is deep in-the-money, you are just waiting for your fixed cash payoff, and increases in volatility can only decrease

---

[8]Note that there is a competing stock-numeraire world where if the bond de-trended by the stock follows a martingale, then $N(d_1)$ in the Black-Scholes formula is the probability that the call finishes in the money (see Crack [2021] for details). It is a Z-score argument similar to the one that establishes $N(d_2)$ as the probability that the call finishes in the money in a world in which the stock de-trended by the bond follows a martingale.

[9]As an aside, you might like to note that the payoff to the European call may also be replicated by using barrier options: you need a "knock-out" call option plus a "knock-in" call option.

your payoff. If you are deep out-of-the-money, you are expecting nothing, and increases in volatility can only increase your payoff. If $c(t)$ is the price of the digital cash-or-nothing option, then somewhere around the at-the-money position, the sign of $\frac{\partial c(t)}{\partial \sigma^2}$ must change.

Rigorously, if $c(t)$ is the price of the digital cash-or-nothing option, then direct calculation (under Black-Scholes assumptions) shows that[10]

$$\frac{\partial c(t)}{\partial \sigma^2} > 0 \text{ if and only if } S(t) < Xe^{-(r+\frac{\sigma^2}{2})(T-t)}.$$

Another (equivalent) way of looking at this is that $\frac{\partial c(t)}{\partial \sigma^2} > 0$ if and only if the probability of finishing in-the-money increases with an increase in σ^2, and this is so if and only if $S(t) < Xe^{-(r+\frac{\sigma^2}{2})(T-t)}$.

Figure B.2 (on p. 173) shows $\frac{\partial \text{ CALL PRICE}}{\partial \sigma^2}$ for the asset-or-nothing digital option, the cash-or-nothing digital option, and the standard call (all options are European). The price of the standard call is just the difference between the prices of the asset-or-nothing digital option and the cash-or-nothing digital option. Differentiation is a linear operation, so the sensitivity of the standard call to volatility is just the difference between the sensitivity of the asset-or-nothing digital option and the cash-or-nothing digital option.

It is clear from Figure B.2 that the price of the standard call is increasing in volatility. This should come as no surprise. A call option is an insurance policy. It puts a floor on your losses. When there is more risk about, the premium (i.e., call price) should be higher. In the same way, you should be happy to pay more for fire insurance if you find out that your next-door neighbor is an arsonist. See Chance (1994) for more details on the sensitivity of option value to the various input parameters.

For the cash-or-nothing, the boundary on the sign of $\frac{\partial c(t)}{\partial \sigma^2}$ is always slightly less than X (see Figure B.2 for a clear illustration). Thus, if you are in-the-money, or at-the-money, more volatility is always bad; if you are very slightly out-of-the-money, more volatility is still bad [when $Xe^{-(r+\frac{\sigma^2}{2})(T-t)} < S(t) \leq X$]; if you are well out-of-the-money, more volatility is always good [when $S(t) < Xe^{-(r+\frac{\sigma^2}{2})(T-t)}$]. This differs from the standard European call option for which $\frac{\partial c(t)}{\partial \sigma^2}$ is always non-negative (see Figure B.2).

You might ask why the boundary on the sign of $\frac{\partial c(t)}{\partial \sigma^2}$ is always slightly less than X, rather than exactly at X. The relationship between volatility and skewness in the (lognormal) distribution of final stock price is where the explanation lies. There are two forces at work: First, an increase in σ^2 tends to spread

---

[10]Note that I am taking vega (i.e., sensitivity of option price to volatility) as $\frac{\partial c}{\partial \sigma^2}$, but that I could equally well have used $\frac{\partial c}{\partial \sigma}$, with the same result. This is because $\frac{\partial c}{\partial \sigma^2} = \frac{\partial c}{\partial \sigma} \Big/ \frac{\partial \sigma^2}{\partial \sigma} = \frac{1}{2\sigma}\frac{\partial c}{\partial \sigma}$. So, $\text{sign}\left(\frac{\partial c}{\partial \sigma^2}\right) = \text{sign}\left(\frac{\partial c}{\partial \sigma}\right)$.

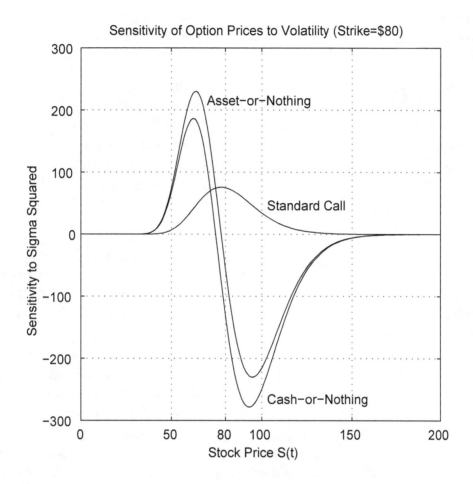

Figure B.2: Sensitivity of Option Prices to Volatility

Note: The figure plots $\frac{\partial \text{ CALL PRICE}}{\partial \sigma^2}$ (i.e., "vega") using parameters $X = 80$, $r = 0.05$, $T - t = 1$, and $\sigma = 0.20$. The asset-or-nothing call price is always more sensitive to σ^2 than the cash-or-nothing call price. The difference between the sensitivities of each digital option is thus non-negative. The standard European call is equivalent to a long position in the asset-or-nothing and a short position in the cash-or-nothing. The response of the standard call price to increases in σ^2 is thus non-negative.

out the distribution of $S(T)$, putting more probability weight into the tails; second, increasing σ^2 drags down the median of the distribution,[11] tending to pull probability weight leftward and out of the right tail, thus increasing the skewness. If the strike price is at or below the median of $S(T)$ (so the option is in-the-money, or very slightly out-of-the-money), then both forces push probability mass leftward, increasing the likelihood of finishing out-of-the-money. However, if the strike price is far above the median of $S(T)$ (so the option is far out-of-the-money), then the increasing spread of the distribution dominates the leftward move of the median, and the probability of finishing in-the-money increases with increasing σ^2. For the forces to be balanced, the option must be struck above the median of the distribution of $S(T)$. The strike price that just balances the influence of both forces is $X = S(t)e^{(r+\frac{\sigma^2}{2})(T-t)}$. At this strike, the option is insensitive to instantaneous changes in σ^2 and it is slightly out-of-the-money: $S(t) = Xe^{-(r+\frac{\sigma^2}{2})(T-t)}$.

Answer 2.12: The naive and time-consuming way to find the delta for the knock-out option (or "barrier option") is to differentiate the closed-form pricing formula for the down-and-out, find $\frac{\partial C}{\partial S}$, and compare it to the same quantity for the standard call.[12] It is more elegant to use common sense and some limiting relationships to deduce the relationships between the deltas of the knock-outs and the standard call.

The delta is the sensitivity of call price to underlying. This means that the option's delta is just the slope when you plot call value, $c(t)$, against underlying value, $S(t)$. Do not get this plot mixed up with the *payoff* diagram (the one with a "kink" for a standard call). See Figure B.1 (on p. 166).

Now, everything you can do with a down-and-out option, you can also do with a standard option. On top of that, you still have a standard option in your hands in cases where the down-and-out gets "knocked out." It follows that the standard call is more versatile than the down-and-out call and must be more expensive. Thus, the value of the standard call must plot above the value of the down-and-out call for any value of the underlying. However, the two calls have the same value for very large $S(t)$—because the down-and-out option is unlikely to get knocked out. Both valuation curves are smooth, so the down-and-out call's valuation curve must be steeper [it starts lower than the standard call and "finishes" in the same place for high $S(t)$]. A steeper valuation curve when plotted against the level of underlying means precisely that the delta is higher for the down-and-out call than for the standard call.

---

[11]The mean of the risk-neutral distribution of $S(T)$ conditional on $S(t)$ is $S(t)e^{r(T-t)}$; the median is $S(t)e^{(r-\frac{1}{2}\sigma^2)(T-t)}$.

[12]The closed-form valuation formula for the down-and-out, together with discussion, is in Merton ([1973, pp. 175–76]; [1992, p. 302]). It takes around 15 minutes to differentiate it by hand carefully and about the same time to program the numerical derivative in MATLAB. The down-and-out option was introduced by Gerard Snyder (1969). See his paper for a look at the operations of the options markets in the late 1960s.

For the up-and-out, you get a different answer. As before, the up-and-out is a knock-out option and is cheaper than the standard call. However, the standard call option and the up-and-out call option have the same value for very small $S(t)$—because the up-and-out option is unlikely to get knocked out. Both valuation curves are smooth, so the up-and-out call's valuation curve must be flatter (it starts in the same place as the standard call and finishes lower). A flatter valuation curve means precisely that the delta is lower for the up-and-out call than for the standard call.

Thus, the following relationships hold for the deltas of the different options:

$$\Delta_{up-and-out\ call} \leq \Delta_{standard\ call} \leq \Delta_{down-and-out\ call}$$

To hedge a short position in a down-and-out call, you need to buy more units of stock than you do to hedge a short position in a standard call. The value of the down-and-out call is more sensitive than the standard call to changes in the value of the underlying stock.

Note that increasing the term to maturity or increasing the knock-out price both increase the likelihood that a down-and-out call will be knocked out. This makes the down-and-out call even cheaper relative to the standard call. In fact, if the down-and-out call is very likely to be knocked out, the plot of down-and-out call price against stock price can become concave. Conversely, if the term to maturity is very short and the knock-out price is very low, the standard call and the down-and-out call have virtually identical prices (because the knock-out is very unlikely to be knocked out).

Answer 2.13: Your observation is that the sample variances are not linear in time and that the differences are statistically significant. This is equivalent to rejecting the null hypothesis of a random walk using a "variance ratio" test (Lo and MacKinlay [1988]).[13] This is contrary to the random walk assumptions of the Black-Scholes model.

The observations are consistent with the empirical findings that some financial stock indices are positively autocorrelated at weekly return intervals (Lo and MacKinlay [1988]).[14] This predictability influences the theoretical value and the empirical estimate of the diffusion coefficient σ (Lo and Wang [1995]). An adjustment can be made to the Black-Scholes formula to account for the predictability that is not part of the original Black-Scholes model. A new diffusion process that captures the predictability can be defined (Lo and Wang [1995]).

With the new specification, the autocorrelation is described using a more complicated drift in the diffusion. The drift is now important for pricing the

---

[13]See also Peterson et al. (1992) for related variance ratio testing in the commodities market; their findings lead them to a brief discussion of option pricing in the presence of autocorrelation.

[14]Autocorrelation in a time series is correlation between observations and themselves lagged. It is also known as "serial correlation." Its presence neither implies, nor is implied by, the presence of a drift (Crack, 2020b).

option. In the old specification, drift was not important (Black and Scholes [1973]; Merton [1973]).

The final pricing formula takes the same form as the original Black and Scholes (1973) formula. However, the way in which the volatility term σ is estimated changes. An increase in autocorrelation may either increase or decrease the value of σ—it depends upon the specification of the drift (Lo and Wang [1995, p. 105]).

The presence of autocorrelation in stock returns is only one example of a real world divergence from the Black and Scholes (1973) assumptions. For example, Thorp (1973) discusses the effect of restrictions on short sales proceeds. See Hammer (1989) for a discussion of other deviations.

Answer 2.14: With no dividends, it is never optimal to exercise the plain vanilla American call option prior to maturity because the option is worth more "alive" than "dead." If you never exercise early, then the "American" feature of the call is not valuable. Thus, the standard American call option and European call option (on a non-dividend-paying stock) have equal values. See Crack (2021) for extensive discussion.

Figure B.3 plots the time value of the call option, $c(t) - \max[S(t) - X, 0]$, against $S(t)$ for the parameter values $X = 80$, $r = 0.05$, $T - t = 1$, and $\sigma = 0.20$. I have replaced the American call value $C(t)$ with the European value $c(t)$ because they are the same thing for plain vanilla call options in the absence of dividends.

The time value (the height in Figure B.3) tends to zero as expiration approaches, and this is regardless of stock price. The existence of positive time value (i.e., value over and above exercise value) means that there is value in waiting to exercise. It is this value that makes the American call more valuable alive than dead. However, this does not mean that you should continue to hold the option. Rather, it means that if you wish to exit the call position, you should sell it, not exercise it. The time value is easily seen by looking at the excess of option price over intrinsic value in the "Listed Options Quotations" (i.e., options on individual stocks) in the *Wall Street Journal* or online.

How does time value arise? There are costs to exercising a call prior to maturity: you lose the interest you would have earned on the strike price and you lose the ability to exercise later. These costs are both intimately linked with the time to maturity, and thus they decline to zero as maturity approaches. There is a benefit to early exercise of a call: you capture any dividend payment on the underlying. In the presence of dividends, you gain the benefits with least cost by waiting until just prior to the ex-dividend day to exercise. In this case, you would exercise only if the benefit outweighs the costs. In practice, these costs of early exercise typically outweigh the benefit until the last ex-dividend date during the life of the option (Cox and Rubinstein [1985, p. 144]). By this time the costs of early exercise have depreciated substantially. A very large expected dividend might also trigger early exercise.

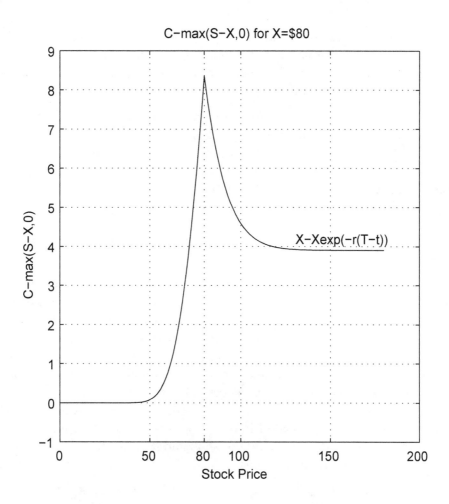

Figure B.3: Time Value of a European Call Option

Note: The difference $c(t) - \max[S(t) - X, 0]$ is the value of not exercising. When the option is deep out-of-the-money, $\max[S(t) - X, 0] = 0$, and $c(t)$ is approximately zero. When the option is deep in-the-money, you save X by not exercising now, but it costs you the present value of exercising at maturity: $X \times e^{-r(T-t)}$. The left-hand limit of $X - X \times e^{-r(T-t)} = X \times \left(1 - e^{-r(T-t)}\right)$ is always non-negative. The "kink" in $\max[S(t) - X, 0]$ puts the "cusp" in the plot of $c(t) - \max[S(t) - X, 0]$ versus $S(t)$ at $S(t) = X$.

Answer 2.15: The naive answer is that as stock price falls, so too does the delta. However, this ignores the influence of the passage of time on your hedge. This is a good question, because you must think in both dimensions.

Two opposing forces are at work here: First, other things being equal, the delta of a call option that is in-the-money rises toward +1 as the option gets closer to expiration;[15] second, other things being equal, as stock price falls, the delta of a call option falls.

If stock price is observed to fall gently over the final two months, and the option remains in-the-money, the approach of the expiration date pushes the delta up to +1. If the fall in stock price is a little stronger, you may see the delta fall somewhat initially (and you will sell stock in your hedge portfolio). However, if the option finishes in-the-money, then the delta rises to +1 at the end of the life of the option (and you will buy stock in your hedge portfolio).

Answer 2.16: Introductory courses typically do not say much about jump processes.

The Black and Scholes (1973) model naively assumes that stock prices are continuous. That is, they assume that you can draw the price history without lifting your pencil from the paper. You need only stand on the floor of an exchange,[16] watch a real-time feed (e.g., on a Bloomberg terminal), or read the WSJ headlines after an "event" to see that prices do not move smoothly. Indeed, the fact that stock prices are typically quoted with a minimum tick size (either exchange-imposed or effective) means that stock prices *cannot* move continuously. You can think of big stock price jumps as being stock price responses to the arrival of information in the market; small stock price jumps might just be due to the random ebb and flow of non-information-based (i.e., liquidity-related) transactions.

A "jump" price process is a price process that has infrequent jumps (i.e., discontinuities) in it. If the jump process is a very simple one, the Black-Scholes/Merton no-arbitrage technique can still be used to hedge and price options on an asset whose price follows the process. If the jump process is more complicated, the no-arbitrage technique breaks down. See the following

---

[15]If the option you sold finishes in-the-money, you need to be long the stock because it will be called away. Of course, if the option is out-of-the-money, the approach of the expiration pushes the delta down to zero. If the option is at-the-money, then (assuming a non-dividend-paying stock) the delta tends to a number slightly greater than one-half as the expiration date approaches (Cox and Rubinstein [1985, figure 5-13, p. 223]).

[16]I have been on the floors of the New York Stock Exchange (NYSE), Chicago Board of Trade (CBOT), Boston Stock Exchange (BSE), and Dunedin Stock Exchange—long since replaced by screen trading—during trading hours. I have also visited the Chicago Board Options Exchange (CBOE), Chicago Mercantile Exchange (CME), Chicago Stock Exchange (CSE), and the old Paris Bourse. The financial futures floor at the CBOT was big enough to fit a 747 jumbo jet with space to spare—and noisy as hell. Conversely, the BSE is small and quieter than your typical MBA computer lab. I forecast that all the Chicago futures exchange floors will soon be deserted—replaced by electronic trading. The NYSE may take a little longer, but I think it will suffer the same fate.

discussion, and go to the references if you need more details. I have included some lengthy comments and references. This is because I think it is relevant, and it is often not covered in introductory courses.

A simple jump process example (that is *not* a diffusion) has $\frac{dS}{S} = \mu dt + (J-1)d\pi$ (Cox and Ross [1976, p. 147]). In this example, $J-1$ is the jump amplitude (where $J \geq 0$), $d\pi$ takes the value $+1$ with probability λdt and 0 with probability[17] $1 - \lambda dt$. The percentage stock price change $\frac{dS}{S}$ can thus jump suddenly to $J-1$ (which may itself be random); such a jump pushes S to SJ.

In this simple example, if J is fixed (i.e., non-random), a riskless hedge portfolio *can* be formed, and options on an asset whose price follows this simple jump process *can* be valued using the Black-Scholes/Merton no-arbitrage technique. This should come as no big surprise. The only real difference between this "pure Poisson process" case, and the simple binomial option pricing situation (Sharpe [1978]; Cox, Ross, and Rubinstein [1979]; Rendleman and Bartter [1979]; Cox and Rubinstein [1985]; Crack [2021]) is that the arrival time of the jump up or jump down is a random variable. You do not need to know *when* the stock price will jump to hedge the risk in a binomial setting. This "pure Poisson process" is a special case of a more general jump diffusion process discussed next.

Consider the jump diffusion process $\frac{dS}{S} = (\alpha - \lambda k)dt + \sigma dZ + dq$ (described in detail in my Footnote 8 to Question 2.16 on p. 30). When $\sigma = 0$ and $Y \equiv dq+1$ is non-random, you get Cox and Ross's simple jump process above, and the no-arbitrage technique can be used to hedge and price options on the jump process.[18] Otherwise, when $\sigma > 0$ and $\text{var}(Y) \geq 0$ it is not possible to form a riskless hedge portfolio or use the no-arbitrage technique (Cox and Ross [1976, p. 147]; Cox and Rubinstein [1985, pp. 361–371]; Merton [1992, p. 316]). Both the (non-jump) diffusion process and the (non-diffusion) simple jump process are the continuous limits of discrete binomial models. However, the jump-diffusion is not. It is for this reason that a riskless hedge cannot be formed in the jump-diffusion case (Cox and Rubinstein [1985, pp. 361–371]).

The fundamental reason that the no-arbitrage technique can be used to hedge and price options in the standard Black-Scholes world is linearity. In continuous time, the Black-Scholes option price is an instantaneously linear function of the stock price. Portfolio building is a linear operation, and it follows that payoffs to the option can be perfectly replicated by building and continuously rebalancing a portfolio of the stock and the bond. Linearity breaks down when the jump term has positive variance—the call price becomes a nonlinear function of the stock price and perfect hedging is not possible (Merton [1992,

---

[17]In this example, π is a continuous time "Poisson process." The term λ is the "intensity" of the process.

[18]I thank John Cox at MIT for explaining to me why such jump processes can be perfectly hedged (personal communication [February 17, 1994]).

p. 316]).

Although the no-arbitrage technique fails to price the option on the jump diffusion process, you can price the option using an *equilibrium* argument. An instantaneous CAPM (capital asset pricing model) approach may be used— as it was in the original Black and Scholes (1973) paper. The information that causes jumps may be assumed to be firm-specific (i.e., unsystematic and diversifiable).[19] You can hedge out the non-jump part of the option and deduce that the remainder (the jump) must have zero beta and, therefore, a riskless rate of return. This yields a partial differential equation that can be solved to give the call option price as an infinite summation:

$$C(S(t), T - t) = \sum_{n=0}^{\infty} \left\{ \frac{\exp[-\lambda(T - t)][\lambda(T - t)]^n}{n!} \times \right.$$

$$\left. E_n\{W[S(t)X_n \exp(-\lambda k(T - t)), (T - t); X, \sigma^2, r]\} \right\}$$

Here X_n is a random variable with the same distribution as the product of n independent and identically distributed random variables each identically distributed to the random variable Y (recall that $Y - 1$ is the random percentage change in stock price when a jump occurs), $X_0 \equiv 1$, E_n is the expectation operator over the distribution of X_n, and $W[S, (T - t); X, \sigma^2, r]$ is the standard Black-Scholes pricing formula (see Merton (1992, pp. 318–320) for a full discussion of the foregoing and Haug [2007, Section 6.9.1] for practical issues).

You cannot perfectly hedge the call when the underlying follows the general jump diffusion $[\sigma > 0, \text{var}(Y) \geq 0]$. However, you can hedge out the continuous parts of the stock and option price movements. This leaves a risky hedge portfolio following a pure jump process (with stochastic jump size). If you follow the Black-Scholes hedge when you are short the option, then most of the time you earn more than the expected rate of return on the risky hedge portfolio. However, if one of those occasional jumps occurs (i.e., news arrives), you suffer a reasonably large loss. In the non-diversifiable jump case, the return to the hedge portfolio when there is a jump balances the return during normal time to some extent, but not well enough to make the equilibrium return on the hedge equal to the riskless rate; as mentioned above, the hedge is risky.

In general, there is no way to adjust the parameters of the hedge technique (σ^2, for example) to get a better hedge (see Merton [1992, pp. 316–317] for a full discussion of the issues).[20]

Finally, if the underlying asset price is modeled as a jump process, the standard Black-Scholes call option formula mis-prices the option. Both the magnitude

---

[19]Note that in situations where the size of the jump is assumed to be systematic, the risk-neutral pricing technique cannot be used to value options. Hull (1997, p. 449, Footnote 14) directs the reader to Naik and Lee (1990) for a discussion of this point.

[20]For theoretical and empirical comparisons of the Merton (1976) jump process call option pricing and the standard Black-Scholes pricing, see Ball and Torous (1985).

---

and the direction of the mis-pricing of the Black-Scholes model relative to the jump model vary with the distributional assumption for the size of the jump component (Trippi et al. [1992]).

Answer 2.17: Most people upon whom I have tested this one make several mistakes. Please note that at time t prior to maturity the call price function is *not* asymptotic to the line with slope 1 rising from the strike price;[21] Merton (1973) demonstrates the correct relationship, discussed below. So, if you made this mistake, stop reading here and go back and try again.

The correct plots appear in Figure B.4. The parameters used are $X = 80$, $r = 0.05$, $T - t = 1$, and $\sigma = 0.20$. The plot of call value against terminal stock price is the classic "kinked" call option payoff (the top plot in Figure B.4). Call value (terminal payoff) rises with slope 1 from the point $S(T) = X$.

The plot of call price versus futures price is a smooth curve that is asymptotic to the line $c = 0$ when the futures price, $F(t, T) = S(t)e^{r(T-t)}$, is very small, and asymptotic to a line rising with slope $e^{-r(T-t)}$ (i.e., slightly less than 1) from the point $F(t, T) = X$ when the futures price is very large (the middle plot in Figure B.4). One way to confirm the slope of this line is to use the chain rule: $\frac{\partial C}{\partial F} = \frac{\partial C}{\partial S} \cdot \frac{\partial S}{\partial F}$, where $\frac{\partial C}{\partial S}$ is the delta (which goes to 1 when F and S are large) and $\frac{\partial S}{\partial F}$ is just $e^{-r(T-t)}$. The slope of the line in this middle plot thus gets closer to one as maturity approaches, but it is strictly less than one at any prior time.

The plot of call price versus stock price, $S(t)$, is a smooth curve that is asymptotic to the line $c = 0$ when the stock price, $S(t)$, is very small, and asymptotic to the line that rises with slope 1 from the point $S(t) = Xe^{-r(T-t)}$ (which equals \$76.10 here) when the stock price is very large.[22] See the bottom plot in Figure B.4. The last two results are tied together by the fact that $F(t, T) = X \Leftrightarrow S(t) = Xe^{-r(T-t)}$.

At time t prior to maturity, the call price is lower if the futures price is equal to \$10 than it is if the stock price is equal to \$10. This is because the futures price represents expected future value in some sense, and this is not worth as much as current value (\$10 today is worth more than \$10 tomorrow).

Answer 2.18: It should take only a few seconds to answer this fundamental question. Black and Scholes (1973) assume an arithmetic Brownian motion in log price. This assumption yields a geometric Brownian motion in price. The volatility of continuously compounded stock returns, σ^2, grows linearly with holding period when stock prices follow a geometric Brownian motion. So, the four-year σ^2 is *four* times the one-year σ^2. It follows that the four-year σ is

---

[21] A curve is "asymptotic" to a line (i.e., an asymptote) if the curve gets closer and closer to the line. For example, $y = \frac{1}{x}$, for $x > 0$ is asymptotic to the line $y = 0$ as $x \to \infty$ and asymptotic to the line $x = 0$ as $y \to \infty$.

[22] Note that this implies that the time value $\{c(t) - \max[S(t) - X, 0]\} \to \{X - Xe^{-r(T-t)}\}$ as $S(t) \to \infty$. See Figure B.3 (on p. 177) for a plot of time value versus stock price.

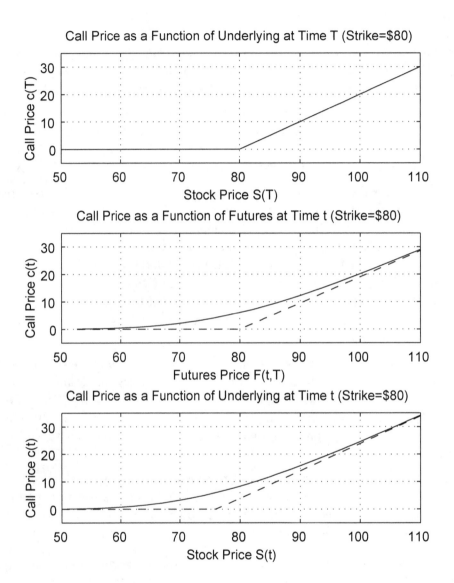

Figure B.4: Call Price as a Function of Different Variables

Note: Call price is plotted as a function of price of underlying and of futures price (see Answer 2.17).

two times the one-year σ. So, the one-year σ of 15% must be doubled to get 30% (all assuming that you use $T - t = 1$ in the Black-Scholes formula in both cases).

If $r > 0$, you must adjust the value of r (r is four times as large when one period is four years as compared to when one period is one year).

Answer 2.19: Suppose that the process $\mathcal{S}(t)$ is an arithmetic Brownian motion of form

$$d\mathcal{S}(t) = \mu dt + \sigma_A dw(t),$$

where μ is the instantaneous drift per unit time, σ_A is the instantaneous volatility of $\mathcal{S}(t)$, and $w(t)$ is a standard Brownian motion (see Crack [2021] for introductory discussion of Brownian motions). Under our assumptions, and under the risk-neutral probability measure, the process is $d\mathcal{S}(t) = \sigma_A dw^*(t)$.

Assume a strike of $\mathcal{X}$. Note that under the risk-neutral probability measure with $r = 0$ the process $\mathcal{S}(t)$ is given by Equation B.2:

$$\mathcal{S}(t) = \sigma_A w^*(t) \qquad (B.2)$$

The call price is the discounted expected payoff under the risk-neutral probability measure, as follows:

$$
\begin{aligned}
c(t) &= e^{-r(T-t)} \, E^*[\max(\mathcal{S}(T) - \mathcal{X}, 0) \mid \mathcal{S}(t)] \\
&= E^*[\max(\mathcal{S}(T) - \mathcal{X}, 0) \mid \mathcal{S}(t)]
\end{aligned}
$$

From Equation B.2, it follows that

$$
\begin{aligned}
\mathcal{S}(T) &= \mathcal{S}(t) + \sigma_A(w^*(T) - w^*(t)) \\
&= \mathcal{S}(t) + \sigma_A \mathcal{W}^*,
\end{aligned}
$$

where $\mathcal{W}^* \equiv w^*(T) - w^*(t)$ is normal $N(0, T-t)$ under the risk-neutral probability measure. Now let "v" play the part of $\mathcal{W}^*$ distributed as $N(0, T-t)$. Then the call price is given by the following integration over the normal density:

$$c(t) = \int_{v_0}^{+\infty} (\mathcal{S}(t) + \sigma_A v - \mathcal{X}) \; f_V(v) \; dv,$$

where

$$f_V(v) = \frac{1}{\sqrt{2\pi}\,\sqrt{T-t}} e^{-\frac{1}{2}\left(\frac{v}{\sqrt{T-t}}\right)^2}$$

is the pdf of $v \sim N(0, T-t)$, and

$$v_0 \equiv \frac{\mathcal{X} - \mathcal{S}(t)}{\sigma_A}$$

is the boundary value of v at which $(\mathcal{S}(t) + \sigma_A v - \mathcal{X})$ changes sign.

The remainder of the proof is left to the reader. The final result is

$$c(t) = \sigma_A \sqrt{T-t} \left\{ \frac{e^{-\frac{1}{2}d^2}}{\sqrt{2\pi}} + N(d)\,d \right\}, \qquad \text{(B.3)}$$

$$\text{where} \quad d = \frac{\mathcal{S}(t) - \mathcal{X}}{\sigma_A \sqrt{T-t}}.$$

The arithmetic Brownian motion pricing formula (equation B.3, above) is not well known. This is because an arithmetic Brownian motion is not a reasonable assumption for a price process: arithmetic Brownian motions can assume negative values. However, the geometric Brownian motion assumed by Black and Scholes (1973) is always non-negative, just as a price process should be. The importance of pricing options on stock catapulted the Black-Scholes formula (and the geometric Brownian motion beneath it) to super-stardom, while the pricing formula for the arithmetic Brownian motion languishes in relative obscurity.

Let's have a little history. Louis Jean-Baptiste Alphonse Bachelier finished his mathematics PhD thesis at the Sorbonne in Paris in January 1900.[23] The topic of his thesis was the pricing of options contracts traded on the Paris Bourse.[24] Bachelier (1900) assumes that stock prices are normally distributed and follow an arithmetic Brownian motion. He also assumes that expected returns on stocks (and on investments in general) are zero. Bachelier was the first to publish payoff diagrams for a European call option. Bachelier was also the first mathematician to use the "reflection principle."[25] Bachelier's derivation of the mathematical properties of Brownian motion predates by five years Albert Einstein's 1905 work on Brownian motion (Einstein [1905]). Bachelier even tested the predictions of his model using actual option prices on the Paris Bourse and found them not too far wrong.[26]

Unfortunately, Bachelier's assumptions violate some basic economic principles. In particular, he violates limited liability, time preference, and risk aversion

---

[23] The Sorbonne was the prestigious University of Paris founded by Robert de Sorbon in 1253. The Sorbonne was split into 13 units during the period 1968–1970. Nowadays, the name "Sorbonne" refers to the original university or to three of the 13 units that retain the title as part of their name. I have had the pleasure of visiting the Sorbonne as a tourist twice. It is on the Left Bank, not far from Notre Dame.

[24] A very brief look at Bachelier's model is in Appendix A of Smith (1976); a full translation appears in Cootner (1964). Note that my option pricing formula, Equation B.3, is mathematically equivalent to equation A.5 in Smith (1976). On an historical point of some coincidence, note that as I write this (for my first edition in 1995) it is Louis Bachelier's 125th birthday. Bachelier was born in Le Havre, France, on March 11th, 1870. See also Zimmerman and Hafner (2007) for a discussion of the Bronzin option pricing work of 1908.

[25] It is also known as the method of "reflected images." If you do not yet know what the reflection principle is, you probably do not need to know. If you are curious, see Harrison (1985, p. 7) for details.

[26] Samuelson (1973, Footnote 2, p. 6) compares Bachelier (1900) and Einstein (1905). He declares Bachelier dominant "in every element of the vector." See Samuelson (1973) for further discussion (and criticism) of Bachelier and other topics in the mathematics of speculative prices.

(see Samuelson [1965, p. 13] for discussion). However, the significant contributions of Bachelier's thesis mean that he is rightfully considered the "father of modern option pricing theory" (Sullivan and Weithers [1991]).

In the special case when $\mathcal{S}(t) = \mathcal{X}$ (the option is struck at-the-money), Equation B.3 reduces to[27]

$$c_A(t) = \sigma_A \sqrt{\frac{T-t}{2\pi}}, \tag{B.4}$$

where my "A" indicates that the underlying process, $\mathcal{S}(t)$, is an *arithmetic* Brownian motion, and σ_A is the standard deviation of the level of $\mathcal{S}(t)$.

Equation B.4 was derived assuming $r = 0$, and $\mathcal{S}(t) = \mathcal{X}$, plus the assumption of arithmetic Brownian motion. You might reasonably ask how does Equation B.4 compare to Black-Scholes for an at-the-money call option when $r = 0$?

The Black-Scholes formula for pricing a standard European call on a non-dividend-paying stock reduces to Equation B.5 in the special case when $r = 0$ and $S(t) = X$ (i.e., the option is struck at-the-money):

$$c_{BS}(t) = S(t) \left[N\left(+\frac{\sigma}{2}\sqrt{T-t} \right) - N\left(-\frac{\sigma}{2}\sqrt{T-t} \right) \right], \tag{B.5}$$

where $S(t)$ follows a *geometric* Brownian Motion, and σ is the standard deviation of continuously compounded returns on the stock price, $S(t)$.

When σ is small, Equation B.5 may be approximated as[28]

$$c_{BS}(t) \approx S(t) \sigma \sqrt{\frac{T-t}{2\pi}}. \tag{B.6}$$

Compare Equation B.6 with Equation B.4. In the arithmetic Brownian motion case, σ_A is the standard deviation of the level of the price process $\mathcal{S}(t)$; in the geometric Brownian motion case, σ is the standard deviation of continuously compounded returns. Standard deviation of price is, however, approximately equal to price times the standard deviation of continuously compounded returns. It follows that the pricing in Equations B.4 and B.6 is consistent, even though the first uses an arithmetic Brownian motion (supposedly incorrect), and the second uses a geometric Brownian motion. Thus, the Black-Scholes formula reduces to the century-old Bachelier formula.

In my book *Basic Black-Scholes*, (Crack [2021]) I demonstrate the general arithmetic Brownian motion case where we assume neither that the option

---

[27]This is equation 4.7 in Samuelson (1973).

[28]This approximation appears in Brenner and Subrahmanyam (1988). They use a Taylor series derivation, but less formally it follows because $[N(z) - N(-z)]$ is just the area under the standard normal pdf from $-z$ to z. With σ small, you can approximate the area by length times height. The length is $\sigma\sqrt{T-t}$; for small σ, the height is close to the height of the standard normal pdf at its peak: $\frac{1}{\sqrt{2\pi}}$ (recall that $\frac{1}{\sqrt{2\pi}} \approx 0.4$).

is at the money, nor that $r = 0$.[29] The formula for the call option price in this case is given by Equations B.7–B.9. See Crack (2021) for full details of the derivation (it first appeared in Crack (2004)). Alexander, Mo, and Stent (2012) present the same formulae with an adjustment for continuous dividends.

$$c(t) = e^{-r(T-t)}\sigma_A\sqrt{\frac{e^{2r(T-t)}-1}{2r}}\left[N'(d)+N(d)\cdot d\right] \qquad \text{(B.7)}$$

$$= e^{-r(T-t)}\sigma_A\sqrt{\frac{e^{2r(T-t)}-1}{2r}}\left[\frac{e^{-\frac{1}{2}d^2}}{\sqrt{2\pi}}+N(d)\cdot d\right] \qquad \text{(B.8)}$$

$$\text{where } d = \frac{S(t)e^{r(T-t)}-X}{\sigma_A\sqrt{\frac{e^{2r(T-t)}-1}{2r}}}. \qquad \text{(B.9)}$$

Answer 2.20: Black-Scholes in your head!? This technique is so well known that some interviewers just ask if you can do it, and if you say yes they move on. It's not worth the gamble if you don't know it.[30]

Traders use the arithmetic Brownian motion approximation (or Black-Scholes reduced formula) from Answer 2.19 as a rough but fundamental call pricing relationship:

$$c(t) \approx \sigma S\sqrt{\frac{T-t}{2\pi}}, \qquad \text{(B.10)}$$

where σ is the standard deviation of returns or where σS is replaced by the standard deviation of prices. You should also note that this versatile little formula prices *both* puts and calls. Why is this? Well, if interest rates are low, and the option is struck at-the-money, then in the absence of dividends a call and put have the same value—just use put-call parity.

Many times interviewees are asked to price an option in their head where the interest rate is zero and the option is struck at-the-money. You should, therefore, know that the option pricing formulae of both Black-Scholes and Bachelier reduce to Equation B.10 and that it works for both for puts and calls. I expect you to be able to evaluate Equation B.10 in your head in less than 10 seconds if asked to in an interview. How can you do this so quickly? Well, $\frac{1}{\sqrt{2\pi}} \approx 0.4$, and for three months, six months, or one year to maturity, you have $\sqrt{0.25} = 0.50$, $\sqrt{0.50} \approx 0.70$, and $\sqrt{1} = 1$, respectively. Of course, it helps that they usually give you easy numbers. For example, if $S = \$100$, $\sigma = 0.40$, and $(T - t) = 0.25$, the formula gives $8 ($0.4 \times 0.4 \times 100 \times 0.5$) whereas Black-Scholes proper gives $7.97—not bad at all! The approximation is usually accurate to within a couple of percentage points.

Answer 2.21: This is a common type of question requiring fundamental knowledge. The only thing that changes between the two options is the time until

---

[29]I thank Mikhail Voropaev for contributing this idea; any errors are mine.
[30]See Haug (2001) for related material.

expiration. The important knowledge here is how the value of a call changes with time to expiration.

You should remember that in the special case where $r = 0$, and the option is struck at-the-money [so that $S(t) = X$], the Black-Scholes European call option pricing formula may be approximated by the following (see discussion in Answer 2.20):

$$c(t) = \sigma_A \sqrt{\frac{T-t}{2\pi}},$$

where σ_A is not standard deviation of continuously compounded returns, but standard deviation of price. From this approximation, you can see that if the call is at-the-money, the call value increases at something like the square root of the term to maturity (if you double term to maturity, value increases by 40% to 50%). You must be very comfortable with this approximation.

The above approximation is a good place to start. However, a full answer recognizes that the response of call value to term to maturity depends heavily upon whether the call is in-the-money, at-the-money, or out-of-the money. Sensitivity to term to maturity decreases as you move into-the-money, down to zero in the limit if you are very deep in-the-money. Sensitivity to term to maturity increases as you move out-of-the-money. Doubling the term to maturity can easily double, triple, or quadruple the value of the call if it is well out-of-the-money. The effect is greater the further out-of-the-money the call is—this is why deep out-of-the-money options are sometimes called "lottery tickets."

You can see this effect clearly if you compare the prices of actively traded equity options and LEAPS.[31] Go to the listed options quotations in the third section of the *Wall Street Journal.* Choose a stock for which both equity options and LEAPS are traded. Compare the prices of call options on your chosen stock that have the same strike, but different terms to maturity (e.g., three months, six months, one year, and two years). If you do this comparison for different strike prices, you should see that an extension in term to maturity has the most impact on call option prices when the options are out-of-the-money. You should see that for call options that are deep out-of-the-money, doubling the term to maturity can easily quadruple the value of the call option.

In simple terms, if you extend the term to maturity, the option has more opportunities to finish in-the-money, the present value of the cost of exercising decreases, and the call value increases. The increase in the call value depends upon the initial likelihood that the call will finish in-the-money. This likelihood

---

[31]LEAPS are "Long-term Equity AnticiPation Securities." That is, LEAPS are long-term options. LEAPS have terms to maturity of up to three years. The term to maturity of standard exchange-traded equity options does not exceed eight months. LEAPS are not exotic options, but exchange-traded standardized options contracts. Like standard equity options, all LEAPS are American-style options. Unlike standard equity options, equity LEAPS all expire in January; index LEAPS all expire in December or January.

is small if the option is well out-of-the-money. Thus an increase in term to maturity produces a proportionately greater increase in the value of an option that is out-of-the-money.[32]

A caveat. The approximation formula $c(t) = \sigma\sqrt{\frac{T-t}{2\pi}}$ prices at-the-money European-style puts and calls when $r = 0$. However, it has its limitations. For example, if $r \neq 0$, then the value of a deep in-the-money European put *decreases* as time to maturity extends. If the put is deep in-the-money, then life is already as good as it gets (the put has limited upside). You want to exercise now and take the money. Extending the life of the option pushes the expected benefit further away and decreases the put's value.

Answer 2.22: I give two different methods for answering this question. If the standard deviation is $20, not $10, then double the answers given.

FIRST SOLUTION
As a loose rule of thumb, the standard deviation of price per period ($10 here) is a rough measure of the average possible upside move or downside move in stock price over the next period. You have approximately half-a-chance of finishing in-the-money, and half-a-chance of finishing out-of-the-money (or "under water," as it is sometimes called). The expected payoff is, therefore, roughly $\left(\frac{1}{2} \times \$0\right) + \left(\frac{1}{2} \times \$10\right) = \$5$. In fact, the shape of the lognormal distribution of final stock price means that the expected payoff is slightly less than $5 (it is around $4).

SECOND SOLUTION
In the case where $r = 0$, and the option is struck at-the-money [so that $S(t) = X$], the Black-Scholes option pricing formula may be approximated by the following (see discussion in Answer 2.20):

$$c(t) = \sigma_A\sqrt{\frac{T-t}{2\pi}},$$

where σ_A is not standard deviation of continuously compounded returns, but standard deviation of price. With $T - t = 1$, and $\frac{1}{\sqrt{2\pi}} \approx 0.40$ (memorize that one), the standard deviation of price of $10 implies a call price of around $4. Note that this technique is more accurate than the first, giving $4 instead of $5.

Answer 2.23: The answer cannot be found exactly in the Black-Scholes framework, but you can get a good estimate.[33] Increasing the implied volatility

---

[32]For a very helpful practitioner view on the interpretation of partial derivatives of call price with respect to each option pricing parameter, see Chance (1994).

[33]Francis Longstaff suggested to me that an important option pricing problem is the handling of "event risk" (personal communication [September 25, 1998]). For example, how do you price a 14-day option on a stock whose CEO is scheduled to make an important announcement in seven days. I think this question is a loose attempt at this issue.

σ by 25% (from 0.20 to 0.25) on one day out of 100 in the option's life is the same (to a first-order approximation) as increasing σ^2 by 50% on one day out of 100 in the option's life.[34] This averages out to something like increasing σ^2 by 0.5% for every day remaining in the option's life (i.e., multiplying the average σ^2 by a factor 1.005).[35] Using the approximation (see p. 186) $c(t) \approx \sigma S(t)\sqrt{\frac{T-t}{2\pi}}$, we see that multiplying σ^2 by M has the same effect on $c(t)$ as multiplying $T - t$ by M. This is because each of σ^2 and $(T - t)$ appear in the option formula under a square root sign—either implicitly or explicitly. It follows that multiplying σ^2 by a factor 1.005 is equivalent to increasing the term to maturity by something like 0.5% (i.e., one-half of a day for a 100-day option). That is, increasing σ^2 by 50% on one day is equivalent to increasing the length of one day by 50%.

Either of the adjustments mentioned increases the value of an at-the-money option by a factor of about $\sqrt{M}$—a quarter of a percent here. Note that the equivalence of the 50% increase in σ^2 on one day and the extension of option life by half a day is a general result—because variance is linear in time. However, the conclusion that either of these adjustments increases option value by about a quarter of a percent applies only to at-the-money options. If an option is deep in-the-money, the adjustments mentioned may have little or no effect on option value; if an option is deep out-of-the-money, the adjustments mentioned may increase the option value by substantially more than a quarter of a percent.

Answer 2.24: A give-away question! A long straddle is a long call plus a long put with the same strike. If you hold the straddle until maturity, then you need a price change of more than $5 either way in the underlying to profit. A smaller price change, however, can lead to profits if it happens before maturity. For example, using Black-Scholes (ignoring that CBOE equity options are American-style), if $\sigma = 0.357$, $T - t = 0.5$, $S = \$25$, and $r = 0.02$, then a straddle struck at $25 costs $5. If the price of the underlying suddenly jumps to $27, then the straddle is suddenly worth $5.50 and you have an immediate 10% gain. See Table B.1 for details.

Answer 2.25: The Eurodollar futures contract is the most popular short-term interest rate futures contract. The contract value used for marking-to-market at the end of the day is $\$10,000 \times [100 - \frac{90}{360}\delta]$, where δ is the settlement discount rate. Between settlements, the market participants determine, through supply and demand, what is considered a fair discount. At maturity, the discount δ

---

[34]The "implied volatility" is the volatility figure implicit within an option price, assuming that market participants value options using the Black-Scholes formula. The "implied vol" appears first in the literature in Latané and Rendleman (1976).

[35]As an aside, note this for the Black-Scholes formula: If we increase the calendar term to maturity, but still call it "one period," then we need to increase σ. However, if we increase $(T - t)$ ("term to maturity" or "the number of periods") without changing the length of one period in the model, we do not need to change σ.

Table B.1: Straddle Prices when the Stock Price Jumps

	Stock Price = $25.00	Stock Price = $27.00
Price of the Call ($X = \$25$)	$2.625	$3.875
Price of the Put ($X = \$25$)	$2.376	$1.626
Price of the Straddle (sum)	$5.001	$5.502

Note: The option prices in the table are calculated using volatility of $\sigma = 0.357$ per annum, time to maturity of $T - t = 0.5$ years, a riskless rate of $r = 0.02$ per annum, and the Black-Scholes formula. A long straddle is a long call plus a long put with the same strike. A straddle struck at $25 costs $5 when stock price is $S = \$25$, but if the stock price jumps immediately to $27, the straddle is worth $5.50, giving an immediate 10% gain, ignoring transactions costs.

must converge to the three-month LIBOR U.S. dollar rate. Note that if the discount is 5%, then $\delta = 5.0$ in the above calculation, not 0.05.

The three-month LIBOR rate is typically about 40 to 50 bps (i.e., 0.40 to 0.50 percentage points) higher than the yield on three-month treasury bills (this compensates for default risk of London banks).[36] The discount rate δ is thus highly correlated with U.S. interest rates. The contract value is highly negatively correlated with δ, and thus highly negatively correlated with U.S. interest rates.

Suppose that you are long a Eurodollar future. If U.S. interest rates rise, the contract value declines, and you finance your loss at a relatively high rate. If U.S. interest rates fall, then the contract value rises, but you invest the marked-to-market gains at relatively low rates. If you hold the forward, rather than the future, you do not have day-to-day gains and losses, so you are not hurt in the same way by these opportunity costs. Other things being equal, you would rather have the Eurodollar forward contract than the Eurodollar futures contract. If the discounts are the same (as stated), then there is a mis-pricing.[37] With the current mis-pricing, I would choose to go long the Eurodollar forward and short the Eurodollar future.

Answer 2.26: It makes much more sense to simulate the underlying and find the

---

[36]This is an estimate only. There is tremendous variation in the spread. The "Ted Spread" is the Eurodollar futures less T-bill futures index point spread (with same delivery month). The Ted Spread was a typical 45.9 bps on June 15, 2009. During the Global Credit Crisis, however, it spiked up to over ten times this level—reaching 465 bps on October 10, 2008—as credit risk fears pushed three-month USD LIBOR up to 4.82% and demand for safety pushed three-month T-bill yields down to 24 bps.

[37]If the underlying were strongly *positively* correlated with U.S. interest rates, then the futures contract would be more attractive than the forward. This is because daily gains can be invested at relatively high rates, while daily losses are financed at relatively low rates (see Hull [1997, pp. 55–56] for more details).

---

payoffs to the call, than it does to simulate the process for the call itself. It is difficult to model the call, because the instantaneous volatility of the call changes whenever the leverage of the call changes (assuming the underlying is of constant volatility). The leverage of the call changes whenever the stock price moves (and it even changes if the stock price does not move—simply because of time decay).

Answer 2.27: A quick review of "mortgage-backs" is in order. Mortgage-backed securities are shares in portfolios of mortgages. The value of all U.S. mortgage-backed securities outstanding was \$9,880,600,000,000 (\$9.8806 trillion) at the end of Q2 2019, according to SIFMA's web site. This compares with \$8.7663 trillion five years earlier (Q2 2014), \$8.390 trillion at the end of 2006, and \$2.606 trillion at the end of 1996. The Q2 2019 total is composed of agency MBS (75%), agency CMO (11%), non-agency CMBS (6%), and non-agency RMBS (8%), where the acronyms stand for mortgage-backed securities, collateralized mortgage obligations, commercial mortgage-backed securities, and residential mortgage-backed securities.

Owners of mortgage-backs are exposed to "prepayment risk," and "extension risk." Prepayment risk is the risk that interest rates will fall, and borrowers will exercise their right to refinance at lower rates (they exercise their call option on the mortgage). The problem is that the holders of the mortgage-backs, therefore, get repaid when interest rates are low—the worst possible time to receive the money. Conversely, extension risk is the risk that interest rates will rise, and borrowers will slow down their rate of repayment—meaning that holders of mortgage-backs get fewer dollars to invest at precisely the best time for them to be investing. Mortgage-back investors thrive when interest rate volatility is low.

The simplest mortgage-back is a "pass-through"—each share in the mortgage pool provides a pro-rata share in the cash flows to the pool, and thus each share has identical risk and return characteristics.

Collateralized mortgage obligations (CMO's) are a type of mortgage-back that splits the mortgage pool up into "tranches" (the French word for "slice"). Unlike a pass-through, which gives equal shares to all holders, the tranches are unequal shares. Take a simple example with only four tranches: "A," "B," "C," and "Z." The A, B, and C shares all receive regular coupons. The A shares are retired (i.e., the principal is repaid) ahead of the other tranches by using the earliest prepayments by borrowers. The B shares are retired, through prepayments, only after the A shares are gone. The C shares are retired, through further prepayments by borrowers, only after the A and B shares are gone. The Z shares receive no payouts whatsoever until all of the A, B, and C shares are gone. You may think of the Z shares as being like zero-coupon bonds with a life equal to the life of the longest-lived mortgages in the pool. CMO tranches thus provide *different* risk-return profiles—in contrast to pass-throughs.

With borrowers long a call on the mortgage (i.e., the right to buy back the mortgage by prepayment), holders of mortgage-backs are short a share of each of these calls from the mortgage pool. You will recall, of course, that long calls have positive convexity and that short calls have negative convexity.

In the absence of the call feature of a mortgage-back (the fact that borrowers have the right to prepay early), the mortgage back has positive convexity as a function of interest rates—just like an ordinary non-callable bond (Sundaresan [1997, p. 393]). However, when interest rates are low, the call feature becomes important to borrowers. If interest rates fall, all borrowers will refinance by the time rates have fallen to some critical value. At this stage, the mortgage-back is worth par. When interest rates are low, the importance of the call feature (a short call position to the mortgage-back holder) means that the mortgage-back can acquire negative convexity.[38] Negative convexity is also called "compression to par" because of the convergence of the security's value to par as interest rates fall (Sundaresan [1997, p. 394]).

Note that although the mortgage-back value may have negative convexity, it is still downward sloping as a function of interest rates. However, if interest rates are low and close to the coupon rate of the mortgage back, then an increase in volatility of interest rates can decrease the value of the security (Sundaresan [1997, p. 394]). This result follows because the holder of the mortgage back is short the calls that the borrowers are long—and calls increase in value with volatility.

Now to the interview question. If you are long mortgage-backs, and you expect a bond market rally, then you expect bond yields to fall and bond prices to rise. Thus, your position will gain in value. The question is, which sign on convexity would maximize the gain (+ or −)? Positive convexity provides a steeper downward sloping plot of security value as a function of interest rates, and this in turn implies a larger gain if rates fall—thus, you prefer positive convexity.[39]

A full answer notes that we have assumed a *parallel* shift in the yield curve. If the yield curve steepens or flattens, the answer could change. Whether additional convexity helps or hurts you depends upon the type of yield-curve shift and the particular bonds under consideration. It needs to be evaluated on a case-by-case basis. See the related discussion beginning on p. 242.

Answer 2.28: The hedging strategy is naive. This is called a "stop-loss strategy" (Hull [1997, p. 310]). At first glance, it replicates the payoff to the call. However, purchases and sales cannot be made at the strike price. When the

---

[38]In fact, this is a feature of any callable bond—if interest rates fall far enough, the call feature kicks in and imparts negative convexity to the security.

[39]Convexity is not such an issue if you expect a bond market rout. When prices fall and rates rise, prepayment becomes less attractive, and the call option in the hands of the borrowers assumes less importance—and so does the negative convexity the call is able to impart to your mortgage-back security value.

stock is near the strike, you cannot know whether it will cross over the strike price or not. You have to wait until the stock price crosses the strike price. This means you end up making purchases at a price slightly higher than the strike and sales at a price slightly lower than the strike. The closer to the strike you try to time your trades, the more frequently you can expect to have to trade. You can get eaten alive by transactions costs (see Hull [1997, p. 310]).

A second criticism is that the timing of the cash flows to the option and the hedge are different—it is not a hedge (see Hull [1997, p. 310]).

> **Advice:** Online psychometric (i.e., personality, aptitude and ability) tests are a quick and cheap way for recruiters to sift out unsuitable candidates early in the process. The tests include verbal comprehension (mostly vocabulary and word meaning), quantitative ability, spatial reasoning, logical reasoning, mathematical ability, diagrams (odd one out, rotations, repeated patterns, compounding patterns (i.e., combine and add or subtract), sequences, etc.). Some look like IQ tests. Many students practice using online examples or dedicated Web sites. You need to practice too, in order to compete.

Answer 2.29: This question and the next are the most popular stochastic calculus interview questions. Although this is ostensibly a stochastic calculus question, the answer relies only upon Riemann calculus. If you were stuck and looking for a hint, then maybe this is enough to get you going.[40] I present two solutions that, at first blush, appear different. Upon closer examination, however, you may see that they are doing exactly the same thing.

FIRST SOLUTION
Let $I_T(\omega)$ denote the integral $\int_0^T w(t, \omega)dt$. In this integral, t measures time along sample paths, and ω is an element of the sample space Ω (i.e., ω corresponds to a particular possible sample path). Since $w(t)$ has continuous paths with probability one (i.e., for almost every $\omega \in \Omega$ the path is continuous), this integral is a Riemann integral evaluated pathwise for any fixed $\omega \in \Omega$. The Riemann integral is just (in its simplest form)

$$I_T = \lim_{n \to \infty} S_n, \text{ where } S_n \equiv \sum_{i=1}^{n} (t_i - t_{i-1})\, w(t_{i-1}), \text{ and}$$

$$t_i \equiv \frac{Ti}{n}, \ 0 = t_0 < t_1 < \ldots < t_n = T.$$

---

[40]I thank Taras Klymchuk and Ian Short for suggesting related solution techniques; any errors are mine.

We may rearrange terms as follows:

$$
\begin{aligned}
S_n &= \sum_{i=1}^{n}(t_i - t_{i-1})\,w(t_{i-1}) \\
&= (t_1 - t_0)w(t_0) + (t_2 - t_1)w(t_1) + \ldots + (t_n - t_{n-1})w(t_{n-1}) \\
&= -t_0 w(t_0) + t_1\left[w(t_0) - w(t_1)\right] + t_2\left[w(t_1) - w(t_2)\right] \\
&\qquad + \ldots + t_{n-1}\left[w(t_{n-2}) - w(t_{n-1})\right] + t_n w(t_{n-1}) \\
&= -t_0 w(t_0) + \sum_{i=1}^{n-1} t_i\left[w(t_{i-1}) - w(t_i)\right] \\
&\quad + t_n \sum_{i=1}^{n-1}\left[w(t_i) - w(t_{i-1})\right] + t_n w(t_0) \quad \text{(a telescoping series)} \\
&= \sum_{i=1}^{n-1}(t_n - t_i)\left[w(t_i) - w(t_{i-1})\right], \quad \text{a.e.} \tag{B.11}
\end{aligned}
$$

The last line, Equation B.11, follows because $w(t_0) \equiv w(0) = 0$ a.e. (i.e. almost everywhere) by definition.

So, S_n is just a weighted sum of increments of a standard Brownian motion. It is well known that such increments are independently normally distributed and that a finite sum of constant-weighted independent normals is also normal. Thus, S_n is normal for each n. Having established normality, we can deduce the mean and variance using algebra or calculus; I will do both.

Algebraic Derivation of Mean and Variance
We have $(t_n - t_i) = Tn/n - Ti/n = T(n - i)/n$, and $(T(n - i)/n)[w(t_i) - w(t_{i-1})] \sim N(0, (n - i)^2 T^3/n^3)$ (because $w(t_i) - w(t_{i-1}) \sim N(0, T/n)$). Thus, $\sum_{i=1}^{n-1}(n - i)^2 = \sum_{i=1}^{n-1} i^2 = n(n - 1)(2n - 1)/6$ (using Answer 1.53), so that $\sum(n-i)^2 T^3/n^3 = n(n-1)(2n-1)T^3/(6n^3) \to T^3/3$ as $n \to \infty$. So, conditional on time 0 information, $I_T(\omega)$ is distributed as $N(0, T^3/3)$.

Calculus Derivation of Mean and Variance
The mean is just $E(I_T) = \int_0^T E[w(t)]dt = 0$. With a mean of zero, the variance is just the second non-central moment

$$
\begin{aligned}
V(I_T) &= E(I_T^2) \\
&= E\left\{\left(\int_0^T w(t)dt\right)\left(\int_0^T w(s)ds\right)\right\} \\
&= \int_0^T \int_0^T E\left[w(t)w(s)\right] dt\, ds.
\end{aligned}
$$

Recall that $w(t)$ is a process with independent increments. Assume, without loss of generality, that $s < t$. Then, $w(t) = w(s) + (w(t) - w(s))$, and $w(t)w(s) = w^2(s) + (w(t) - w(s))w(s)$. It follows that

$$
E\left[w(t)w(s)\right] = E\left[w^2(s)\right] = s,
$$

using independent increments and that $w(s)$ has a variance of s. More generally, $E\left[w(t)w(s)\right] = \min(t,s)$. Thus, we the variance of the integral is

$$
\begin{aligned}
V(I_T) &= \int_0^T \int_0^T E\left[w(t)w(s)\right] dt ds \\
&= \int_0^T \int_0^T \min(t,s) dt ds \\
&= \int_0^T \left(\int_0^s t\, dt + \int_s^T s\, dt \right) ds \\
&= \int_0^T \left(\frac{s^2}{2} + s(T-s) \right) ds \\
&= \int_0^T \left(sT - \frac{s^2}{2} \right) ds = \left(\frac{T^3}{2} - \frac{T^3}{6} \right) = \frac{T^3}{3},
\end{aligned}
$$

demonstrating again that $I_T(\omega)$ is distributed as $N(0, T^3/3)$.

SECOND SOLUTION

This shorter second solution follows exactly the same steps as the first, but without the explicit expansions.[41]

Begin by noting that $d(tw(t)) = t\, dw(t) + w(t) dt$. Integrating from 0 to T yields $Tw(T) = \int_0^T t\, dw(t) + \int_0^T w(t) dt$. Rearranging, and using $w(T) = \int_0^T dw(t)$, yields $\int_0^T w(t) dt = \int_0^T (T-t) dw(t)$. (This is just the continuous limit of Equation B.11.) Given that increments in a Brownian motion are normally distributed with mean 0, examination of $\int_0^T (T-t) dw(t)$ allows us to deduce that $\int_0^T w(t) dt$ must be normally distributed with mean 0. Given the zero mean, the variance of $\int_0^T w(t) dt$ is just the second non-central moment of $\int_0^T (T-t) dw(t)$. Mentally unpicking the $dw(t)$ term and squaring it, then using $dw \cdot dw = dt$ (Merton [1992, p. 123]), we get that the variance we seek is $\int_0^T (T-t)^2 dt$. Changing variables, say to $s = T - t$, and flipping the limits on the integral, yields $\int_0^T (T-t)^2 dt = \int_0^T s^2 ds = T^3/3$, as before.

Answer 2.30: Do you need a hint? This problem requires Itô's Lemma and not much else. Now go back to the problem and stop peeking at the solutions.[42]

---

[41]I thank Adrien Brandejsky for suggesting this solution technique; any errors are mine.

[42]I had the pleasure of attending a symposium in honor of Norbert Wiener at MIT in October 1994 ("The Legacy of Norbert Wiener: A Centennial Symposium"). Two seats to my left sat Kiyoshi Itô—of Itô's Lemma fame. Although 79 at the time, Professor Itô did not appear old. He was of small build and very distinguished looking. He spoke clearly in somewhat halting English, and his good-natured humor was infectious. Previous and future Nobel Prize winners, respectively, Paul Samuelson and Robert Merton also spoke, and it seems that Itô's Lemma was in fact a footnote in a paper of Itô's. They joked that it should be called "Itô's Footnote" instead—but that does not have the same ring to it. In 2006, at age 91, Itô was awarded the Gauss Prize in Mathematics (Protter [2007]). Itô died in 2008 aged 93. Samuelson died in 2009 aged 94.

If we apply Itô's Lemma to $F(t, w) \equiv \frac{w^2(t)}{2}$, we find[43]

$$dF = F_t dt + F_w dw + \frac{1}{2} F_{ww} (dw)^2 = w(t) dw(t) + \frac{1}{2} dt.$$

This notation means precisely

$$F(T) - F(0) = \int_0^T w(t) dw(t) + \frac{1}{2} \int_0^T dt = \int_0^T w(t) dw(t) + \frac{T}{2}.$$

Given the definition of $F(t)$, it follows immediately that

$$\int_0^T w(t) dw(t) = \frac{w^2(T) - T}{2} \quad \text{a.e.}$$

It should be noted that the expected value of the right-hand side of the equality is zero. This is consistent with the expected value of the left-hand side of the equality being zero also.

Answer 2.31:   For $w^n(t)$ to be a martingale, we need to show that for $0 \le s \le t$, $E[w^n(t)|\mathcal{F}_s] = w^n(s)$, or, equivalently, that $E[w^n(t) - w^n(s)|\mathcal{F}_s] = 0$. So, let us introduce the increment $w(t) - w(s)$, write $w^n(t) = [(w(t) - w(s)) + w(s)]^n$, and use the binomial theorem $(a + b)^n = \sum_{k=0}^n \binom{n}{k} a^k b^{n-k}$.

$$
\begin{aligned}
E[w^n(t)|\mathcal{F}_s] &= E\left\{[(w(t) - w(s)) + w(s)]^n | \mathcal{F}_s\right\} \\
&= E\left[\sum_{k=0}^n \binom{n}{k} [w(t) - w(s)]^k w^{n-k}(s) \Bigg| \mathcal{F}_s\right] \\
&= E\left[\sum_{k=0}^n \binom{n}{k} [w(t) - w(s)]^k \Bigg| \mathcal{F}_s\right] w^{n-k}(s) \\
&= \sum_{k=0}^n \binom{n}{k} E\left[(w(t) - w(s))^k\right] w^{n-k}(s),
\end{aligned}
$$

where the last step follows because the increment $w(t) - w(s)$ is independent of the filtration $\mathcal{F}_s$.

We know that $w(t) - w(s) \sim N(0, t - s)$, so we need to use the properties of the normal distribution. Assume that $X \sim N(0, \sigma^2)$, then what is the value of the raw moment $E\left(X^k\right)$? Well,

$$
\begin{aligned}
E\left(X^k\right) &= \int_{x=-\infty}^{+\infty} \frac{1}{\sqrt{2\pi}\sigma} x^k e^{-\frac{1}{2}\left(\frac{x}{\sigma}\right)^2} dx \\
&= \begin{cases} 0, & \text{if } k > 0 \text{ odd} \\ 2\int_{x=0}^{+\infty} \frac{1}{\sqrt{2\pi}\sigma} x^k e^{-\frac{1}{2}\left(\frac{x}{\sigma}\right)^2} dx, & \text{if } k > 0 \text{ even.} \end{cases}
\end{aligned}
$$

---

[43]I thank Taras Klymchuk for suggesting this solution technique; any errors are mine.

Now assume, say, $k = 2m$, for natural number m. Let $w = \frac{1}{2}\left(\frac{x}{\sigma}\right)^2$, so that $x = \sigma\sqrt{2w}$ and $dx = \sigma(2w)^{-\frac{1}{2}}dw$. Then we get

$$
\begin{aligned}
2\int_{x=0}^{+\infty} \frac{1}{\sqrt{2\pi}\sigma} x^k e^{-\frac{1}{2}\left(\frac{x}{\sigma}\right)^2} dx &= 2\int_{w=0}^{+\infty} \frac{1}{\sqrt{2\pi}\sigma} \sigma^{2m} 2^m w^m e^{-w} \sigma 2^{-\frac{1}{2}} w^{-\frac{1}{2}} dw \\
&= \sigma^{2m} \frac{2^m}{\sqrt{\pi}} \int_{w=0}^{+\infty} w^{\left(m+\frac{1}{2}\right)-1} e^{-w} dw \\
&= \sigma^{2m} \frac{2^m}{\sqrt{\pi}} \Gamma\left(m + \frac{1}{2}\right) \\
&= \sigma^{2m}(2m-1)!! \\
&= \sigma^{k}(k-1)!!
\end{aligned}
$$

where the double exclamation is the double factorial,[44] and I used the property of the gamma function that $\Gamma\left(m + \frac{1}{2}\right) = \frac{(2m-1)!!\sqrt{\pi}}{2^m}$ (Abramowitz and Stegun, 1972, p. 255).

Combining all of the above, we deduce that

$$
\begin{aligned}
E[w^n(t)|\mathcal{F}_s] &= \sum_{k=0}^{n} \binom{n}{k} E\left[(w(t) - w(s))^k\right] w^{n-k}(s) \\
&= w^n(s) + \sum_{k=1}^{n} \binom{n}{k} E\left[(w(t) - w(s))^k\right] w^{n-k}(s) \\
&= w^n(s) + \underbrace{\sum_{\substack{k=1 \\ k \text{ even}}}^{n} \binom{n}{k} (t-s)^{\frac{k}{2}}(k-1)!! \; w^{n-k}(s)}_{\text{positive for all } k}.
\end{aligned}
$$

$$
\therefore \; E\left[w^n(t) - w^n(s)|\mathcal{F}_s\right] = \underbrace{\sum_{\substack{k=1 \\ k \text{ even}}}^{n} \binom{n}{k} (t-s)^{\frac{k}{2}}(k-1)!! \; w^{n-k}(s)}_{\text{positive for all } k}.
$$

The RHS term is identically zero only in the case that $n = 1$ (in which case the summation is empty). Thus, $w^n(t)$ is a martingale only in the case that $n = 1$.

Answer 2.32: Most people incorrectly deduce that the derivative security is worth \$1. If you got this answer, go back right now and think some more. I present three solution techniques: the first uses standard no-arbitrage arguments; the second uses partial differential equations (PDE's); the third uses stopping times.[45]

---

[44]The double factorial is defined as $n!! = \begin{cases} 1, & \text{if } n = 0 \text{ or } n = 1 \\ n \cdot (n-2)!!, & \text{if } n \geq 2. \end{cases}$
For example, $1!! = 1$, $2!! = 2$, $3!! = 3 \cdot 1$, $4!! = 4 \cdot 2$, $5!! = 5 \cdot 3 \cdot 1$, and $6!! = 6 \cdot 4 \cdot 2$.

[45]If you want a good introductory book on PDE's, I recommend Farlow (1993). I loved this book when I was a student. I still find it a breath of fresh air compared to my other math books.

FIRST SOLUTION

You are an investment banker. Assume there exists a derivative security that promises one dollar when IBM hits $100 for the first time. If this security is marketable at *more* than $0.75, then you should issue 100 of them and use $75 of the proceeds to buy one share of IBM. If IBM ever hits $100, sell the stock and pay $1 to each security holder as contracted. You sell the securities, perfectly hedge them, and still have money in your pocket. By no-arbitrage, the security cannot sell for more than $0.75.

The converse is that if this security costs *less* than $0.75, you should buy 100 of these securities financed by a short position in one IBM share. For this to establish $0.75 as a lower bound on the security price (and, therefore, to pinpoint the price at $0.75—the solution given to the interviewee by the Wall Street firm), you need to assume that you can roll over a short position *indefinitely*. This assumption seems reasonable for moderate amounts of capital. However, it is not clear to me that this is a reasonable interpretation of "ignore any short sale restrictions" when larger quantities of capital are involved. As one colleague said to me: "If it were possible to short forever, I'd short stocks with face value of a billion dollars, consume the billion, and roll over my short position forever." This seems to be an arbitrage opportunity.

We conclude that $0.75 is a clear upper bound by no-arbitrage, and thus $1 cannot be the correct answer. Whether or not $0.75 is also a lower bound is arguable (but it seems to make sense for moderate amounts of capital). The second solution technique also establishes $0.75 as the value of the security.

SECOND SOLUTION

This technique is more advanced and may be beyond the average candidate.[46] The derivative value V must satisfy the Black-Scholes PDE (Wilmott et al. [1993]):

$$\frac{\partial V}{\partial t} + \frac{1}{2}\sigma^2 S^2 \frac{\partial^2 V}{\partial S^2} + rS\frac{\partial V}{\partial S} - rV = 0$$

The boundary conditions that make sense for $V(S,t)$ are

$$V(S = 100, \text{ any } s > t) = \$1, \text{ and}$$
$$V(S = 0, \text{ any } s > t) = \$0.$$

Let us simplify our lives by searching initially for a solution that is affine in S: $V(S,t) = kS(t) + l$, for some constants k and l.[47]

The two boundary conditions imply that

$$(k \times \$100) + l = \$1, \text{ and}$$
$$(k \times \$0) + l = \$0.$$

---

[46]I thank Alan J. Marcus for suggesting this type of solution technique. I am responsible for any errors.

[47]An affine function involves both a linear portion, kS, and a constant, l. On a two-dimensional plot, a linear function goes through the origin; whereas an affine function may have a non-zero intercept.

From these we deduce that $k = \frac{1}{100}$, and $l = 0$. The functional form $V(S, t) = \frac{1}{100} S(t)$ satisfies the Black-Scholes PDE and the two boundary conditions and is thus the derivative value. In the special case where $S(t) = \$75$, we get $V = \$0.75$, as for the first technique.

THIRD SOLUTION

Following Shreve (2004, p. 297), we will take a "first passage" or "stopping time" approach. This technique is even more advanced than the previous one.[48]

Let now be time $t = 0$ and consider a derivative with lifespan T that pays \$1 if stock price $S(t)$ hits a barrier at level $B > S(0)$ before time T. In our case $B = \$100$ and $S(0) = \$75$. In the Black-Scholes world we have risk-neutral stochastic differential equation $dS(t) = rS\,dt + \sigma S(t)\,d\widetilde{W}(t)$ with solution

$$S(t) = S(0)e^{\left(r - \frac{1}{2}\sigma^2\right)t + \sigma \widetilde{W}} = S(0)e^{\sigma \widehat{W}},$$

where $\widetilde{W}(t)$ is a standard Brownian motion, $\widehat{W}(t) \equiv \alpha t + \widetilde{W}(t)$, and $\alpha \equiv \frac{1}{\sigma}\left(r - \frac{1}{2}\sigma^2\right)$.

Let $\widehat{M}(T) \equiv \max_{0 \le t \le T} \widehat{W}(t)$, then $\max_{0 \le t \le T} S(t) = S(0)e^{\sigma \widehat{M}(t)}$. The stock price hits the barrier B before time T if and only if this maximum stock price is larger than B. That is, $S(0)e^{\sigma \widehat{M}(t)} > B$. Simple algebra shows us that

$$
\begin{aligned}
\widetilde{P}\left(\max_{0 \le t \le T} S(t) > B\right) &= \widetilde{P}(S(0)\, e^{\sigma \widehat{M}(t)} > B) \\
&= 1 - \widetilde{P}(S(0)\, e^{\sigma \widehat{M}(t)} \le B) \\
&= 1 - \widetilde{P}\left(\widehat{M}(t) \le \frac{1}{\sigma}\ln\left(\frac{B}{S(0)}\right)\right) \\
&= 1 - \widetilde{P}(\widehat{M}(t) \le b),
\end{aligned}
$$

where $b \equiv \frac{1}{\sigma}\ln\left(\frac{B}{S(0)}\right)$. We can use Shreve (2004, Corollary 7.2.2, p. 297) to deduce immediately that

$$\widetilde{P}(\widehat{M}(t) \le b) = N\left(\frac{b - \alpha T}{\sqrt{T}}\right) - e^{2\alpha b} N\left(\frac{-b - \alpha T}{\sqrt{T}}\right), \quad b \ge 0.$$

---

[48]I thank Olaf Torne for suggesting this type of solution technique; any errors are mine.

It follows that the risk-neutral probability that we get our \$1 is[49]

$$\tilde{P}\left(\max_{0\le t\le T} S(t) > B\right) =$$

$$= 1 - \left[N\left(\frac{b - \alpha T}{\sqrt{T}}\right) - e^{2\alpha b}N\left(\frac{-b - \alpha T}{\sqrt{T}}\right)\right]$$

$$= N\left(\frac{-b + \alpha T}{\sqrt{T}}\right) + \left(\frac{B}{S(0)}\right)^{\left(\frac{2r}{\sigma^2}-1\right)} N\left(\frac{-b - \alpha T}{\sqrt{T}}\right)$$

$$= \left[N\left(\frac{\ln\left(\frac{S(0)}{B}\right) + (r - \frac{1}{2}\sigma^2)T}{\sigma\sqrt{T}}\right)\right.$$

$$\left. + \left(\frac{S(0)}{B}\right)^{\left(1 - \frac{2r}{\sigma^2}\right)} N\left(\frac{\ln\left(\frac{S(0)}{B}\right) - (r - \frac{1}{2}\sigma^2)T}{\sigma\sqrt{T}}\right)\right] \quad (*)$$

Equation $(*)$ gives the risk-neutral probability of the stock price touching the barrier and generating the payoff. If we multiply this probability by the \$1 payoff, we get the risk-neutral expected *future* payoff. If the interest rate is zero, then we do not need to discount, and plugging $r = 0$ into equation $(*)$ gives the value of the finitely-lived instrument that pays \$1 when the stock price hits B. If we take the limit as $T \to \infty$, the first $N(\cdot)$ term $\to 0$ (because its argument goes to $-\infty$), and the second $N(\cdot)$ term $\to 1$ (because its argument goes to $+\infty$). We are left with $\$1 \cdot \left(\frac{S(0)}{B}\right)$, which is just \$0.75 in our case.

From equation $(*)$, you should be able to deduce the risk-neutral probability that the stock price eventually hits the barrier as

$$\lim_{T\to\infty} \tilde{P}(\text{hit B}) = \begin{cases} 1 & ; \text{ if } r \ge \frac{1}{2}\sigma^2, \\ \left(\frac{S(0)}{B}\right)^{\left(1 - \frac{2r}{\sigma^2}\right)} & ; \text{ if } 0 \le r < \frac{1}{2}\sigma^2. \end{cases}$$

Extension: Some candidates have very recently been asked this question in the case $r > 0$. My first two solutions do not rely upon $r = 0$, so the answer must be the same. Can we demonstrate this using this third solution technique? Well, to discount the expected future value at rate r we need to know how long to discount for. Let τ be the time at which $S(t)$ first hits B. This "first passage time" is distributed Inverse Gaussian with the following pdf:[50]

$$f(\tau) = \frac{\ln\left(\frac{B}{S(0)}\right)}{\sigma\sqrt{2\pi\tau^3}} e^{-\frac{1}{2}\left(\frac{\ln\left(\frac{B}{S(0)}\right) - (r - \frac{1}{2}\sigma^2)\tau}{\sigma\sqrt{\tau}}\right)^2} \quad \text{where} \quad \tau \ge 0$$

---

[49]I used $\ln(A) = -\ln\left(\frac{1}{A}\right)$ for $A > 0$, $1 - N(x) = N(-x)$, $A^x = \left(\frac{1}{A}\right)^{-x}$, and $e^{[g\ln(h)]} = h^g$.

[50]Given time taken, the distance traveled by a Wiener process is Gaussian, but given distance traveled, the time taken is Inverse Gaussian. So, the distribution of the first passage time for $\ln S(t)$ to hit $\ln B$ is also Inverse Gaussian (Crack [1998]).

The general functional form of the Inverse Gaussian is

$$f(x) = \sqrt{\frac{\lambda}{2\pi x^3}}\, e^{-\frac{\lambda}{2}\left(\frac{x-\mu}{\mu\sqrt{x}}\right)^2} \quad \text{where} \quad x \geq 0,\ \lambda > 0,\ \mu > 0.$$

In our case $x = \tau$, $\lambda = \frac{\left[\ln\left(\frac{B}{S(0)}\right)\right]^2}{\sigma^2}$ and $\mu = \frac{\ln\left(\frac{B}{S(0)}\right)}{\left(r-\frac{1}{2}\sigma^2\right)}$. With $B > S(0)$, the condition $\mu > 0$ implies that $r > \frac{1}{2}\sigma^2$, else we do not have a valid pdf for $f(\tau)$. If we proceed assuming $r > \frac{1}{2}\sigma^2$, our discount factor is the expected value of $e^{-r(\tau)}$ with respect to $f(\tau)$ such that $\tau \leq T$:

$$E[e^{-r(\tau)}I_{\{\tau \leq T\}}(\tau)],$$

where

$$I_X(x) \equiv \left\{\begin{array}{ll} 1; & \text{if } x \in X, \\ 0; & \text{otherwise.} \end{array}\right.$$

So, we need to find the following discounted expected payoff:

$$\lim_{T\to\infty}\left\{E[e^{-r(\tau)}I_{\{\tau\leq T\}}(\tau)]\cdot \$1\cdot\left[N\left(\frac{\ln\left(\frac{S(0)}{B}\right)+(r-\frac{1}{2}\sigma^2)T}{\sigma\sqrt{T}}\right)\right.\right.$$
$$\left.\left.+\left(\frac{S(0)}{B}\right)^{\left(1-\frac{2r}{\sigma^2}\right)}N\left(\frac{\ln\left(\frac{S(0)}{B}\right)-(r-\frac{1}{2}\sigma^2)T}{\sigma\sqrt{T}}\right)\right]\right\}$$

For $r > \frac{1}{2}\sigma^2$, everything is surprisingly well behaved as $T \to \infty$. The discounting term $E[e^{-r(\tau)}I_{\{\tau\leq T\}}(\tau)] \to E[e^{-r(\tau)}]$, and it takes a page of tedious yet simple algebra to show that $E[e^{-r(\tau)}] = \frac{S(0)}{B}$ (hint: complete the square in the exponent). As we take the limit $T \to \infty$, the first $N(\cdot)$ term $\to 1$ (because its argument goes to $+\infty$), and the second $N(\cdot)$ term $\to 0$ (because its argument goes to $-\infty$). We are left again with $\$1 \cdot \left(\frac{S(0)}{B}\right)$, which is just $\$0.75$ as before. I find it interesting that in the two cases $r = 0$ and $r > \frac{1}{2}\sigma^2$ the limiting behavior of the two cumulative normal terms is opposite, but with the same end result. In the case $0 < r \leq \frac{1}{2}\sigma^2$, the instrument's value is the same, but I do not have a formal proof using Shreve's notation.

Finally, note that regardless of the value of r, the value of the finitely-lived instrument depends upon volatility, but the value of the perpetual instrument is independent of volatility.

> **Advice:** One out of every three males I have ever interviewed put his finger up his nose at some point during the interview. I am not joking. They seem to be unaware of it. Perhaps it is nerves. Some of them spend an incredible amount of time with a finger or fingers up their nose. It is difficult to take the candidate seriously after that. They expect me to shake hands with them at the end of the interview, but I always find a way out of it. Keep your hands off your face during the interview!

Answer 2.33: There are two ways to proceed: the first way is to work out the pricing formula from first principles; the second way is to use Black-Scholes option pricing as it stands, and attempt to obtain a similarity solution via adjustments that account for the power payoff.

FIRST SOLUTION

I was unable to find a published pricing formula for the power call (with payoff $\max[S^\alpha - X, 0]$) or for the power put (with payoff $\max[X - S^\alpha, 0]$), so I followed a straight discounted expected payoff approach under risk-neutral probabilities. It is relatively straightforward to show that the value at time t of European power call and put options maturing at time T is

$$c(t) = S^\alpha(t)e^{m(T-t)}N(d'_1) - e^{-r(T-t)}XN(d'_2), \quad (**) \quad \text{and}$$

$$p(t) = e^{-r(T-t)}XN(-d'_2) - S^\alpha(t)e^{m(T-t)}N(-d'_1), \quad \text{where}$$

$$d'_1 = \frac{\ln\left(\frac{S(t)}{K}\right) + (r + (\alpha - \frac{1}{2})\sigma^2)(T - t)}{\sigma\sqrt{T - t}},$$

$$d'_2 = \frac{\ln\left(\frac{S(t)}{K}\right) + (r - \frac{1}{2}\sigma^2)(T - t)}{\sigma\sqrt{T - t}} = d'_1 - \alpha\sigma\sqrt{T - t},$$

$$K \equiv X^{\frac{1}{\alpha}}, \quad \text{and} \quad m \equiv \left(r + \frac{\alpha}{2}\sigma^2\right)(\alpha - 1).$$

In the case $\alpha = 1$, the power option pricing formulae reduce to the standard Black-Scholes call and put pricing formulae.

The "delta" of the power call can be found by differentiating the power call pricing formula with respect to $S(t)$. The delta for the power call is given by

$$\Delta_{power\ call} \equiv \frac{\partial c(t)}{\partial S(t)}$$

$$= \alpha S^{(\alpha-1)}e^{m(T-t)}N(d'_1)$$

$$+ \frac{X^{(1-\frac{1}{\alpha})}n(d'_2 + \sigma\sqrt{T - t})[e^{-\frac{1}{2}(T-t)\sigma^2(\alpha-1)^2} - 1]}{\sigma\sqrt{T - t}},$$

where $n(\cdot)$ is the standard normal pdf function $n(x) \equiv \frac{1}{\sqrt{2\pi}}e^{-\frac{1}{2}x^2}$, and m, d'_1, and d'_2 are as defined above.

It is interesting to note that because d'_2 has the same functional form as the original Black-Scholes d_2, then the term $d'_2 + \sigma\sqrt{T-t}$ appearing in the delta has the same functional form as the original Black-Scholes d_1. However, this differs from the power call's d'_1 which contains an α term.

How does the power call's delta behave as $S(t)$ gets large? Well, as $S(t)$ gets large, both $d'_1, d'_2 \to \infty$. Thus, $N(d'_1) \to 1$, and $n(d'_2 + \sigma\sqrt{T-t}) \to 0$. It follows that

$$\Delta_{power\ call} \approx \alpha S^{(\alpha-1)} e^{m(T-t)}, \quad \text{for large } S(t).$$

It follows that if $S(t)$ is large, then as $(T-t) \to 0$, we get that

$$\Delta_{power\ call} \approx \alpha S^{(\alpha-1)}.$$

This should come as no surprise: If the power call is deep in-the-money, and there is little time to maturity, then its sensitivity to changes in $S(t)$ will be about the same as the sensitivity of $S^\alpha(t)$ to changes in $S(t)$. The latter sensitivity is just

$$\frac{\partial S^\alpha(t)}{\partial S(t)} = \alpha S^{(\alpha-1)}.$$

One implication of this is that the delta of a power call continues to change as $S(t)$ increases.

What may come as a surprise is the shape of the power call option pricing function (see Figure B.5). If $\alpha > 1$, the plot of $c(t)$ versus $S(t)$ is *steeper* than and above the plot of $\max(S^\alpha - X, 0)$ for large $S(t)$ (it decays down toward the payoff as maturity approaches). If $\alpha < 1$, the plot of $c(t)$ versus $S(t)$ is less steep than and *below* the plot of $\max(S^\alpha - X, 0)$ for large $S(t)$ (it decays up toward the payoff as maturity approaches). Only in the case $\alpha = 1$ do the results agree with those for the standard call: The plot of call value as a function of stock price is less steep than and above the plot of $\max(S - X, 0)$. In all cases, the plot of $c(t)$ as a function of $S(t)$ is above the plot of $\max(S^\alpha - X, 0)$ for small $S(t)$.

Mathematically, the approximation $\Delta_{power\ call} \approx \alpha S^{(\alpha-1)} e^{m(T-t)}$ drives the results for large $S(t)$ (together with the fact that m is positive if $\alpha > 1$ and negative if $\alpha < 1$). Economically, the time value of the option drives the results. When $\alpha > 1$, the power of S is so high that the option value grows more quickly with increasing S than does the intrinsic value. When $\alpha < 1$, the option value grows less quickly than does the intrinsic value, and the European nature of the option means that there is "negative time value" for having to wait for such a low payout.

The payoff diagram for the power call is a little strange because the "kink" does not occur at $S = X$, but at $S = X^{\frac{1}{\alpha}}$—see Figure B.5. For example, if $\alpha = 2$, the payoff diagram is flat until $S(T) = \sqrt{X}$ and then is an upward sloping portion of the parabola $S^2(T) - X$. If $\alpha > 1$, the delta of the power call will be higher than the delta of a standard call with strike $X^{\frac{1}{\alpha}}$ because the payoff diagram is steeper. Conversely, if $\alpha < 1$, the delta of the power call will be lower than the delta of a standard call with strike $X^{\frac{1}{\alpha}}$ because the payoff diagram is less steep.

In the power option pricing formulae, d_2' has the same functional form as the d_2 in the regular Black-Scholes. The only difference is that you have $\ln\left(\frac{S(t)}{K}\right)$, where $K = X^{\frac{1}{\alpha}}$, in place of $\ln\left(\frac{S(t)}{X}\right)$. The reasoning follows a Z-score argument (see details in Crack [2021]). In the standard Black-Scholes formula, $N(d_2)$ is the (risk-neutral) probability that the call finishes in-the-money; it is the probability that $S(T) > X$. In the power call option formula, $N(d_2')$ is the (risk-neutral) probability that the power call finishes in-the-money. For the power call, this is the probability that $S^\alpha(T) > X$. This is the same as the probability that $S > X^{\frac{1}{\alpha}}$. This probability is in turn just the standard $N(d_2)$, in the case where the strike is given by $K \equiv X^{\frac{1}{\alpha}}$.

To extend the formulae to the case of continuous dividends at rate ρ, replace $S(t)$ by $S(t)e^{-\rho(T-t)}$ throughout the power option pricing formulae to yield

$$c(t) = S^\alpha(t)e^{(m-\alpha\rho)(T-t)}N(d_1') - e^{-r(T-t)}XN(d_2'), \quad \text{and}$$

$$p(t) = e^{-r(T-t)}XN(-d_2') - S^\alpha(t)e^{(m-\alpha\rho)(T-t)}N(-d_1'), \quad \text{where}$$

$$d_1' = \frac{\ln\left(\frac{S(t)}{K}\right) + (r - \rho + (\alpha - \frac{1}{2})\sigma^2)(T - t)}{\sigma\sqrt{T - t}},$$

$$d_2' = \frac{\ln\left(\frac{S(t)}{K}\right) + (r - \rho - \frac{1}{2}\sigma^2)(T - t)}{\sigma\sqrt{T - t}} = d_1' - \alpha\sigma\sqrt{T - t},$$

$$K \equiv X^{\frac{1}{\alpha}}, \quad \text{and} \quad m \equiv \left(r + \frac{\alpha}{2}\sigma^2\right)(\alpha - 1).$$

> **Story:** A headhunter sent me a candidate to interview. After two minutes in the interview room, I could see that the candidate had inflated his CV. I knew it, and he knew I knew it. He was embarrassed and uncomfortable. I felt that both he and the headhunter had completely wasted my time. Your CV is in the cross-hairs. Putting something false on it is a stupid thing to do. Do not do it! Your interviewer is not an idiot!

SECOND SOLUTION

We can attempt to use what we already know about Black-Scholes to arrive at a similarity solution. If we apply Itô's Lemma to $V \equiv S^\alpha$ where $dS = rSdt + \sigma Sdw$, we obtain $dV = r'Vdt + \sigma'Vdw$, where $r' \equiv \alpha r + \frac{1}{2}\alpha(\alpha - 1)\sigma^2$, and $\sigma' \equiv \alpha\sigma$ (exercise). We see that V follows a geometric Brownian motion, and we might be tempted to deduce a similarity solution for the power call (with no dividends) as in (***) below.

$$c'(t) = V(t)N(d_1') - e^{-r'(T-t)}XN(d_2'), \quad (***) \quad \text{where}$$

$$d_1' = \frac{\ln\left(\frac{V(t)}{X}\right) + (r' + \frac{1}{2}\sigma'^2)(T-t)}{\sigma'\sqrt{T-t}}, \quad \text{and}$$

$$d_2' = d_1' - \sigma'\sqrt{T-t}.$$

This is, however, only an approximation to the power call value. Both $S(t)$ and $V(t)$ follow geometric Brownian motions, but they differ in that although the r term in dS is the correct rate to discount the strike price X, the r' term in dV is not. It is this difference that undermines the similarity solution approach. The difference between r and r' thus determines the accuracy of the approximation; see the exercise following.

> **Exercise:** We defined $m \equiv \left(r + \frac{\alpha}{2}\sigma^2\right)(\alpha-1)$ on p. 202. Please demonstrate your algebraic dexterity here by showing that $m = r' - r$, that d_1' and d_2' in (***) are identical to those in (**) on p. 202, and that the correct power call formula $c(t)$ given by (**) on p. 202 satisfies $c(t) = e^{m(T-t)}c'(t)$ where $c'(t)$ is the similarity solution given in (***) above. Now deduce that the accuracy of the similarity solution is determined by how far $m(T-t)$ is from zero. In practice, if α is far from one (say above 1.2 or below 0.8), or time to maturity is longer than about six months, or implied volatility is bigger than about 0.40, then the approximation is poor.

JARROW AND TURNBULL'S POWERED CALL

Jarrow and Turnbull ask their readers to value a call with payoff $[S(T)-K]^2$ if $S(T) \geq K$ and zero otherwise (Jarrow and Turnbull [1996, p. 175]). Assuming a Black-Scholes world, it is easy to show that the value of this call at time t prior to maturity is

$$c(t) = S^2(t)e^{(r+\sigma^2)(T-t)}N(d_0) - 2KS(t)N(d_1)$$
$$+ e^{-r(T-t)}K^2N(d_2), \quad \text{where}$$

$$d_l = \frac{\ln\left(\frac{S(t)}{K}\right) + \left(r + \left[\frac{3}{2} - l\right]\sigma^2\right)(T-t)}{\sigma\sqrt{T-t}}, \quad \text{for } l = 0, 1, 2.$$

For the powered call with general payoff

$$c(T) = \begin{cases} [S(T) - K]^\alpha & ; S(T) \geq K \\ 0 & ; \text{otherwise}, \end{cases}$$

for non-negative integer α, we can employ the following result (Crack [1997])

$$E^* \left[f(\alpha, T) \right] = S^\alpha(t)e^{\alpha\left(r + \left[\frac{\alpha-1}{2}\right]\sigma^2\right)(T-t)}N(d_{2-\alpha}), \quad (B.12)$$

where E^* is expectation with respect to the risk-neutral probability measure,

$$f(\alpha, T) = \begin{cases} S^\alpha(T); & \text{if } S(T) \geq K, \\ 0; & \text{otherwise,} \end{cases}$$

and d_l is as above. Combining Equation B.12 with the binomial theorem we obtain the general pricing formula

$$c(t) = \sum_{j=0}^{\alpha} (-K)^{\alpha-j} \binom{\alpha}{j} S^j(t) e^{\left[(j-1)\left(r+j\frac{\sigma^2}{2}\right)(T-t)\right]} N(d_{2-j}), \text{ where}$$

$$d_l = \frac{\ln\left(\frac{S(t)}{K}\right) + \left(r + \left[\frac{3}{2} - l\right]\sigma^2\right)(T-t)}{\sigma\sqrt{T-t}}, \quad l = 2, 1, \ldots, 2 - \alpha,$$

and $\binom{\alpha}{j} \equiv \frac{\alpha!}{j!(\alpha-j)!}$ is the usual binomial coefficient (see also Haug [2007, p. 119]). The reader should check that in the special case $\alpha = 2$, the general formula reduces to that previously given, and that in the special case $\alpha = 1$, the general formula reduces to standard Black-Scholes pricing.[51]

Answer 2.34: If the Black-Scholes assumptions are correct, then the implied volatilities of options (those backed out of the Black-Scholes pricing formula given the other pricing parameters) should fall on a horizontal line when plotted against strike prices of the options used. However, the patterns that result include smiles and skewed lines depending upon the underlying asset and the time period (Hammer [1989]; Sullivan [1993]; Murphy [1994]; Derman and Kani [1994]). Before the Crash of 1987, you typically got smiles when you plotted the implied volatilities against strikes. Nowadays you are more likely to get skews, or smirks.[52]

What is happening may be viewed in some different and related ways. Option prices are determined by supply and demand, not by theoretical formulae. The traders who are determining the option prices are implicitly modifying the Black-Scholes assumptions to account for volatility that changes both with time and with stock price level. This is contrary to the Black and Scholes (1973) assumption of constant volatility irrespective of stock price or time to maturity. That is, traders assume $\sigma = \sigma(S(t), t)$, whereas Black and Scholes assume σ is just a constant.[53]

If volatility is changing with both level of the underlying and time to maturity, then the distribution of future stock price is no longer lognormal. The distribution must be something different. Black-Scholes option pricing takes

---

[51]Haug (2007, pp. 118–119) gives some of these formulae and cites Crack (1997, 2004).

[52]Another related deviation from Black-Scholes pricing is that implied volatilities when plotted against term to maturity produce a "term-structure of volatility." That is, traders use different volatilities to value long-maturity and short-maturity options (Derman and Kani [1994, pp. 2–3]; Hull [1997, pp. 503–504]).

[53]Black (1976) is the earliest paper I know of that acknowledges that $\sigma \uparrow$ as $S \downarrow$, and vice versa.

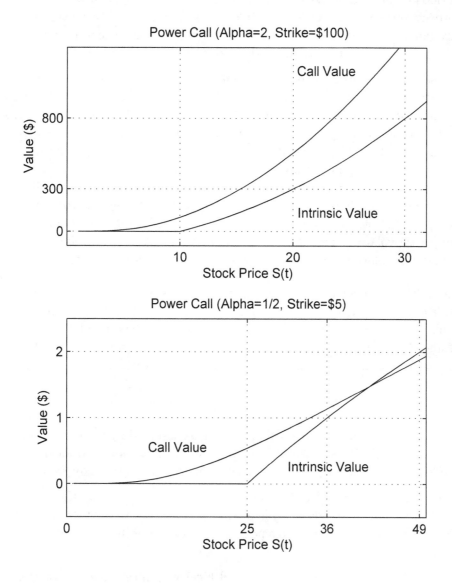

Figure B.5: Power Calls with $\alpha > 1$, and $\alpha < 1$

Note: The power call prices are plotted as a function of price of underlying. Note that the "kink" in the payoff diagram does not occur at the strike K, but rather at $K^{\frac{1}{\alpha}}$ (see Question 2.33).

discounted expected payoffs relative to a lognormal distribution. As volatility changes through time, you are likely to get periods of little activity and periods of intense activity. These periods produce peakedness and fat tails respectively (together called "leptokurtosis"), in stock returns distributions. Fat tails are likely to lead to some sort of smile effect, because they increase the chance of payoffs away-from-the-money.[54]

These irregularities have led to "stochastic volatility" models that account for volatility changing as a function of both time and stock price level (Hull and White [1987]; Scott[1987]; Wiggins [1987]; Heston [1993]; Hull [1997]). Applications to FOREX options include Chesney and Scott (1989) and Melino and Turnbull (1990). The effect of stochastic volatility on options values is similar to the effect of a jump component: both increase the probability that out-of-the-money options will finish in-the-money and increase the probability that in-the-money options will finish out-of-the-money (Wiggins [1987, pp. 360–361]). Whether the smile is skewed left, skewed right, or symmetric in a stochastic volatility model depends upon the sign of the correlation between changes in volatility and changes in stock price (Hull [1997, Section 19.3]).

Answer 2.35: A local volatility model is a stochastic volatility model with the additional condition that the volatility varies only with the level of the asset price and with time, say, $\sigma_t = \sigma(S(t), t)$. The stochastic volatility model is assumed to produce option prices consistent with, or calibrated to, the prices of traded options. For example, the underlying risk-neutral process might be

$$dS(t) = r(t)S(t)dt + \sigma(S(t), t)S(t)dw(t),$$

where $w(t)$ is a standard Brownian motion, as assumed by Dupire (1994). Derman and Kani (1994a, 1994b) and Rubinstein (1994) are also local volatility models, with local (or "move") volatility inferred endogenously from a tree.

The volatility is "local" in the sense that it is driven only by the level of the asset price and time, both visible at that point in the tree for example, rather than being driven by an exogenous source of variability, like an additional stochastic process.

Stochastic volatility models are not all local volatility models. For example, the Heston (1993) model assumes that the stochastic volatility is driven by its own stochastic process with its own Brownian motion. So, because the volatility process depends upon more than just stock price and time, it is not a local volatility model.

Rubinstein (1994, p. 809) points out that vega (i.e., sensitivity of option price to volatility) no longer has a clear meaning in a model with stochastic local volatility.

---

[54]The interaction of skewness and kurtosis of returns gives rise to many different possible smile effects (Hull [1997, Section 19.3]; Krause [1998, pp. 145-148]).

Answer 2.36: This question is probably supposed to invoke misleading memories of the barrier option parity relationship: Other things being equal, a down-and-out call plus a down-and-in call is the same as a standard call. However, a double-barrier knock-out is not the same as an up-and-out together with a down-and-out. The latter pair of options is more valuable than the double-barrier knock-out. The most obvious reason is that if the underlying moves one way, then the double knock-out is knocked out, but a portfolio of a down-and-out plus a down-and-in still contains one option. That is, the pair of knock-outs is more versatile—and thus more valuable.

A double-barrier knock-out can be priced using lattice (e.g., binomial) methods. It may also be priced using the Kunitomo-Ikeda formula (Kunitomo and Ikeda [1992]; Musiela and Rutkowski [1997, p. 211]; or the user-friendly Haug [2007, p. 156]). The Kunitomo-Ikeda formula is an infinite series. Typically, only the leading few terms are needed for practical purposes (Kunitomo and Ikeda [1992, p. 286]). More terms may be needed if volatility is high, term to maturity is long, or the distance between the barriers is small (in each case this increases the likelihood of knockout and the pricing is more difficult).

Answer 2.37: The prices of the digital asset-or-nothing, $da(t)$, and the digital cash-or-nothing (with a "bet" size of $1), $dc(t, \$1)$, are just the two parts of the Black-Scholes formula

$$
\begin{aligned}
c(t) &= da(t) - X dc(t, \$1), \text{ where} \\
da(t) &= S(t)N(d_1), \\
dc(t, \$1) &= e^{-r(T-t)}N(d_2), \\
d_1 &= \frac{\ln\left(\frac{S(t)}{X}\right) + (r + \frac{1}{2}\sigma^2)(T-t)}{\sigma\sqrt{T-t}}, \text{ and,} \\
d_2 &= d_1 - \sigma\sqrt{T-t}.
\end{aligned}
$$

Black-Scholes derivations using discounted expected payoffs under risk-neutral probabilities (e.g. Crack [2021]) contain implicit derivations of both digital option values. These may be identified if the initial step is re-expressed as

$$
\begin{aligned}
da(t) &= e^{-r(T-t)} E^*[S(T)\mathcal{I}_{S(T)>X} \mid S(t)], \text{ and,} \\
dc(t, \$1) &= e^{-r(T-t)} E^*[\mathcal{I}_{S(T)>X} \mid S(t)],
\end{aligned}
$$

where $\mathcal{I}_{S(T)>X}$ is the indicator function

$$
\mathcal{I}_{S(T)>X} = \begin{cases} 1 \text{ if } S(T) > X, \\ 0 \text{ if } S(T) \leq X. \end{cases}
$$

Answer 2.38: A path-dependent option is one where the final payoff depends upon the stock price path followed. If the stock price ends up between the barriers, the option has different values, depending upon whether it was

209

knocked in or knocked out (or both). Path-dependent options can typically be priced using Monte-Carlo methods. However, Monte-Carlo does not work for American-style options. Standard lattice techniques (e.g., binomial option pricing) do not usually work for path-dependent options.[55] However, you can price the "out-in" derivative using standard lattice methods, as follows. The parity relationship for knock-outs says that a down-and-out plus a down-and-in is a standard option. We can generalize this to conclude that an out-in plus a double-barrier knock-out is the same as an up-and-out (other things being equal). It follows that the out-in is worth the excess of the value of the up-and-out over the double-barrier knock-out. Both these knock-outs can be priced using standard lattice techniques.

Answer 2.39: Let $G(\cdot)$ denote the gold price. Now is time t, and time T is six months from now. The naive (and incorrect) step is to conclude that a volatility of $\sigma = \$60$ per annum translates to a six-month volatility of $\$30$. In fact, volatility grows with the square root of the term. Thus, $\$60$ per year translates to about $\sqrt{\frac{1}{2}} \times \$60 \approx \$42$ per half-year.

How do we find the probability that the option finishes in-the-money, $P(G(T) > 430)$? With $r = 0$ there is no drift in the risk-neutral world, so the distribution of $G(T)$ is centered on $G(t) = \$400$, with standard deviation roughly $\$42$. Thus

$$
\begin{aligned}
P(G(T) > 430) &= P(G(T) - G(t) > 30) \\
&= P\left(\frac{G(T) - G(t)}{42} > \frac{30}{42}\right) \\
&\approx 1 - N\left(\frac{3}{4}\right),
\end{aligned}
$$

where $N(\cdot)$ is the cumulative standard normal function. The last step follows because $\frac{G(T)-G(t)}{42}$ is roughly standard normal. We know that $N(0) = 0.50$, and $N(1) = 0.84$, so $N\left(\frac{3}{4}\right) \approx 0.75$.

We conclude that there is roughly a 25% chance that the digital option finishes in-the-money. With a bet size of $\$1$ million, and a riskless interest rate of zero, the discounted expected payoff (in a risk-neutral world) is roughly $\$250,000$. The erroneous $\sigma = \$30$ gives an incorrect value of only about $\$160,000$.

Answer 2.40: Let us review quickly standard American options before looking at the perpetual option. American options are harder to price than European ones. Puts are harder to price than calls. An American put is hardest of all to price because early exercise can in general be optimal at any time for an American-style put. This differs from an American-style call, for which early

---

[55]Standard lattice techniques can be modified to allow pricing of path-dependent options. However, a couple of conditions involving complexity of the payoffs need to be satisfied (Hull and White [1993]; Hull [1997]).

exercise is optimal only at a few dates during the option's life (just prior to ex-dividend days). In fact, the problem is so hard that no exact pricing formula exists for standard American put options.

Black and Scholes (1973) value European-style puts and calls. If a stock does not pay dividends, then a European call and an American call have the same value (there is no incentive to exercise early). Thus, American calls on non-dividend-paying stocks can be valued using Black-Scholes. The introduction of dividends complicates matters. However, an approximate pricing formula (Black [1975]) and an exact pricing formula (Roll [1977b]; Geske [1979]; Whaley [1981]) for American calls on dividend-paying stocks are known (see Hull [1997, Chapter 11]). American puts are more complicated. The dividend issue is not as important for puts as for calls because it is the receipt of the strike, not the dividends, that encourages early exercise of a put. Although no exact American put pricing formula exists, there are approximations (Parkinson [1977]; MacMillan [1986]; Barone-Adesi and Whaley [1987]). See the summaries in Tables B.2 and B.3.

Now to the perpetual American put. Extending the life of an option in perpetuity eases the pricing burden (removing the dependence on time turns a PDE into an ODE). Pricing the perpetual American put was a question on a problem set I had as a student in Robert C. Merton's derivatives course at Harvard in 1991. I reproduce my solution here.

Let V denote the value of a perpetual American put option on a stock. Let S denote the stock price. Let X denote the strike price. Assume that the stock pays continuous dividends at rate ρ. Let σ and r denote the volatility of stock returns and the riskless interest rate respectively. The Black-Scholes PDE is given by (Wilmott et al. [1993])

$$\frac{\partial V}{\partial t} + \frac{1}{2}\sigma^2 S^2 \frac{\partial^2 V}{\partial S^2} + (r - \rho)S\frac{\partial V}{\partial S} - rV = 0.$$

However, for a *perpetual* put, time decay must be zero (it cannot age if it can live forever). Thus, the PDE becomes an ODE (though I am keeping the partial derivative notation):

$$\frac{1}{2}\sigma^2 S^2 \frac{\partial^2 V}{\partial S^2} + (r - \rho)S\frac{\partial V}{\partial S} - rV = 0$$

Let $\underline{S}$ denote the lower exercise boundary (this is how low the stock has to go before exercise of the put becomes optimal—it has to be determined). Then, we have the boundary conditions

$$\begin{aligned} V(S = \underline{S}) &= X - \underline{S}, \\ \left.\frac{\partial V}{\partial S}\right|_{S=\underline{S}} &= -1, \\ V(S) &\leq X. \end{aligned}$$

The second condition is the Samuelson "high-contact" condition.

All of this ODE's solutions may be represented as a linear combination of any two linearly independent solutions. It follows that

$$V(S) = A_1 V^1(S) + A_2 V^2(S),$$

where A_1 and A_2 are constants, and V^1 and V^2 are linearly independent solutions of the ODE. My guess is that $V^1 = S^{\lambda_1}$, and $V^2 = S^{\lambda_2}$ for some constants λ_1, and λ_2.[56] Substitution of V^i into the ODE yields (for $i = 1, 2$, and for $\underline{S} \leq S$)

$$\left[\frac{1}{2}\sigma^2 \lambda_i(\lambda_i - 1) + (r - \rho)\lambda_i - r \right] S^{\lambda_i} = 0.$$

Rearranging and collecting terms in λ_i, we get for $i = 1, 2$

$$\frac{1}{2}\sigma^2 \lambda_i^2 + \left(r - \rho - \frac{1}{2}\sigma^2 \right) \lambda_i - r = 0.$$

This is a quadratic formula, with solutions for λ_i:

$$\lambda_1 = \frac{-\left(r - \rho - \frac{1}{2}\sigma^2\right) + \sqrt{\left(r - \rho - \frac{1}{2}\sigma^2\right)^2 + 2\sigma^2 r}}{\sigma^2}, \quad \text{and}$$

$$\lambda_2 = \frac{-\left(r - \rho - \frac{1}{2}\sigma^2\right) - \sqrt{\left(r - \rho - \frac{1}{2}\sigma^2\right)^2 + 2\sigma^2 r}}{\sigma^2}$$

The solutions for λ_i can be seen to satisfy $\lambda_1 > 0$ if $r > 0$, and $\lambda_2 < 0$ if $r > 0$. Let us now consider the behavior of the general solution we have derived: $V(S) = A_1 S^{\lambda_1} + A_2 S^{\lambda_2}$. First of all, with $\lambda_1 > 0$, and $\lambda_2 < 0$, then

$$\lim_{S \to +\infty} \left(A_1 S^{\lambda_1} + A_2 S^{\lambda_2} \right) = \pm\infty, \quad \text{if } |A_1| > 0.$$

However, the boundary conditions put both upper and lower finite bounds on the value of the put. Therefore, $A_1 = 0$, and $V(S) = A_2 S^{\lambda_2}$. Now, the first boundary condition tells us that

$$V(\underline{S}) = A_2 \underline{S}^{\lambda_2} = X - \underline{S},$$

so it follows that $A_2 = \frac{X - \underline{S}}{\underline{S}^{\lambda_2}}$, which yields

$$V(S) = \left(\frac{X - \underline{S}}{\underline{S}^{\lambda_2}} \right) S^{\lambda_2} = (X - \underline{S}) \left(\frac{S}{\underline{S}} \right)^{\lambda_2}.$$

---

[56]Why make this guess? Look at the ODE: the degree of the derivatives of V and the degree of S in the coefficients move together (both two, then both one, then both zero). This suggests solutions that are powers of S.

To pinpoint the solution, we must determine the value of the lower exercise boundary $\underline{S}$. The second of our boundary conditions says $\frac{\partial V}{\partial S}\big|_{S=\underline{S}} = -1$. We can solve for $\underline{S}$ using this.

$$\frac{\partial V}{\partial S} = \lambda_2(X - \underline{S})\left(\frac{S^{\lambda_2-1}}{\underline{S}^{\lambda_2}}\right)$$

$$\Rightarrow \quad \frac{\partial V}{\partial S}\bigg|_{S=\underline{S}} = \lambda_2\frac{(X - \underline{S})}{\underline{S}} = -1$$

$$\Rightarrow \lambda_2(X - \underline{S}) = -\underline{S}$$

$$\Rightarrow \quad \underline{S} = \frac{\lambda_2 X}{\lambda_2 - 1}.$$

Thus, for $S \geq \underline{S} \equiv \frac{\lambda_2 X}{\lambda_2-1}$, the perpetual American put is worth

$$V(S) = (X - \underline{S})\left(\frac{S}{\underline{S}}\right)^{\lambda_2} = \left(\frac{X}{1 - \lambda_2}\right)\left[\frac{(\lambda_2 - 1)S}{\lambda_2 X}\right]^{\lambda_2}, \quad \text{where}$$

$$\lambda_2 = \frac{-\left(r - \rho - \frac{1}{2}\sigma^2\right) - \sqrt{\left(r - \rho - \frac{1}{2}\sigma^2\right)^2 + 2\sigma^2 r}}{\sigma^2}.$$

For $0 \leq S \leq \frac{\lambda_1 X}{(\lambda_1-1)} \equiv \overline{S}$, it may be shown using similar techniques that a perpetual American call is worth

$$V(S) = \left(\frac{X}{\lambda_1 - 1}\right)\left[\frac{(\lambda_1 - 1)S}{\lambda_1 X}\right]^{\lambda_1}, \quad \text{where}$$

$$\lambda_1 = \frac{-\left(r - \rho - \frac{1}{2}\sigma^2\right) + \sqrt{\left(r - \rho - \frac{1}{2}\sigma^2\right)^2 + 2\sigma^2 r}}{\sigma^2}.$$

Note that (theoretically at least) a perpetual European call is worth the same as the stock, whereas a perpetual European put is worth zero (look at the limiting behavior of the Black-Scholes formula).[57]

Answer 2.41: If you subtract LIBOR, denoted "L," from both payments, it seems that Party B is paying $24\% - 3 \times L$. This is three times $8\% - L$. The quoted swap is, therefore, equivalent to three swaps, each of which is a swap of LIBOR for 8% fixed (where Party A pays LIBOR, and Party B pays 8%).

Answer 2.42: If you sold the option, you should hold about one-half a share to hedge. If you bought the option, you should short about one-half a share to hedge. If you are at-the-money, there is about a fifty-fifty chance the option finishes in-the-money; and with this expectation, you need about one-half a share to hedge.

---

[57]Note that in the case of the perpetual American call, $\lim_{\rho \to 0} \lambda_1 = 1$, and $\lim_{\lambda_1 \to 1} V(S) = S$. That is, with no dividends, the perpetual American call has the same value as the stock—just like the perpetual European call.

©2021 Timothy Falcon Crack   213   All Rights Reserved Worldwide

Table B.2: Pricing Methods Summary: Plain Vanilla Options

	European-Style		American-Style	
	Put	Call	Put	Call
No dividends	Black-Scholes put formula	Black-Scholes call formula	No exact formula (use approximation formula, tree, or finite differences)	Black-Scholes call formula (early exercise is never optimal)
Lump sum dividend D	Use $S^*=S-PV(D)$ in Black-Scholes	Use $S^*=S-PV(D)$ in Black-Scholes	No exact formula (use approximation formula, tree, or finite differences)	Roll-Geske-Whaley formula, or Black's pseudo formula
Continuous dividends at rate ρ	Use $S^*=Se^{-\rho(T-t)}$ in Black-Scholes (Merton's formula)	Use $S^*=Se^{-\rho(T-t)}$ in Black-Scholes (Merton's formula)	No exact formula (use approximation formula, tree, or finite differences)	Adjust Roll-Geske-Whaley formula
$S=\left(\frac{USD}{FX}\right)$	Use $\rho=r_{FX}$ in Merton's formula (Garman-Kohlhagen/Grabbe formula)	Use $\rho=r_{FX}$ in Merton's formula (Garman-Kohlhagen/Grabbe formula)	Use $\rho=r_{FX}$ in the above	Use $\rho=r_{FX}$ in the above
All cases: Numerical	Monte Carlo, lattice, or finite differences		Lattice or finite differences	

Note: Pricing methods for European- or American-style plain vanilla puts or calls where the underlying pays no dividends, pays a lump sum dividend, pays continuous dividends, or is a foreign currency.

Table B.3: Pricing Methods Summary: Exotic Options

European-Style		American-Style	
Path-Independent	Path-Dependent	Path-Independent	Path-Dependent
Lattice, Monte Carlo, or finite difference	Monte Carlo, finite difference, lattice (difficult)	Lattice or finite differences	Lattice (difficult) or finite differences
... or a formula if you can derive it			

Note: Summary of pricing methods for exotic options that are European- or American-style, path-independent or path-dependent.

Answer 2.43:   Mean reversion is the tendency for a variable to return to some sort of long-run mean. Interest rates are generally considered to be mean-reverting: they go up, they go down, but they eventually return to some sort of long-term average. In the case of a mean-reverting stock price, the stock price would tend to be pulled back to the average if the price rises or falls very far. This may reduce volatility and make the option cheaper.

A model of mean reversion makes sense for interest rates, and for stock returns, but it is by no means clear to me that it makes sense for stock *prices*. Bates argues that strong mean reversion in stock prices is implausible because of speculative opportunities available from buying when $S < \bar{S}$ and selling when $S > \bar{S}$ (Bates [1995, pp. 7–8]). Lo and Wang say that autocorrelation in asset *returns* can increase or decrease σ (and the option price) and that it depends upon the specification of the drift in the model (Lo and Wang [1995, p. 105]).

Mean reversion in prices can easily yield negative autocorrelation in both prices and returns at some horizon. If we have autocorrelation in returns, then we do not have a GBM, the Black-Scholes model is invalid, and the drift term in the price process may be very important (Lo and Wang [1995]). Conversely, if we have a GBM, then we have no autocorrelation in returns and the drift term is unimportant for pricing options.[58]

At short horizons (e.g., daily or weekly), stock index returns used to be positively autocorrelated (Lo and MacKinlay [1988]) but this result has all but disappeared now (Crack [2020b]). At longer horizons (e.g., three or four years), Fama and French (1988) and Poterba and Summers (1988) say that stock returns are negatively autocorrelated (i.e., mean reverting). However, evidence for this is weak (Richardson [1993]). Lo and MacKinlay (1988, p. 61) say that longer-term positive autocorrelation is not inconsistent with shorter-term negative autocorrelation (i.e., mean reversion). Peterson et al. (1992) and Lo and Wang (1995) discuss option pricing when asset returns are autocorrelated. Crack and Ledoit (2010) discuss hypothesis testing when asset returns are autocorrelated.

Answer 2.44: Hedging can increase your risk if you are forced to both buy short-dated options and hedge them. In this case, to hedge, you need to short the stock. If the stock price rises up to the strike, and the options (be they puts or calls) expire worthless, then you lose on both the options and the short stock position. By hedging, you end up worse off than if you had not hedged.

Answer 2.45: This is a common question. You can hedge the written put by shorting an asset whose returns are correlated with returns on the underlying stock. Ideally, this would just be the stock itself. However, it is not always possible to short stock. There are single-stock futures contracts on about 1,000 leading U.S. stocks (see www.OneChicago.com), but that still leaves about 4,000 listed U.S. stocks and another 5,000 OTC stocks without single-stock futures (Crack [2020b, 2021]). You could short index futures instead but that would give you an imperfect hedge. You need to know either the beta or the correlation of the stock returns relative to the index returns to apportion the hedge correctly. You could also short the stock of a close competitor. If the stock is heavily influenced by a commodity (e.g., gold, silver, oil, corn), you could short commodity futures.

---

[58]Can you prove to your satisfaction that a GBM in prices implies very strong positive autocorrelation in prices? See Crack (2020b, Chapter 1) for further discussion.

Answer 2.46: People are fed by the area, A, of the pizza. $A = \pi r^2 = \pi \left(\frac{d}{2}\right)^2 = \frac{\pi}{4}d^2$, where d is the diameter. Thus, $d = \sqrt{\frac{4}{\pi}}\sqrt{A}$. Multiplying A by $\frac{8}{6}$ requires a multiplicative change of $\sqrt{\frac{8}{6}}$ in d. That is, $d' = \sqrt{\frac{8}{6}}d = 13.86$ inches. Without a calculator, the square root of $(1+X)$ is roughly $(1+\frac{X}{2})$, so $\sqrt{\frac{8}{6}} \approx \sqrt{1.33} \approx 1.15$. Fifteen percent of 12 is 1.8, so the answer is roughly 13.8 inches.

Why is this a derivatives question? Using the approximation $c = S\sigma\sqrt{\frac{T-t}{2\pi}}$, a question with the same answer is: a six-month at-the-money call has price $12; what is the price of the eight-month call?

Answer 2.47: You want to be short a put if you expect the put to fall in price (e.g., the underlying is expected to rise, volatility to expected to fall, etc.).

Answer 2.48: A fair price for future delivery of an asset depends upon the spot price and the cost of carry. The cost of carry includes the cost of money (i.e., an interest rate), dividend income, storage costs, and the convenience yield. The only difference between the two pieces of land is the entrance fee to the beach. This is a dividend that lowers the forward price of the beach relative to the field.

Answer 2.49: There are two important points: use of logarithms, and division by $T-1$. Begin by calculating continuously compounded returns (as used in Black-Scholes):

$$
\begin{aligned}
X_t &\equiv \ln(1 + R_t) \\
&= \ln\left(1 + \frac{P_t - P_{t-1}}{P_{t-1}}\right) \\
&= \ln\left(\frac{P_t}{P_{t-1}}\right)
\end{aligned}
$$

With 30 stock prices, you get $T = 29$ returns. Now calculate the standard sample mean and variance. Remember to divide by $T-1 = 28$ in the variance estimator to get an unbiased small sample estimator of historical volatility (DeGroot [1989, p. 413]).

$$
\begin{aligned}
\hat{\mu} &= \frac{1}{T}\sum_{t=1}^{T} X_t \\
\hat{\sigma}^2 &= \frac{1}{T-1}\sum_{t=1}^{T}(X_t - \hat{\mu})^2.
\end{aligned}
$$

Some people may even leave off the "$-\hat{\mu}$" in the $\hat{\sigma}^2$ calculation because mean daily stock returns are typically so tiny compared to volatility, but I prefer to leave it in.

Answer 2.50: The key is default risk, but let's start with a quick swap curve review. Swap rates are fixed rates quoted by dealers against the floating leg (e.g., six-month USD LIBOR) of an interest rate swap. The "swap buyer" is the fixed-rate payer and is said to be "long the swap" (although I have also heard the reverse). The swap curve is inferred from quoted swap rates for different maturities in the same manner that a zero-coupon yield curve (i.e., a "spot curve") is bootstrapped from the yields on coupon bearing bonds of different maturities (corporates or treasuries). Swaps dealers can do customized deals offering different quoted swap rates to companies of different credit rating; however, dealers tend to quote the same swap rate to companies of different credit rating but ask for different amounts of collateral based on the rating (personal communication with a NY dealer [April, 1999]).[59] The collateral and subsequent margin calls essentially resolve the credit issues. Johannes and Sundaresan (2003, p. 9) state that the "key to effective credit risk mitigation is frequent margin calls." They state that more than 65% of plain vanilla derivatives, and especially interest rate swaps, are collateralized and that at least 74% mark to market at at least a daily frequency.

The settlement features of an interest rate swap mean that default risk in a swap is higher than in a eurodollar futures contract but lower than in a bond (Minton [1997, p. 253]). The reasoning is as follows. The settlement rate for the futures contract is reset daily by market forces, but the swap typically resets only every six months. Both the futures contract and the swap are marked-to-market and use margins, but the futures contract is backed by the triple-A-rated futures clearing corporation as a counterparty of last resort and so the futures contract is less credit-risky than the swap. The swap differs from the bond because no principal changes hands.[60] At initiation, the value of a swap contract is zero; but during the life of the swap, as interest rates rise and fall, the value of the contract can become positive or negative, respectively, to the swap buyer. Although a bondholder is always worried about default risk, the swap buyer worries about default risk only when the swap has positive value. Default on a swap is thus less likely than default on a bond because default on a bond requires only that the company be in financial distress, whereas default on a swap requires both that the company be in financial distress and that the remaining value of the swap be positive. The joint probability of both events needed for swap default is less than the single probability needed for bond default (Minton [1997, p. 262–263, p. 267]).

It follows that the coupon rate on a bond will be higher than the quoted swap rate for a swap of the same maturity. This is true for all maturities, so bootstrapping the swap curve from swap rates of swaps of different maturities and bootstrapping the zero-coupon yield curve (i.e., the spot curve) from coupon

---

[59]Minton (1997, p. 252) confirms that the plain vanilla swap quotes in her (1992 and earlier) sample assume no credit enhancement (e.g., margins or marking to market).

[60]Although true for an interest rate swap, this is not so in a forex swap, where principal changes hands at initiation and conclusion of the life of the swap.

rates of corporate bonds (e.g., AA-rated) of different maturities produces a swap curve strictly below the zero-coupon yield curve.[61] It follows that when you discount the cash flows to the bond using the swap curve, you get a number above that which you would get when you discount the cash flows to the bond using the zero-coupon yield curve (i.e., above par).

Answer 2.51: Try a simple economics argument. The option must cost the same as a replicating portfolio—else there is money to be made. This result is driven by no-arbitrage and is thus independent of risk preferences. I can ease my calculations by assuming risk-neutrality for everyone in the economy. In such an economy in equilibrium, the required return (and thus the expected growth rate and also the discount rate) for all traded securities is the riskless rate. I price the option as if we are in this economy (and the option pricing is immune to this assumption).

Answer 2.52: Options live in the future, not the past: Today is the first day of the rest of the life of a traded option. Setting aside problems with volatility smiles and skews, the implied volatility (or "implied standard deviation") is a market-consensus forecast of volatility over the remaining life of the option. It would be logical, therefore, that implied volatility is a better predictor of future volatility than is historical volatility. Indeed, this is found empirically for both FOREX (Xu and Taylor [1995]) and for equity indices (Fleming [1998]).

Answer 2.53: Which is worth more, a European-style call that is 10% out-of-the-money or a European-style put that is 10% out-of-the-money?[62]

The short answer is that the call is worth more because option value is discounted expected payoff relative to the distribution of possible payoffs, and the call's long right tail of possible high payoffs (and low probability of occurrence) dominates the put's stunted left tail of low payoffs (and high probability of occurrence).

Let us assume that $S = 100$, so that the call has strike $X_c = S \times 1.1 = 110$, and the put has strike $X_p = S/1.1 = 90.909090...$ (we could use $X_p = 90$ but some of the exact relationships quoted below would then be approximations only). Assume there are no dividends.

The distribution of stock prices at expiration is lognormal in the Black-Scholes model and is thus positively skewed with its mean higher than the median,

---

[61]In early 1999, just before the Tech Bubble, two-year swap rates were about 40 bps higher than U.S. treasuries (which were at 500 bps), about 5 bps lower than the yields on AAA-rated debt, about 30 bps lower than the yields on AA-rated debt and about 40 bps lower than the yields on BBB-rated debt. For comparison, ten years later in mid-2009, coming out of the Global Credit Crisis, these rates/spreads were 45 bps, 120 bps, 3 bps, 75 bps, and 575 bps respectively. Five years later still, in August 2014, these rates/spreads for a five-year maturity were 36 bps, 165 bps, 0 bps, 11 bps, and 68 bps, respectively.

[62]I thank Veeken Chaglassian for helpful advice on this answer; any errors are mine.

which is in turn higher than the mode (the peak). The median of the distribution of future stock prices is $Se^{(r-\frac{1}{2}\sigma^2)(T-t)}$, where $(T-t)$ is the time to maturity.

To make clear some subtle points, let us consider two special cases. First, suppose that the interest rate satisfies $r = \frac{1}{2}\sigma^2$ (e.g., $r = 12.5\%$ for $\sigma = 50\%$ and $(T-t) = 1$), then the median of the distribution of $S(T)$ equals $S(t)$ at 100. In that case, even though the distribution of $S(T)$ is skewed, the risk-neutral probability that $S(T) > X_c$ is the same as the risk-neutral probability that $S(T) < X_p$.[63] That is, the call and put are exactly equally likely to finish in the money (this exact result is only approximate if we use $X_p = 90$). For the numbers I just gave ($r = 12.5\%$, $\sigma = 50\%$, $(T-t) = 1$, $S(t) = \$100$, $X_c = \$110$, and $X_p = \$90.909090...$) the call is worth about \$20.95 and the put is worth about \$9.56. That is, the call is worth more than twice what the put is worth, even though the call and put have the same probability of ending up in the money. This premium in the value of the call is driven by the product of the upside payoffs (in the long right tail of the distribution of $S(T)$), and their probability of occurring.

Second, suppose that the interest rate is zero, $r = 0$. Then, using the same numbers again, the risk-neutral probability that the call finishes in-the-money is about 33.0%, and the risk-neutral probability that the put finishes in the money is about 52.4%. Even though the put is much more likely to finish in-the-money, the call is worth about \$16.10 and the put is worth about \$14.63 (the call is worth exactly 10% more that the put;[64] this exact result is only approximate if we use $X_p = 90$).

My two special cases show that if we were to look only at the probability of finishing in-the-money, we would be misled. It is the (discounted) product of probabilities and payoffs that determine value, and in this case the right-skewed distribution of final stock price gives the call the higher price.

Answer 2.54: The value of the derivative, V, must satisfy the Black-Scholes PDE (Wilmott et al. [1993]):

$$\frac{\partial V}{\partial t} + \frac{1}{2}\sigma^2 S^2 \frac{\partial^2 V}{\partial S^2} + rS\frac{\partial V}{\partial S} - rV = 0$$

These derivatives are just the theta (Θ), gamma (Γ), and delta (Δ), respectively, so we rewrite the PDE as

$$\Theta + \frac{1}{2}\sigma^2 S^2 \Gamma + rS\Delta - rV = 0.$$

---

[63]Can you show that when $r = \frac{1}{2}\sigma^2$, $X_c = S \times (1+f)$, and $X_p = S/(1+f)$, for some scaling factor $f > 0$, we get that $d_2^{\text{call}} = -d_2^{\text{put}}$? It then follows that the call and put with these strikes have the same probability of finishing in-the-money.

[64]Can you manipulate the Black-Scholes formula to show that in the case $r = 0$, $c(S(t), X_c = K) = \frac{K}{S}p(S, X_p = S^2/K)$? That is, if $S = 100$, $X_c = 110$, and $X_p = 10,000/110 \approx 90.909090$, then $c = 1.1 \times p$.

The last two terms may be written as $r(S\Delta - V)$, and they offset to some extent. The entire PDE adds to zero, so that leaves $\Theta + \frac{1}{2}\sigma^2 S^2 \Gamma$ taking a value close to zero. This means that Θ and Γ are typically going to be of opposite signs. Not only that, but their magnitudes are going to be correlated. For example, if Θ is large and negative then Γ is probably large and positive (e.g., an at-the-money call close to maturity has these properties).

There are two exceptions amongst plain vanilla puts and calls. These were mentioned on p. 164: Θ can be positive for a deep in-the-money European call (if the dividend yield is high enough), and Θ can also be positive for a deep in-the-money European put. As long as these options are not so deep in-the-money that they have zero Γ, then they can have both positive Θ and positive Γ.

Answer 2.55: If you said you have an 80% chance of getting \$20, and a 20% chance of getting nothing, giving an expected payoff of \$16, which you then discount at zero to get an answer of \$16 for the call value, you are wrong! Sure enough, the call does have an expected payoff of \$16 in the real world, but the discount rate is not zero. The discount rate is some leveraged version of the discount rate on the stock, and you do not have that information. Try again, then come back here for the answer below.

We do not know the discount rate on the stock. We do not know the discount rate on the option. We must use risk-neutral valuation. The risk-neutral probability π^* of an up move in the stock satisfies

$$S = e^{-r(\Delta t)}\left[\pi^* Su + (1 - \pi^*)Sd\right],$$
$$\text{that is, } \$100 = \pi^* \$130 + (1 - \pi^*)\$70,$$

where r is the riskless rate (zero here), u is the multiplicative "up" growth factor in the stock (1.30 here), and d is the multiplicative "down" growth factor in the stock (0.70 here). See Crack (2021) or you favorite option pricing book for deeper details of binomial/lattice pricing. Simple algebra yields $\pi^* = 0.50$. The value of the call is then

$$c = e^{-r(\Delta t)}\left[\pi^* \max(0, Su - X) + (1 - \pi^*)\max(0, Sd - X)\right]$$
$$= 1 \cdot [0.50 \cdot (\$130 - \$110) + 0.50 \cdot (\$0)] = \$10.$$

Story: 1. Man wore jogging suit to interview for position as financial vice president. 2. Interrupted to phone his therapist for advice on answering specific interview questions.

Interview Horror Stories from Recruiters
Reprinted by kind permission of *MBA Style Magazine*
©1996–2021 MBA Style Magazine, www.mbastyle.com

Answer 2.56:   The product call pricing formula is so simple that you could simply say "here is the answer, it looks like regular dividend-adjusted Black-Scholes but you replace $S(t)$ by the product $S_1(t) \times S_2(t)$, and you replace σ by $\sigma' \equiv \sqrt{\sigma_1^2 + \sigma_2^2 + 2\rho\sigma_1\sigma_2}$ where ρ is the instantaneous correlation between the Wiener processes (i.e., Brownian motions) driving S_1 and S_2, and of course the answer is symmetric in S_1, S_2, and their associated 'dividend yields'." However, the derivation is very instructive in risk-neutral pricing, PDE's, and similarity solutions, and I cannot find it in my books so I think it belongs here.

One application of the product call is to the pricing of foreign equity options struck in a domestic currency (Haug [2007, pp. 226–228]). For example, a U.S. investor has the right to buy one share of NTT corporation stock (trading in Tokyo at JPY price S_2), but the call option strike price is in USD.[65] In this case, the payoff is $\max[S_1(T) \times S_2(T) - X, 0]$, where S_1 is the $\frac{USD}{JPY}$ exchange rate, S_2 is the JPY price of NTT per share, and T is the expiration date.

Make the following definitions:

$$
\begin{aligned}
S_1(t) &= \frac{USD}{JPY}(t) \\
S_2(t) &= \frac{JPY}{\text{Share of NTT}}(t) \\
r_{US} &= \text{US riskless interest rate} \\
r_{JP} &= \text{Japanese riskless interest rate} \\
q &= \text{NTT's continuous dividend yield} \\
dS_1 &= r_1 S_1 dt + \sigma_1 S_1 dw_1 \\
dS_2 &= r_2 S_2 dt + \sigma_2 S_2 dw_2 \\
\sigma_1 &= \text{Volatility of } dS_1/S_1 \text{ process} \\
\sigma_2 &= \text{Volatility of } dS_2/S_2 \text{ process} \\
r_1 &= \text{Drift of } dS_1/S_1 \text{ process} \\
r_2 &= \text{Drift of } dS_2/S_2 \text{ process} \\
\rho dt &= E[(dw_1) \cdot (dw_2)] = \text{instantaneous correlation} \\
X &= \text{USD-denominated strike price}
\end{aligned}
$$

So, what exactly are r_1 and r_2 in a risk-neutral world? The answer depends upon whether we look from a U.S. or a Japanese perspective (Hull [1997, p. 301]). We shall use the U.S. perspective. For S_1 from the U.S. perspective, the risk-neutral process has $r_1 = r_{US} - r_{JP}$. For S_2 from the Japanese perspective, $r_2 = r_{JP} - q$, but from the U.S. perspective, $r_2 = r_{JP} - q + (-\rho) \cdot \sigma_1\sigma_2$, where $-\rho$ is the instantaneous correlation between the Wiener processes driv-

---

[65]Please note that this is *not* a quanto option. Quantos are currency translated options, and so is this, but a quanto takes the JPY price of the foreign security and simply replaces the JPY symbol with a USD symbol when calculating the payoff (Haug [2007, p. 228]; Hull [1997, p. 298]; Wilmott [1998, p. 155]). The JPY security payoff is said to be "quantoed" into USD.

ing the two JPY-denominated processes $S_2(t)$ and $\frac{JPY}{USD}(t)$. This correlation is the negative of that between the Wiener processes driving $S_2(t)$ and $S_1(t) = \frac{1}{\frac{JPY}{USD}(t)}$ (Hull [1997, p. 301]). Thus, the risk-neutral drifts from the U.S. perspective are

$$r_1 = r_{US} - r_{JP}, \text{ and } r_2 = r_{JP} - q - \rho\sigma_1\sigma_2,$$

but we shall continue to work with r_1, and r_2, and then plug these in at the end. From our stochastic calculus training we know that as long as dynamic replication is possible, then de-trended prices of traded assets are martingales in the risk-neutral economy (Huang [1992]; Crack [2021, Section 4.4]). A bullet-point review is called for before proceeding.

• *RISK – NEUTRAL PRICING REVIEW* •

- The technical requirement for dynamic replication to be possible is described nicely in Jarrow and Rudd (1983). Essentially, it requires that for very small time horizons the value of the derivative and the value of the underlying(s) be perfectly linearly correlated. A diffusion or a simple jump process satisfies this, but if the underlying stock price follows a jump-diffusion process (regardless of whether the jump size is deterministic, stochastic, diversifiable, or non-diversifiable), then a replicating portfolio cannot be formed, and the no-arbitrage pricing method fails (Cox and Rubinstein [1985, chapter 7]; Merton [1992]).

- If dynamic replication is possible, then by no-arbitrage the value of the derivative equals the start-up cost of a replicating portfolio.

- If the replication recipe is known (perhaps via an equilibrium CAPM pricing approach as in the original Black and Scholes [1973] paper), then no two economic agents can disagree on the correct arbitrage-free price of the derivative. Thus, regardless of what we assume about the preferences of the agents in the economy, the pricing of the derivative will be the same.

- We ease our calculations substantially by proceeding *as if* the agents in the economy are risk-neutral.[66] That is, although they see the risk, they ignore it completely.

- People in a risk-neutral economy care only about expected return. In equilibrium all traded assets must offer the same expected return (or investors would still be shorting low-yield securities to invest in high-yield ones and we would not yet be in equilibrium). Existence of a government-backed fixed-rate riskless asset means that the riskless rate is the equilibrium required return on all securities in this hypothetical world.

---

[66]Important: We are not assuming anyone is really risk-neutral. It is simply that options prices are immune to assumptions about risk preferences, and this proves to be a very helpful assumption.

- If risk is not priced by agents in the economy, then traded security prices (including derivatives) are simply discounted expected payoffs where discounting uses the riskless rate, and all traded security prices are assumed to drift upwards at the riskless rate (less any dividend yield, of course—so that total yield is the riskless rate). If risk were priced, then discount rates would need to be risk adjusted, perhaps via the CAPM (Arnold, Crack and Schwartz [2009, 2010]).

- Let $B(t) \equiv e^{rt}$ denote the price of a riskless money market instrument (i.e., you invest \$1 at time 0, and it grows at riskless rate r). Then $B(t)$ drifts upward at the riskless rate. The money market account serves as a benchmark for performance in both the real and risk-neutral worlds. It seems natural to express other asset prices in terms of units of this asset.[67] That is, instead of looking at security price $P(t)$, look at $\frac{P(t)}{B(t)}$.

- With $B(t)$ drifting upward at the riskless rate, and $P(t)$ expected to drift upward at the same rate in equilibrium in the risk-neutral world, it follows that $\frac{P(t)}{B(t)}$ is expected to have no drift. That is, for any $\Delta t > 0$,

$$E^* \left[\frac{P(t + \Delta t)}{B(t + \Delta t)} \middle| \frac{P(t)}{B(t)} \right] = \frac{P(t)}{B(t)},$$

  where E^* denotes expectation in the risk-neutral world.

- Let $P^\dagger(t) \equiv \frac{P(t)}{B(t)}$, then the previous result says that for any $\Delta t > 0$,

$$E^* \left[P^\dagger(t + \Delta t) \middle| P^\dagger(t) \right] = P^\dagger(t).$$

  That is, the best guess of where $P^\dagger$ will be in the future (in the risk-neutral world) is where it is today. This is akin to the efficient markets hypothesis. A random variable with this property is called a "martingale."

- When we assume that traded securities' prices have required returns equal to the riskless rate in the risk-neutral world, we are really just redistributing the probabilities we associate with possible final security price outcomes.[68] However, some things stay the same. For example, if a stock price outcome occurs with probability **0** in the real world, then it still occurs with probability **0** in the risk-neutral world (thus, the range of possible outcomes does not change, only their probability of occurrence; and the transformation of probabilities moves the expected return on IBM, say, from 12% per annum to whatever the T-bill yield happens to be). Similarly, if a stock price outcome occurs with probability **1** in the real world, then it still occurs with probability **1** in the risk-neutral world.

---

[67]This is referred to as a change of "numeraire." A numeraire is a base unit of measurement. This is similar to changing units of measurement from USD to GBP, say, except that here we choose a USD-denominated money market account instead of GBP.

[68]Note the word "traded" here. A futures price, for example, is not the price of a traded asset, so its drift need not be r.

- In probability theory, a mathematical function that allocates probability weight to outcomes in the sample space is called a "measure." Two measures that reassign probabilities to outcomes without changing the range of possible outcomes (as above) are called "equivalent measures."[69]

- Thus, in the risk-neutral world, we reallocate probabilities in an equivalent manner (i.e., same range of possible outcomes), and the price of any traded asset—when "de-trended" by the money market account—follows a martingale. The probability measure (i.e., allocation of probabilities to outcomes) in the risk-neutral world is thus called an "equivalent martingale measure." You see this expression in the more advanced literature.

- Two natural derivative pricing methods fall out of all of the above. The first uses discounted expected payoffs, the second uses PDE's.

- First Method (Cox and Ross [1976]): The martingale property applied to de-trended derivative price V (i.e., $V^\dagger = V/B = Ve^{-rt}$) implies

$$
\begin{aligned}
V^\dagger(t) &= E^*\left[V^\dagger(T)\,\middle|\,V^\dagger(t)\right] \\
\Rightarrow V(t)e^{-rt} &= E^*\left[V(T)e^{-rT}\,|\,V(t)\right] \\
\Rightarrow V(t) &= e^{-r(T-t)}E^*\left[V(T)\,|\,V(t)\right].
\end{aligned}
$$

I derive Black-Scholes in Crack [2021] using precisely this approach: discounted expected payoff in a risk-neutral world.

- Second Method (Harrison and Kreps [1979]): Let V be the derivative price we seek, then the martingale property applied to de-trended V (i.e., $V^\dagger = V/B = Ve^{-rt}$) implies that $dV^\dagger$ has no time trend (i.e., no drift). We can apply Itô's Lemma to $V^\dagger$ to calculate

$$
dV^\dagger = [\text{time trend}]dt + \sum_i [\text{diffusion coefficients}]_i dw_i,
$$

where dw_i is the ith Brownian motion driving the underlyings. If V is a function of $S(t)$ and t only, and $dS(t) = rSdt + \sigma Sdw$ then

$$
\begin{aligned}
dV^\dagger(S(t),t) &= d[V(S(t),t)e^{-rt}] \\
&\overset{\text{Itô}}{=} \left(V_S dS + V_t dt + \frac{1}{2}V_{SS}(dS)^2\right)e^{-rt} \\
&\qquad\qquad\qquad\qquad\qquad -rVe^{-rt}dt \\
&= \left(\frac{1}{2}V_{SS}\sigma^2 S^2 + V_S rS + V_t - rV\right)e^{-rt}dt \\
&\qquad\qquad\qquad\qquad\qquad +V_S\sigma Se^{-rt}dw,
\end{aligned}
$$

where $(dw \cdot dw) = dt$, $(dt \cdot dw) = 0$ and $(dt \cdot dt) = 0$ (Merton [1992, pp. 122–123]).

---

[69]The relationship between the two measures is captured by the Radon-Nikodym derivative. See Baxter and Rennie (1998, p. 65) for simple intuition, Musiela and Rutkowski (1992, pp. 114, 121) for the advanced mathematics, and Arnold, Crack and Schwartz (2010) for an application.

- However, $V^\dagger = Ve^{-rt}$ is a martingale in the risk-neutral world by construction, so there is no drift term. Thus, we deduce that

$$\frac{1}{2}V_{SS}\sigma^2 S^2 + V_S rS + V_t - rV = 0.$$

Given the boundary conditions, we may solve this (Black-Scholes) PDE to find the option value $V(S(t), t)$. Different processes for dS yield different PDEs. We now value the product call.

- $\mathcal{END\ OF\ RISK-NEUTRAL\ PRICING\ REVIEW}$ •

Story: 1. Said he wasn't interested because the position paid too much. 2. While I was on a long-distance phone call, the applicant took out a copy of Penthouse, and looked through the photos only, stopping longest at the centerfold.

Interview Horror Stories from Recruiters
Reprinted by kind permission of *MBA Style Magazine*
©1996–2021 MBA Style Magazine, `www.mbastyle.com`

The time-t value of the European-style product call expiring at time-T is simply its discounted expected payoff in a risk-neutral world:

$$V(S_1(t), S_2(t), t) = e^{-r_{US}(T-t)} E^*\{\max[S_1(t)S_2(t) - X|\Omega_t]\},$$

where E^* denotes expectation taken with respect to the risk-neutral probability measure from the U.S. perspective, and Ω_t is the time-t information set. We could work this out directly (it would be a double integral with respect to the two Brownian motions), but let us instead use the PDE approach.

Given the nature of the product call, I am going to guess that the solution is a function of only two variables, not three: $V(S_1, S_2, t) = \kappa H(\eta, t)$ for some constant κ and $\eta = S_1 \cdot S_2$ (see analogous guess in Wilmott [1998, p. 155]). I will need to use Itô's Lemma soon so I will now work out all the partial derivatives for the change of variables:

$$\begin{aligned}
\frac{\partial}{\partial S_1} &= \frac{\partial \eta}{\partial S_1}\frac{\partial}{\partial \eta} = S_2\frac{\partial}{\partial \eta} \\
\frac{\partial}{\partial S_2} &= \frac{\partial \eta}{\partial S_2}\frac{\partial}{\partial \eta} = S_1\frac{\partial}{\partial \eta} \\
\frac{\partial^2}{\partial S_1^2} &= S_2\frac{\partial \eta}{\partial S_1}\frac{\partial^2}{\partial \eta^2} = S_2^2\frac{\partial^2}{\partial \eta^2} \\
\frac{\partial^2}{\partial S_2^2} &= S_1\frac{\partial \eta}{\partial S_2}\frac{\partial^2}{\partial \eta^2} = S_1^2\frac{\partial^2}{\partial \eta^2} \\
\frac{\partial^2}{\partial S_1 \partial S_2} &= \frac{\partial}{\partial \eta} + S_2\frac{\partial \eta}{\partial S_2}\frac{\partial^2}{\partial \eta^2} = \frac{\partial}{\partial \eta} + S_1 S_2\frac{\partial^2}{\partial \eta^2},
\end{aligned}$$

and $\frac{\partial}{\partial t}$ is unchanged.

From our risk-neutral pricing review, we know $Ve^{-r_{US}t}$ is a martingale in the risk-neutral world, so it has no time trend. We need only find the coefficient of dt in $d[Ve^{-r_{US}t}]$ and equate it to zero. There are two Brownian motions, so we need the two dimensional Itô's Lemma (Merton [1992, p. 122]; Hull [1997, p. 304]), and $d[Ve^{-r_{US}t}]$ is itself a geometric Brownian motion (GBM):

$$
\begin{aligned}
&d[Ve^{-r_{US}t}] \\
&= -r_{US}Ve^{-r_{US}t}dt + e^{-r_{US}t}dV \\
&\overset{\text{Itô}}{=} -r_{US}Ve^{-r_{US}t}dt + e^{-r_{US}t} \times \left(\frac{\partial V}{\partial t}dt + \frac{\partial V}{\partial S_1}dS_1 + \frac{\partial V}{\partial S_2}dS_2 \right. \\
&\quad + \left. \frac{1}{2}\frac{\partial^2 V}{\partial S_1^2}(dS_1)^2 + \frac{1}{2}\frac{\partial^2 V}{\partial S_2^2}(dS_2)^2 + \frac{\partial^2 V}{\partial S_1 \partial S_2}(dS_1 \cdot dS_2) \right) \\
&= e^{-r_{US}t} \times \left\{ \left[-r_{US}V + \frac{\partial V}{\partial t} + \frac{\partial V}{\partial S_1}r_1 S_1 + \frac{\partial V}{\partial S_2}r_2 S_2 \right.\right. \\
&\quad + \left. \frac{1}{2}\frac{\partial^2 V}{\partial S_1^2}\sigma_1^2 S_1^2 + \frac{1}{2}\frac{\partial^2 V}{\partial S_2^2}\sigma_2^2 S_2^2 + \frac{\partial^2 V}{\partial S_1 \partial S_2}\rho\sigma_1\sigma_2 S_1 S_2 \right] dt \\
&\quad + \left. \left[\frac{\partial V}{\partial S_1}\sigma_1 S_1 dw_1 + \frac{\partial V}{\partial S_2}\sigma_2 S_2 dw_2 \right] \right\}, \text{ which is a GBM,}
\end{aligned}
$$

where we used the earlier definitions of dS_1, dS_2, and so on. We now take the time trend coefficient of dt, equate it to zero, use the change of variables $V(S_1, S_2, t) = \kappa H(\eta, t)$, where $\eta = S_1 S_2$, and drop the common terms $e^{-r_{US}t}\kappa$:

$$
-r_{US}H + H_t + r_1 S_1 S_2 H_\eta + r_2 S_1 S_2 H_\eta + \frac{1}{2}\sigma_1^2 S_1^2 S_2^2 H_{\eta\eta}
$$

$$
+\frac{1}{2}\sigma_2^2 S_1^2 S_2^2 H_{\eta\eta} + S_1 S_2 \sigma_1 \sigma_2 \rho [H_\eta + S_1 S_2 H_{\eta\eta}] = 0
$$

Now collect terms and use $\eta = S_1 S_2$:

$$
H_t + \eta H_\eta (r_1 + r_2 + \rho\sigma_1\sigma_2) + \frac{1}{2}(\sigma_1^2 + \sigma_2^2 + 2\rho\sigma_1\sigma_2)\eta^2 H_{\eta\eta} - r_{US}H = 0
$$

Now plug in $r_1 = r_{US} - r_{JP}$ and $r_2 = r_{JP} - q - \rho\sigma_1\sigma_2$, and let $\sigma' \equiv \sqrt{\sigma_1^2 + \sigma_2^2 + 2\rho\sigma_1\sigma_2}$ to deduce

$$
H_t + \eta H_\eta (r_{US} - q) + \frac{1}{2}\sigma'^2 \eta^2 H_{\eta\eta} - r_{US}H = 0.
$$

This PDE is the regular Black-Scholes PDE with continuous dividends and special volatility σ'. Recalling our definition of η, we get a "similarity solution" by using what we already know about the Black-Scholes solution to this PDE:

$$c(t) = S_1(t)S_2(t)e^{-q(T-t)}N(d_1) - e^{-r_{US}(T-t)}XN(d_2), \text{ where}$$

$$d_1 = \frac{\ln\left(\frac{S_1(t)S_2(t)}{X}\right) + (r_{US} - q + \frac{1}{2}\sigma'^2)(T-t)}{\sigma'\sqrt{T-t}},$$

$$d_2 = d_1 - \sigma'\sqrt{T-t}, \text{ and}$$

$$\sigma' = \sqrt{\sigma_1^2 + \sigma_2^2 + 2\rho\sigma_1\sigma_2}$$

Reassuringly, this is identical to equation (5.35) in Haug (2007, p. 227).

Advice: As an interviewer, I find telephone interviews difficult. Body language and nuances of voice are lost. Be sure to use a landline not a mobile/cell phone, hold the speaker close to your mouth, and speak a bit louder than usual. If you insist on using a mobile/cell, make sure it is fully charged.

Answer 2.57: An Asian option is an average rate option. The underlying is a time series average of prices. Changes in average prices are much less volatile than changes in consecutive prices. Other things being equal, this lower volatility makes Asian options less expensive than plain vanilla options.

Answer 2.58: If the riskless rate is positive, and there are no dividends, early exercise is not optimal for an American-style call, and the European and American call have the same value. If the riskless rate is zero, then there is no incentive for early exercise of an American-style put. In this case, the European and American put have the same value.

Of course, that's little consolation to you if you are short an American-style option, a retail investor decides to exercise non-optimally, and you are assigned.

Answer 2.59: The one thing to watch out for here is that there are $(N+1)$ terms in the summation in both cases.

In the case of a recombining tree the answer is $1+2+3+4+\cdots+N+(N+1) = \sum_{i=1}^{N+1} i = \frac{(N+1)(N+2)}{2}$ (using the answer to Question 1.4 but with $(N+1)$ in place of n).

In the case of the non-recombining tree, there are $2^0 + 2^1 + 2^2 + \cdots + 2^N = \sum_{i=0}^{N} 2^i = 2^{N+1} - 1$ nodes. There is a simple trick to get this last result if you cannot recall it. Let $S = \sum_{i=0}^{N} 2^i$, then multiply both sides by 2: $2S = \sum_{i=1}^{N+1} 2^i$. The RHS is just $S - 1 + 2^{N+1}$, so you have $2S = S - 1 + 2^{N+1}$, and you can solve directly for S.

Just out of interest, let me mention that this question came from a big name investment bank, and the candidate who answered it got both answers wrong. He did not realize it at the time and was not told he was wrong by the interviewer. A simple manual check of the formula compared to a diagram in the case $N = 1$ or $N = 2$ would have been enough to show him he was wrong!

Answer 2.60: The derivatives will give more leverage than the stock, so you should use a derivative. If you can only go long, then buying a call option is expensive because you are paying for the embedded downside protection of a put option via put-call parity type arguments (see Crack [2021, Section 3.6]). With non-stochastic interest rates, the forward and futures prices are the same (Cox and Rubinstein [1985, p. 62]). It comes down to a question of margin/collateral. If the forward contract requires no collateral, and the futures contract requires a margin deposit, then the forward contract will provide more "bang for your buck."

Answer 2.61: I think the interviewer wants a directional answer only and an explanation. So, if you are peeking here for advice, then go away and figure out only whether the call price should rise or fall.

Most stocks have positive betas, and the call option (as a leveraged investment in the stock) will therefore have a very large positive beta and a high positive expected return. For example, suppose a \$50 stock has a beta of $\beta_S = 1.10$. Then an at-the-money six-month European call option on the stock (assume $r = 0.05$, $\sigma = 0.30$) has a beta of $\beta_c = 6.719837$ under Black-Scholes assumptions.[70] This is an "instantaneous beta" because as soon as the stock price changes, the degree of leverage in the call changes and the call's beta changes (but it will still be higher than the stock's beta). So, the expected return on the option is positive and tomorrow's expected price is higher than today's.

See also the answer to the next question where I take this one step further and use Itô's Lemma to derive an approximate numerical answer for the specific numerical example given above.

Answer 2.62: Now, how do we reconcile Answer 2.61 (call price expected to rise) with negative theta (i.e., time decay)? An option's theta is the sensitivity of the option price to the passage of time holding all else constant. You cannot look at this in isolation because all else is not held constant over the next 24 hours. To reconcile the positive expected return on the option with the negative theta, we need a formula that uses a total differential.

If we were working with deterministic functions, we would simply write

$$ dc = \frac{\partial c}{\partial t} dt + \frac{\partial c}{\partial S} dS = \Theta dt + \Delta dS. \quad (\dagger) $$

We could then talk about how delta is positive (i.e., $\Delta \equiv \frac{\partial c}{\partial S} > 0$) and how the expected value of dS is positive (because stock price is expected to rise on average) and how this outweighs the negative time decay term (i.e., the negative theta: $\Theta \equiv \frac{\partial c}{\partial t} < 0$) and so on. This is, however, quite wrong here!

---

[70]The relationship is $\beta_c = \Omega \beta_S$, where $\Omega \equiv \frac{N(d_1) \cdot S}{c} = \frac{\Delta \cdot S}{c}$ is the elasticity of the call price with respect to the stock price (Cox and Rubinstein [1985, p. 190]). In this example we have $c = 4.817438$, $S = 50$, and $N(d_1) = \Delta = 0.588589$.

Continuing with the numerical at-the-money call example from Answer 2.61, on the stock with beta 1.10, and using a 10% expected return for a CAPM Market portfolio (see notes at the end of this section), I have the following numbers: $\Theta = -5.357262$, $dt = \frac{1}{365}$, $\Delta = 0.588589$, $E(dS) \approx 0.013679$ (see notes at end of this question). So, $\Delta E(dS) \approx \$0.008051$, but $\Theta dt = -\$0.014677$, so the total differential above (i.e., equation (†)) would give $E(dc) = -\$0.006626$ which contradicts that fact that the expected return on the call is positive.

What is missing is that the total differential above (i.e., equation (†)) applies only to deterministic functions. The call price is stochastic, driven by the stochastic S. We cannot use the stated total differential because it has a term missing! We need Itô's Lemma:

$$
\begin{aligned}
dc &= \frac{\partial c}{\partial t}dt + \frac{\partial c}{\partial S}dS + \frac{1}{2}\frac{\partial^2 c}{\partial S^2}(dS)^2 \\
&= \Theta dt + \Delta dS + \frac{1}{2}\Gamma(dS)^2,
\end{aligned}
$$

where $\Gamma \equiv \frac{\partial^2 c}{\partial S^2}$. Continuing the numerical example above, we have $\Gamma = 0.036681$, and $E[(dS)^2] \approx \$0.617039$ (see notes at end of this question), so then we get

$$
\begin{aligned}
E(dc) &= \Theta dt + \Delta E(dS) + \frac{1}{2}\Gamma E\left[(dS)^2\right] \\
&\approx \left(-5.357262 \cdot \frac{1}{365}\right) + (0.588589 \cdot 0.013679) \\
&\qquad\qquad\qquad + \left(\frac{1}{2} \cdot 0.036681 \cdot 0.617039\right) \\
&= -0.014677 + 0.008051 + 0.011317 \\
&= \$0.004691.
\end{aligned}
$$

This is roughly a 10 bps increase in value from $c = \$4.817438$. That is, the time decay contributes a negative component to the expected change in the call price, but the expected values of the stochastic terms contribute positive values that more than offset the time decay.

We can now continue our answer to Question 2.61 and assert that for this particular example, Itô's Lemma implies that $c = \$4.817438$ today and $E(c + dt) \approx 4.817438 + 0.004691 = 4.822129$ tomorrow.

In simple terms, the contributions to the expected change in call price are: a negative term for the time decay, a positive term for the call's delta and the positive expected return on the stock, and a positive return for the call's gamma and the volatility of the stock.

Notes for readers who want more details: My numerical example is given to make the analysis concrete and to show relative magnitudes; I have given many decimal places so you can reproduce it. No interviewer expects this sort of detail. The numerical example uses $dt = \frac{1}{365}$ but this infinitesimal notation is not strictly correct for a non-infinitesimal time step. The same can be said of using the notation dS and dc for non-infinitesimal moves in the stock and call prices, respectively. I am simply going to ignore this loose use of notation and continue. If you are not happy with that then you are not ready to interview with a finance firm. I gave numbers for $E(dS)$ and $E[(dS)^2]$ without saying where they came from. Here are the minimum details: If μ is expected return on the stock such that $E[S(t+dt)] = S(t)e^{\mu dt}$, then in a Black-Scholes world we may write (loosely) $S(t+dt) = S(t)e^{(\mu-\frac{1}{2}\sigma^2)dt+\sigma\sqrt{dt}\cdot\epsilon}$, where $\epsilon \sim N(0,1)$. In this case, $dS = S(t+dt) - S(t)$, and we can use the properties of normal and lognormal distributions (see Question 4.33) to deduce that $E(dS) = S(t)(e^{\mu dt} - 1)$ and $E[(dS)^2] = S^2(t)(e^{2(\mu+\frac{1}{2}\sigma^2)dt} - 2e^{\mu dt} + 1)$. You can also reproduce the value of $E(dc)$ almost exactly by using the CAPM information in the answer. Note however that the $E(dc)$ number implied by the CAPM will match the $E(dc)$ value calculated using Itô's Lemma only in the limit as $dt \to 0$.[71] If you want to use the CAPM then you should use what approximates an instantaneous CAPM (a CAPM defined only over the time step dt). I used $dt = \frac{1}{365}$, $r = 0.05$, $Rf = e^{r\cdot dt} - 1$, $r_M = \ln(1+0.10)$, $E(R_M) = e^{r_M \cdot dt} - 1$, $\mu_{S,simple} = Rf + \beta_S(E(R_M) - Rf)$, $\mu = \frac{1}{dt}\ln(1+\mu_{S,simple})$, $\beta_c = \Delta \cdot S \cdot \beta_S/c$, $\mu_{c,simple} = Rf + \beta_c(E(R_M) - Rf)$, $E(dc)_{CAPM} = c \cdot \mu_{c,simple}$.

---

[71]This is because the CAPM relationship between β_c and β_S given in Footnote 70 is only true in an instantaneous CAPM, and this holds only for an infinitesimal time step. If I look at the ratio of the $E(dc)$ from the CAPM argument to that from the Itô's Lemma argument, I get 97.6508% for $dt = 10/365$, 99.7603% for $dt = 1/365$, 99.9760% for $dt = 0.1/365$, 99.9976% for $dt = 0.01/365$, and 99.9998% for $dt = 0.001/365$.

Appendix C

Other Financial Economics Answers

This appendix contains answers to the questions posed in Chapter 3.

Answer 3.1: This is a very old problem, and a common interview question. The probability that the first head occurs on toss k is $\left(\frac{1}{2}\right)^k$; this event carries with it a payoff of $\$2^k$. The contribution of toss k to the expected payoff is thus $\left(\frac{1}{2}\right)^k \times \$2^k = \$1$. This is the same for each k. The expected payoff to the game as a whole is the summation over all k of these payoffs. This is $\$1 + \$1 + \$1 + \cdots = \$\infty$. The expected payoff to the game is infinite!

This is called the "St. Petersburg Game." The fact that the expected payoff to the game is infinite, and that no one in his or her right mind would pay more than a few hundred dollars to play, is why it is sometimes called the "St. Petersburg Paradox." There are several ways that you can think about this sensibly.

One way is to note that "value" is not the same thing as "expected payoff";[1] value equals *utility* of expected payoff. Most people cannot distinguish between very large amounts of money.[2] This means that $\$2^{50}$ is not worth twice $\$2^{49}$. However, these very large amounts are counted in exactly this way when calculating expected payoff to the game as a whole. If you think that $\$2^k = \$2^{50}$ (essentially) for all $k \geq 50$, then the expected payoff to the game is finite:

$$\$50 + \$2^{50} \times \left(\frac{1}{2^{51}} + \frac{1}{2^{52}} + \frac{1}{2^{53}} + \ldots \right) = \$51$$

A spread could be quoted around this, maybe ($10, $200). How much would you pay your customer to play? How much would you charge your customer?

---

[1] It is important to note that the Weak Law of Large Numbers fails if the expectation is not finite (Feller [1968, pp. 251]).

[2] Bernoulli ([1738]; [1954]) suggests that utility of payoffs should depend upon how wealthy you are. For a practitioner's view of utility, see Kritzman (1992a).

A second way to think about this is in terms of default risk.[3] We need to quote the bid (what we pay) and the ask (what the customer pays). For the bid, it is the customer's default risk we need to worry about. Let us assume a wealthy customer who defaults above one million dollars. In this case, the customer defaults after (about) 20 tosses. Assuming the investment bank is of large scale, a payoff from the customer between two dollars and one million dollars is of relatively small size. The investment bank takes such bets every day, and this one is uncorrelated with all the others. At this level, we could argue that the investment bank is risk-neutral and so the bid is exactly \$20 with no risk premium.

For the ask, it is the company that risks bankruptcy and default. Let us assume that the company files for bankruptcy after losing one billion dollars (on the order of magnitude of Barings, and Metallgesellschaft)—approximately $\$2^{30}$. The expected value of the game to the customer is thus about \$30— the bank defaults after 30 tosses. However, your career and the holdings of all the shareholders can be destroyed by this bet, so you had better add a considerable risk premium. You might want to go all the way up to \$200 and quote a bid-ask of (\$20, \$200)—it depends upon your degree of risk aversion.

Each of these two solutions uses a truncation method. Another related way to think about this is in terms of feasibility. If it does take more than 50 tosses to get a head, then the payoff is not feasible because $\$2^{50}$ is more dollars than there are atoms in the universe, and whoever sold the ticket to the game is—by the laws of physics—unable to pay. See also Feller (1968, pp. 251–253).

Answer 3.2: This is a frequent question. Assuming continuously compounded returns follow an arithmetic Brownian motion (see Crack [2021]), variance of returns grows linearly with the compounding period. This is because consecutive returns in a random walk are independent, and the variance of a sum of independent random variables is just the sum of the variances. This means that the four-year σ^2 equals four times the one-year σ^2. It follows that the four-year σ is two times the one-year σ. The answer is, therefore, 20%. See also Question 2.18.

Answer 3.3: This is a very common term-structure question. You should be able to do this in your head almost instantly. Think of it this way: the rate over the first five years and the rate over the second five years must average out to give the rate over the full 10 years. That is, the average of 10% and the unknown forward rate must give 15%. The unknown must be 20%. To work it out quickly, note that the unknown (20%) is as far above the average (15%) as the known (10%) is below it.

---

[3]I thank Olivier Ledoit for suggesting this solution technique; any errors are mine.

In fact, if you work it out exactly, the forward rate is

$$\left[\frac{(1.15)^{10}}{(1.10)^5} \right]^{\frac{1}{5}} - 1 = 20.227\%.$$

You are making a "first-order" approximation when you do the simple averaging, but you end up quite close. For a practitioner's viewpoint on the term-structure of interest rates, take a look at Kritzman (1993b).

Answer 3.4: There are many different types of bond yield. The "yield" on a bond is usually the "internal rate of return" or "yield-to-maturity" or "promised yield"; it is what you earn if you hold the bond to maturity assuming a constant reinvestment rate. In practice, given that reinvestment rates can vary significantly from your initial promised yield, your actual return can be higher or lower.

The "rate of return" on a bond is the internal rate of return of the realized cash flows to the bond-holder including reinvestment. If the bond is sold before maturity, the (realized) rate of return can be positive or negative.

Suppose you buy a bond promising 5%, but interest rates rise dramatically soon after your purchase. If you then sell the bond, you record a capital loss and a negative rate of return. However, if you hold the bond to maturity, you get your promised 5% plus a bit more because of higher reinvestment rates on the coupons.

Answer 3.5: Chaos theory came out of MIT in the early 1960's. Professor Edward N. Lorenz (Professor Emeritus in the department of Earth, Atmospheric and Planetary Science from 1987 until his death in early 2008) discovered that computer-simulated nonlinear mathematical equations describing the evolution of weather patterns are very sensitive to the starting values of the variables (Lorenz [1963]).[4]

This "sensitive dependence on initial conditions" is the first of three characteristics most often associated with chaos theory. The second characteristic is that the nonlinear systems describing chaotic systems are non-random. That is, they are "deterministic," not "stochastic." However, the output of the (often very simple nonlinear) systems can appear quite random. The third characteristic is "self-similarity": the physical system looks similar at different levels of magnification. It is self-similarity that gives rise to the "fractals" that you may have seen elsewhere. Fractals are often associated with the mathematician Benoit Mandelbrot (who died aged 85 in 2010 while a Professor Emeritus of Mathematics at Yale).

---

[4]I had the pleasure of attending some Independent Activities Period (IAP) classes taught by Prof. Lorenz at MIT in 1994/1995. He reminded me a little of a slim Dave Thomas (you know, the Wendy's guy). Although in his late seventies he seemed younger and very good-natured. Lorenz died in 2008 aged 90.

There are several different definitions of "chaos" in the literature. These definitions are beyond the scope of this book. See Brock et al. (1991, pp. 8–17) for further details. For a low-level broad introduction to chaos, see Gleick (1987).

Can you use chaos theory in finance? This was a hot topic in the late 1980's and early 1990's. Many academic economics and finance papers were written on the subject. The few that made any sense found nothing reliable. The others were written by ignorant people who jumped on the bandwagon; they should never have published their empty papers.

After reading more than 150 journal articles and half a dozen books on chaos theory and writing a 100-page Masters-level thesis on chaos theory applied to financial economics and publishing one paper in the *Journal of Finance*, I am quite pessimistic. My co-author and I hypothesized considerable discreteness-induced bias in the popular "BDS test" for chaos in equity data (Crack and Ledoit [1996]). Our hypothesis has now been confirmed (Krämer and Runde [1997]).

If you want to predict stock returns, I recommend that you use neural nets or some other nonlinear technique. In my opinion, any predictability that you can discern with chaos theory (e.g., "nearest neighbor" prediction techniques) is better investigated using the other nonlinear techniques available to you. Give it up—chaos theory is great in the physical sciences, but it is a lost cause in finance.

Answer 3.6: Look at Table C.1 on p. 243. The slope of the price-yield curve is $-\frac{D}{(1+r)}P$, where D is Macaulay duration, P is bond price, and r is yield. Changing slope (i.e., curvature) is driven almost entirely by changing P, because Macaulay duration, D, changes very little with changing yield, r (Crack and Nawalkha [2001]). D does, however, fall slowly with rising yield for a standard bond with coupons, and this does contribute marginally to curvature.

Note that curvature (i.e., changing slope) of the plot does *not* always imply that the Macaulay duration of a bond is changing (Crack and Nawalkha [2001])! This is a common misconception (it is easy to misconstrue this in Fabozzi and Fabozzi [1995, pp. 97–98]). For example, consider a zero-coupon bond with ten years to maturity. The plot of bond value versus bond yield is downward sloping with curvature. Whatever the yield, however, the bond's duration is ten years because it is a ten-year zero

A mathematical explanation of the convexity: you know that the curve slopes downward, it goes to a vertical asymptote at yield -1 and a horizontal asymptote at yield infinity. You know that the curve must be smooth because the pricing relationship is simple and well-behaved. The only way to get a well-behaved smooth curve in this situation is to have it be convex.

Answer 3.7: This question is an interesting intersection of theory and empirical reality. The question is not necessarily well-posed, but you should do your best to answer it. I give what I think is the best answer possible.

If the empirical security market line (SML) is wholly above the theoretical one, this means that stocks are under-priced relative to the CAPM. I propose two possible causes: First, maybe there is only one risk factor (the Market), but market participants require higher compensation per unit of beta-risk than suggested by the CAPM; second, maybe there is more than one risk factor, and market participants require compensation for factors not mentioned by the CAPM. Conversely, if the empirical SML is wholly below the theoretical one, then stocks are overpriced relative to the CAPM. In this case, market participants do not require as much compensation per unit of beta-risk as theory suggests.

I think the best answer is to say that the CAPM does not account for all priced risk factors. It is likely, however, that beta is priced. It follows that stocks require a premium over and above that suggested by CAPM, and you could think of this as an empirical SML plotting above the theoretical one. For more on factor models and estimation, see Kritzman (1993a).

There have been several papers pronouncing the CAPM either dead or alive (Wallace [1980]; Fama and French [1992]; Black [1993]; Fama and French [1996]). For a friendly introduction to the CAPM, see Mullins (1992). Ferguson and Shockley (2003) show that even if the traditional single-factor CAPM holds, use of an equity-only proxy for the World Market Portfolio of Risky Assets leads to an errors-in-variables mis-estimation of CAPM betas. This error in turn means that variables related to leverage will help to explain returns because they serve as instruments for the missing beta risk. The upshot of all this is that many empirical anomalies we see are in fact consistent with the single-beta CAPM.

You should note that there are some theoretical problems with both the question and my answer. It is quite difficult (if not impossible) to get either of the empirical SML's mentioned. This is not because the CAPM is "correct," or because there is only one risk factor. Rather, it is because there is a *very* tight mathematical relationship between betas and returns (Sharpe [1964]; Roll [1977a]). You would certainly need that the market proxy is not mean-variance efficient to get the plots suggested. It is probably not sufficient to simply assume that there are risk factors not accounted for by the CAPM. Go with the answer above, but realize that there is more here than meets the eye.

Answer 3.8: This question is very similar to Question 3.3 (and is just as common). You should be able to do it in your head almost instantly. If you cannot, then go back and try Question 3.3 again before reading on.

The rate over the first year and the rate over the second year must average out to give the rate over the full two years. That is, the average of 7.15% and the unknown forward rate must give 7.60%. The unknown rate must be around 8.05% (remember, it is as far above 7.60% as 7.15% is below 7.60%).

In fact, if you work it out exactly, the forward rate is

$$\left[\frac{(1.0760)^2}{(1.0715)^1}\right] - 1 = 8.052\%.$$

You are making a "first-order" approximation when doing the simple averaging, and the answer is quite accurate.

Answer 3.9: This is introductory finance theory; it uses no-arbitrage and not much more. Assume for the sake of simplicity that interest rates are constant at r per unit time, today is time t, and the forward contract matures at time T. The forward price, $F(t,T)$, is related to the spot price, $S(t)$, as follows:

$$F(t,T) = S(t)e^{r(T-t)} \geq S(t)$$

The discount bond sells at a forward *premium* because of no-arbitrage.

The coupon bond is a different story. If you assume a continuous coupon of ρ per unit time, then the forward price, $F(t,T)$, is related to the spot price, $S(t)$, as follows:

$$F(t,T) = S(t)e^{(r-\rho)(T-t)} \leq S(t),$$

where the inequality follows because we were told that $r \leq \rho$. The coupon bond sells at a forward *discount* because of no-arbitrage.

For a practitioner's view on futures, forwards, and hedging, see Kritzman (1993c).

Answer 3.10: This is a classic question, and a very good test of your dexterity with elementary finance theory. If you have not yet figured it out, and you are peeking at the answers for a hint, I strongly recommend that you go back to the question and try again; read no further. If you are still reading, here is a hint: think about your investment horizon, and an immunization strategy. Now go back and try again.

Your investment horizon is very short. You want to profit from the change in the relationship between short- and long-term rates. However, you want to protect yourself from shifts in the level of the yield curve. That is, you want your position to be insensitive to parallel shifts in the yield curve, but positively sensitive to a steepening. This suggests that you should go short long-term debt, go long short-term debt, and match both the duration and price of the positions (i.e., use very low coupon short-term debt and very high coupon long-term debt).[5]

You may think of this as a "zero-duration" portfolio (to match your horizon). However, in just the same way that a zero net investment stock portfolio has no well-defined beta but can still be market-neutral, a zero net investment bond

---

[5]If you cannot match durations of the positions, you can match on the product of duration × price. However, this will no longer be a zero net investment strategy.

portfolio has no well-defined duration but can still be insensitive to parallel shifts in the yield curve.

Traders tell me that this strategy originated with the Salomon Bond arbitrage ("bond-arb") group. However, it is now so well known that profits may be slim. See also Chincarini (2012, Box 2.2, pp.17–18).

For more on "Yield Curve Strategies," see the excellent papers by Jones (1991) and Litterman and Scheinkman (1991). Jones describes the statistical relationship between changes in level, slope, and curvature of the yield curve.

Answer 3.11: For a standard bond, with annual coupons, the Macaulay duration (Macaulay [1938]) is just the weighted-average term-to-maturity of the bond,

$$D \equiv \frac{\sum_{t=1}^{T} \frac{C_t \times t}{(1+r)^t}}{\sum_{s=1}^{T} \frac{C_s}{(1+r)^s}} \tag{C.1}$$

$$= \sum_{t=1}^{T} \omega_t \times t, \tag{C.2}$$

where

$$\omega_t \equiv \frac{\frac{C_t}{(1+r)^t}}{\sum_{s=1}^{T} \frac{C_s}{(1+r)^s}} = \frac{PV(C_t)}{V},$$

C_t are the annual cash flows (both coupon and principal), r is the annual YTM, T is the count of periods until maturity, $PV(\cdot)$ denotes present value, and V is bond value. Note that the weights ω_t sum to one, and that duration is measured in units of time, as is the term-to-maturity.

The weights ω_t are applied to the timing of the bond's cash flows. Each weight is equal to the present value of the particular cash flow as a proportion of the total value of the bond. It follows that the duration of a zero-coupon bond equals its term-to-maturity—because the weight of the final cash flow is +1.

If the bond pays m coupons per annum (e.g., $m = 2$ in the case of a semi-annual bond), then Equations C.1 and C.2 are replaced by Equations C.3.

$$D \equiv \frac{1}{m} \frac{\sum_{i=1}^{mT} \frac{C_i \times i}{(1+r/m)^i}}{\sum_{j=1}^{mT} \frac{C_j}{(1+r/m)^j}} = \frac{\sum_{i=1}^{mT} \frac{C_i \times i/m}{(1+r/m)^i}}{\sum_{j=1}^{mT} \frac{C_j}{(1+r/m)^j}} \tag{C.3}$$

$$= \frac{1}{m} \sum_{i=1}^{mT} \omega_i \times i = \sum_{i=1}^{mT} \omega_i \times i/m ,$$

where

$$\omega_i \equiv \frac{\frac{C_i}{(1+r/m)^i}}{\sum_{j=1}^{mT} \frac{C_i}{(1+r/m)^j}} = \frac{PV(C_i)}{V},$$

C_i are the periodic cash flows (e.g., semi-annual coupons and principal if $m = 2$), and r/m is the periodic interest rate.

Duration is a measure of how sensitive a bond's price is to changes in interest rates. Duration is related to, but differs from, the slope of the plot of bond price versus yield-to-maturity (Crack and Nawalkha [2001]).

I find the following construction to be an instructive way of understanding how duration works.[6] Suppose that you have a liability due in the future and that you buy a bond now with the intention of using the bond (and its reinvested coupons) to meet the liability (the maturity of the bond is assumed to be greater than or equal to the maturity of the liability). Suppose that the present value of the bond is identical to the present value of the liability. Suppose that you open a bank account that earns the market interest rate (i.e., the yield-to-maturity of the bond). You deposit all cash in-flows from the bond in the bank account and let them compound through time (with no taxes or transaction costs). When your liability falls due, you sell your bond and close your bank account. Call the proceeds of the bond sale together with your final bank balance the "Terminal Value."

Can you meet your liability with the Terminal Value? Well, there are two risks involved. A fall in interest rates immediately after you purchase the bond pushes up the price at which you are able to sell your bond. However, a fall in interest rates also decreases your final bank balance because you earn less interest on the coupons. The opposite obtains with a rise in interest rates. That is, higher interest rates decrease the price at which you can sell the bond, but your closing bank balance is higher because you earn more interest on the coupons. These two risks are known as *price risk* and *coupon reinvestment rate risk*, respectively.

Price risk and coupon reinvestment rate risk have opposite influences on the Terminal Value. The Terminal Value differs depending upon which influence is strongest. It can be proved that if your liability falls due before the weighted-average term-to-maturity of your bond, the price risk has the stronger influence on Terminal Value. If, however, your liability falls due after the weighted-average term-to-maturity of your bond, the coupon reinvestment rate risk has the stronger influence on Terminal Value. If your liability falls due precisely at the weighted-average term-to-maturity of the bond, the Terminal Value is relatively insensitive to an immediate change in interest rates. By definition, the weighted-average term-to-maturity of the bond is just its Macaulay duration.

Redington (1952, p. 289) introduced the word "immunization" to refer to a particular type of liability matching involving "investment of the assets in such a way that the existing [insurance] business is immune to a general change in the rate of interest." He also says that the distribution of the term of the fixed income assets in relation to the term of the liabilities should be "in such a way as to reduce the possibility of loss arising from a change in interest rates" (Redington, 1952, p. 289). This requires both that the value of the

---

[6]I have not seen my construction in the literature. Kritzman (2003, Chapter 7), however, comes close to this explanation when he gives some elementary insights into duration and convexity.

assets and liabilities match and that the durations of assets and liabilities match (Redington, 1952, p. 290). Note that an initial immunized position protects you from exactly one immediate parallel shock to a flat term-structure (Redington, 1952, p. 292; Shiu, 1990). This shock is assumed to be very small (Redington, 1952, p. 290; Shiu, 1990). You are no longer immunized after that shock has hit because it changes present values and duration. Although you are no longer immunized, you still have a non-immunized hedge in place. That is, you still get your planned future Terminal Value as long as no more shocks hit.

Note that you must re-balance after each shock to stay immunized. In fact, to stay immunized, you must rebalance even if no shocks hit. This is because, absent a zero-coupon bond position, changes in bond duration are not in lock-step with the passage of time. So, your horizon and your bond's duration decrease at different speeds, and you become non-immunized.

I must emphasize that my bank account/Terminal Value construction is an artificial one. The fact that you must rebalance your position as time passes (in order to remain immunized) means that you cannot stick with the same bond until the liability is due. Indeed, the only bond that you can hold until the liability falls due (while remaining immunized) is a zero-coupon bond with maturity equal to the maturity of the liability; and in this case, the absence of coupons removes the need for the bank account in the construction.

So, if you can open a bank account that pays the yield-to-maturity on your bond, purchase a coupon bond with duration and present value the same as those of the liability, and deposit all coupons in the bank account until the liability falls due, then, if there is one and only one small parallel shock to the flat term-structure of interest rates between now and your liability falling due, and if that single shift in interest rates occurs immediately, then the Terminal Value will meet your liability (although you will not be immunized against a second shock). You are not, however, immunized against a large or non-parallel shift in the yield curve (Redington, 1952, p. 290, 294; Shiu, 1990).[7]

Other things being equal, duration increases with increasing term-to-maturity.[8] Other things being equal, duration decreases with increasing coupons (larger cash flows early on decrease the proportional importance of the repayment of principal at maturity).

Compared to duration, convexity is a higher-order measure of sensitivity of bond price to interest rates. Convexity is a scaled measure the rate at which the sensitivity of bond price to interest rates changes with changing interest rates (Crack and Nawalkha [2001]). Convexity is related to, but differs from,

---

[7]See Reitano (1992), Zheng (2007), and Poitras (2013) for discussion of immunization in these more complicated cases.

[8]Deeply-discounted coupon-bearing bonds (i.e., bonds paying coupons far below current market rates) can be an exception (Fisher and Weil [1971, Table 4, p. 418]).

the rate of change of slope of the plot of bond price versus yield-to-maturity. See the summary in Table C.1. For a practitioner's view of Macaulay duration and convexity, see Kritzman (1992b).[9]

How do the definitions of duration and convexity arise? Suppose the price of an annual-coupon bond, P, is expanded in terms of yield-to-maturity, r, using a second-order Taylor series (that is, one that stops at the quadratic term):[10]

$$P(r + \Delta r) - P(r) \approx \frac{\partial P(r)}{\partial r} \times \Delta r + \frac{\frac{\partial^2 P(r)}{\partial r^2}}{2!} \times (\Delta r)^2$$

Letting $\Delta P \equiv P(r + \Delta r) - P(r)$, use $P(r) = \sum_{t=1}^{T} \frac{C_t}{(1+r)^t}$ to find that[11]

$$\Delta P \approx \frac{-\Delta r}{1+r} \sum_{t=1}^{T} \frac{t \times C_t}{(1+r)^t} + \frac{(\Delta r)^2}{2!(1+r)^2} \sum_{t=1}^{T} \frac{t \times (t+1) \times C_t}{(1+r)^t}.$$

Now divide both sides by P to get

$$\frac{\Delta P}{P} \approx \frac{-\Delta r}{1+r} D + \frac{(\Delta r)^2}{2!} \mathcal{C},$$

where

$$D \equiv \frac{1}{P} \sum_{t=1}^{T} \frac{t \times C_t}{(1+r)^t}$$

is the standard Macaulay duration, and

$$\mathcal{C} \equiv \frac{1}{(1+r)^2 P} \sum_{t=1}^{T} \frac{t \times (t+1) \times C_t}{(1+r)^t}$$

is a measure of curvature, or "convexity," in the plot of bond price versus yield-to-maturity. Other things (i.e., duration and price) being equal, $\mathcal{C}$ increases with increasing coupons. Even a zero-coupon bond has positive convexity (because $C_1 = C_2 = \cdots = C_{T-1} = 0$, but $C_T = \text{Face} > 0$).

---

[9]The standard Macaulay duration is a relatively simple concept. People on The Street expect you to know that they use more complex tools. For example, the standard Macaulay duration can be generalized to allow for immunization against parallel shifts in yield curves that are *not* flat. This generalization was originally proposed by Macaulay (1938), but was made popular by Fisher and Weil (1971). An even more sophisticated measure of duration is presented by Cox, Ingersoll, and Ross (1979). Duration measures for bonds with embedded options are also important (Mehran and Homaifar [1993]).

[10]Note that this is similar to expressing the change in the price of a call option (given a change in the level of the underlying) in terms of the "delta" and the "gamma." The delta is the rate of change of call price with respect to underlying, and the gamma measures the "convexity" of call price with respect to underlying.

[11]I used the result $\frac{\partial P(r)}{\partial r} = \sum_{t=1}^{T} \frac{\partial}{\partial r} \frac{C_t}{(1+r)^t} = \frac{-1}{1+r} \sum_{t=1}^{T} \frac{t \times C_t}{(1+r)^t}$ and an analogous result for $\frac{\partial^2 P(r)}{\partial r^2}$.

In addition to immunization, duration and convexity enable you to estimate the impact on bond price of a change in interest rates. A "first-order" estimate uses duration; a "second-order" estimate uses duration and convexity. Higher-order approximations are more accurate.

Take a 20-year bond paying an annual coupon of 7%. Assume a face value of $1,000. Assume that the term-structure is flat at 10%. The price of the bond is $744.59 under these assumptions.

If the entire term-structure rises by one percentage point (i.e., 0.01), what is the new price of the bond? This can be estimated using the equation we derived previously:[12]

$$\frac{\Delta P}{P} \approx \frac{-\Delta r}{1+r}D + \frac{(\Delta r)^2}{2!}\, \mathcal{C}$$

The Macaulay duration of this bond is calculated as 10.0018 years, the convexity $\mathcal{C}$ can be calculated as 130.04676, $\Delta r = +0.01$, $r = 0.10$, and $P = \$744.59$, thus:

$$
\begin{aligned}
\Delta P &\approx \frac{-\Delta r}{1+r}D \times P + \frac{(\Delta r)^2}{2!}\, \mathcal{C} \times P \\
&= \frac{-0.01}{1.10} \times 10 \times \$744.59 + \frac{(0.01)^2}{2} \times 130.04676 \times \$744.59 \\
&= -\$67.69 + \$4.84 \\
&= -\$62.85
\end{aligned}
$$

Thus, $P(r + \Delta r) \approx P + \Delta P = \$744.59 - \$62.85 = \$681.74$. *Direct evaluation* gives the answer as $681.47 (the estimate is 27 cents too high and would have been out by roughly $5 if not for the convexity term).

If the entire term-structure falls by one percentage point (i.e., 0.01), the change in bond price is estimated as follows:

$$
\begin{aligned}
\Delta P &\approx \frac{-\Delta r}{1+r}D \times P + \frac{(\Delta r)^2}{2!}\, \mathcal{C} \times P \\
&= \frac{+0.01}{1.10} \times 10 \times \$744.59 + \frac{(0.01)^2}{2} \times 130.04676 \times \$744.59 \\
&= +\$67.69 + \$4.84 \\
&= +\$72.53
\end{aligned}
$$

Thus, $P(r + \Delta r) \approx P + \Delta P = \$744.59 + \$72.53 = \$817.12$. *Direct evaluation* gives the answer as $817.43 (the estimate is 31 cents too low and would have been out by roughly $5 if not for the convexity term).[13]

---

[12]Note that the term $\frac{D}{1+r}$ that multiplies $-\Delta r$ is often called the "modified duration," frequently denoted D^*. It follows that the first-order approximation using modified duration is $\Delta P \approx -\Delta r D^* P$.

[13]Why am I *estimating* the change in bond price when direct evaluation gives the exact answer? For purposes of demonstration, it is convenient to be able to show you exactly how the duration

Note that the "27 cents too high" and the "31 cents too low" in the above examples can be reduced to pennies (at least) by using a third term in the expansion—a measure of rate of change of convexity with respect to yield. Mehran and Homaifar (1993) refer to this third term as "velocity," though that name is not commonly used. Thus, they represent change in bond price as a function of duration, convexity, and velocity—see Mehran and Homaifar (1993) for more details.[14]

Macaulay duration may be written using a closed-form formula (i.e., with no summation term). Let us define the following function:

$$d(F, C, r, T) = \frac{1+r}{r} - \frac{\left\{(1+r) + T\left[\frac{C}{F} - r\right]\right\}}{\frac{C}{F}\left[(1+r)^T - 1\right] + r}, \quad \text{where } r \neq 0. \quad (C.4)$$

Then for a standard bond with annual coupons of C, and face value F, the Macaulay duration in Equations C.1 and C.2 may be rewritten as $D = d(F, C, r, T)$. If the bond pays m coupons per annum (e.g., $m = 2$ in the case of a semi-annual bond) still totaling C, then Equations C.3 may be rewritten as $D = \frac{1}{m}d(F, C/m, r/m, mT)$. The proof of this result uses the standard closed-form formula for an annuity and, although not difficult, may be a little tedious—a similar type of expression exists for convexity.

Note that $D^* = D/(1+r)$ in Table C.1 generalizes to $D^* = D/(1+r/m)$ in the case of a bond paying m coupons per period. So, taking the limit as $m \to \infty$ (i.e., as we move to continuous compounding), we get $D = D^*$, as mentioned in the caption to Table C.1.

Finally, let me exorcise a myth. Most of the foregoing is predicated on parallel shifts in yield curves. Other things (i.e., price and duration) being equal, the higher the convexity of a bond, the better off you are if there is a parallel shift (up or down) in a yield curve: hence the myth that you should pay for convexity.[15] In reality, these shifts are anything but parallel (Jones [1991]; Litterman and Scheinkman [1991]). Other things (i.e., price and duration) being equal, if the yield curve steepens, additional convexity will probably hurt you. Whether additional convexity helps or hurts depends upon the bonds you consider, and the "twist" in the yield curve that occurs. Crack and

---

and convexity measures work and where the approximations break down. This simple example is a good way to do that. In a real world situation, you might know the current value of your bond portfolio and its duration and convexity. It may be easier (and much faster) to *estimate* how your portfolio changes in value with changes in interest rates—using current value, duration, and convexity—than it is to *directly evaluate* each bond individually.

[14]People on The Street tell me that duration measures accounting for embedded options are important. Mehran and Homaifar (1993) discuss duration and convexity for bonds with embedded options. Before looking at Mehran and Homaifar (1993), be sure that both your mathematics and finance are up to scratch. They have the ideas correct, but their notation is contrary to conventional symbolic mathematics.

[15]This win-win situation is not kosher. A model that allows only parallel shifts in the yield curve freely admits arbitrage opportunities: match on price and duration and go long high convexity and short low convexity (Shiu, 1990; Lacey and Nawalkha 1993).

Table C.1: Duration/Convexity Summary (Annual Coupon Bond)

The bond pays C_t for $t = 1, \ldots, T$, and has discretely compounded annual yield r.	
Bond Price	$P = \sum_{t=1}^{T} C_t (1+r)^{-t}$
Modified Duration	$D^* \equiv \dfrac{-\frac{\partial P}{\partial r}}{P}$ $= \dfrac{\sum_{t=1}^{T} t\, C_t (1+r)^{-(t+1)}}{P} = \dfrac{1}{(1+r)} \sum_{t=1}^{T} t\, \omega_t,$ where $\omega_t \equiv \dfrac{C_t(1+r)^{-t}}{P}$ & $\sum_{t=1}^{T} \omega_t = 1.$
Macaulay Duration	$D = D^*(1+r) = \sum_{t=1}^{T} t\, \omega_t$ where $\omega_t \equiv \dfrac{C_t(1+r)^{-t}}{P}$ & $\sum_{t=1}^{T} \omega_t = 1.$
Bond Convexity	$\mathcal{C} \equiv \dfrac{\frac{\partial^2 P}{\partial r^2}}{P}$ $= \dfrac{\sum_{t=1}^{T} t\,(t+1)\, C_t (1+r)^{-(t+2)}}{P}$ $= \dfrac{1}{(1+r)^2} \sum_{t=1}^{T} t\,(t+1)\, \omega_t,$ where $\omega_t \equiv \dfrac{C_t(1+r)^{-t}}{P}$ & $\sum_{t=1}^{T} \omega_t = 1.$
Slope of Price-Yield Curve	$\text{Slope} = \dfrac{\partial P}{\partial r} = -D^* P = -\dfrac{D}{(1+r)} P$
Curvature of Price-Yield Curve	$\text{Curvature} = \dfrac{\partial^2 P}{\partial r^2} = \mathcal{C} P$
Taylor Series	$\Delta P \approx \dfrac{\partial P}{\partial r}(\Delta r) + \frac{1}{2}\dfrac{\partial^2 P}{\partial r^2}(\Delta r)^2 = -D^* P(\Delta r) + \frac{1}{2}\mathcal{C} P(\Delta r)^2$

Note: In the table, D is Macaulay duration, D^* is modified duration, P is bond price, and $\mathcal{C}$ is convexity. Try proving that $\frac{\partial D^*}{\partial r} = (D^*)^2 - \mathcal{C}$. Many of these relationships simplify substantially when we use continuously compounded yields. For example, D and D^* are identical using continuously compounded yields y, so $\frac{\partial D}{\partial y} = D^2 - \mathcal{C}$, which in turn equals zero if the bond is a pure discount bond (Crack and Nawalkha [2001]).

Nawalkha (2000) derive simple expressions that allow bond portfolio managers to capture the combined effects of term-structure height, slope and curvature shifts on duration, convexity, and higher-order bond risk measures. See Kahn and Lochoff (1990) and Lacey and Nawalkha (1993) for empirical evidence.

Answer 3.12: From empirical investigations, it is known that stock returns do not have constant variance through time and that periods of high (low) volatility tend to follow periods of high (low) volatility (Fama [1965]; Akgiray [1989]). The GARCH model attempts to capture this empirical fact.

Suppose you estimate a simple linear model like $r_{it} = \alpha_i + \beta_i r_{mt} + u_{it}$ (return on stock i at time t is a constant plus a constant times return on the market plus a residual). If you do not take account of changes in the variance of u_{it} through time, you can draw faulty statistical inferences about α_i and β_i. Note that the standard ordinary least squares (OLS) regression does not account for changing variance. In remedying this problem, the GARCH estimation captures a portion of stock price behavior that might otherwise be interpreted as non-normality and might lead to faulty inferences.

The GARCH model is a generalization of the ARCH model first presented in Engle (1982).[16] The formal GARCH(1,1) model for the residuals of a market model of stock returns is[17]

$$r_{it} = \alpha_i + \beta_i r_{mt} + u_{it}$$
$$u_{it}|\mathcal{F}_{i\,t-1} \sim N(0, h_{it})$$
$$h_{it} = \gamma_{0i} + \gamma_{1i} u_{i\,t-1}^2 + \gamma_{2i} h_{i\,t-1}.$$

The residuals, u_{it}, may be assumed to be independently distributed across stocks i. The market return, r_{mt}, is assumed common to all stocks. $\mathcal{F}_{i\,t-1}$ is the information set relative to stock i available just prior to date t; $\mathcal{F}_{i\,t-1}$ contains $u_{i\,t-1}$, $h_{i\,t-1}$ and all past returns on stock i. Note that conditional normality is not required for the GARCH model (Bollerslev [1987]).

The GARCH model estimation differs from a straightforward ordinary least squares (OLS) estimation; you do not have a nice closed-form expression for $\hat{\alpha}_i$ or $\hat{\beta}_i$. In the GARCH estimation, you typically run OLS to get an initial guess for α_i and β_i. Then you adjust guesses of the γ_{ji}'s, α_i and β_i until you obtain what seem to be the most likely parameter estimates. This is a "maximum likelihood estimation" technique.[18]

---

[16]The review paper by Bera and Higgins (1993) is the best overview of ARCH and GARCH models that I have seen. Following this, you might look at Bera et al. (1988) as an introduction to ARCH, and also as an introduction to Engle (1982). For an introduction to statistical models for financial market volatility, see Engle (1993) and his references. For a higher-level review of ARCH modelling in finance, see Bollerslev et al. (1992). For a concise overview of the broad econometric peculiarities of the ARCH(1) model, see Hendry (1986).

[17]If you remove the term $h_{i\,t-1}$ from the second moment of the GARCH(1,1) model, you get the ARCH(1) model.

[18]See Berndt et al. (1974) for details on a good maximum likelihood estimation technique. See Bollerslev (1986) and Greene (1993) for more on the GARCH model.

Answer 3.13: The question does not specify whether you hold T-bonds or corporate bonds. In the case of a T-bond holding, you can reduce your exposure (i.e., hedge) by shorting T-bond futures contracts. Each Chicago Board of Trade (CBOT) T-bond contract covers a face value of \$100,000 of T-bonds. If the duration of your bond is the same as the duration of the cheapest-to-deliver (CTD) T-bond, then you short $\frac{\$50,000,000}{\$100,000} = 500$ contracts.[19] If the duration of your bond is different from the duration of the CTD T-bond, then you adjust for durations: go short $\frac{D_B}{D_F} \times \frac{\$50,000,000}{\$100,000} = \frac{D_B}{D_F} \times 500$ contracts, where D_B is the duration of your bonds, and D_F is the duration of the CTD T-bond.

Note that you could hedge by shorting Eurodollar futures (the underlying is the interest rate on a three-month \$1 million Eurodollar deposit). However, the short end of the yield curve does not move with the long end. It, therefore, makes sense to use a hedging instrument whose underlying interest has maturity as close as possible to the portfolio to be hedged.

If you hold corporate bonds, then you can still hedge using T-bond futures (Kuberek and Pefley, 1983; Edwards and Ma, 1992, p. 343), but changes in default risk premia will move the price of your corporate bond with little or no effect on the T-bond futures. This is really an example of cross hedging. You can get the hedging ratio by regressing say, monthly, price changes of your corporate bond on monthly price changes of the near-month T-bond futures. If the coefficient were β, then you would replace the ratio of durations with β, to get $\beta \times \frac{\$50,000,000}{\$100,000} = \beta \times 500$ contracts.[20]

Answer 3.14: "Brady bonds" are sovereign bonds issued by developing countries in exchange for previously rescheduled bank loans. They are either "Par" bonds or "Discount" bonds. The former were issued at the par value of the loans but carry a below-market interest rate; the latter were issued at a discount from the face value of the former loans but carry a (floating) market interest rate. About a quarter of the market value of Brady bonds is collateralized by U.S. Treasury issues. The size of this collateralization means that Brady bonds are sensitive to changes in U.S. interest rates. In fact, something like a quarter of the variation in price movements of Brady bonds is (statistically) explained by moves in U.S. Treasuries (sometimes with a lag of one day). Mexico has retired all its Brady bonds, but the arguments apply more generally, so I kept the question.[21]

Let us assume that the yield on the Brady bond increases by 25 bps (i.e., one quarter of the U.S. Treasury yield change). If we assume that the duration of the Brady bond is about 15 years, that the bond is trading at around par of

---

[19]For more details on the CTD bond, see Hull (1997, pp. 92–93); for details on duration-based hedging, see Hull (1997, pp. 102–104).

[20]If you regress changes in corporate yields on changes in T-bond yields, to get coefficient β_Y, you would replace the previous ratio of durations $\frac{D_B}{D_F}$ by $\frac{D_B}{D_F} \times \beta_Y \times \frac{(1+y_T)}{(1+y_B)} \times \frac{\$50,000,000}{\$100,000}$ contracts, where y_T and y_B are the yields on the T-bonds and corporate bonds, respectively.

[21]This summary benefited from an unpublished research report prepared for Merrill Lynch by a group of my former students from when I was a teaching assistant at MIT.

$1,000, and that the Mexican yield curve is flat at around 8%, then the price response would be (denoting yield by y)

$$
\begin{aligned}
\Delta P &\approx -DP\frac{\Delta y}{(1+y)}\\
&= -15 \times \$1{,}000 \times \frac{0.0025}{1.08}\\
&= -\$15{,}000 \times \frac{0.0025}{1.08}\\
&= -\frac{\$37.50}{1.08} \approx -\$35.
\end{aligned}
$$

With these assumptions, my guess is that the Brady bond price goes down by about three or four percentage points.

Answer 3.15: This question is similar to Question 3.10. The zero-coupon corporate bond has the same duration as longer-term coupon-bearing treasuries. You should short the corporate bond and buy treasuries that have the same duration and value as the corporate bond. By matching on duration and value, you create a zero-net investment portfolio that reaps profits.

Of course, you could just trade the treasuries, going long long-term bonds and short short-term bonds.

Answer 3.16: First of all, the 5/10 time span is not relevant. The same result holds for a 1/2-year time span. That is, if the one-year interest rate is 10%, and two-year interest rate is 15%, then the forward rate for the second year is close to, but strictly greater than, 20%. Second, the order of the rates is not important. That is, if the two-year rate is 15%, and the forward rate for the second year is 10%, then the one-year rate is close to, but strictly greater than, 20%. Third, the result holds for effective (i.e., simple) interest rates but does not hold for continuously compounded interest rates (for which the approximation is exact).

The argument relies upon the way in which the interest on your interest accumulates. If you are offered 10% for the first year and 20% for the second year, you will not do as well as if you are offered the average (15%) for two years. Although the interest on the principal is the same in both cases (and equal to 30%), the interest on the interest is not the same (15% of 15% equals 2.25% and exceeds 20% of 10%, which is only 2%). To avoid arbitrage, the "plug" rate has to exceed 20%. That was the "plain English" approach.

The result can be proved using math. Let R_1 and R_2 be two different interest rates, then

$$\left(\frac{R_1 + R_2}{2}\right)^2 - R_1 R_2 = \frac{1}{4}(R_1^2 + 2R_1 R_2 + R_2^2 - 4R_1 R_2)$$

$$= \frac{1}{4}(R_1^2 - 2R_1 R_2 + R_2^2)$$

$$= \frac{1}{4}(R_1 - R_2)^2 > 0.$$

It follows that $\left(\frac{R_1+R_2}{2}\right)^2 > R_1 R_2$. This means that the interest on the interest is better at the average rate than at the product of rates—as stated above.

The result may also be written as $\left(\frac{R_1+R_2}{2}\right) > \sqrt{R_1 R_2}$. This is a special case of a more general result that an arithmetic average exceeds a geometric average. This result is true beyond the case $n = 2$ and can be extended to encompass quadratic and harmonic averages also.

Let $\mathcal{Q}$, $\mathcal{A}$, $\mathcal{G}$, and $\mathcal{H}$ denote the quadratic, arithmetic, geometric, and harmonic averages, respectively, of the **positive** real numbers x_1, x_2, ..., x_n as follows:

$$\mathcal{Q} \equiv \sqrt{\frac{1}{n}\sum_{i=1}^{n} x_i^2} = \sqrt{\frac{x_1^2 + x_2^2 + \cdots + x_n^2}{n}},$$

$$\mathcal{A} \equiv \frac{1}{n}\sum_{i=1}^{n} x_i = \frac{x_1 + x_2 + \cdots + x_n}{n},$$

$$\mathcal{G} \equiv \sqrt[n]{\Pi_{i=1}^{n} x_i} = \sqrt[n]{x_1 x_2 \ldots x_n}, \quad \text{and}$$

$$\mathcal{H} \equiv \frac{n}{\sum_{i=1}^{n} \frac{1}{x_i}} = \frac{n}{\frac{1}{x_1} + \frac{1}{x_2} + \cdots + \frac{1}{x_n}}$$

Then the following result holds (Spiegel [1968]):[22]

$$\mathcal{Q} \geq \mathcal{A} \geq \mathcal{G} \geq \mathcal{H},$$

and the inequalities are equalities only in the special case where

$$x_1 = x_2 = \cdots = x_n.$$

Note that $\mathcal{Q} \geq \mathcal{A}$ is a special case of $var(X) = E(X^2) - [E(X)]^2 \geq 0$, when X is uniform and discrete with n values. That is, $E(X^2) \geq [E(X)]^2$ implies $\sqrt{E(X^2)} \geq E(X)$, and thus $\mathcal{Q} \geq \mathcal{A}$. The result $\mathcal{Q} \geq \mathcal{A}$ also follows from the

---

[22]To help you remember the letter rankings $\mathcal{A} \geq \mathcal{G} \geq \mathcal{H}$, note that it is the same as the ranking of the letters A, G, and H in the Latin alphabet.

Cauchy-Schwarz inequality applied to x_is and 1s. That is,

$$\left(\sum_{i=1}^{n} x_i^2\right) \cdot \left(\sum_{i=1}^{n} 1^2\right) \geq \left(\sum_{i=1}^{n} x_i \cdot 1\right)^2$$

$$\Rightarrow \left(\sum_{i=1}^{n} x_i^2\right) \cdot n \geq \left(\sum_{i=1}^{n} x_i\right)^2$$

$$\Rightarrow \sum_{i=1}^{n} x_i^2 \bigg/ n \geq \left(\sum_{i=1}^{n} x_i\right)^2 \bigg/ n^2,$$

which implies $\sqrt{\sum_{i=1}^{n} x_i^2/n} \geq \sum_{i=1}^{n} x_i/n$, as required.

There is an extensive discussion of arithmetic versus geometric means and associated biases in Crack (2020b, Section 2.1).

Answer 3.17: If the one-year rate is 12%, and the two-year rate is 18%, then the forward rate for the second year is 24% to a first-order approximation (it is exactly 24% if these are continuously compounded rates). Let us assume this is 12% per half-year in the second year. Then your discounted expected payoff to the game is approximately

$$\left(\frac{1}{2} \times -\$2\right) + \left(\frac{1}{2} \times \frac{\$7}{(1.12)(1.12)}\right) \approx -\$1 + \frac{\$3.50}{1.25}$$

$$= -\$1 + \frac{14}{5}$$

$$= \$1.80.$$

If you can play repeatedly, then you are risk-neutral, and you would pay anything up to about $1.80 to play this game. If you can play only once, then you might argue that the amount is so small you are still risk-neutral. If you multiply everything by a factor of one million, then you'll need to add a risk premium to the discount rates, and you will not pay as much to play.[23]

Answer 3.18: No one wants to trade with the informed (i.e., insider) trader because you almost always lose to someone who is better informed than you are (Glosten and Milgrom [1985]). The identity of the informed trader has not been announced. This means that *any* trade could be a losing trade. Traders will, therefore, be reluctant to trade. This leads directly to decreased trading volume.

Here is another way to look at it. Uncertainty over the identity of the informed trader means that traders widen their bid-ask spreads to compensate (on average) for any potential losses. Wider bid-ask spreads is one component of a decrease in liquidity, and it is usually associated with a decreased volume of trade (Chordia and Subrahmanyam [1995]).

---

[23]The risk premium as a function of the size of the bet is discussed by Tversky and Kahneman (1981) and Kahneman and Tversky (1982). Tversky and Kahneman (1974) is an earlier article you might like to read before reading these two.

Answer 3.19: The very first thing I check (see the next question!) is whether $\rho = \frac{\min(\sigma_1, \sigma_2)}{\max(\sigma_1, \sigma_2)}$. Finding that it is not (because this ratio is $2/3$ here and $\rho = 0.50$), we proceed as follows.

Let $\sigma_1 = 0.20$, $\sigma_2 = 0.30$, and $\rho = 0.50$ be the standard deviations and correlation, respectively. Let ω be the weight put into Stock 1. The portfolio variance is just $\sigma^2 = \omega^2 \sigma_1^2 + (1-\omega)^2 \sigma_2^2 + 2\omega(1-\omega)\sigma_1\sigma_2\rho$. Differentiate this with respect to ω to get

$$
\begin{aligned}
\frac{\partial \sigma^2}{\partial \omega} &= 2\omega\sigma_1^2 - 2(1-\omega)\sigma_2^2 + 2(1-\omega)\sigma_1\sigma_2\rho - 2\omega\sigma_1\sigma_2\rho \\
&= 2[\omega(\sigma_1^2 + \sigma_2^2 - 2\sigma_1\sigma_2\rho) - \sigma_2^2 + \sigma_1\sigma_2\rho].
\end{aligned}
\tag{C.5}
$$

This is zero when $\omega = \frac{\sigma_2(\sigma_2 - \sigma_1\rho)}{\sigma_1^2 + \sigma_2^2 - 2\sigma_1\sigma_2\rho}$, assuming $\sigma_1^2 + \sigma_2^2 - 2\sigma_1\sigma_2\rho \neq 0$. In our particular case this ratio is $\omega = \frac{0.06}{0.07} = 0.8571...$ and this gives $\sigma = 0.1964$.

It is good practice to check the second order condition: $\frac{\partial^2 \sigma^2}{\partial \omega^2} = 2(\sigma_1^2 + \sigma_2^2 - 2\sigma_1\sigma_2\rho) = 0.14 > 0$, so it is a minimum.

Answer 3.20: In the previous question I said that the very first thing I check is whether $\rho = \frac{\min(\sigma_1, \sigma_2)}{\max(\sigma_1, \sigma_2)}$. It was not in that question, but it is in this one (i.e, $\sqrt{\frac{0.10}{0.40}} = 0.50$), so the approach is different.

I have never seen it written down in a book, but it is well known that there are several cases for ρ in the two-asset portfolio (these can each be deduced from the first order condition, setting Equation C.5 equal to zero, in Answer 3.19):

- $\rho = -1$: then $\omega = \frac{\sigma_2}{\sigma_1 + \sigma_2}$, and $\sigma = 0$. This is the case of perfect negative correlation and a zero-risk portfolio. No shorting is required.

- $-1 < \rho < \frac{\min(\sigma_1, \sigma_2)}{\max(\sigma_1, \sigma_2)}$: then $\omega = \frac{\sigma_2(\sigma_2 - \sigma_1\rho)}{\sigma_1^2 + \sigma_2^2 - 2\sigma_1\sigma_2\rho}$, this does not involve short selling, and variance reduction occurs below that of either asset. This is the case in Question 3.19.

- $\rho = \frac{\min(\sigma_1, \sigma_2)}{\max(\sigma_1, \sigma_2)} \neq 1$: then all money goes into the lowest volatility asset to minimize volatility (so $\omega = 1$ if $\sigma_1 < \sigma_2$, and $\omega = 0$ if $\sigma_2 < \sigma_1$), and $\sigma = \min(\sigma_1, \sigma_2)$.

- $\frac{\min(\sigma_1, \sigma_2)}{\max(\sigma_1, \sigma_2)} < \rho < 1$: then $\omega = \frac{\sigma_2(\sigma_2 - \sigma_1\rho)}{\sigma_1^2 + \sigma_2^2 - 2\sigma_1\sigma_2\rho}$, this does involve short selling, and variance reduction occurs below that of either asset.

- $\rho = 1$ and $\sigma_1 \neq \sigma_2$: then $\omega = \frac{\sigma_2}{\sigma_2 - \sigma_1}$, and the high volatility asset is shorted to over-invest in the low volatility asset, and the optimum is a zero-risk portfolio.

- $\rho = 1$ and $\sigma_1 = \sigma_2$: then there is no unique solution for the weights; any ω gives the minimum-risk portfolio, with variance equal to that of both assets.

This question is for the middle case above, and we should put all our money into the low volatility asset. Unlike the previous question, you just have to remember the ratio of the standard deviations (only one ratio is feasible for the standard deviations because the reciprocal ratio would be bigger than 1), and if the correlation equals the feasible ratio then all money goes into the low volatility asset. The interviewer is trying to find out whether you know this result.

Story: A reader sent me the following e-mail: "...I bought your book... ...I just opened it to the first problem and was somewhat taken back by your solution. If you worked out the math, you would know that your answer is wrong. If you do not want to work out the math, then you could qualitatively grasp the mistake like so: ... ...Of course, to be quantitatively correct, you have to do the math. Always do the math... ...Hopefully, not too many interviewers have read this answer—or there will be lots of poor quants that will be turned away for being smart. Sincerely, YT."

Like many an overconfident quant, YT jumped into the math without *thinking* about the problem. Just as a pickpocket bumps you from the left while his accomplice takes money out of your right pocket, many of these questions are set up to distract you. You must be hard wired to ignore the superficial "pickpocket answer" and home in on the deeper response that is required.

I sent YT a tactful e-mail telling him politely why he was mistaken and why no math was needed. I even gave him a challenge quant question to solve to save face, but he did not respond. I think that his failure to respond was because he was unable to handle any criticism or admit his mistake (that would be consistent with his condescending e-mail). This is not what employers are looking for! Suppose an interviewer pushes you so hard or so far that you supply the wrong answer to a quant question. If the interviewer points out your mistake (and they do not always) then you should behave like a team member who is happy to accept constructive criticism. Do not get defensive, do not supply any BS; just take it and roll with the punches.

Appendix D

Statistics Answers

This appendix contains answers to the questions posed in Chapter 4.

Answer 4.1: Before giving an algebraic answer, I think you should have a guess. This shows that you can guess, and it gives you a baseline number to compare your algebraic answer with, which could produce a warning red flag if you make a mistake with the algebra.

Obviously, when you buy your first cereal box, you get one of the four toys with probability one on that draw. As you acquire different toys, however, the likelihood that you get the next one in only one draw falls. For example, by the time you already have three of the four toys, you only have one chance in four that the next draw will give you the fourth. So, the absolute minimum number of purchases required is four, but you could buy 100 boxes, and not get all four toys—though this latter outcome seems very unlikely. Weighing these odds up, my gut instinct is that it should take something like 10 draws on average to get all four toys.

Now let us solve the problem algebraically. Consider first the more general problem of having T toys. (As an aside, note that the answer we seek must also be the same as if we roll a T-sided die and we ask how many rolls do we expect to have to make in order to have seen all T sides appear.)

Let us give a simple recursion argument. Suppose that T is the number of different toys we seek. Let us suppose that we are currently attempting to get our t^{th} toy, having already found $(t-1)$ different toys. We can immediately see that the probability, p_t that we get the tth toy in only one draw is $[T-(t-1)]/T$. For example, when seeking the first toy, $p_1 = 1$, and when seeking the second toy, $p_2 = (T-1)/T$, and so on.

Let N_t be the number of draws required to obtain the tth toy, having already found $(t-1)$ different toys. Then there is probability p_t that we get the tth toy in one draw, and probability $(1-p_t)$ that we have to draw again. Given independence of outcomes on different draws, it follows that we have a simple recursion for $E(N_t)$ given by

$$E(N_t) = p_t \cdot 1 + (1 - p_t) \cdot [1 + E(N_t)].$$

Solving for $E(N_t)$ yields $E(N_t) = 1/p_t$.

Let N be the total number of draws required, then $N = N_1 + N_2 + \cdots + N_T$. It follows that the expected total number of draws is given by

$$
\begin{aligned}
E(N) &= E(N_1 + N_2 + \cdots + N_{T-1} + N_T) \\
&= E(N_1) + E(N_2) + \cdots + E(N_{T-1}) + E(N_T) \\
&= \frac{1}{p_1} + \frac{1}{p_2} + \cdots + \frac{1}{p_{T-1}} + \frac{1}{p_T} \\
&= \frac{T}{T} + \frac{T}{(T-1)} + \cdots + \frac{T}{2} + \frac{T}{1} \\
&= T \cdot \sum_{t=1}^{T} \frac{1}{t}.
\end{aligned}
$$

In the case $T = 4$, $E(N) = 4 \cdot (\frac{1}{1} + \frac{1}{2} + \frac{1}{3} + \frac{1}{4}) = 8\frac{1}{3}$, not far from my ballpark answer of 10.

Alternatively, when trying to obtain the tth toy, consider each cereal box purchase as a Bernoulli trial with probability of success p_t. Then the geometric distribution $f_{N_t}(n) = P(N_t = n) = p_t \cdot q_t^{n-1}$ for $n \geq 1$, counts the number of trials up to and including the first success (Spiegel, 1975; Evans et al., 1993). This version of the geometric distribution has mean $E(N_t) = 1/p_t$, and variance $V(N_t) = q_t/p_t^2$. So, we get a mean of $E(N) = T \cdot \sum_{t=1}^{T} \frac{1}{t}$, as above, and (left as an exercise), a variance of $V(N) = \sum_{t=1}^{T} V(N_t) = T \cdot \sum_{t=1}^{T} \left(\frac{T-t}{t^2} \right)$. In the case $T = 4$, these yield a mean of $8\frac{1}{3}$ cereal boxes, a variance of $4 \left(\frac{3}{1} + \frac{2}{4} + \frac{1}{9} + \frac{0}{16} \right) = 14\frac{4}{9}$ cereal boxes, and, thus, a standard deviation of $\sqrt{14\frac{4}{9}} \approx 3.8$ cereal boxes. So, in practice, for $T = 4$ toys, it is very unlikely that you will need to buy more than about 25 cereal boxes.

Finally, and I do not think this was expected, here is another chance to use the Euler-Mascheroni approximation to the partial sums of the harmonic series $\sum_{t=1}^{\infty} \frac{1}{t}$. For large T, $\sum_{t=1}^{T} \frac{1}{t} \approx \ln(T) + \frac{1}{2T} + \gamma$, where $\gamma \approx 0.5772156649$ is the Euler-Mascheroni constant. It follows that $E(N) \approx T \left(\ln(T) + \frac{1}{2T} + \gamma \right)$. In fact, this approximation is very accurate, yielding answers within a tenth of a percent (in relative terms) of the actual answer for $T > 5$.

Answer 4.2: Imagine the surface $f(x, y) = x \cdot y$ plotted above the unit square. We need to find the area of that part of the domain where $f(x, y) = x \cdot y > 1/2$. If we project this down onto the x–y space, we need only find the area within the unit square above the isovalue curve $x \cdot y = 1/2$. That is, we need the area within the unit square that is above $y = 1/(2x)$.

A quick sketch shows that this area is only in the top-right quarter of the unit square. Given the function's concavity, the area must be slightly greater than one-half of one-quarter of one. So, my initial ballpark guess is a number slightly greater than 0.125.

Thus, the answer must be one-half less the area below $y = 1/(2x)$ for $x \geq 1/2$. The answer is given as follows.

$$
\begin{aligned}
P &= \frac{1}{2} - \int_{x=1/2}^{x=1} \frac{1}{2x} dx \\
&= \frac{1}{2} - \int_{x=1/2}^{x=1} \frac{1}{2} x^{-1} dx \\
&= \frac{1}{2} \left(1 - \left. \ln(x) \right|_{x=1/2}^{x=1} \right) \\
&= \frac{1}{2} \left[1 + \ln \left(\frac{1}{2} \right) \right] \approx 0.1534,
\end{aligned}
$$

which is in line with my ballpark guess.

Answer 4.3: If $X \sim N(\mu, \sigma^2)$, then $f_X(x) = \frac{1}{\sqrt{2\pi}\sigma} e^{-\frac{1}{2}\left(\frac{x-\mu}{\sigma}\right)^2}$. In my experience, the most common error is to leave the σ out of the denominator of the initial term. The constant factor ensures that the pdf integrates to 1.

Answer 4.4: Suppose that $X \sim N(\mu, \sigma^2)$, as in the previous question, then $E(X^2) = \mu^2 + \sigma^2$. I find this particularly easy to remember because of the symmetry in the answer. Note, of course, that this result can be deduced directly from the widely used result

$$
\text{var}(X) = E\left(X^2\right) - [E(X)]^2,
$$

just by solving for $E(X^2)$.

The raw, or "non-central," moments $E(X^n)$, $n \in \mathbb{Z}$, $n \geq 0$ are quite messy. So, let me calculate the easier central moment $E[(X - \mu)^n]$ result first, and then derive a formula for the non-central moments (which depends upon the central moments in the standard normal case), and then I will give a table of both the central and non-central moments up to order 10.

If $X \sim N(\mu, \sigma^2)$, then $(X - \mu) \sim N(0, \sigma^2)$, and we deduce from the derivation in Answer 2.31 that the central moments are given by

$$
E\left[(X - \mu)^n\right] = \begin{cases} 0, & \text{if } n > 0 \text{ odd} \\ \sigma^n (n-1)!!, & \text{if } n > 0 \text{ even}, \end{cases} \tag{D.1}
$$

where the double exclamation denotes the double factorial, as defined in Footnote 44 on p. 197. Of course, the zero result when n is odd follows immediately by symmetry.

Now note that if $X \sim N(\mu, \sigma^2)$, then $X = \sigma Z + \mu$, where $Z \sim N(0, 1)$. It follows, using the binomial theorem, $(a + b)^n = \sum_{k=0}^{n} \binom{n}{k} a^k b^{n-k}$, that

$$
\begin{aligned}
E(X^n) &= E\left[(\sigma Z + \mu)^n\right] \\
&= E\left[\sum_{k=0}^{n} \binom{n}{k}(\sigma Z)^k \mu^{n-k}\right] \\
&= \sum_{k=0}^{n} \binom{n}{k}\sigma^k E\left(Z^k\right)\mu^{n-k} \quad\quad\quad\text{(D.2)} \\
&= \begin{cases} \mu, & \text{if } n = 1 \\ \mu^n + \sum_{j=1}^{\text{floor}(n/2)} \binom{n}{2j}\sigma^{2j}(2j-1)!!\mu^{n-2j}, & \text{if } n \geq 2, \end{cases} \quad\text{(D.3)}
\end{aligned}
$$

where the last line follows from Equation D.1 in the special case $\mu = 0$ and $\sigma = 1$, and floor$(\cdot)$ is the floor function that rounds down to the nearest integer. Equation D.3 may be rewritten more concisely, though perhaps less clearly, as Equation D.4.

$$
E(X^n) = \sum_{j=0}^{\text{floor}(n/2)} \binom{n}{2j}\sigma^{2j}[2\cdot\max(j,1) - 1]!!\mu^{n-2j}, \; n \in \mathbb{Z}, \; n \geq 0 \quad\text{(D.4)}
$$

A couple of years after deriving Equation D.4, I discovered Winkelbauer (2014), which must implicitly contain it, and related results.

Table D.1 gives the central and non-central moments of $X \sim N(\mu, \sigma^2)$ up to order 10. Note that the final term in the summation in Equation D.2 is just $E\left[(X - \mu)^n\right]$, as given by Equation D.1, and that this is true whether n is even or odd. That is,

$$
E(X^n) = E\left[(X - \mu)^n\right] + \text{Adjustment}(n; \mu, \sigma), \quad\quad\text{(D.5)}
$$

where Adjustment$(n; \mu, \sigma) = 0$, if $\mu = 0$. Of course, Equation D.5 is tautologically true, but I think it is helpful to view it this way. Note that in the case $n = 2$, Equation D.5 reduces to $E(X^2) = \text{var}(X) + [E(X)]^2$, and if we move $[E(X)]^2$ to the other side, we are back right where this answer started.

Answer 4.5: Suppose that X and Y are independent random variables each distributed standard normal: $X \sim N(0,1)$, and $Y \sim N(0,1)$. What are the variance and the standard deviation of $X - Y$?

I suspect that the minus sign confuses some people. Just remember that when random variables are independent, the variance of the sum is the sum of the variances. Also, recall that var$(aY) = a^2\text{var}(Y)$ for constant a and random

Table D.1: Moments of $X \sim N(\mu, \sigma^2)$

Order n	Central Moment $E\left[(X - \mu)^n\right]$	Non-Central Moment $E(X^n)$
1	0	μ
2	σ^2	$\mu^2 + \sigma^2$
3	0	$\mu^3 + 3\mu\sigma^2$
4	$3\sigma^4$	$\mu^4 + 6\mu^2\sigma^2 + 3\sigma^4$
5	0	$\mu^5 + 10\mu^3\sigma^2 + 15\mu\sigma^4$
6	$15\sigma^6$	$\mu^6 + 15\mu^4\sigma^2 + 45\mu^2\sigma^4 + 15\sigma^6$
7	0	$\mu^7 + 21\mu^5\sigma^2 + 105\mu^3\sigma^4 + 105\mu\sigma^6$
8	$105\sigma^8$	$\mu^8 + 28\mu^6\sigma^2 + 210\mu^4\sigma^4 + 420\mu^2\sigma^6 + 105\sigma^8$
9	0	$\mu^9 + 36\mu^7\sigma^2 + 378\mu^5\sigma^4 + 1260\mu^3\sigma^6 + 945\mu\sigma^8$
10	$945\sigma^{10}$	$\mu^{10} + 45\mu^8\sigma^2 + 630\mu^6\sigma^4 + 3150\mu^4\sigma^6 + 4725\mu^2\sigma^8 + 945\sigma^{10}$

Note: This table uses Equation D.1 and Equation D.3 to give the central and non-central moments of $X \sim N(\mu, \sigma^2)$ up to order 10. Note that in every case, the central moment $E\left[(X - \mu)^n\right]$ is equal to the term in σ^n that appears in the non-central moment $E(X^n)$; this term is trivial for n odd. Also, obviously, if $\mu = 0$, the two moments are identical.

variably Y. So, we get that

$$
\begin{aligned}
\mathrm{var}(X - Y) &= \mathrm{var}(X - Y) \\
&= \mathrm{var}[X + (-Y)] \\
&= \mathrm{var}(X) + \mathrm{var}(-Y) \\
&= \mathrm{var}(X) + (-1)^2\mathrm{var}(Y) \\
&= \mathrm{var}(X) + \mathrm{var}(Y) \\
&= 2.
\end{aligned}
$$

It follows that the standard deviation of $X - Y$ is $\sqrt{2}$.

The result that $\mathrm{var}(X - Y) = \mathrm{var}(X) + \mathrm{var}(Y) = \mathrm{var}(X + Y)$ is true for any independent random variables X and Y. The key drivers are that when random variables are independent, the variance of the sum is the sum of the variances, and that $\mathrm{var}(-Y) = \mathrm{var}(Y)$.

In the particular case (of standard normal random variables), another way to think about this is that because Y is symmetric about zero, the signed random variable $-Y$ is, from a probabilistic standpoint, the same as the random variable Y. That is, if $Y \sim N(0,1)$, then $-Y \sim N(0,1)$ also. So, $X + Y$ and $X - Y$ are then probabilistically the same. That is, the random variables $X+Y$ and $X-Y$ have the same mean, the same variance, the same skewness, the same kurtosis, etc. In other cases (e.g., X and Y lognormal or chi-squared, or normal with non-zero mean), the variance result still holds, but the other results need not.

Answer 4.6: This sort of question is common. Begin by calculating the expected payoff to the game. This is given by the summation over the product of potential outcomes times their probability of occurrence:

$$\left(\tfrac{1}{6} \times \$1\right) + \left(\tfrac{1}{6} \times \$2\right) + \left(\tfrac{1}{6} \times \$3\right) + \left(\tfrac{1}{6} \times \$4\right) + \left(\tfrac{1}{6} \times \$5\right) + \left(\tfrac{1}{6} \times \$6\right) = \$3.50$$

If you are selling tickets to repeated plays of this game, you are effectively risk-neutral.[1] This means you should charge the expected payoff (\$3.50) plus a margin for profit. You choose how wide to make the margin—it depends on your overhead, monopoly power, greed, and so on. You cannot charge \$6.00 or above, since no one will play. If the game is to be played only once, then you are risk-averse. You should charge the expected value, plus your profit margin, plus a risk premium. The risk premium depends upon how risk-averse you are.

Answer 4.7: I give an elegant answer first, and then a hammer-and-tongs solution that could be useful for variations of the game.

FIRST SOLUTION

The original game is stated as "You toss five coins and I toss four coins. You win if you get strictly more heads." This game is isomorphic to an analytically simpler game.[2] "You toss four coins and I toss four coins. Whomever gets the most heads wins immediately. If we are tied, however, then you toss one more coin to decide the outcome." By observation, both stages of this second game are completely symmetric. So, we each have a probability one-half of winning.

SECOND SOLUTION

A simple sketch of the joint probability mass function of our outcomes, and an appeal to symmetry, gives the answer as $1/2$ without any calculation. I derive the answer graphically, with more details than you need.

The key to this more complex solution is to recognize that when $p = 1/2$, the binomial probability mass function $B(N, p)$ of either player is symmetric, and

---

[1] This is an application of the "Weak Law of Large Numbers." The law says, essentially, that if you independently draw repeated observations from the same random distribution, then for very many drawings, the sample mean is very close to the population mean (DeGroot [1989, p. 229–231]). In other words, after many repeated plays of the game, the ticket seller can be sure that his average payout per game is very close to the expected payout per game. Because all that matters is the expected payout, not the variance of payouts, the ticket seller is effectively risk-neutral. Similarly, casinos are effectively risk-neutral. With repeated plays, and odds slightly in the favor of "the house," the casino expects to be the winner for sure in the long run.

[2] I thank Tommaso Sechi for suggesting this elegant approach.

Table D.2: Binomial Joint pmf: Two Tosses versus One Toss

		$Y\ [P(Y=y)]$		
$P(X=x, Y=y)$		$0\ \left[\frac{1}{4}\right]$	$1\ \left[\frac{1}{2}\right]$	$2\ \left[\frac{1}{4}\right]$
$X\ [P(X=x)]$	$0\ \left[\frac{1}{2}\right]$	$\frac{1}{8}$	$\frac{2}{8}$	$\frac{1}{8}$
	$1\ \left[\frac{1}{2}\right]$	$\frac{1}{8}$	$\frac{2}{8}$	$\frac{1}{8}$

Y is the number of heads in two tosses of a fair coin. X is the number of heads in one toss of a fair coin. The binomial marginal probability mass functions $P(X=x)$ and $P(Y=y)$ are shown in square brackets. The tosses are all independent. So, the binomial joint probability mass function $P(X=x, Y=y)$ is the product of the marginals. The sum of the shaded cells is $P(Y > X) = 1/2$.

that two people tossing coins independently of each other means that the joint probability mass function is just the product of the marginals.[3]

To make the intuition clear, I will consider first the simpler case where you toss only two coins and I toss only one. I give all the fine details to make it clear, which may be useful in variations of the game, but in fact, no calculation is needed. Each toss is a Bernoulli trial with probability of success (i.e., a head) equal to $1/2$. The tosses are independent, so the count of heads Y that you get is distributed binomial: $P(Y=y) = \binom{N}{y}p^y q^{N-y}$, where $N=2$, $p=\frac{1}{2}$, $q \equiv 1-p = \frac{1}{2}$. So, $P(Y=y) = \binom{2}{y}\left(\frac{1}{2}\right)^y \left(\frac{1}{2}\right)^{2-y} = \binom{2}{y}\left(\frac{1}{2}\right)^2$. Similarly, with X as the number of heads in one toss of a fair coin, $P(X=x) = \binom{1}{x}\left(\frac{1}{2}\right)^1$. The marginals are thus given by

$$P(Y=y) = \begin{cases} \frac{1}{4}, & y=0, \\ \frac{1}{2}, & y=1, \\ \frac{1}{4}, & y=2, \end{cases} \quad \text{and} \quad P(X=x) = \begin{cases} \frac{1}{2}, & x=0, \\ \frac{1}{2}, & x=1. \end{cases}$$

The random variables Y and X are statistically independent of each other, so the joint probability mass function is just the product of the marginals $P(X=x, Y=y) = P(X=x) \cdot P(Y=y)$ as shown in Table D.2. Simple visual inspection of Table D.2 shows that in the simple case of two and one tosses, we get $P(Y > X) = 1/2$ (i.e., the sum of the shaded cells).

Although I gave the formal calculation of the marginal and joint probability mass functions in this simplified case, this calculation is not needed. The two

---

[3]The binomial distribution $B(N,p)$ has skewness $\frac{q-p}{\sqrt{Npq}}$ and kurtosis $3 - \frac{6}{N} + \frac{1}{Npq}$; these go to zero and three, respectively, as $N \to \infty$ (i.e., the distribution converges to normality). See Evans et al. (1993) for more details.

Table D.3: Binomial Joint pmf: Five Tosses versus Four Tosses

		$Y \ [P(Y=y)]$					
$P(X=x, Y=y)$		$0\left[\frac{1}{32}\right]$	$1\left[\frac{5}{32}\right]$	$2\left[\frac{10}{32}\right]$	$3\left[\frac{10}{32}\right]$	$4\left[\frac{5}{32}\right]$	$5\left[\frac{1}{32}\right]$
$X \ [P(X=x)]$	$0\left[\frac{1}{16}\right]$	$\frac{1}{512}$	$\frac{5}{512}$	$\frac{10}{512}$	$\frac{10}{512}$	$\frac{5}{512}$	$\frac{1}{512}$
	$1\left[\frac{4}{16}\right]$	$\frac{4}{512}$	$\frac{20}{512}$	$\frac{40}{512}$	$\frac{40}{512}$	$\frac{20}{512}$	$\frac{4}{512}$
	$2\left[\frac{6}{16}\right]$	$\frac{6}{512}$	$\frac{30}{512}$	$\frac{60}{512}$	$\frac{60}{512}$	$\frac{30}{512}$	$\frac{6}{512}$
	$3\left[\frac{4}{16}\right]$	$\frac{4}{512}$	$\frac{20}{512}$	$\frac{40}{512}$	$\frac{40}{512}$	$\frac{20}{512}$	$\frac{4}{512}$
	$4\left[\frac{1}{16}\right]$	$\frac{1}{512}$	$\frac{5}{512}$	$\frac{10}{512}$	$\frac{10}{512}$	$\frac{5}{512}$	$\frac{1}{512}$

Y is the number of heads in five tosses of a fair coin. X is the number of heads in four tosses of a fair coin. The binomial marginal probability mass functions $P(X=x) = \binom{4}{x}\left(\frac{1}{2}\right)^4$ and $P(Y=y) = \binom{5}{y}\left(\frac{1}{2}\right)^5$ are shown in square brackets. The tosses are all independent. So, the binomial joint probability mass function $P(X=x, Y=y)$ is the product of the marginals. The symmetrical marginals mean that the joint probability mass function is symmetric in all respects. If you take a pair of scissors and cut out the shaded cells as a single inverted staircase, then rotate that through 180 degrees, the contents perfectly match the contents of the un-shaded cells. So, by symmetry, $P(Y > X) = 1/2$.

marginal binomial distributions shown in square brackets in Table D.2 are symmetric because $p = 1/2$. With both marginals symmetric, it must be that the sum of the joint probabilities in the shaded cells and the sum of the joint probabilities in the un-shaded cells are the same. The two sums must add to one, so the sum of the shaded cells must be $P(Y > X) = 1/2$.

Table D.3 shows an analogous table for the case of you tossing five coins and me tossing four coins. Again, I have given all the details of the marginal and joint probability mass functions, but in fact, no numbers are required to do the calculation. I have given them only to fill in the fine details to back up the answer.

Story: 1. Announced she hadn't had lunch and proceeded to eat a hamburger and french fries in the interviewer's office. 2. Without saying a word, candidate stood up and walked out during the middle of the interview.

Interview Horror Stories from Recruiters
Reprinted by kind permission of *MBA Style Magazine*
©1996–2021 MBA Style Magazine, www.mbastyle.com

Answer 4.8:   Another die-rolling question; they are very popular. You want to get as many dollars as possible. You let me roll once and look at which number comes up. You must compare this number to the possible payoffs on the remaining two rolls. If it seems likely that you can do better by not stopping the game, then you proceed, otherwise you stop me.[4]

You must work backwards to deduce the best strategy. This is analogous to pricing an American-style option using a tree method. So, suppose that you have seen the second roll and are trying to decide whether to ask for a third. You must compare the outcome of the second roll to the distribution of possible outcomes on the third roll:

Table D.4: Distribution of Payoff to Third Roll of a Die

Maximum Payoff	$1	$2	$3	$4	$5	$6
Probability	$\frac{1}{6}$	$\frac{1}{6}$	$\frac{1}{6}$	$\frac{1}{6}$	$\frac{1}{6}$	$\frac{1}{6}$

The expected value of the distribution in Table D.4 is $3.50; the variance is $2.92; the standard deviation is $1.71. If you see a 4 or higher on the second roll, you might stop the game because you probably will not do better. If you get a 3 or lower, you might continue because you expect to do better.

Now, stepping backwards again, suppose that you have just seen the first roll. You must decide whether to ask for a second roll (which may lead to a third). You must compare the outcome of the first roll to the distribution of possible outcomes if you proceed to a second (and possibly third) roll.

If you ask for the second roll, there is one-half a chance that it yields a 1, 2, or 3, and one-half a chance that it yields a 4, 5, or 6. Using the argument above, in the first case (1, 2, or 3 on roll two) you proceed to a third roll; in the second case (4, 5, or 6 on roll 2) you do not proceed. There is thus one-half a chance that you proceed to a third roll (expected value $3.50 from

---

[4]I thank Bingjian Ni for suggesting the solution technique; any errors are mine.

Table D.4), and one-half a chance that you stop the game at roll two (expected value $\frac{\$4+\$5+\$6}{3}$). It follows that the expected value of asking for a second roll is

$$\left(\frac{1}{2} \times \$3.50\right) + \left[\frac{1}{2} \times \left(\frac{\$4 + \$5 + \$6}{3}\right)\right] = \$4.25.$$

Thus, you would ask for a second roll only if you get a 1, 2, 3, or 4 on roll one. If you have a 5 or 6 on roll one, you should stop the game.

In simple terms, then, the strategy is to stop the game at roll number one if a 5 or 6 appears (probability $\frac{1}{3}$), otherwise continue (probability $\frac{2}{3}$). If you continue, stop the game at roll number two if a 4, 5, or 6 appears, otherwise continue.

Please note that my argument involving expected payoffs assumes that you are risk-neutral; your stopping rule might use lower acceptable payoffs if you are risk-averse, or higher payoffs if you are risk-loving.[5]

The overall expected value of the game may now be calculated.

$$\text{Value} = \left(\frac{2}{3} \times \$4.25\right) + \left[\frac{1}{3} \times \left(\frac{\$5 + \$6}{2}\right)\right] = \frac{\$14}{3} \approx \$4.67.$$

If you are charging entry to repeated plays of this game, you are effectively risk-neutral.[6] You charge the expected value (\$4.67) plus a commission. You add a risk premium to the ticket price if there is only one or a few plays of the game; the more plays, the lower the risk premium. You would never charge more than six dollars because the player can never earn more than six dollars.

In the amended game (where I roll the die three times and pay you the maximum number of the three rolls), you need the distribution of the maximum payoff to three rolls of a die; this distribution is given in Table D.5.[7]

Table D.5: Distribution of Maximum Payoff in Three Rolls of a Die

Maximum Payoff	$1	$2	$3	$4	$5	$6
Probability	$\frac{1}{216}$	$\frac{7}{216}$	$\frac{19}{216}$	$\frac{37}{216}$	$\frac{61}{216}$	$\frac{91}{216}$

The mean of the distribution of the maximum payoff from three rolls of the die is $\$\frac{1071}{216} = \$4.96$; the variance is $\$\frac{61047}{46656} = \$1.31$; and the standard deviation is

---

[5]In addition, you should question my treatment of discreteness. For example, although you cannot roll a "$3\frac{1}{2}$" or a "$4\frac{1}{4}$," I use these as cutoff points when deciding whether to proceed or not.

[6]This is the "Weak Law of Large Numbers" again. See Footnote 1 (on p. 256) and DeGroot (1989, p. 229–231).

[7]Can you use elementary statistics to prove that this probability distribution is described by $\text{Prob}(Max = m) = \frac{m^3 - (m-1)^3}{216} = \frac{3m(m-1)+1}{216}$, where m is the maximum of three rolls of the die? If you cannot, you need to work on your statistics.

$1.14 (all calculated using information in Table D.5). You should, therefore, charge a ticket price of $4.96 plus some profit margin for repeated plays. Again, you cannot charge more than six dollars because no one will play the game.

The second game is more expensive than the first game ($4.96 > $4.67) because it strictly dominates it. That is, the payoff to the second game is never less than, and often exceeds, the payoff to the first game. This is because the second game *guarantees* the maximum of three rolls without risk, but the first game does not.

Answer 4.9: The correlation is still ρ. Adding a constant or multiplying by a constant has no impact on the correlation. Go back to first principals and write out correlation as the ratio of covariance to the product of standard deviations. Adding a constant to X has no effect on either the numerator or denominator. Multiplying X by five multiplies both the numerator and denominator by five.

Answer 4.10: This has been a very popular question. Assume that neither of you peek into your envelopes. Assume that you have X in your envelope, where X has a fifty-fifty chance of being either m or $2m$. This means that your opponent's envelope has a fifty-fifty chance of containing $2X$ or $\frac{1}{2}X$. The expected value of switching is

$$\left(\frac{1}{2} \times \$2X\right) + \left(\frac{1}{2} \times \$\frac{1}{2}X\right) = \$1.25X.$$

The expected *benefit* of switching is, therefore, $0.25X$. On this basis, it looks as though you should switch envelopes. Of course, if your opponent does not peek, and she has Y in her envelope, exactly the same argument shows that she has an expected benefit to switching of $0.25Y$. So, it looks as though she should switch also. This is the first part of the "Exchange Paradox": it seems that you *both* benefit from switching.

Now, suppose that neither of you peek and that you do switch envelopes once. If you still do not peek, then a repeat of exactly the same argument suggests an expected benefit of 0.25 of the contents of your envelope if you switch again. The same applies to your opponent. This is the second part of the "Exchange Paradox": it seems that you could happily switch forever (like a dog chasing its own tail). The foregoing is the naive answer.

The problem is twofold: First, you are assuming that value is expected payoff (this is so only if you are genuinely risk-neutral);[8] second, your "prior" beliefs

---

[8]An aside is in order. In corporate finance, the present value of a projected random payout is the discounted expected cash flow. The discounting is done at a rate that incorporates risk (e.g., using the CAPM), and the expectation is a mathematical one using real world probabilities (Brealey and Myers [1991]). An alternative to the real world expected cash flow coupled with the risk-adjusted discount rate is a risk-neutral world expected cash flow coupled with a riskless discount rate. The former is popular in corporate finance; the latter is popular in option pricing (see Arnold and Crack [2004] and Arnold, Crack and Schwartz [2009, 2010]). With no discounting (e.g., the envelope question), value is expected payoff only if you are risk-neutral.

are that you have a fifty-fifty chance of having either $\$m$ or $\$2m$. The first problem is a function of your individual risk preferences and is difficult to address. The second problem can be tackled using two approaches: the first approach is to reconsider the nature of your prior; the second approach is to "update" your prior probability assessment (this is "Bayesian" statistics as opposed to "classical" statistics).

The first approach is to reconsider the nature of your priors. Our previous (paradoxical) calculation yielded $\$1.25X$ as the expected payoff to switching. However, this assumes that for any given X, it is equally likely that your opponent has $\$2X$ or $\$\frac{1}{2}X$. If you do not peek, then you are assuming a "diffuse level prior" because you assume this equality of likelihood for *any* X. Your prior is, therefore, not a valid pdf because the probabilities—across X—do not sum to **1**. However, for any *particular m*, it is equally likely that you received one of $\$m$ or $\$2m$. Thus, for any particular m, your priors are a pdf and any paradoxes should disappear. The expected value of switching should be zero. This is easily demonstrated. Let $P(\$m)$ denote the probability that *you* got $\$m$ (the lower amount); let $E(V)$ denote the expected value to switching; then $E(V)$ is given by

$$
\begin{aligned}
E(V) &= [E(V|\$m) \times P(\$m)] + [E(V|\$2m) \times P(\$2m)] \\
&= \left(+\$m \times \frac{1}{2}\right) + \left(-\$m \times \frac{1}{2}\right) \\
&= \$0.
\end{aligned}
$$

The expected value is zero, and you are thus indifferent—resolving the paradox.[9] Note that $E(V|\$m) = +\$m$ because, conditional on your having been given the envelope containing only $\$m$, you gain $\$m$ by switching.

The second approach is to update your prior. To update your prior, you need information. The most obvious source of information is to peek into your envelope. So, assume that both you and your opponent peek into your envelopes. Now it gets subjective. If you see an amount that *seems* very high, then you update your prior probabilities: the probability that you have the high-value envelope increases, and the probability that you have the low-value envelope decreases. You no longer see value in switching envelopes.[10] If you see an amount that *seems* very low, then you see value in switching. The problem now is that you must subjectively assess the amount in the envelope as being either "low" or "high." The "Bayesian Resolution of the Exchange Paradox" is covered in detail in Christensen and Utts (1992).

If you have both peeked, and you do switch, then you will not switch again. This is because one of you gained, and that person will not want to lose by

---

[9]I thank Andres Almazan for suggesting this type of solution technique; any errors are mine.

[10]However, you might argue that if you see an amount that seems so high that even one-half of it is more money than you can comprehend, you might switch envelopes just for the hell of it; it is worth the gamble.

switching back. A similar question (but with an upper bound on the quantities possible) appears in Dixit and Nalebuff (1991, Chapter 13). The Dixit and Nalebuff book on strategic thinking is well worth a look.

Answer 4.11: This is a very common question and has been in use since at least 1990. Well, the first thing to notice is that you are trying to replicate a $100 bet on Team A to win the series and you are doing this via a series of small bets. At each step, there are two possible outcomes: Team A wins, or Team A loses. With replication, time steps, and binomial outcomes, the obvious thing to do is build a lattice for a replicating strategy (see Figure D.1). To deduce the betting strategy in Figure D.1, I first drew the lattice and identified the boundary nodes at which the game must end (marked with large dots). You start with $100 in wealth. In the case where Team A has won four games, you must end up with an accumulated wealth of $200 through $100 in betting profits; In the case where Team B has won four games, you must end up with an accumulated wealth of $0 through $100 in betting losses. It is simple to step back from each pair of ending nodes (starting with the right-most pair) to deduce how much you must bet in each case (working back to $31.25 on the first game) in order to end up replicating the payoffs at the boundary. If you follow this betting strategy, you are *guaranteed* to replicate the payoff to betting $100 on Team A to win the series. The given probabilities are "red herrings" because you do not need any probabilities, physical world or risk-neutral, to solve this problem. Note, finally, that I have assumed that you earn no interest on your wealth.

Answer 4.12: There are many different possible answers; I give only two. Toss the coin twice. If you get HT, give the apple to the first child. If you get TH, give the apple to the second child. If you get HH, give the apple to the third child. If you get TT, then start again. This effectively takes TT out of the sample space.

A second solution is to toss the coin three times and assign the outcomes to the three children. Let T win. If one child beats the other two (i.e., the outcome is some permutation of $\{T, H, H\}$), then give the apple to the child who was allocated the T. Otherwise, toss three more times. This is isomorphic to a tournament where each child competes against each other child until one child beats both others.

Answer 4.13: For my first answer in Answer 4.12: If you toss the coin twice and get TT, then you have to start again. There is thus a chance that you will take more than 2 tosses to complete the strategy. We can use a recursion to find the expected number of tosses. Let N be the number of tosses required, then there is a three quarter chance that N will be 2, but a one-quarter chance that you have to start again (in the TT outcome). Thus $E(N) = \left[\frac{3}{4} \cdot 2\right] + \left[\frac{1}{4} \cdot (2 + E(N))\right] = 2 + \frac{E(N)}{4}$. Simple algebra now yields $E(N) = \frac{8}{3} = 2\frac{2}{3}$.

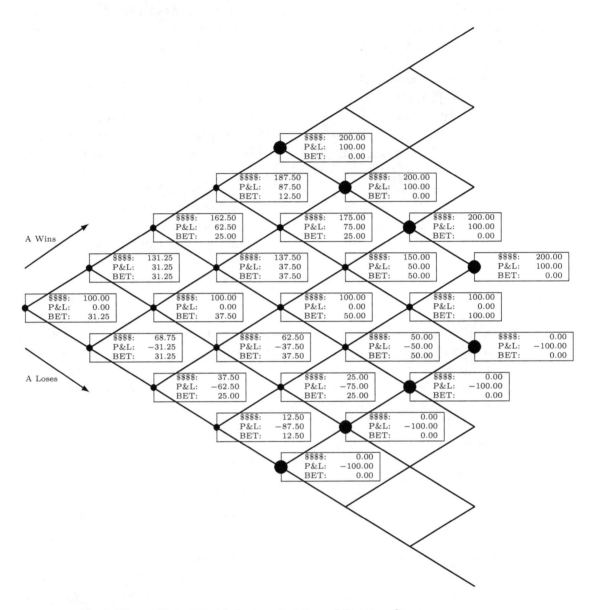

Figure D.1: World Series: Lattice of Betting Strategy

Note: See Answer 4.11 Each step has two possible outcomes for the game: Team A wins (the up step), or Team A loses (the down step). You start with $100 in wealth. Each box shows how much wealth you have ("$$$$"), your cumulative profit or loss ("P&L") and the bet you place on Team A winning ("BET"). A large dot on a node indicates the end of the series (i.e., one team has reached four wins).

Alternatively,[11] consider each double-toss as a Bernoulli trial with probability of success $p = 3/4$ (i.e., we have a success if anything but a TT occurs). Then the geometric distribution $f_X(x) = P(X = x) = p \cdot q^{x-1}$ for $x \geq 1$ counts the number of trials up to and including the first success (Spiegel, 1975; Evans et al., 1993). We have $E(X) = 1/p = 4/3$, and thus $E(N) = 2 \cdot E(X) = \frac{8}{3}$, as before.

From my second answer in Answer 4.12: We will need at least three tosses in this case, but there are five chances in eight that we will need more than three tosses. Using a recursive argument similar to that above, we figure that the expected number of tosses in this case is $E(N) = 8$.

Answer 4.14: To simulate an event with probability $1/3$ using a fair coin, toss the coin twice. If you get HH, let that be your event with probability $1/3$. If you get HT or TH, let that be your event with probability $2/3$. If you get TT, then ignore it, and toss twice again. By removing TT from the sample space, the outcomes are restricted to three equally likely possibilities.

Answer 4.15: Start with a simple case first: What if you only need the expected number of tosses required to get *one* head? Let N be the number of coin tosses, then we want to find $E(N|1H)$ (expected number of tosses given that you seek only one head). Toss the coin once. Either you get a head (with probability p) or you get a tail. If you get a tail, then you are recursively back where you started. That is, there is probability p that $N = 1$, and probability $1-p$ that you still have $E(N|1H)$ tosses to go after the one you already tossed. In other words,

$$E(N|1H) = (p \cdot 1) + (1 - p) \cdot [1 + E(N|1H)].$$

Solving for $E(N|1H)$ gives $E(N|1H) = \frac{1}{p}$. Check: the higher is p, the lower is $E(N|1H)$, and when $p = 0.50$ (a fair coin), $E(N|1H) = 2$, all of which seems reasonable.

Now consider the case of two heads in a row. Well, to get two heads in a row, you first need one head "in a row," which requires the expected $\frac{1}{p}$ tosses just calculated. If you have this one head already, then there is probability p that your next toss will be a head, and probability $(1 - p)$ that you are back where you started having performed $E(N|1H)$ plus one tosses already. In other words,

$$\begin{aligned} E(N|2H) &= p \cdot [E(N|1H) + 1] + (1 - p) \cdot [E(N|1H) + 1 + E(N|2H)] \\ &= E(N|1H) + 1 + (1 - p) \cdot E(N|2H). \end{aligned}$$

This last line implies that

$$E(N|2H) = \frac{E(N|1H) + 1}{p} = \frac{1+p}{p^2}.$$

---

[11]I thank Mark Cawston for discussions regarding this answer; any errors are mine.

In the case of a fair coin, this gives $E(N|2H) = 6$. Exactly the same reasoning in the case of three heads in a row leads us to

$$E(N|3H) = \frac{E(N|2H) + 1}{p} = \frac{1 + p + p^2}{p^3}.$$

In the case of a fair coin, this gives $E(N|3H) = 14$. It should be clear that there is a pattern: in the case of J heads in a row,

$$E(N|JH) = \frac{\sum_{i=0}^{i=J-1} p^i}{p^J}.$$

This can be proved formally using numerical induction if you wish.

Answer 4.16: When repeatedly tossing a fair coin, what is the probability that you will see the sequence HTH before you see the sequence HHT?

At first blush, you might say that with a fair coin and equally likely outcomes, and independent tosses, any of the eight possible triplets is as likely as any other, and so the answer is 50%. Although any triplet is equally likely in three tosses, it does not necessarily follow that you are equally likely to see any one triplet before another in repeated tosses. This is because one outcome can prevent another outcome.

For example, suppose we had been asked how likely it is that we will see triplet HHH before triplet THH. In this case, the only way that you will see HHH before THH, is if the first three tosses are heads, which happens with probability one eighth. If you see anything other than three heads in the first three tosses, then THH must occur before HHH. This is because each of the other seven triplets includes a T, and once you have seen a T, you only need to see the first two Hs of HHH to see THH. So, seeing a T prevents you from seeing HHH before THH.

For the case in hand, how likely are you to see HTH before HHT? Well, both triplets need an H to get started. So, we can completely ignore any outcome until we get an H. For this reason, my tree in Figure D.2 starts with an H. Now the argument is quite simple. If there is a second H (i.e., the upper branch of the first fork), then HHT must "win" (i.e., occur first) eventually. The only way that HHT would not win is if there were an infinite sequence of Hs—which happens with probability zero.

If the first H is followed by a T (i.e., the lower branch of the first fork in Figure D.2), then either the next toss is an H, and HTH wins, or the next toss is a T, and we restart the game.

Given that the lower branch of the second fork restarts the game, we can treat this outcome as if it is not in the sample space at all. This is perfectly analogous to Answer 4.12, where we tossed a coin twice to give an apple to one of three children with equal probability, but we restarted the game if TT occurred.

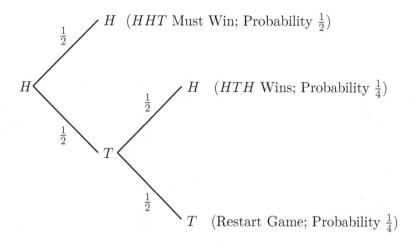

H (HHT Must Win; Probability $\frac{1}{2}$)

$\frac{1}{2}$

H

$\frac{1}{2}$

$\frac{1}{2}$

H (HTH Wins; Probability $\frac{1}{4}$)

T

$\frac{1}{2}$

T (Restart Game; Probability $\frac{1}{4}$)

Figure D.2: Coin Toss Triplets: HTH versus HHT

Note: Both HTH and HHT start with an H. A second H assures HHT of a win (because then the only way that HHT does not win is if an infinite sequence of Hs occur, which happens with probability zero). Two Ts in a row restarts the game.

So, removing the lower branch of the second fork from the sample space leaves us only with HHT being twice as likely to win as HTH. Grossing up the probabilities gives HHT a 2/3 probability of winning and HTH a 1/3 probability of winning.[12]

Answer 4.17: When tossing a fair coin, the number of tosses, N, needed to obtain the outcome HTH is a random variable. What is $E(N)$? This question differs from the previous question in two ways. First, we are counting tosses here, rather than focusing solely on probability of outcomes. So, we need to count the tosses needed to get that first H in this case. Second, there is no competition between triplets vying for their first appearance. So, no outcome prevents us from eventually getting HTH.

In Figure D.3 I have repeated the tree from Figure D.2, but I have added the earlier fork needed to get the first H. We now look at Figure D.3 and use a recursive argument twice. With N as the number of tosses needed to get HTH, we look at probabilistic outcomes on the first fork of the tree. If we toss a T first, then we have burned one toss, and we restart again with $E(N)$ additional tosses expected. So, an initial T outcome gives a half a chance that we take $[1 + E(N)]$ tosses. If, instead, we toss an initial H, then we have burned one toss, and we now need to ask what is $E(X|H)$, where $X|H$ is the count of <u>extra</u> tosses required conditional upon having obtained the initial H.

---

[12]More formally, we are rescaling the probabilities in the tree by dividing them through by $P(\neg HTT) = 3/4$. So, for example, $P(HHT|\neg HTT) = \frac{P(HHT \cap \neg HTT)}{P(\neg HTT)} = \frac{1/2}{3/4} = \frac{2}{3}$, where $\neg$ is the logical not symbol.

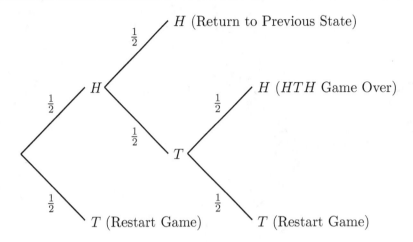

Figure D.3: Coin Toss Triplets: Tosses to get HTH

Note: HTH start with an H. An initial T restarts the game. A second H returns the game to the previous state. Getting TT restarts the game.

So, an initial H outcome gives a half a chance that we take $[1 + E(X|H)]$ tosses. Thus, we have Equation D.6

$$
\begin{aligned}
E(N) &= \frac{1}{2} \cdot [1 + E(N)] + \frac{1}{2} \cdot [1 + E(X|H)] \\
&= 1 + \frac{1}{2} \cdot E(N) + \frac{1}{2} \cdot E(X|H)
\end{aligned}
\tag{D.6}
$$

Now we must solve for $E(X|H)$. Looking at Figure D.3, we see there is a half a chance that we get a second H, and then we have burned another toss, and are back to where we were with an additional $E(X|H)$ tosses required. Multiplying probabilities down the lower branch of the second fork with the branches of the third fork, we see there is one quarter of a chance that we use two extra tosses and the game is over, and one quarter of a chance that we burn two extra tosses and are back to the start with $E(N)$ tosses left. Putting these together, we get Equation D.7.

$$
\begin{aligned}
E(X|H) &= \frac{1}{2} \cdot [1 + E(X|H)] + \left(\frac{1}{4} \cdot 2\right) + \frac{1}{4} \cdot [2 + E(N)] \\
&= 1\frac{1}{2} + \frac{1}{2} \cdot E(X|H) + \frac{1}{4} \cdot E(N) \\
\Rightarrow \frac{1}{2} \cdot E(X|H) &= 1\frac{1}{2} + \frac{1}{4} \cdot E(N) \\
\Rightarrow E(X|H) &= 3 + \frac{1}{2} \cdot E(N)
\end{aligned}
\tag{D.7}
$$

Plugging Equation D.7 into Equation D.6, yields Equation D.8.

$$
\begin{aligned}
E(N) &= 1 + \frac{1}{2} \cdot E(N) + \frac{1}{2} \cdot \left[3 + \frac{1}{2} \cdot E(N) \right] \\
&= 2\frac{1}{2} + \frac{3}{4} \cdot E(N) \\
\Rightarrow \frac{1}{4} \cdot E(N) &= 2\frac{1}{2} \\
\Rightarrow E(N) &= 10
\end{aligned}
\tag{D.8}
$$

So, on average, there are 10 tosses until we see HTH.

Answer 4.18: This is elementary statistics, and one of the easiest questions in this book. The rules of the game have effectively removed the 1 from the sample space (i.e., the collection of possible outcomes). It follows that there are five possible outcomes (2 to 6), and each is equally likely. The expected outcome is simply

$$
\frac{\sum_{i=2}^{i=6} i}{5} = \$4.
$$

To do the sum in your head, remember that the dots on the opposing faces of the die add to seven. The sum must be three times seven, less one to give 20. Now divide by five to get the expected payoff of $4.

Answer 4.19: The naive answer is that the probability is just $\frac{2}{52} \approx 4\%$. This is incorrect. There are four chances that the first card dealt to you (out of a deck of 52) is a King. Conditional on the first card being a King, there are three chances that the second card dealt to you (out of the remaining deck of 51) is a King. Conditional probability says that

$$P(\text{Both are Kings}) =$$
$$P(\text{Second is a King} \mid \text{First is a King}) \times P(\text{First is a King})$$

where " $\mid$ " is read as "conditional upon," or "given." This is a special case of the more general conditional probability result:

$$P(A \cap B) = P(A \mid B) \times P(B)$$

Thus, $P(\text{Both are Kings}) = \frac{3}{51} \times \frac{4}{52} = \frac{1}{17} \times \frac{1}{13} = \frac{1}{221} \approx 0.5\%$. Therefore, you have roughly one chance in 200 of getting exactly two Kings dealt to you.[13]

I wish you to avoid a common form of confusion. Please note that although you multiply probabilities to get the answer, and such multiplication is often done when dealing with independent events, the events here (King on first

---

[13]I thank Arta Babaee for pointing out that this answer is identical to $\binom{4}{2} / \binom{52}{2} = \frac{4!/(2!2!)}{52!/(2!50!)} = \frac{4}{52} \times \frac{3}{51}$. That is, of all possible pairs of cards you might be dealt, how many ways are there to get a pair of kings.

card, and King on second card given King on first card) are *dependent*, not independent. That is, you calculate the probability that the second card is a King given that, or *dependent upon*, the first card being a King.

I wish to emphasize that the above procedure is different from that for figuring out the probability that, for example, you get two heads in two tosses of a fair coin (this probability is $\frac{1}{2} \times \frac{1}{2} = \frac{1}{4}$). The outcomes of the coin tosses are genuinely *independent*, and this is why you can multiply their probabilities directly. That is, $P(H_1 \cap H_2) = P(H_2|H_1) \times P(H_1) = P(H_2) \times P(H_1)$ because the probability of a head on the second coin toss is not influenced by the event that you get a head on the first coin toss (i.e., the conditional probability formula still applies but it reduces to the product of probabilities if the events are independent). However, the probability that you get a King on the second card dealt *is* influenced by the event that you get a King on the first card dealt. That is why the conditional probability theory is used. Be sure you understand the distinction and how and where to apply each method. If it is not clear, go to your favorite statistics book for a review (e.g., see Feller [1968, Chapter V]).

Answer 4.20: The "Let's Make a Deal" or "Monty Hall" problem is very frequently asked. Many people find it very difficult.

Assume that you choose Door 3. The host opens Door 2 and offers you the chance to switch to Door 1. Should you do it? If you have decided that it does not matter whether you switch doors or not (indifference), or that you should definitely not switch (aversion), then you should go back and think again before reading any further. Stop here and try again.

Let me begin with very simple intuition. My experience, however, is that many readers cannot accept the simple intuition, and for them I provide a formal proof using Bayes' Theorem.

SIMPLE INTUITION

Assume for a moment that you have already decided that you will switch doors. What then is the probability that you will find the prize behind the door you switch to? Well, you win the prize if you *originally* chose one of the two doors that has nothing behind it. In that case, the host shows you the other empty door, and switching yields the prize. So, the problem reduces to figuring the probability that you originally chose one of the two doors that has nothing behind it. That unconditional probability is just two thirds by construction. You thus have probability two thirds that you win by switching and one third that you lose by switching. So, you should switch![14]

FORMAL BAYES' THEOREM PROOF

If you are to play this game repeatedly, two-thirds of the time you profit by switching, and one-third of the time you lose by switching. Let B_k denote the

---

[14]I thank Jun Chung for this simple argument; any errors are mine.

event that the prize is behind Door number k ("B" for b̲ehind). Let H_j denote the event that you see the host open Door number j ("H" for h̲ost).

The unconditional probabilities of the location of prizes (probabilities calculated without conditioning on which door the host opens) are simply $P(B_1) = P(B_2) = P(B_3) = \frac{1}{3}$. What you need to know is the conditional probability $P(B_1|H_2)$. That is, the probability that the prize is behind Door 1 given that you see (or "conditional on") the host open Door 2. We use a straightforward application of conditional expectations and Bayes' Theorem (see Feller [1968, Chapter V]), as follows:

$$P(B_1|H_2) = \frac{P(B_1 \cap H_2)}{P(H_2)} = \frac{P(H_2 \cap B_1)}{P(H_2)} = \frac{P(H_2|B_1) \times P(B_1)}{P(H_2)}$$

You know that $P(B_1) = \frac{1}{3}$, but what about $P(H_2|B_1)$ and $P(H_2)$? You know that the host is going to show you an empty door other than the door you choose (assume through all of this that it is Door 3 that you choose). The host's door must be revealed empty and cannot be the same door that you choose. Therefore, it must be that if you choose Door 3, then $P(H_2|B_1) = 1$.

Now, $P(H_2)$ is given by

$$\begin{aligned} P(H_2) &= [P(H_2|B_1) \times P(B_1)] + [P(H_2|B_2) \times P(B_2)] \\ &+ [P(H_2|B_3) \times P(B_3)], \end{aligned}$$

so some extra terms need to be calculated to get $P(H_2)$.

Well, the host's door must be shown to be empty, so it must be that $P(H_2|B_2) = 0$. The host is impartial, so it must be that $P(H_2|B_3) = \frac{1}{2}$ [and $P(H_1|B_3) = \frac{1}{2}$]. Thus, $P(H_2)$ is given by

$$\begin{aligned} P(H_2) &= [P(H_2|B_1) \times P(B_1)] + [P(H_2|B_2) \times P(B_2)] \\ &+ [P(H_2|B_3) \times P(B_3)] \\ &= \left(1 \times \frac{1}{3}\right) + \left(0 \times \frac{1}{3}\right) + \left(\frac{1}{2} \times \frac{1}{3}\right) = \frac{1}{2}. \end{aligned}$$

It follows that the probability of finding the prize if you switch doors is two-thirds:

$$P(B_1|H_2) = \frac{P(H_2|B_1) \times P(B_1)}{P(H_2)} = \frac{1 \times \frac{1}{3}}{\frac{1}{2}} = \frac{2}{3}$$

The summary in Table D.6 may clarify matters further. You choose Door 3. The host must choose an empty door to open. If the prize is behind Door 1, he *must* open Door 2 [$P(H_2|B_1) = 1$]. However, if the prize is behind Door 3, he can *choose* between Doors 1 and 2 [$P(H_2|B_3) = \frac{1}{2}$]. If you see Door 2, it is either because the prize is behind Door 1, and the host had no choice, or it is because the prize is behind Door 3, and the host randomly chose between Doors 1 and 2. It, therefore, follows that if you choose Door 3, and Door 2 is

Table D.6: The Monty Hall Problem

Assume You Choose Door 3			
Prize Location B_j	Host Opens H_i	Unconditional Probability $P(H_i \cap B_j)$	Conditional Probability $P(H_i|B_j)$
1	2	$\frac{1}{3}$	1
2	1	$\frac{1}{3}$	1
3	1	$\frac{1}{6}$	$\frac{1}{2}$
	2	$\frac{1}{6}$	$\frac{1}{2}$

revealed empty by the host, the prize is twice as likely to be behind Door 1 as it is to be behind Door 3. Continuing along this line of thought, we may take a frequentist approach. Suppose you play the game repeatedly and always choose Door 3. If you look at all the times the host reveals Door 2 empty, you will find that two-thirds of the time the prize lies behind Door 1, and one-third of the time it is behind Door 3. Seeing Door 2 empty is thus a stronger signal that Door 1 has the prize than it is that Door 3 has it. This argument is more general, of course. Whichever door you choose, seeing the host reveal an empty door is a signal that you should switch.

Answer 4.21: There are two interpretations. If we assume that the game can be played repeatedly with an audience member always revealing a door to be empty, then we must also assume that the audience member knows the location of the prize. Otherwise, how can he or she always reveal an empty door in repeated play? In this case, if we make the same uniformly random assumptions about prize placement and empty doors revealed as in the previous question, then the audience member is, in effect, wearing the host's hat, and the argument is the same as in the previous question: You should always switch.

Suppose instead that the host of this week's show has, just for a one-off special occasion (his 60th birthday, say), decided to let an audience member (who is ignorant of the prize's location) reveal another door. Suppose it just happens to turn out to be empty. We cannot now talk about a frequentist approach and repeated plays of the game because in repeated plays, the audience member would reveal the prize one third of the time, and that is not the situation we find ourselves in. The ignorant audience member has, on this occasion, just happened to show us an empty door. The audience member has blindly removed one door from the sample space, and we have a 50/50 chance of winning (and also of losing) if we switch. We are therefore indifferent.

Answer 4.22: This question is solved most efficiently by trying a few possible combinations, not by some time-consuming feat of constrained linear optimization. You should begin with extreme distributions, or with symmetrical distributions. It is in the extremes or in symmetry that solutions to such problems usually lie.

The probability of selecting a white marble is maximized (at almost $\frac{3}{4}$) by placing one white marble in one jar and the remaining 99 marbles in the other. The probability of selecting a white marble is minimized (at $\frac{1}{4}$) by placing all 100 marbles in one jar (assuming you do not get a second chance if the jar you choose is empty). If zero marbles in one jar is not an acceptable answer to you, then you minimize the probability of a white marble (at just over $\frac{1}{4}$) by maximizing the probability of a black one. That is, put one black marble in one jar and the remaining 99 marbles in the other.

Answer 4.23: This is a tough "game theory" problem. Early editions of my book included a full and formal solution to this problem. It was more than five pages long and far too detailed. I have now cut my answer down to bare bones key issues only.[15]

Mr. 30 and Mr. 60 are going to shoot at each other because they do not see you as an immediate threat; you do not die first because Mr. 60 and Mr. 30 are shooting it out; you do not want to be put into a shoot-out where your opponent is a very good shot and gets to shoot first; if Mr. 30 gets to shoot before Mr. 60, it is less likely that you end up facing Mr. 60 than if Mr. 60 gets to shoot first, so you shoot in the air; if the direction of play is reversed, and Mr. 60 gets to shoot before Mr. 30, then you should help out Mr. 30 (and yourself) by shooting at Mr. 60 also, otherwise, leave it to Mr. 30; the cost of stepping in and shooting at Mr. 60 is that if you hit Mr. 60, you lose your chance to shoot first in the final shootout with Mr. 30; the benefit of stepping in and shooting at Mr. 60 is that you increase the likelihood of your facing Mr. 30 rather than Mr. 60 in the final shoot-out; there is a delicate balance between leaving it to Mr. 30 and stepping in to help him out, and it changes with the direction of play. Finally, there is a slim chance that everyone shoots at the sky, but this requires some sort of cooperation.

Answer 4.24: If you take the three-point shot, you have a 40% chance of winning. If you take the two-point shot, you have a 70% chance of a tie, and conditional on a tie you have a 50% chance of winning in overtime. Informally, the probability of winning if you take the two-point shot is thus 70% multiplied by 50%, which is 35%. This is lower than for the 40% for the three-point shot, so you should take the three-pointer.

More formally, let "W" denote <u>w</u>inning, let "2" denote taking the two-point shot, let "T" denote sinking the two-pointer and getting a <u>t</u>ie, and let "T^C"

---

[15]I thank Olivier Ledoit for this solution technique; any errors are mine.

denote missing the two-pointer and not getting the tie (the "C" is for complement, that is, the remainder of the sample space). Then

$$
\begin{aligned}
P(W|2) &= P(W|T)P(T|2) + P\left(W|T^C\right)P\left(T^C|2\right) \\
&= (0.50 \times 0.70) + (0 \times 0.30) \\
&= 0.35.
\end{aligned}
$$

Answer 4.25: This is one of the easier problems. If the cost is \$1.50 per spin, and
you may play as often as you want, then yes, you should play. The expected
payoff is \$1.80 per spin ($\sum_{i=1}^{i=5} \text{Payoff}_i \times \frac{1}{5} = \$1.80$). If you can play as often as
you want, you are risk-neutral (in the long run, your average payoff will equal
the expected payoff), and you expect to make \$0.30 per spin on average.

If you get only one spin, then whether you play or not depends upon whether
the expected \$0.30 gain is sufficient to compensate you for the risk of losing
\$0.50 (the \$1.50 cost less the \$1.00 worst possible payoff). With amounts
this small, you would probably take the bet. It is like spending \$1.50 on a
lottery ticket—it is too small to care about. If the numbers were larger, say
everything multiplied by one billion, and if your job is lost if you lose, then
you are significantly more risk-averse, and your boss would not want you to
take the bet.

Answer 4.26: Assuming no special information on your part, each sports match
presents a fifty-fifty chance of winning. Assuming each match is independent
of each other, then winning is analogous to tossing a fair coin four times in
a row and trying to get four heads. This probability is only $\left(\frac{1}{2}\right)^4 = \frac{1}{16}$. The
odds of winning are thus much worse than the odds offered by the bookie, and
you should not play unless you are a risk-seeker. If the odds were raised to
25-to-1, this would be an attractive bet.

Answer 4.27: This is a simple question, but, strictly speaking, it is not well
posed. You cannot ask for "the standard deviation of $(1, 2, 3, 4, 5)$" without
supplying further information. You should ask the interviewer which of the
following cases he or she means. The first solution assumes we have drawn a
sample and we are *estimating* the population parameter. The second solution
assumes we are dealing with the full sample space and we are *calculating* the
true population parameter.

FIRST SOLUTION
Perhaps the interviewer wants the standard deviation of these numbers assuming they are a sample drawn from some data generating process. In that case,
we need to know whether they are sampled independently of each other and
whether the process is stable. If not, the answer can be quite difficult. So, let
us assume that the observations are independent and identically distributed.
We can find the sample standard deviation with and without a small sample
adjustment.

The sample standard deviation without adjustment is just the square root of the average of the sum of squared deviations from the mean. The mean is 3. So, we get $\hat{\sigma} = \sqrt{\frac{1}{5}\sum_{i=1}^{i=5}(i-3)^2} = \sqrt{\frac{10}{5}} = \sqrt{2} \approx 1.4142$. I expect you to know $\sqrt{2}$ to four decimal places.

If we use the small sample adjustment,[16] where we divide by $N-1$, we instead get $\hat{\sigma} = \sqrt{\frac{10}{4}} = \sqrt{2.5}$.

SECOND SOLUTION

Perhaps the interviewer wants us to assume that $(1,2,3,4,5)$ is the full sample space of possible outcomes for a random variable, and that each is equally likely. That is, a uniform discrete distribution from 1 to 5. In that case, the standard deviation is just the square root of the expected squared deviation from the mean, with the outcomes weighted by true probabilities.

The mean of $(1, 2, 3, 4, 5)$ is 3. The squared deviations are 4, 1, 0, 1, 4, each with probability $\frac{1}{5}$. The expected squared deviation is 2. The standard deviation is thus $\sqrt{2} \approx 1.4142$.

Answer 4.28:   Given that no shot was fired on the first pull of the trigger, there are four possible states of the world corresponding to where the firing pin struck most recently (as indicted in Figure D.4). If I do not spin the cylin-

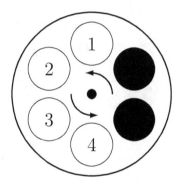

Figure D.4: Russian Roulette: Revolver Cylinder

Note: The revolver cylinder is shown with two contiguous rounds and four empty chambers. A direction of spin is indicated; it differs for different revolver models, but does not change the conclusion.

der, only the first possible state of the world has fatal implications for you (i.e., there is only one chance in four of not having to discuss your CV). If I spin the cylinder before I pull the trigger again, however, then both live rounds

---

[16]Note that Bessel's correction (i.e., to divide by $N-1$ instead of N) gives us an unbiased variance estimator, $E(\hat{\sigma}^2) = \sigma^2$, when the sample is independent and identically distributed. Note, however, that the standard deviation estimator is still biased (see further discussion in Crack [2020b]).

are in play, and the odds of you being killed increase to one in three. So, you do not want me to spin it.

Another way to look at this is that on the first pull of the trigger, the firing pin did not strike the *first* of the two contiguous rounds. Assuming no spin of the cylinder, then on the second pull of the trigger, the firing pin will not strike the *second* of the two contiguous rounds. After a spin the cylinder, however, *both* rounds are in play, yielding a higher probability of death for you.

Answer 4.29: Before we look at the formal math, let's use some informal intuition. There is one chance in a thousand (unconditionally) that you plucked the two-headed coin (which would certainly explain 10 heads in a row). There is also about one chance in a thousand that a fair coin would give 10 heads in a row (because $\left(\frac{1}{2}\right)^{10} = \frac{1}{1024} \approx \frac{1}{1000}$). Looking at the event (10 heads), I'd have to say that the coin is roughly equally likely to be two-headed or fair.

Now turn to the formal math – a direct application of Bayes' Theorem. Let "TH" denote the event that your coin is the two-headed one. Let "$10H$" denote the event that you toss one of the pennies and get 10 heads. Let X^c denote the complement of an event X. Then

$$
\begin{aligned}
P(TH|10H) &= \frac{P(TH \cap 10H)}{P(10H)} \\
&= \frac{P(10H|TH)P(TH)}{P(10H|TH)P(TH) + P(10H|TH^c)P(TH^c)} \\
&= \frac{1 \times \frac{1}{1000}}{\left[1 \times \frac{1}{1000}\right] + \left[\left(\frac{1}{2}\right)^{10} \times \frac{999}{1000}\right]} \approx \frac{1}{2},
\end{aligned}
$$

where I used the facts that $2^{10} = 1024 \approx 1000$, and $\frac{999}{1000} \approx 1$. So, given the 10 heads, you have about a half a chance that you have the two-headed coin—as per our intuition.

Answer 4.30: You win with probability 1/3. Wind is effectively absent from the sample space—it does not affect your chances of winning or losing. You lose with probability 1/3 at the first turn. You thus have only a 2/3 possibility of even getting to turn a second card. If you do get to turn the second card, there is 50% chance that it will be Fire and you lose, and a 50% chance it will not be, and you win. Thus the probability of winning is 50% of 2/3.

Alternatively,[17] of the three cards that matter, you win if Fire is the last card selected. The probability that one card out of n is the last selected in a random sequence is $1/n$, which is 1/3 in this case.

Answer 4.31: Assuming that the players have fifty-fifty probabilities of playing

---

[17]I thank Mark Cawston for discussions regarding this answer; any errors are mine.

Red or Blue,[18] each player has the same expected payoff: $1. Player B has a variance of payoffs given by

$$\left[(0-1)^2 \times \frac{1}{2}\right] + \left[(2-1)^2 \times \frac{1}{2}\right] = 1,$$

whereas player A has a variance of payoffs given by

$$\left[(1-1)^2 \times \frac{1}{4}\right] + \left[(3-1)^2 \times \frac{1}{4}\right] + \left[(0-1)^2 \times \frac{1}{2}\right] = 1.5.$$

Thus, if you are risk averse, player B's position is favored (it offers the same expected return, but less risk).

Answer 4.32: We seek $F_{P|H}(p) = P(\tilde{P} \le p|H) = P(A|H)$, where "$A$" denotes the event that $\tilde{P} \le p$, and "H" denotes the event that you get a head.[19] I put a tilde over the P to emphasize that we are talking about the probability of a probability. That is, the probability, $\tilde{P}$, that we get a head is itself a random variable; we are unsure of its value. So, there is a distribution of possible values of p, and each corresponds to a particular possible degree of bias in a coin. The probability of a probability is a "second-order probability" (Peijnenburg and Atkinson, 2013).

We may apply Bayes' Theorem, but we need to be mindful that when we write "$P(H)$" for example, this is not just the unconditional probability that we get a head, which is the random variable $\tilde{P}$, but rather in our case it is to be understood as the (unconditional) probability-weighted average probability over all possible values of p. That is, we are unwinding (or "regressing") one level of probability, by exploiting the unconditional distribution and Bayes' Theorem.

Let $f_P(p) \equiv 1$, $0 \le p \le 1$ denote the unconditional pdf of $\tilde{P}$. We apply Bayes' Theorem directly for $p \in [0, 1]$ to get

$$\begin{aligned} F_{P|H}(p) &= P(A|H) \\ &= \frac{P(A \cap H)}{P(H)} \\ &= \frac{\int_{p'=0}^{p'=p} p' f_P(p') dp'}{\int_{p'=0}^{p'=1} p' f_P(p') dp'} \\ &= \frac{(p^2/2)}{(1/2)} = p^2. \end{aligned}$$

---

[18]Recall that for a solution to be a Nash equilibrium, it has to be the case that no unilateral change in strategy for any single player is profitable to that player. A mixed strategy (Nash) equilibrium exists where B plays Red with probability $\frac{1}{4}$ and A plays Red with probability $\frac{1}{2}$. In this case, the expected payoff to playing Red equals the expected payoff to playing Blue for each player. A's expected payoff is $\frac{3}{4}$, whereas B's is 1. Thus, B is favored. I thank Alex Butler for this argument; any errors are mine. If instead the winnings come out of the other player's pocket, can you show that a Nash equilibrium exists where each player plays Red with probability 3/8?

[19]I thank Avishalom Shalit and Alex Vigodner for discussions regarding this answer; any errors are mine.

As $p \to 1$, $F_{P|H}(p) \to 1$, and as $p \to 0$, $F_{P|H}(p) \to 0$ (just checking). This cdf produces the pdf $f_{P|H}(p) = 2p$. This pdf is left-skewed and has a mean of $2/3$—slightly above $1/2$ as you might have expected.

Let "$750H/1000$" denote the event that you flip the coin 1,000 times and get 750 heads. In this case, with N so large, intuitively, the (conditional) distribution function is going to look much like the step function[20]

$$F_{(P|750H/1000)}(p) \approx \begin{cases} 0, & 0 \le p < 0.75, \\ 1, & 0.75 \le p \le 1. \end{cases}$$

Although $N = 1,000$ is large, it is not extraordinarily large. So, how close to a step function will $F_{(P|750H/1000)}(p)$ be? Using the same logic as the previous case, we get

$$F_{(P|750H/1000)}(p) = \left. \frac{\int_{p'=0}^{p'=p} f_{B(N,p')}(x) f_P(p') dp'}{\int_{p'=0}^{p'=1} f_{B(N,p')}(x) f_P(p') dp'} \right|_{x=750}, \qquad (D.9)$$

where $f_{B(N,p)}(x) = \binom{N}{x} p^x (1-p)^{N-x}$ is the binomial probability that we get x heads in N tosses, and $f_P(p)$ is the uniform density on $[0, 1]$.

Both the numerator and denominator in Equation D.9 are uniform-probability-weighted averages (over p) of the binomial probability that we get 750 heads (for a given p). The binomial expressions are not easily to work with, or to have intuition for. With large N, however, and assuming p is not too close to 0 or 1, we may approximate the binomial distribution with the normal distribution. So, we may replace $f_{B(N,p)}(x)$ with $f_{N(\mu,\sigma)}(x) = \frac{1}{\sqrt{2\pi\sigma^2}} e^{-\frac{1}{2}\left(\frac{x-\mu}{\sigma}\right)^2}$ where $\mu(p) = Np$ and $\sigma(p) = \sqrt{Np(1-p)}$. This yields Equation D.10.

$$F_{(P|750H/1000)}(p) \approx \left. \frac{\int_{p'=0}^{p'=p} f_{N(\mu(p'),\sigma(p'))}(x) f_P(p') dp'}{\int_{p'=0}^{p'=1} f_{N(\mu(p'),\sigma(p'))}(x) f_P(p') dp'} \right|_{x=750} \qquad (D.10)$$

Equation D.10 is still too messy to evaluate, but the integrand in the numerator is the normal pdf $f_{N(\mu(p),\sigma(p))}(x)$, and we know that 99% of the probability mass of a normal distribution is within roughly plus or minus 2.58 standard deviations of the mean.

Suppose for a moment that p is fixed at $p = 0.75$ and that it is x that we are going to vary in the numerator of Equation D.10 (in fact, the opposite is true). With $N = 1,000$, $\mu(p) = Np = 750$ and $\sigma(p) = \sqrt{Np(1-p)} = \sqrt{1000 \cdot 0.75 \cdot 0.25} = \sqrt{187.5} \approx 13.7$. So, the values of $f_{N(\mu(p),\sigma(p))}(x)$ that matter would be bounded by roughly 750 ± 35. If we squint, we get the normal pdf taking significant values for $715 \le x \le 785$, say. Now, in fact, it is $x = 750$ that is fixed, and the integral in Equation D.10 is over p, not x.

---

[20]This conclusion relies upon a Weak Law of Large Numbers argument (see Footnote 1 [on p. 256], and DeGroot [1989, p. 229–231]).

Even so, for large N, varying p with fixed x, and asking how far Np is from x is almost the same as varying x with fixed p, and asking how far x is from Np (and the variation in $\sigma(p)$ is not enough to make much of a difference).

We conclude, therefore, that the conditional cdf of $\tilde{P}$ looks much like a step function, but instead of a sudden step up at $p = 0.75$, there is a sloped step from something like $p = 0.715$ to something like $p = 0.785$. The larger is N (assuming $x = 0.75N$), the steeper would be the step.[21]

Answer 4.33: This is well known. More generally, if $X \sim N(\mu, \sigma^2)$, then $E(e^X) = e^{\mu + \frac{1}{2}\sigma^2}$. If X is normal, then e^X is lognormal. So, this is the sort of knowledge that arises in analytical Black-Scholes derivatives work, or in setting up a Monte-Carlo simulation of price paths in a Black-Scholes world. See Crack (2021, Section 2.2) for detailed discussion and examples. It is straightforward to prove this from first principles because the normal pdf has an $e^{(\cdot)}$ kernel in it, and you just have to add the exponents, complete the square, and integrate out to see what is left over.

Answer 4.34: Both games have the same expected payoff: \$3.5 million. However, the second game has much less volatility than the first. The Weak Law of Large Numbers says that your actual payoff will be much closer to the expected payoff in Game Two. As a risk-averse individual, you choose Game Two.

Answer 4.35: The short answer is that it will be roughly $\pm\frac{1}{\sqrt{1,000}}$ which is roughly $\pm\frac{1}{\sqrt{900}}$ which is $\pm\frac{1}{30}$ which is roughly $\pm 3\%$.

The long answer is still quite simple. Suppose you sample N people and record a 1 if they say they will vote for Candidate A and a 0 otherwise. You have N binomial trials. Let X_i denote the outcome of the ith trial, then

$$X_i = \begin{cases} 1, & \text{with probability } p, \\ 0, & \text{with probability } (1-p). \end{cases}$$

Let $Y = \sum_{i=1}^{i=N} X_i$, then Y/N is the estimator of p. It follows that

$$E(Y/N) = E(Y)/N = \sum_{i=1}^{i=N} E(X_i)/N = N \cdot p/N = p,$$

and letting "$V(\cdot)$" denote variance, we have

$$V(Y/N) = V(Y)/(N^2) \overset{*}{=} \sum_{i=1}^{i=N} V(X_i)/(N^2) \overset{**}{=} N \cdot p(1-p)/N^2 = \frac{p(1-p)}{N},$$

---

[21]Numerical evaluation of Equation D.10 shows that $F_{(P|750H/1000)}(0.715) \approx 0.0075$ and that $F_{(P|750H/1000)}(0.785) \approx 0.9967$. For $N = 100,000$ (and $x = 75,000$), the same values are achieved at $p = 0.7466$ and $p = 0.7536$. These results are consistent with the Weak Law of Large Numbers intuition that for very large N, the sample mean converges to the population mean.

where " * " follows because the variance of the sum equals the sum of the variance when the random variables are independent, and " ** " follows directly from the definition of X_i using the definition of variance as probability-weighted deviation about the mean: $V(X_i) = (1-p)^2 \cdot p + p^2 \cdot (1-p) = p(1-p)$. it follows that the standard error of Y/N is the square root of its variance: $\mathrm{SE}(Y/N) = \sqrt{\frac{p(1-p)}{N}}$.

In the particular case of the question we have $\hat{p} = 0.60$, so our best guess for the standard error is $\sqrt{\frac{\hat{p}(1-\hat{p})}{N}} = \sqrt{\frac{0.60 \cdot 0.40}{1000}} = 0.01549$. So, a 95% confidence interval would be

$$\hat{p} \pm 1.96 \cdot \sqrt{\frac{\hat{p}(1-\hat{p})}{N}} = 0.60 \pm 1.96 \cdot 0.01549 = 0.60 \pm 0.0304.$$

That is, the margin of error is roughly plus/minus 3%, which is what I said two-dozen lines above! So, how did I know that before working out the details? The key lies in two approximations. First, the 95% confidence interval for $\hat{p}$ is $\hat{p} \pm 1.96$ times the standard error, so let us just take that as ± 2.00 times the standard error. Now, the standard error itself is $\sqrt{\frac{p(1-p)}{N}}$, but for most cases of interest, p is roughly 0.50 (otherwise it would not be much of a horse race). So, $p(1-p)$ is roughly 0.25. In fact, $p(1-p)$ is an inverted parabola in p and it has slope zero at $p = 0.50$. So, there is a range about $p = 0.50$ where approximating $p(1-p)$ by 0.25 is good. For example, with $\hat{p} = 0.60$ we get $\hat{p}(1-\hat{p}) = 0.24$ which is very close.

So, we get a confidence interval which is

$$\hat{p} \pm (\text{roughly } 2) \times \sqrt{\frac{\text{roughly } 0.25}{N}},$$

but $\sqrt{0.25} = 0.50$, and 2 times this gives 1. So, we get a 95% confidence interval which is roughly

$$\hat{p} \pm \sqrt{\frac{1}{N}}.$$

This is a good approximation unless $\hat{p}$ is quite far from 0.50.

It is good if you can calculate approximate square roots of powers of 10 in your head: $\sqrt{1,000} \approx 30$, $\sqrt{10,000} = 100$, $\sqrt{100,000} \approx 300$, and so on. ...and you need to be able to invert them too (e.g., $1/30 \approx 0.03$).

Answer 4.36:   This is an old/common interview question. It is a direct application of Bayes' Theorem. Question 4.29 was also a Bayes' Theorem question. In that case we tried some informal intuition before doing the math; let us try that here too.

Most people do not have the disease. If we were to randomly select from the disease-free population (which is 99.5% of the sample here, so that is not too far from what we are actually doing), we would get a positive test result 7% of the time. If we are randomly selecting from the *entire* population, we get a diseased person 0.5% of the time. So, overall it seems that for roughly 7.5% of the draws, we get a positive, but for only 0.5% of the draws would they have the disease. Given a positive test result, we focus only on the roughly 7.5% of the population that returns a positive. With this restriction, the likelihood of the person having the disease is the ratio of those with the disease to those with a positive: roughly 0.005/0.075. This ratio is just 2/3 with the decimal place moved, so our guess is 6.67%.

Now let us do the math. Let "+" denote a positive on the test. Let "D" denote the presence of the disease, and let "D^c" denote the complement of being diseased (i.e., no disease). Then from Bayes' Theorem

$$
\begin{aligned}
P(D|+) &= \frac{P(D \cap +)}{P(+)} \\
&= \frac{P(+|D)P(D)}{P(+|D)P(D) + P(+|D^c)P(D^c)} \\
&= \frac{(1 \times 0.005)}{(1 \times 0.005) + (0.07 \times 0.995)} \\
&\approx \frac{0.005}{0.07465} \\
&\approx 0.06698.
\end{aligned}
$$

So, our 6.67% estimate is not far off.

If the percentage with the disease were only 0.05%, then the answer would drop to 0.007096% (which is almost exactly the ratio of $P(D)$ to $[P(+|D^c)+P(D)]$—the dominant terms in the above calculations).

Answer 4.37: A "stars and bars" approach is the easiest.[22] Let each star denote a thousand-dollar investment and each bar denote a line of demarcation between funds. Then ★★★★★|★★★★★★★★||★★★★★★★| has 20 stars and four bars to indicate an allocation of ($5,000;$8,000;$0;$7,000;$0).

There are $\binom{24}{4} = \frac{24!}{4!(24-4)!} = \frac{24 \cdot 23 \cdot 22 \cdot 21}{4 \cdot 3 \cdot 2 \cdot 1} = 10,626$ ways to allocate the four bars to the 24 possible locations for the 24 symbols I used. The general answer is $\binom{N+k-1}{k-1}$ for N-thousand dollars invested into k funds. Please confirm that in the case $N = 20, k = 2$ this formula gives the simple answer $N + 1 = 21$.

A less elegant approach is to consider 20 independent generalized Bernoulli trials where we roll a five-sided die and record each result as a five-tuple with a 1 in the position corresponding to the die's outcome and zeroes otherwise. The five-tuple containing the cumulative total count of outcomes is distributed multinomial (DeGroot [1989, p. 297]). The number of possible fungible (i.e., financially indistinguishable) allocations of bills to buckets must be the same as

---

[22]I thank Chun Han for suggesting this approach to me; any errors are mine.

the size of the sample space in this generalized experiment. For a multinomial with N generalized Bernoulli trials (each of k outcomes) the sample space is of size $\binom{N+k-1}{k-1}$, as above.[23]

Story: I spoke with a gay employee at a big-name Wall Street investment bank. I told him that some of my students were about to fly out to New York to interview. He told me: "Make sure they have nice suits, good hair-cuts, and wear their wedding rings."

Answer 4.38: The nature of the problem allows us to practice many different skills: statistical inference, probability, combinatorics, recursion, induction, algebraic approximations, etc.

This question is a particular case of a more general question: How many chips, N, should go randomly into some cookie dough to give a probability of at least p that each of k cookies randomly cut from the batch contains at least m chips? The interviewer's particular case uses the high probability $p = 0.90$ and the low hurdle $m = 1$ chips per cookie.

Well, if you have fewer than 100 chips, then at least one cookie does not have a chip, so 100 is the lower bound on any feasible answer. You should take an initial gut instinct guess before any formal analysis. My gut instinct is that something like $N = 500$ chips is enough because I would then be fairly sure that each cookie in the batch gets a chip. Is 500 enough? We will look at two exact solutions and several approximations to find out.

EXACT SOLUTIONS

#1: Inclusion-Exclusion.[24] If p is the probability that every cookie has at least $m = 1$ chips, then $1 - p$ is the probability of the event that some cookie has no chips. This event in turn is a union of events involving individual cookies having no chips. Let A_i^0 be the event that cookie i has no chips, then the inclusion-exclusion formula (see discussion on p. 95) yields

$$
\begin{aligned}
1 - p &= P\left(A_1^0 \cup A_2^0 \cup \cdots \cup A_k^0\right) \\
&= P\left(\bigcup_{i=1}^{k} A_i^0\right) \\
&= \sum_{i=1}^{k} P\left(A_i^0\right) - \sum_{1 \le i < j \le k} P\left(A_i^0 \cap A_j^0\right) + \\
&\quad \sum_{1 \le i < j < l \le k} P\left(A_i^0 \cap A_j^0 \cap A_l^0\right) - \cdots + (-1)^{k+1} P\left(A_1^0 \cap A_2^0 \cap \cdots \cap A_k^0\right) \\
&= \sum_{i=1}^{k} (-1)^{i+1} \sum_{\substack{\{j_1, j_2, \ldots, j_i\} \subseteq \{1,2,\ldots,k\} \\ j_1 < j_2 < \cdots < j_i}} P\left(\bigcap_{j \in \{j_1, j_2, \ldots, j_i\}} A_j^0\right).
\end{aligned}
$$

---

[23]Lyons and Hutcheson (1996).
[24]I thank Nate Coehlo for suggesting this approach; any errors are mine.

The ith term from this summation is a signed summation over probabilities of the form

$$P\left(\bigcap_{j\in\{j_1,j_2,\dots,j_i\}} A_j^0 \right) = P\left(A_{j_1}^0 \cap A_{j_2}^0 \cap \cdots \cap A_{j_i}^0 \right).$$

There are $\binom{k}{i}$ such probabilities that satisfy $\{j_1, j_2, \dots, j_i\} \subseteq \{1, 2, \dots, k\}$ and $j_1 < j_2 < \cdots < j_i$ (i.e., i numbers chosen without regard to order from k numbers) and, by symmetry, each such probability is identical. So, we just need to figure out the probability of getting a particular sub-batch of i chip-less cookies, $\{j_1, j_2, \dots, j_i\}$, in the batch of k cookies. For any given chip arriving in the dough, there is a probability $\frac{i}{k}$ that the chip lands in this sub-batch and a probability $\frac{k-i}{k}$ that the chip misses this sub-batch. The N chips arrive independently, so there is probability $\left(\frac{k-i}{k} \right)^N$ that this sub-batch of i cookies ends up chip-less. Plugging these results back into the above gives

$$
\begin{aligned}
1 - p &= \sum_{i=1}^{k} (-1)^{i+1} \sum_{\substack{\{j_1,j_2,\dots,j_i\}\subseteq\{1,2,\dots,k\} \\ j_1<j_2<\cdots<j_i}} P\left(\bigcap_{j\in\{j_1,j_2,\dots,j_i\}} A_j^0 \right) \\
&= \sum_{i=1}^{k} (-1)^{i+1} \binom{k}{i} \left(\frac{k-i}{k} \right)^N, \text{ for } N \geq k. \quad\quad (D.11)
\end{aligned}
$$

Note that the final, k^{th}, term in the summation is identically zero because the cookies cannot all be chip-less. If we plug $p = 0.90$ and $k = 100$ into Equation D.11 and solve for N, we need a computer to find $N = 682.52$. So, $N = 683$ chips will do the job. Do not worry about needing a computer to solve this; Your interviewer will either have stopped you before you got to this point or will have given you a computer.

I am now able to use Equation D.11 to find that my gut instinct guess of $N = 500$ chips gives a probability of only $p = 51.2\%$ that I will get at least $m = 1$ chip in each of $k = 100$ cookies. At the other extreme, it would have taken $N = 916$ chips to obtain $p = 99\%$.

#2: Recursion.[25] An exact solution can also be found using a recursion approach. Let $B_{k,N}$ count the number of ways that we can put N chips into k cookies. There are k choices for the first chip, k choices for the second chip, etc. So, $B_{k,N} = k^N$. Let $C_{k,N}$ count the number of ways that we can put N chips into k cookies where every cookie gets at least one chip (call this outcome a "success"). Well, as mentioned above, $C_{k,N} = 0$ if $N < k$. We must also have $C_{1,N} = 1$ for all $N \geq 1$ (there is only one way to place N chips into one cookie). We can get a recursion going as follows: In order to get a success when placing the Nth chip, it must be either that the previous $N - 1$ chips already distributed a chip to each cookie (success already!) and the Nth chip can go into any of the k cookies, or the previous $N - 1$ chips distributed a chip

---

[25]I thank Torsten Schöneborn for suggesting this approach; any errors are mine.

to $k-1$ of the cookies and the Nth chip will go into the empty cookie; there are k ways that the latter event could take place. This produces the following recursion formula:

$$
\begin{aligned}
C_{k,N} &= k \cdot C_{k,N-1} + k \cdot C_{k-1,N-1} \\
&= k \cdot [C_{k,N-1} + C_{k-1,N-1}]
\end{aligned}
$$

If we let $P_{k,N}$ be the probability that we get a success (i.e., at least one chip per cookie) from N chips placed into k cookies, then

$$
\begin{aligned}
P_{k,N} &= \frac{C_{k,N}}{B_{k,N}} \\
&= \frac{k \cdot [C_{k,N-1} + C_{k-1,N-1}]}{k^N} \\
&= P_{k,N-1} + P_{k-1,N-1} \cdot \left(\frac{k-1}{k}\right)^{N-1} , \qquad (D.12)
\end{aligned}
$$

with initial conditions $P_{k,N} = 0$ if $N < k$ and $P_{1,1} = 1$ for all $N \geq 1$ (from above). Although the recursion does not automatically generate a closed-form solution, we can compare Equation D.12 with Equation D.11, above, to deduce that

$$
P_{k,N} = p = 1 - \sum_{i=1}^{k}(-1)^{i+1}\binom{k}{i}\left(\frac{k-i}{k}\right)^{N}, \quad \text{for } N \geq k. \qquad (D.13)
$$

A tedious proof by induction (omitted) easily shows that $P_{k,N}$ given in Equation D.13 does indeed satisfy the recursion shown in Equation D.12 and the initial condition $P_{1,1} = 1$ for all $N \geq 1$.

From an implementation standpoint, the recursion in Equation D.12 is easier to execute accurately for large numbers than the closed-form solution in Equation D.13—because the latter involves large factorials in the binomial coefficients.[26]

APPROXIMATE SOLUTIONS

I present two approximate solutions that can be figured using a handheld calculator. The first uses the union bound; the second relies upon near independence.

#1: Union Bound. The union bound relies upon Boole's Inequality, which uses just the first term from the inclusion-exclusion formula:

$$
P\left(\bigcup_{i=1}^{k} A_i^0\right) \leq \sum_{i=1}^{k} P\left(A_i^0\right)
$$

---

[26]Note, however, that there are recursive approaches to calculating binomial coefficients that include large numbers: we can use $\binom{k}{i} = \frac{k}{i} \cdot \binom{k-1}{i-1}$. So, for example, $\binom{100}{6} = \frac{100}{6} \cdot \frac{99}{5} \cdot \frac{98}{4} \cdot \frac{97}{3} \cdot \frac{96}{2} \cdot \frac{95}{1}$.

That is, the probability of at least one of the events occurring is bounded above by the sum of the probabilities of each of the events. In our case,

$$
\begin{aligned}
1 - P_{k,N} &= P\left(\bigcup_{i=1}^{k} A_i^0\right) \\
&\leq \sum_{i=1}^{k} P\left(A_i^0\right) \\
&= (-1)^{1+1}\binom{k}{1}\left(\frac{k-1}{k}\right)^N, \quad \text{from the } i = 1 \text{ term in Equation D.11} \\
&= k\cdot\left(\frac{k-1}{k}\right)^N.
\end{aligned}
$$

Thus, $P_{k,N} \geq 1 - k\cdot\left(\frac{k-1}{k}\right)^N$. In our case, we get $P_{k,N} \geq 1 - 100\cdot\left(\frac{99}{100}\right)^N$. If we plug the known solution $N = 683$ into this we get $P_{k,N} \geq 89.6\%$, which is correct ($N = 683$ actually gives $P_{k,N} = 90.0\%$). If instead we set $P_{k,N} = 0.90$ and solve for N, we get $N \leq \frac{\log(0.001)}{\log(0.99)} = 687.3$, so, $N = 688$ is an upper bound on a sufficient number of chips.

#2: Assumed Independence. When the number of chips N is large relative to the number of cookies k, and when the minimum number of chips m required in each cookie is small, then the event that there are at least m chips in one cookie is very nearly independent of the event that there are at least m chips in another cookie. We can exploit this to get an excellent approximation to the exact solution.

Consider our case where $k = 100$ cookies and we want at least $m = 1$ chip per cookie. From the above, we know that the probability that there are no chips in the first cookie is

$$
P(A_1^0) = \left(\frac{k-1}{k}\right)^N.
$$

It follows that the probability that there is at least one chip in the first cookie is $\left[1 - \left(\frac{k-1}{k}\right)^N\right]$. Each cookie has the same statistical properties, so, with near independence, the probability that there is at least one chip in every cookie is

$$
p \approx \left[1 - \left(\frac{k-1}{k}\right)^N\right]^k.
$$

Solving for N gives $N \approx \frac{\ln\left(1-p^{\frac{1}{k}}\right)}{\ln\left(1-\frac{1}{k}\right)} = \frac{\ln(1-0.9^{0.01})}{\ln(0.99)} = 682.17$. So, 683 chips will suffice, and we can figure this with a handheld calculator.

This answer relies upon the near independence between the event that there is at least one chip in one cookie and the event that there is at least one chip in another cookie.[27] For the case of at least $m = 1$ chip per cookie, I think my assumed-independence solution for N is either exactly correct, or underestimates N by only 1 for all k. I have also seen a solution that uses the Poisson distribution in the $m = 1$ case, assumes independence, and yields an answer that is algebraically very close to each of solutions presented here.

#3: Another Approximation. Finally, and this might be difficult to do in an interview, I plotted the assumed-independence solution for the $m = 1$ case, $N \approx \ln\left(1 - p^{\frac{1}{k}}\right) / \ln\left(1 - \frac{1}{k}\right)$, and the solution appeared to me to behave like $N = k \cdot \ln(b \cdot k)$ where b is a function of p only. Comparing the two functional forms revealed

$$ b \approx \left[\ln\left(\frac{1}{p}\right)\right]^{-1} \cdot p^{\frac{1}{k}} \approx \left[\ln\left(\frac{1}{p}\right)\right]^{-1}. $$

This yielded the approximate solution

$$ \begin{aligned} N &\approx k \cdot \ln\left\{\left[\ln\left(\frac{1}{p}\right)\right]^{-1} \cdot k\right\} \\ &= k \cdot \{\ln(k) - \ln[-\ln(p)]\}. \end{aligned} $$

This solution is almost as accurate as the assumed-independence solution. For example, when $k = 100$ cookies, and $p = 0.90$, the exact solution for the $m = 1$ case is 683, the assumed-independence solution is 683, and the above approximation yields 686 (an error of less than a half percent). Similarly, when $k = 500$ cookies, and $p = 0.90$, the exact solution for the $m = 1$ case is 4,229, the assumed-independence solution is 4,229, and the above approximation yields 4,233 (an error of less than a tenth of a percent).

Answer 4.39: I present two solutions: the first is a full "hammer-and-tongs" solution; the second uses a recursive argument similar to Answer 4.15. Questions requiring recursive proofs have become popular in interviews; look up "recursive argument" in the index to find other examples in this book.

FIRST SOLUTION
When the game stops (i.e., you rolled a 4, 5, or 6), you have a $\frac{2}{3}$ chance of seeing the accumulated score (i.e., you got a 4 or 5 out of a possible 4, 5, or 6 to stop the game). The accumulated score is 0 with probability $\frac{1}{2}$, 1 with probability $\left(\frac{1}{2}\right)^2$, 2 with probability $\left(\frac{1}{2}\right)^3$, and so on. So, the expected payoff is given by

$$ \frac{2}{3} \cdot \sum_{i=0}^{\infty} j \cdot \left(\frac{1}{2}\right)^{j+1} = \frac{1}{3} \cdot \sum_{i=0}^{\infty} \frac{j}{2^j} = \frac{2}{3}, $$

---

[27]Let N_i be the number of chips in the ith cookie. Then, for $N = 683$ and $k = 100$ the events $\mathcal{A} = (N_i \geq m)$ and $\mathcal{B} = (N_j \geq m)$ for $i \neq j$ are effectively numerically indistinguishable from independent for small m. I simulated $\frac{P(\mathcal{A}) \cdot P(\mathcal{B})}{P(\mathcal{A} \cap \mathcal{B})}$ for various m and found the ratio was 1 ± 0.000001 for $m = 1$, 1 ± 0.0001 for $m = 2$, 1 ± 0.0002 for $m = 3$, 1 ± 0.0003 for $m = 4$, 1 ± 0.001 for $m = 5$, 1 ± 0.02 for $m = 6$–10, 1 ± 0.10 for $m = 11$–16, and too rare to simulate for $m \geq 17$.

using the result that $\sum_{i=0}^{\infty} \frac{j}{2^j} = 2$ (see Footnote 11 on p. 74).

SECOND SOLUTION[28]

Let N be the random number of times you roll a 1, 2, or 3, before a 4, 5, or 6 appears. If you now roll the die once, there is a half a chance that $N = 0$ and the game stops, and there is a half a chance that you get a 1, 2, or 3, and you are otherwise recursively back where you started (expecting to roll an additional $E(N)$ 1's, 2's, or 3's before the game ends). If we write this algebraically, we get

$$E(N) = \left(0 \cdot \frac{1}{2}\right) + \left[(1 + E(N)) \cdot \frac{1}{2}\right].$$

We can solve this directly to get $E(N) = 1$.[29] When the game does end, we get paid only if we roll a 4 or 5. In other words, conditional upon the game ending, we have a two thirds chance of being paid N. Our expected payoff is thus $\frac{2}{3} \cdot E(N) = \frac{2}{3}$, as before.

Answer 4.40: I first heard about the "broken stick problem" appearing in MBA interviews back in the early 1990's. It is still used today. This classic question deserves justice here.

Let me present two solutions for obtaining the probability that a triangle can be formed from three bits. The first solution is based on a general proof using polygons and polytopes due to Bull (1948) and I shall draw upon that solution to answer the next question. The second solution is much shorter and is an expansion of an equivalent argument using just a circle (Rushton, 1949).

FIRST SOLUTION

Bull (1948) considers the case where a stick is broken randomly into n pieces. He says that a necessary and sufficient condition for a polygon of n or fewer angles to be made out of the n pieces is that no one piece can be of a length that exceeds the sum of the lengths of the others. Equivalently, each piece must be not greater in length than half the length of the stick.[30]

Following Bull... ...let x, y, and $1 - x - y$ denote the lengths of the three separate pieces formed from a stick of unit length. If x and y are taken as axes of coordinates in two dimensions, then all ways of breaking the stick (regardless of whether a triangle can be formed or not) are represented by points inside and on the triangle formed by the coordinate axes and the line $x + y = 1$ (i.e., the boundary and interior of the triangle O–A_1–A_2 in Figure D.5). If this statement is not immediately obvious, then think of it as follows. There

---

[28]I thank Simon West for suggesting this technique; any errors are mine.

[29]Alternatively, we may use the geometric distribution, as we did in Answers 4.1 and 4.13, with $p = 1/2$, to find $E(N+1) = 1/p = 2$. I thank Mark Cawston for discussions regarding this answer; any errors are mine.

[30]Bull implicitly allows for two degenerate cases: triangles with zero area when one piece has length $\frac{1}{2}$; and, one or two pieces having zero length. For randomly placed breaks, these cases happen with probability zero; my allowing them does not change the final answer.

are three pieces of lengths x, y, and $1 - x - y$. It must be the case that each piece has non-negative length: $x \geq 0$, $y \geq 0$, and $1 - x - y \geq 0$. After rearranging the latter inequality, these three conditions say $x \geq 0$, $y \geq 0$, and $x + y \leq 1$. The intersection of these three conditions is the boundary and interior of the triangle O–A_1–A_2 in Figure D.5, as stated.

The points in Figure D.5 representing ways of breaking the stick that allow a triangle to be formed are those points inside and on the area bounded by the lines $x = \frac{1}{2}$, $y = \frac{1}{2}$, and $x + y = \frac{1}{2}$ (i.e., the shaded area in Figure D.5). If this is not immediately obvious, think of the conditions required: each piece must not be greater in length than half the length of the stick: $x \leq \frac{1}{2}$, $y \leq \frac{1}{2}$, and $1 - x - y \leq \frac{1}{2}$ (or, $x + y \geq \frac{1}{2}$). The intersection of these three conditions is the boundary and interior of the shaded triangle B_{12}–A_1'–A_2' in Figure D.5.

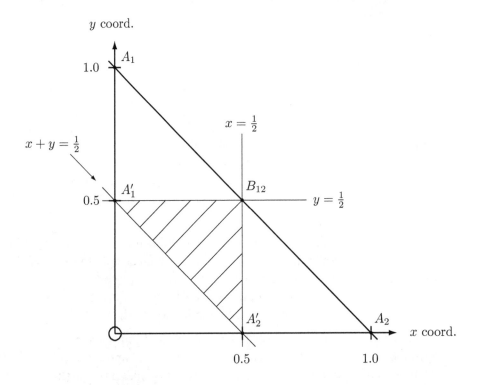

Figure D.5: Broken Stick Problem: Form a Triangle

Note: Any particular x and y coordinate pair within the triangle O–A_1–A_2 corresponds to a broken stick with three pieces of lengths x, y, and $1 - x - y$, respectively. If the x and y coordinate pair fall within the shaded triangle B_{12}–A_1'–A_2' then the three pieces can be used to construct a triangle—for in this case no one piece can be of a length that exceeds the sum of the lengths of the others, or, equivalently, each piece must be not greater in length than half the length of the stick.

Random breaking of the stick means that the possible triplets of pieces $(x, y, 1-x-y)$ obtained are represented by coordinate pairs (x, y) distributed uniformly over the triangle O–A_1–A_2 in Figure D.5. The shaded triangle B_{12}–A_1'–A_2' corresponds to pieces that can be used to build a triangle. The probability you can form a triangle is thus

$$P(3) = \frac{\text{AREA}(\text{triangle } B_{12}\text{–}A_1'\text{–}A_2')}{\text{AREA}(\text{triangle } O\text{–}A_1\text{–}A_2)} = \frac{\frac{1}{2} - 3 \cdot \left(\frac{1}{4 \cdot 2}\right)}{\frac{1}{2}} = 1 - (3 \cdot 1/4) = \frac{1}{4}.$$

Visual inspection of Figure D.5 yields the same solution, solving the question.

Bull (1948) presents a geometric proof for the case of four pieces. His proof is the three-dimensional analogy of my Figure D.5. He has three axes, x, y, z, and a tetrahedron representing all ways of forming a polygon of four or fewer angles from the pieces. At the origin, and along each axis are tetrahedrons that must be excluded if a polygon is to be formed. So, instead of my two axes and three triangles to exclude, Bull has three axes and four tetrahedrons to exclude. I won't draw the picture, but here are the calculations: The volume of a tetrahedron is $\frac{1}{3} \cdot A \cdot h$, where A is base area and h is height. The large tetrahedron has $A = \frac{1}{2}$ and $h = 1$; the four small ones have $A = \frac{1}{8}$ and $h = \frac{1}{2}$. So, the answer for $n = 4$ is $P(4) = \frac{(\frac{1}{3} \cdot \frac{1}{2} \cdot 1) - 4 \cdot (\frac{1}{3} \cdot \frac{1}{8} \cdot \frac{1}{2})}{(\frac{1}{3} \cdot \frac{1}{2} \cdot 1)} = 1 - (4 \cdot 6/48) = \frac{1}{2}$.

In the general n-piece proof, Bull has an $(n-1)$-dimensional polytope with n polytopes to be excluded.[31] The same relative probability argument yields $P(n) = \frac{\frac{1}{(n-1)!} - n \cdot \left(\frac{1}{2^{n-1}(n-1)!}\right)}{\frac{1}{(n-1)!}} = 1 - \frac{n}{2^{n-1}}$. As n gets large, $P(n)$ goes to 1 (e.g., if I break a stick randomly into 100 pieces, it is very likely that I can lay the pieces out to form a polygon of 100 or fewer angles.)

SECOND SOLUTION

Rushton (1949) gives a very elegant re-statement of the n-segment problem in terms of placing points at random on the circumference of a circle.[32] Assume that we sprinkle n points randomly upon the circumference of a circle. Label these points as X_1, X_2, ..., X_n. Now cut the circle at point X_n, open it up, and flatten it out to a straight line. Label the end that was adjacent to X_n as O. There are n line segments: O–X_1, X_1–X_2, ..., X_{n-1}–X_n.

Let us solve for the likelihood that we cannot form an n-sided polygon from these segments. We cannot form the polygon if there exists a line segment longer than half the length of O–X_n. Each segment is equally likely to be longer than half the length of O–X_n. (As an aside, note that each such case corresponds to the points we sprinkled all falling upon a semi-circle of the original circle). The probability that the first segment fulfils this condition is the probability that the remaining $n - 1$ points lie upon the second half

---

[31]A polytope is "a finite region of n-dimensional space enclosed by a finite number of hyperplanes (`mathworld.wolfram.com`)."

[32]I thank Aidong Chen for helpful discussions regarding this solution; any errors are mine.

of the line $O\text{–}X_n$. With randomly sprinkled points, each has a fair coin toss likelihood of landing on either half of the line $O\text{–}X_n$. So, the probability that the first segment fulfils this condition is $1/2^{n-1}$. The probability that there is one segment of length greater than half the length of the circumference (note there can be at most one), is the sum of the probabilities that each particular segment could be so (because these are mutually exclusive): $n/2^{n-1}$. So, the favorable probability is $P(n) = 1 - n/2^{n-1}$, yielding $P(3) = 1/4$, as before. Figure D.6 shows the sample space for the n-segment broken stick problem.

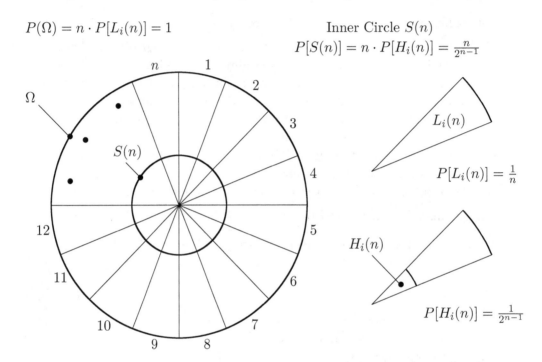

$$P(\Omega) = n \cdot P[L_i(n)] = 1 \qquad\qquad \text{Inner Circle } S(n)$$
$$P[S(n)] = n \cdot P[H_i(n)] = \frac{n}{2^{n-1}}$$

$$P[L_i(n)] = \frac{1}{n}$$

$$P[H_i(n)] = \frac{1}{2^{n-1}}$$

Figure D.6: Venn Diagram for Broken Stick Problem

The sample space for the n-segment broken stick problem. Do not confuse the circle in the figure with the circle in Rushton's original argument. Randomly break a stick of unit length into n segments. The sample space is Ω. $L_i(n)$ is the event that the ith segment is the longest. $H_i(n)$ is the event that the ith segment is of length larger than one-half. The width of each slice $L_i(n)$ of the sample space pie decreases as n increases. $S(n)$ is the event that there exists a segment of length larger than one-half (there can be at most one), in which case all points sprinkled on the circle in Rushton's argument fall upon a semi-circle. The probability we can form a polygon from the n segments is $P(n) = 1 - P[S(n)] = 1 - n/2^{n-1}$, which is the area between the two circles. Note that the area of the inner circle goes to zero as $n \to \infty$. That is, $lim_{n\to\infty}P[S(n)] = 0$. This implies that $lim_{n\to\infty}P(n) = 1$.

Answer 4.41: *FIRST SOLUTION*

Unlike Answer 4.40, a triangle need not be formed here. To derive the pdf for the longest piece we will derive the cdf first and then differentiate it. We shall work with the properties of Figure D.5.

Let L denote the random longest piece, and l denote a particular value of L. We want to find the cdf $F_L(l) = P(L \leq l)$. We know that $L \equiv \max(x, y, 1 - x - y)$, so the event $L \leq l$ happens if and only if $x \leq l$, $y \leq l$ and $1 - x - y \leq l$. The latter may be rearranged as $x + y \geq 1 - l$. Following the arguments in Answer 1.40, we need only find the relative area contained within the region bounded by the lines $x = l$, $y = l$ and $x + y = 1 - l$ (but also within the original triangle O–A_1–A_2) in Figure D.5. There are two cases: $0.5 \leq l \leq 1$ (see Figure D.7), and $\frac{1}{3} \leq l \leq 0.5$ (see Figure D.8). These correspond to the cases where you cannot, and can, respectively, form a triangle from the pieces. The figure captions contain the algebra. The cdf of the longest piece is

$$F_L(l) = \begin{cases} [1 - 3(1 - l)^2], & 0.5 \leq l \leq 1 \\ (3l - 1)^2, & \frac{1}{3} \leq l \leq 0.5, \end{cases}$$

and the pdf of the length of the longest piece is[33]

$$f_L(l) = \begin{cases} 6(1 - l), & 0.5 \leq l \leq 1 \\ 6(3l - 1), & \frac{1}{3} \leq l \leq 0.5. \end{cases}$$

So, the expected length of the longest piece of broken stick is

$$
\begin{aligned}
E(L) &= \int_{\frac{1}{3}}^{1} l \cdot f_L(l) dl = \int_{\frac{1}{3}}^{0.5} l \cdot 6(3l - 1) dl + \int_{0.5}^{1} l \cdot 6(1 - l) dl \\
&= \left(6l^3 - 3l^2 \right) \Big|_{\frac{1}{3}}^{0.5} + \left(3l^2 - 2l^3 \right) \Big|_{0.5}^{1} \\
&= \left[\left(\frac{6}{8} - \frac{3}{4} \right) - \left(\frac{6}{27} - \frac{3}{9} \right) \right] + \left[(3 - 2) - \left(\frac{3}{4} - \frac{2}{8} \right) \right] = \frac{11}{18}.
\end{aligned}
$$

I leave you to use the same technique to confirm that the expected length S of the shortest piece[34] is $E(S) = \frac{2}{18} = \frac{1}{9}$.

SECOND SOLUTION[35]

For an alternative derivation of the pdf for the length of the longest piece, assume, without loss of generality, that x is the longest piece. If so, then (x, y) falls within the diagonal-hatched kite-shaped region of Figure D.9 bounded by the inequalities $x \geq y$, $2x + y \geq 1$ (i.e., $x \geq 1 - x - y$), $x + y \leq 1$, and $y \geq 0$. The vertices of this kite are at $(0.5, 0)$, $(1, 0)$, $(0.5, 0.5)$, and $(\frac{1}{3}, \frac{1}{3})$. The

---

[33]Can you sketch the pdf to confirm that it is right-skewed and triangular?

[34]There is only one case. I get $F_S(s) = [1 - (1 - 3s)^2]$, and $f_S(s) = 6(1 - 3s)$, for $0 \leq s \leq \frac{1}{3}$. I deduce that $E(M) = \frac{5}{18}$ for the middle-length piece because $E(S + M + L) = 1$.

[35]I thank Mr. Lee for suggesting this technique; any errors are mine.

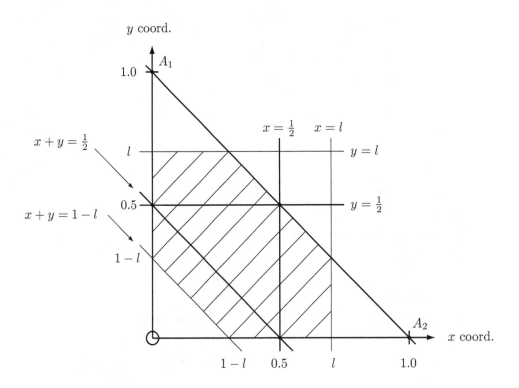

Figure D.7: Broken Stick Problem, $F_L(l) = P(L \leq l)$, Case: $0.5 \leq l \leq 1$

Note: The cdf of the length of the longest piece is given by the shaded relative probability area bounded by the three conditions $x \leq l$, $y \leq l$ and $x+y \geq 1-l$ (but also within the original triangle $O\text{--}A_1\text{--}A_2$). In the case $l \geq 0.5$ this is simply the relative area obtained by excluding the three equal-sized un-shaded triangles. Each of the three un-shaded triangles has area $\frac{1}{2}(1-l)^2$, so the cdf value is simply $F_L(l) = P(L \leq l) = \frac{\frac{1}{2} - 3 \cdot \left[\frac{1}{2}(1-l)^2\right]}{\frac{1}{2}} = [1 - 3(1-l)^2]$. This yields pdf $f_L(l) = 6(1-l)$ in the case $0.5 \leq l \leq 1$.

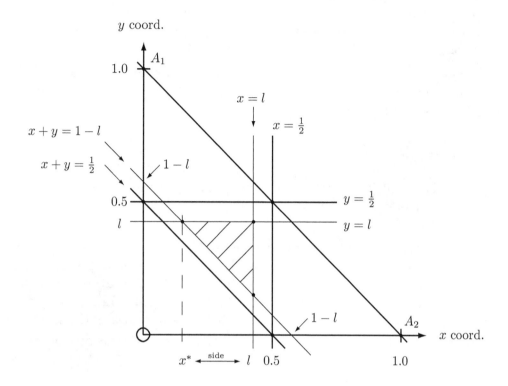

Figure D.8: Broken Stick Problem, $F_L(l) = P(L \leq l)$, Case: $\frac{1}{3} \leq l \leq 0.5$

Note: As in Figure D.7, the cdf of the length of the longest piece is given by the shaded relative probability area bounded by the three conditions $x \leq l$, $y \leq l$ and $x+y \geq 1-l$ (but also within the original triangle O–A_1–A_2). In the case $l \leq 0.5$ this is simply the relative area of the shaded triangle. Close inspection shows that as l drops, the area of the triangle reduces until $l = \frac{1}{3}$ at which point the area is zero. This corresponds to the simple intuition that the longest piece of stick cannot be smaller than $\frac{1}{3}$ in length (else it is not the longest). One way to get the area of the shaded triangle is to deduce the value of x^* so that we can deduce the side length $l - x^*$. To find x^* note that it is the value of x at which the lines $x + y = 1 - l$ and $y = l$ intersect. If we plug the latter into the former, we can solve for x^*: $x^* + l = 1 - l$ implies $x^* = 1 - 2l$. The side length is thus $l - x^* = l - (1 - 2l) = 3l - 1$. The shaded triangle thus has area $\frac{1}{2}(3l - 1)^2$. So, the cdf value is simply $F_L(l) = P(L \leq l) = \frac{\frac{1}{2}(3l-1)^2}{\frac{1}{2}} = (3l - 1)^2$. This yields pdf $f_L(l) = 6(3l - 1)$ in the case $\frac{1}{3} \leq l \leq 0.5$.

conditional joint distribution $f_{X,Y|L_x(3)}(x,y)$ of (x,y), where $L_x(3)$ is the event that x is the longest of three pieces, is uniform with value 6 over this kite-shaped region (i.e., just the uniform joint distribution $f_{X,Y}(x,y) = 2$ over the triangle O–A_1–A_2 of area 0.5, but rescaled to account for the kite occupying only one-third of the area of the triangle O–A_1–A_2).

The marginal pdf $f_{X|L_x(3)}(x)$ of x, conditional upon x being the longest piece, is now obtained by integrating out y. For $\frac{1}{3} \le x \le 0.5$, $f_{X|L_x(3)}(x) = \int_{y=1-2x}^{y=x} 6dy = 6(3x-1)$, and for $0.5 \le x \le 1$,

$$f_{X|L_x(3)}(x) = \int_{y=0}^{y=1-x} f_{X,Y|L_x(3)}(x,y)dy = \int_{y=0}^{y=1-x} 6dy = 6(1-x),$$

as derived already. The proof proceeds as previously. Note that only for points within the interior of the triangle B_{12}–A_1'–A_2' can a triangle be formed from the three pieces.

A similar argument applies if x is assumed to be the shortest piece, but the relevant region is then the horizontal-hatched triangle in Figure D.9 bounded by the inequalities $x \le y$, $2x + y \le 1$ (i.e., $x \le 1 - x - y$), and $x \ge 0$. The vertices of the triangle are at $(0,0)$, $(\frac{1}{3}, \frac{1}{3})$, and $(0,1)$. In this case, for $0 \le x \le \frac{1}{3}$, $f_{X,Y|S_x(3)}(x) = 6$, where $S_x(3)$ is the event that x is the shortest of three pieces. Then, $f_{X|S_x(3)}(x) = \int_{y=x}^{y=1-2x} 6dy = 6(1-3x)$, as previously.

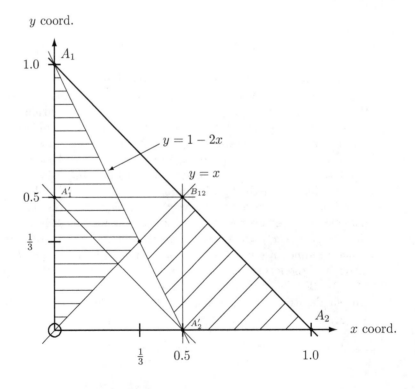

Figure D.9: Broken Stick Problem: x is Longest or Shortest Piece

Answer 4.42:   Like Question 4.39, this question can be solved using infinite series, or using a simple recursion proof.

FIRST SOLUTION

There is a $\frac{1}{2}$ chance that the game ends with two tosses, a $\left(\frac{1}{2}\right)^2$ chance that it ends with four tosses, a $\left(\frac{1}{2}\right)^3$ chance that it ends with six tosses, ..., a $\left(\frac{1}{2}\right)^n$ chance that it ends with $2n$ tosses, and so on. Thus the expected number N of tosses is

$$E(N) = \sum_{i=1}^{\infty} 2n \cdot \left(\frac{1}{2}\right)^n = \sum_{i=1}^{\infty} \frac{2n}{2^n} = 4,$$

using the result that $\sum_{i=0}^{\infty} \frac{n}{2^n} = 2$ (see Footnote 11 on p. 74).

SECOND SOLUTION Let N be the number of coin tosses required to reach Box 4. After two coin tosses, there is a half a chance that you are in Box 4 and the game is over after two tosses, and a half a chance that you are recursively back at the beginning again still expecting $E(N)$ more tosses:

$$E(N) = \left(2 \cdot \frac{1}{2}\right) + \left[(2 + E(N)) \cdot \frac{1}{2}\right].$$

We can solve this directly to get $E(N) = 4$.

Answer 4.43:   You know only that I have two children and that one is a girl. My family has (implicitly) conducted two Bernoulli trials. Without the information that one child is a girl, there are four possible equally likely outcomes: GG, GB, BG, BB. With the information that one child is a girl, the last outcome is excluded, and the sample space describing the randomness you are confronted with is three equally likely outcomes: GG, GB, BG. The probability of GG is thus $\frac{1}{3}$. See Answer 4.44 for more details.

Story: "During his interview with me, a candidate bit his fingernails and proceeded to bleed onto his tie. When I asked him if he wanted a Band-Aid, he said that he chewed his nails all the time and that he'd be fine. He continued to chew away."

AUDREY W. HELLINGER
Chicago Office of Martin H. Bauman
Associates, New York

"Doomed Days: The Worst Mistakes Recruiters Have Ever Seen,"
The Wall Street Journal, February 25, 1995, pR4.
Reprinted by permission of *The Wall Street Journal*
©1995 Dow Jones and Company, Inc.
All Rights Reserved Worldwide.

Answer 4.44:   You know only that I have two children and that one is a girl you are facing at my front door. Now the argument changes from the previous question. The only randomness is the gender of the child you cannot see. The sample space describing this randomness is just G and B. The probability that I have two girls is thus $\frac{1}{2}$.

Like in Answer 4.43, without seeing my child, there are four possible equally likely outcomes: GG, GB, BG, BB. Having pinpointed the gender of Child #1 (we might as well call her that), however, the latter two outcomes are excluded, and the sample space describing the randomness you are confronted with is two equally likely outcomes: GG, GB. The probability of GG is thus $\frac{1}{2}$.

If they press you for the formal derivation so you can point your finger at the difference between the Answers 4.43 and 4.44, you can use Bayes' Theorem. In Answer 4.43 you are seeking $P(G \cap G|\text{told } G)$:

$$
\begin{aligned}
P(G \cap G|\text{told } G) &= \frac{P(G \cap G \cap \text{told } G)}{P(\text{told } G)} = \frac{P(\text{told } G \cap (G \cap G))}{P(\text{told } G)} \\
&= \frac{P(\text{told } G|G \cap G) \cdot P(G \cap G)}{P(\text{told } G|G \cap G) \cdot P(G \cap G) + \mathbf{P(\textbf{told } \textbf{G}|\textbf{B} \cap \textbf{G})} \cdot P(B \cap G) + P(\text{told } G|B \cap B) \cdot P(B \cap B)} \\
&= \frac{1 \cdot \frac{1}{4}}{1 \cdot \frac{1}{4} + \mathbf{1} \cdot \frac{1}{2} + 0 \cdot \frac{1}{4}} = \frac{1}{3}
\end{aligned}
$$

In Answer 4.44 you are seeking $P(G \cap G|\text{see } G)$:

$$
\begin{aligned}
P(G \cap G|\text{see } G) &= \frac{P(G \cap G \cap \text{see } G)}{P(\text{see } G)} = \frac{P(\text{see } G \cap (G \cap G))}{P(\text{see } G)} \\
&= \frac{P(\text{see } G|G \cap G) \cdot P(G \cap G)}{P(\text{see } G|G \cap G) \cdot P(G \cap G) + \mathbf{P(\textbf{see } \textbf{G}|\textbf{B} \cap \textbf{G})} \cdot P(B \cap G) + P(\text{see } G|B \cap B) \cdot P(B \cap B)} \\
&= \frac{1 \cdot \frac{1}{4}}{1 \cdot \frac{1}{4} + \mathbf{\frac{1}{2}} \cdot \frac{1}{2} + 0 \cdot \frac{1}{4}} = \frac{1}{2}
\end{aligned}
$$

I used bold font to show where the two derivations differ: $P(\text{told } G|B \cap G) = 1$, but $P(\text{see } G|B \cap G) = \frac{1}{2}$. Otherwise everything is the same.

Answer 4.45: To figure out the probability that we will meet under the big clock, I have assumed that we arrive randomly in the interval 1PM–2PM. For each moment of that hour, I have asked myself the following question. If I arrive at that moment, when would you have to arrive in order for us to meet? The answer is shaded in Figure D.10, where for each of my arrival times x (on the horizontal), I have shaded on the vertical the time range from $y_{min}(x) = \max(1\text{PM}, x - 15 \text{ minutes})$ to $y_{max}(x) = \min(2\text{PM}, x + 15 \text{ minutes})$. If I arrive at time x and you arrive at time $y(x) \in [y_{min}(x), y_{max}(x)]$, then we shall meet.

From Figure D.10 we see that the probability we meet is the ratio of the area of the shaded region (mutual arrival times when we meet) divided by the area of the square (all possible mutual arrival times): $\frac{7}{16}$.

Answer 4.46: To obtain three heads or three tails, the coin must be tossed a minimum of three times. At most five tosses are required, because it is impossible to toss the coin five times without obtaining three matching outcomes. So, the game will stop after either three, four, or five tosses.

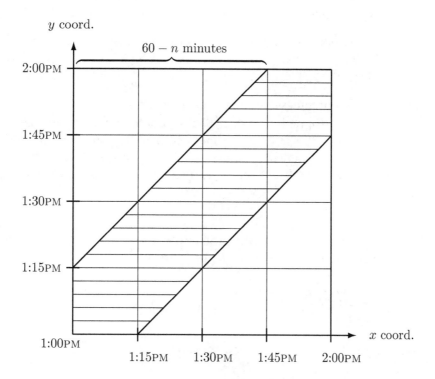

y coord.

$60 - n$ minutes

2:00PM

1:45PM

1:30PM

1:15PM

1:00PM

1:15PM   1:30PM   1:45PM   2:00PM

x coord.

Figure D.10: Meeting Under the Big Clock

Note: We agree to meet between 1PM and 2PM, but wait no more than 15 minutes for each other, and not to arrive before 1PM or stay beyond 2PM. My arrival time is x, and in order to meet up with you, you must arrive at time $y(x) \in [y_{min}(x), y_{max}(x)]$, where $y_{min}(x) = \max(1\text{PM}, x - 15 \text{ minutes})$ and $y_{max}(x) = \min(2\text{PM}, x + 15 \text{ minutes})$. The probability we meet is the relative area of the shaded region divided by the area of the square: $\frac{7}{16}$.

The shaded area is the area of the big square (60^2 minutes) less the area of the un-shaded square (i.e., the two un-shaded triangles of total area $(60 - 15)^2$ minutes). More generally, for $0 \leq n \leq 60$ where n is maximum number of minutes we agree to wait, the probability we meet is $p_{meet}(n) = \frac{60^2 - (60-n)^2}{60^2} = \frac{n(120-n)}{3600}$.

This gives $p_{meet}(n) = \frac{n(120-n)}{3600} = \begin{cases} 0 & \text{if } n = 0, \\ 1/4 & \text{if } n = 60 - \sqrt{2700}, \\ \mathbf{7/16} & \text{if } \mathbf{n = 15}, \\ 1/2 & \text{if } n = 60 - \sqrt{1800}, \\ 3/4 & \text{if } n = 30, \\ 1 & \text{if } n = 60. \end{cases}$

The three-toss outcomes are HHH and TTT, each with probability $\frac{1}{8} = \frac{2}{16}$ (it will be easier to do this using sixteenths), yielding total probability $\frac{4}{16}$.

The four-toss outcomes must each begin with a permutation of HHT (followed by an H) or a permutation of TTH (followed by a T): HHTH, HTHH, THHH, TTHT, THTT, HTTT, each with probability $\frac{1}{16}$, yielding total probability $\frac{6}{16}$.

The five-toss outcomes must each begin with a permutation of HHTT (else we would have stopped already). The fifth outcome must end the game (with either H or T). Given that the end happens for sure on the fifth toss, in this case we need only count the permutations of HHTT, each occurring with probability $\frac{1}{16}$: HHTT, HTHT, THHT, TTHH, THTH, HTTH, yielding total probability $\frac{6}{16}$.

So, our analysis yields three tosses with probability $\frac{4}{16}$, four tosses with probability $\frac{6}{16}$, and five tosses with probability $\frac{6}{16}$. Let T be the number of tosses required to end the game, then $E(T)$ is given by

$$E(T) = \left(3 \cdot \frac{4}{16}\right) + \left(4 \cdot \frac{6}{16}\right) + \left(5 \cdot \frac{6}{16}\right) = \frac{12 + 24 + 30}{16} = \frac{66}{16} = 4\frac{1}{8}.$$

Although not asked for, can you prove that $\text{var}(T) = \frac{39}{64}$?

Answer 4.47: A bias towards either heads or tails in the coin in Question 4.46 is a bias in favor of "more of the same." Given that the stopping rule is "three of the same," the expected number of tosses required to end the game must decrease in this case.

So, if the probability of a head is one-half, and T is the number of tosses required to end the game, $E(T) = 4\frac{1}{8}$, and it cannot be higher. If, however, the probability of a head is two-thirds (or, given symmetry, if it is one-third), the expected number of tosses to end the game drops to $E(T) = 107/27 \approx 3.96$. If the probability of a head is 3/4 (or, given symmetry, if it is 1/4), the expected number of tosses to end the game drops to $E(T) = 483/128 \approx 3.77$. If the probability of a head is one (or, given symmetry, if it is zero), the expected number of tosses to end the game drops to $E(T) = 3$, and it cannot be lower.

Answer 4.48: The mathematics for the length of longest runs in the general case of N tosses is quite complex (Binswanger and Embrechts, 1994). The case of four or five tosses is, however, quite manageable.

In the case $N = 4$, the longest runs must be of length one, two, three, or four. A quick sketch of the tree, with 16 possible outcomes, reveals two runs of length one (HTHT, and the same with H and T transposed), eight runs of length two (HHTH, HHTT, HTHH, HTTH, and the same with H and T transposed), four runs of length three (HHHT, HTTT, and the same with H and T transposed), and two runs of length four (HHHH, and the same with

H and T transposed). So, we get that

$$E[L(4)] = \left(1 \cdot \frac{2}{16}\right) + \left(2 \cdot \frac{8}{16}\right) + \left(3 \cdot \frac{4}{16}\right) + \left(4 \cdot \frac{2}{16}\right)$$
$$= \frac{2 + 16 + 12 + 8}{16}$$
$$= \frac{38}{16} = 2\frac{6}{16} = 2\frac{3}{8}.$$

In the case $N = 5$, the longest runs must be of length one, two, three, four, or five. A quick sketch of the tree, with 32 possible outcomes reveals two runs of length one (HTHTH, and the same with H and T transposed), 14 runs of length two (HHTHH, HHTHT, HHTTH, HTHHT, HTHTT, HTTHH, HTTHT, and the same with H and T transposed), 10 runs of length three (HHHTH, HHHTT, HHTTT, HTHHH, HTTTH, and the same with H and T transposed), four runs of length four (HHHHT, HTTTT, and the same with H and T transposed), and two runs of length five (HHHHH, and the same with H and T transposed). So, we get that

$$E[L(5)] = \left(1 \cdot \frac{2}{32}\right) + \left(2 \cdot \frac{14}{32}\right) + \left(3 \cdot \frac{10}{32}\right) + \left(4 \cdot \frac{4}{3}\right) + \left(5 \cdot \frac{2}{32}\right)$$
$$= \frac{2 + 28 + 30 + 16 + 10}{32}$$
$$= \frac{86}{32} = 2\frac{11}{16}.$$

It follows that $E[L(5)] - E[L(4)] = \frac{5}{16}$. Expressing that in decimal form brings us back to Question 1.26. Five-sixteenths is one-sixteenth above one-quarter. So, we just have to add 0.0625 to 0.2500 to get 0.3125.

Answer 4.49: There are $6^3 = 216$ distinct outcomes from rolling three dice. For the difference between the maximum and minimum outcomes of three dice (i.e., the range) to be exactly four, you must either have a maximum of a 6 and a minimum or a 2, or a maximum or a 5 and a minimum of a 1.

Let us consider the first case (max=6, min=2). What is the third number? It must be a 2, 3, 4, 5, or 6. So, the unordered outcomes are 226, 236, 246, 256, and 266. Paying attention to order, the first can occur three ways (i.e., the 6 is first, second, or third), the next three can be permuted in six ways each, and the last can occur in three ways (i.e., the 2 is first, second, or third). So, there are 3+18+3=24 ways to obtain a range of exactly four, with a maximum of a 6 and a minimum of a 2.

Similarly, there are 24 different ways to obtain a range of exactly four when the maximum is a 5 and the minimum is a 1. So, there are 48 possible ways, out of 216, to obtain a range of exactly four. After some simplifications, we see that $\frac{48}{216} = 2/9$.

Ninths always appear as repeated fractions. For example, $\frac{1}{9} = 0.111\dot{1}$, where the dot above the number means that it is repeated. So, $\frac{n}{9} = 0.nnn\dot{n}$, and in our case, $\frac{2}{9} = 0.222\dot{2}$.

More generally, you can use the same technique to show that the range takes value zero with probability $\frac{6}{216}$ (i.e., the six cases where all three dice have identical numbers on them), one with probability $\frac{30}{216}$, two with probability $\frac{48}{216}$, three with probability $\frac{54}{216}$, four with probability $\frac{48}{216}$, five with probability $\frac{30}{216}$, and cannot take the value six. So, the expected value of the range, which was not asked for, is $630/216 = 2.916\dot{6}$.

Answer 4.50: The initial value $P(0) = 100$ is irrelevant, except that it is non-zero. With these odds, the population will not last long at all.

Let G be the number of generations until extinction. Then there is half a chance that the population will be extinct in one generation, and half a chance that it will survive for one more generation (and we then we are faced with the same question again). So, a simple recursion says that

$$E(G) = \left(\frac{1}{2} \cdot 1\right) + \left[\frac{1}{2} \cdot (1 + E(G))\right].$$

Solving for $E(G)$ yields $E(G) = 2$.

Note that this question is analogous to Question 4.39. So, we can use the geometric distribution argument to find $E(G) = 1/p = 1/\frac{1}{2} = 2$, as done there.

Answer 4.51: Given C coins, and the requirement that you flip them in groups of g adjacent coins, let us assume that $C \geq 3$ (ignoring the very simple cases $C = 1$ and $C = 2$). Let us also assume that $1 \leq g \leq C$. (If $g > C$, we can think of g in modulo-C terms, looking at the coins that do get flipped.)

Let $gcd(C, g)$ denote the greatest common divisor of C and g. For example, $gcd(7, 3) = 1$, but $gcd(12, 9) = 3$. Let me begin with the specific case where $gcd(C, g) = 1$ and g is odd. Our particular case ($C = 7, g = 3$) satisfies these assumptions.

Let us number the coins from 1 to C, like the numbers of the hours on an analog clock face with C hours. Let the coin in the middle of any group of g coins to be flipped be our reference point (recall that we are assuming g is odd, so a middle coin exists). There are C such possible reference points.

Let us pick a coin flipping strategy. For any reference coin c, say, we have to choose whether to flip the group centered on c or not. Note that the order of our flipping decisions is irrelevant because either two groups of coins to be flipped do not overlap, and so order is unimportant, or two groups of coins to be flipped do overlap, in which case, any coin in the overlap is flipped twice, and is left unchanged regardless of the order of the flips. Note also that we would never flip any group more than once, because all that does is consume flips (which we wish to minimize), to no effect. For example, if we flip some group twice, then the same strategy but excluding those two flips gives the same outcome, or if we flip some group three times, that is the same as flipping once. So, let us assume all flipping strategies have any such redundant flips removed.

Then, given that we have to make the decision to flip, or not, any group centered on c, for $c = 1, 2, \ldots, C$, and we will not flip any group more than once, it follows that there are exactly 2^C possible coin flipping strategies.

Suppose we flip every group of g coins. That is, when we focus on each coin, c, for $c = 1, 2, \ldots, C$, we say yes, we will flip the group of coins centered on coin c. For example, in the case $C = 7$ and $g = 3$ this would mean that we flip the $C = 7$ coin groups (7,1,2), (1,2,3), (2,3,4), (3,4,5), (4,5,6), (5,6,7), and (6,7,1). Then, the even distribution of the $C \times g$ individual coin flips means that we have flipped every one of the C individual coins g times. Given that g is odd, we have flipped every coin from heads-up to heads-down, which was to be done.

Note also that, because order does not matter, the sequence of consecutively-overlapping coin flips stated above has the same outcome as this sequence of consecutively non-overlapping coin flip groups: (1,2,3), (4,5,6), (7,1,2), (3,4,5), (6,7,1), (2,3,4), and (5,6,7). This ordering of flips, though equivalent, will be easier to work with at the next step.

How can we prove that flipping all C groups of g coins is the minimum number of moves needed to achieve the all-coins-turned-over outcome? Well, in the case where $gcd(C, g) = 1$ and g is odd, we will prove in a moment that there exists a strategy to achieve any possible outcome. There are 2^C possible outcomes, and, as argued above, 2^C strategies, so, it follows that, in this case, there is a one-to-one correspondence between outcomes and strategies. Not only is flipping all C coins the most efficient way to turn all individual coins over, it is the only way to do so.

How do we know that in the case where $gcd(C, g) = 1$ and g is odd, any possible outcome is able to be achieved? The answer is that there exists a strategy to flip any particular coin you care to point at. For example, in the case $C = 7$ and $g = 3$, suppose you wish to flip only coin $c = 1$. Then, all you need do is execute the first five of the above-mentioned, consecutively non-overlapping coin flip groups: (1,2,3), (4,5,6), (7,1,2), (3,4,5), (6,7,1). Then, you will have flipped coins 1–7 twice, followed by flipping coin $c = 1$ once. Similarly, if we wanted to flip only coin $c = 2$, we would take five of the consecutively non-overlapping coin flip groups, but beginning at a different part of the sequence: (2,3,4), (5,6,7), (1,2,3), (4,5,6), and (7,1,2). Similarly for any other individual coin.

It follows that if we can flip any individual coin of our choice, then we can achieve any outcome we desire. For example, to flip coins $c = 1$ and $c = 2$, we

APPENDIX D. STATISTICS ANSWERS

would combine the two above sets of five groups of three flips, but remove the three sets of redundant pairs, yielding: (3,4,5), (6,7,1), (2,3,4), (5,6,7).

The key to being able to flip any individual coin is that we can keep K of the original C consecutively non-overlapping coin flip groups, and contained within them is an even number, E, say, of flips of all coins, followed by one extra flip, or, alternatively, we find that contained within them is an even number E flips of all but the last coin. For example, in the case $C = 7$ and $g = 3$, we kept $K = 5$ groups of $g = 3$ flips, and they contained $E = 2$ flips of all $C = 7$ coins, plus one extra flip. In the case $C = 8$ and $g = 3$, however, we flip the fist coin using the following consecutively non-overlapping coin flip groups: (1,2,3), (4,5,6), (7,8,1), (2,3,4), (5,6,7). So, in this case, we keep $K = 5$ groups of $g = 3$ coins, that contain $E = 2$ flips of all but the last coin.

More generally, if $gcd(C, g) = 1$ and g is odd, there exists K (which is odd) and E (which is even) such that $(K \cdot g) = (E \cdot C) \pm 1$. (Note that K must be odd, given that $(E \cdot C) \pm 1$ is odd and g is odd.) That is, we can flip any coin we wish to point at, and so, any outcome can be achieved, and so the count of strategies equals the count of possible outcomes, and so flipping all C consecutively non-overlapping coin flip groups is the only strategy, and thus the most efficient strategy, to flip every individual coin.

Finally, we need to consider some other cases. Suppose that C is perfectly divisible by g (i.e., $gcd(C, g) = g$). For example, $C = 9$ and $g = 3$. Then it takes exactly C/g flips of non-overlapping groups of coins to flip all individual coins.

Otherwise, you cannot flip all coins. For example, if $gcd(C, g) = 1$ but g is even, like the case $C = 7$ and $g = 2$, it is not possible to flip all coins, or a single coin, because the groups cycle around in even pairs. You can, however, flip all but a single coin in this case. Similarly, if $gcd(C, g) \neq 1$ and $gcd(C, g) \neq g$, like the case $C = 6$ and $g = 4$, then it is not possible to flip all coins. Note also that even in some simple cases where it is not the case that both $gcd(C, g) = 1$ and g is odd, the strategies are no longer necessarily unique. For example, in the case $C = 3$ and $g = 2$, the coin flip group (1,2) produces the same outcome as the combination of (2,3) and (3,1). So, in this case, with only 2^C strategies, and some giving the same outcomes, not all 2^C outcomes are achievable.

Answer 4.52: In order for the maximum of three dice outcomes to be a four, the maximum must be less than or equal to 4, but not less than or equal to 3. So,

$$
\begin{aligned}
P(\max = 4) &= P(\max \leq 4) - P(\max \leq 3) \\
&= \left(\frac{4}{6} \cdot \frac{4}{6} \cdot \frac{4}{6} \right) - \left(\frac{3}{6} \cdot \frac{3}{6} \cdot \frac{3}{6} \right) \\
&= \frac{4^3 - 3^3}{6^3} = \frac{64 - 27}{216} = \frac{37}{216},
\end{aligned}
$$

using the independence of the dice rolls, and the fact that if the maximum is

©2021 Timothy Falcon Crack   302   All Rights Reserved Worldwide

less than or equal to a number, then so is every number showing. My rusty long division yields 0.171 to three decimal places.

In fact, my first attempt at this calculation used a visual approach. I imagined a 6×6 macro-cube that looks like a Rubik's cube, where the outcomes on any single dice are recorded along one of the axes. Then the 216 micro-cubes making up the macro-cube represent all possible outcomes. So, outcomes with all numbers less than or equal to 4 take up a 4×4 sub-cube. Similarly, outcomes with all numbers less than or equal to 3 take up a 3×3 sub-cube of the 4×4 sub-cube. Thus, of the 216 possible outcomes, the count where the maximum is exactly 4 must be the same as the count of the remaining micro-cubes when the 3×3 cube is subtracted from the 4×4 cube: $4^3 - 3^3$, as above.

Although not requested, the same "difference of cubes" technique reveals that the probability of the maximum being a 1 is $1/216$ (when all three dice return a 1), being a 2 is $7/216$, being a 3 is $19/216$, being a 4 is $37/216$, being a 5 is $61/216$, and a being 6 is $91/216$. This yields $E(\text{max}) = 1,071/216 = 119/24 = 4.958\dot{3}$.

Challenge: Can you use the difference of cubes approach, along with the cubic answer to Question 1.53, to show that the expected *minimum* when throwing three dice is given by the following?

$$
\begin{aligned}
E(\text{min}) &= \left(1^3 + 2^3 + 3^3 + 4^3 + 5^3 + 6^3\right)\big/6^3 \\
&= \frac{6^2 \cdot 7^2/4}{6^3} \\
&= 441/216 = 49/24 = 2.041\dot{6}
\end{aligned}
$$

Answer 4.53: A Poisson process exhibits a random arrival (or departure, or other event) pattern as follows: First, the number of arrivals in any two disjoint intervals of time must be independent of each other; second, for a very short time interval δt, the probability of at least one arrival during that interval is roughly proportional to the length of the time interval: $\lambda \delta t + o(\delta t)$, where λ is the intensity, or arrival rate, of the process and $o(\delta t)$ is a function that approaches zero as $\delta t \to 0$; and third, the probability that there are more than one arrivals during time interval δt is also $o(\delta t)$ (DeGroot, 1989, pp. 254–255).

Under these assumptions, the inter-arrival times X_i of a Poisson process are distributed exponential, $f_X(x) = \lambda e^{-\lambda x}$ for $x \geq 0$, where λ is the arrival rate, and the mean of X_i is $1/\lambda$ (DeGroot, 1989, p. 290).

The count of occurrences in any fixed interval of time of length δt will be distributed Poisson with mean $\lambda \delta t$ (DeGroot, 1989, p. 255).[36]

---

[36]Y has a Poisson distribution with mean $\theta > 0$ if $f_Y(y) = \frac{e^{-\theta}\theta^y}{y!}$ for $y = 0, 1, 2, \ldots$ and zero otherwise (DeGroot, 1989, p. 252).

We have observed $X_1 = 2$, $X_2 = 12$, and $X_3 > 7$. So, $\bar{X} = \frac{X_1+X_2+X_3}{3} > \frac{21}{3} = 7$ minutes. Our best guess of λ is $\lambda = 1/\bar{X} < 1/7 \approx 0.14286$ arrivals per minute. That is, $1/7$ is slightly larger than our best guess will be if we wait to observe the next arrival. Of course, three observations (or two and a half in this case), is a very small sample. We need more data.

Answer 4.54: Let p be the probability of seeing any car drive by in 30 minutes. I want to relate p to the stated probability of seeing any car drive by during one hour. Let us assume that cars arrive as a Poisson process, with a fixed rate of arrivals per unit time and independent arrivals in any non-overlapping periods. Then the probability of no cars in one hour is the product of the probability of no cars in each half-hour. We are using the result that $P(A \cap B) = P(A)P(B)$ if A and B are independent events—and in this case each event is the complement of the event that a car arrives in the non-overlapping half hours. So, we deduce that $1 - 0.36 = (1 - p)(1 - p)$. It follows that $p = 0.20$.

Note that the naive answer here is to simply conclude that p (probability of a car in 30 minutes) equals half the 36% number (i.e., half the probability of a car in 60 minutes). This is not sensible, for the same reason that $p = 0.20$ in the next 30 minutes does not yield $p = 1.00$ in the next 2.5 hours, or $p = 1.20$ (impossible) in the next three hours: the probability of independent events is not additive. Note that the probability of mutually exclusive events is additive, but mutually exclusive events cannot be independent (unless at least one occurs with probability zero).

Answer 4.55: Yes, this is an example of something called Simpson's Paradox (DeGroot, 1989, p. 548). There are several slightly different flavors of Simpson's Paradox. They are each special cases of "statistical mix effects" (Armstrong and Wattenberg, 2014). Mix effects mean that aggregate numbers can be affected by changes in the relative size of subpopulations as well as the relative values within those subpopulations (Armstrong and Wattenberg, 2014).

In the case at hand, suppose Italy made 120 passes in the first half, with 60 being successful (50%), and the U.S. made 50 passes, with only 10 being successful (20%). In the second half, suppose Italy improved, making 60 passes, with all 60 being successful (100%), and the U.S. also improved, making 200 passes with 190 being successful (95%). Italy looked better in each half, but over the match as a whole, Italy had only a 66.66% success rate (120/180), whereas the U.S. had an 80% success rate (200/250).

Armstrong and Wattenberg (2014) give the famous example of UC Berkeley graduate admissions. It was found that 44% of male applicants were accepted, whereas only 35% of female applicants were accepted. Rather than being discrimination by Berkeley, however, departments with higher acceptance rates had proportionally more male applicants. In fact, by disaggregating the data,

Bickel, Hammel, and O'Connell (1975) found a small but significant bias in favor of the female applicants.

Here is another example of a mix effect. Suppose my students sign up for class at the start of the semester. You would not be surprised to find that the average height of the men is larger than the average height of the women. The overall average will be between the averages of the two sexes. Suppose, however, that a female student signs up late because she was playing in a sports match out of town. Suppose that this new student is tall for a woman, but still of height less than the previous overall average. Then, although the average height of the women goes up and the average height of the men is unchanged, the average height of the class as a whole must go down.

Answer 4.56: With fair coins, the symmetry in payoffs must give an expected payoff of zero. You get payoff -6 (HH) with probability $1/4$, +5 (HT or TH) with probability $1/2$, and -4 (TT) with probability $1/4$, so the expected payoff is

$$\left(-6 \cdot \frac{1}{4}\right) + \left(5 \cdot \frac{1}{2}\right) + \left(-4 \cdot \frac{1}{4}\right) = 0.$$

The variance of payoffs is

$$\left((-6)^2 \cdot \frac{1}{4}\right) + \left(5^2 \cdot \frac{1}{2}\right) + \left((-4)^2 \cdot \frac{1}{4}\right) = \frac{36 + 50 + 16}{4} = \frac{51}{2} = 25.5.$$

Suppose you play the game N times, where N is a large number. Then, sure enough, the expected payoff is zero for every game, and therefore zero overall, but you have a problem.

Let X_n be the dollar payoff to the nth game. Let $D(N) \equiv \sum_{n=1}^{N} X_n$ be the total dollar payoff to playing N games. Then we have that

$$E[D(N)] = E\left(\sum_{n=1}^{N} X_n\right) = \sum_{n=1}^{N} E(X_n) = 0, \text{ and}$$

$$V[D(N)] = V\left(\sum_{n=1}^{N} X_n\right) = \sum_{n=1}^{N} V(X_n) = N \cdot \frac{51}{2},$$

where $V(\cdot)$ denotes variance. For large N, a standard central limit theorem result will yield that $D(N)$ is roughly normally distributed, centered on zero, but with standard deviation $\sqrt{N \cdot 51/2}$. Thus, as N grows, so too does the standard deviation of the accumulated payoffs.

If you play 20,000 games, then, sure enough, $E[D(N)] = 0$, but $V[D(N)] = 510,000$, which means the standard deviation of your payoffs is \$714.14, rounding to pennies. If you play one million games, then $V[D(N)] = 25,500,000$, yielding a standard deviation of payoffs of \$5,049.75, rounding to pennies. For two million games, the standard deviation of the payoff is \$7,141.43, rounding to pennies. In the last case, there is a roughly 5% chance that your gain or loss will exceed 1.96 standard deviations (i.e., a 5% chance of gains or losses beyond plus or minus $13,997.20, respectively).

Samuelson (1963) would argue that from a utility standpoint, playing the original game once is unattractive because it has positive risk, but an expected payoff of zero. He would argue that playing it many times is all the more unattractive.

Answer 4.57:   Reconsider the game from Question 4.56, but allow that your coin has probability p (of your choice) of getting a head, and your opponent's coin has probability p' (of his or her choice, after knowing p) of getting a head.

So, you get payoff -6 (HH) with probability $p \cdot p'$, +5 (HT or TH) with probability $[p \cdot (1 - p') + (1 - p) \cdot p']$, and -4 (TT) with probability $(1 - p) \cdot (1 - p')$. Let X_n denote your payoff to the nth game, then

$$
\begin{aligned}
E(X_n) &= (-6 \cdot p \cdot p') + (5 \cdot [p \cdot (1 - p') + (1 - p) \cdot p']) \\
&\qquad\qquad\qquad\qquad + (-4 \cdot (1 - p) \cdot (1 - p')) \\
&= -20pp' + 9p + 9p' - 4 \\
&= (9 - 20p) \cdot p' + 9p - 4 \\
&= b \cdot p' + a, \qquad\qquad\qquad\qquad\qquad\qquad\qquad\text{(D.14)}
\end{aligned}
$$

a linear function of p', where the coefficient is $b = (9 - 20p)$ and the intercept is $a = 9p - 4$ (see Figure D.11).

If $p'(p)$ is chosen by your opponent as a function of p in order to minimize your expected payoff, then optimal $p'(p)$ will be found by minimizing this expected payoff, Equation D.14, with respect to p. There are three cases, depending upon the sign of the slope b.

If $b > 0$, your opponent wants to minimize $b \cdot p' + a$ and chooses the lowest possible p' value (i.e., $p' = 0$). In this case, the expected payoff is $a = 9p - 4$. Note, however, that $b > 0$ implies $9 - 20p > 0$ implies $p < 9/20$. So, the expected payoff is $a = 9p - 4 < 81/20 - 4 = \$\,1/20$ (i.e., you get an expected payoff strictly less than $\$\,1/20$).

If $b < 0$, your opponent wants to minimize $b \cdot p' + a$ and chooses the highest possible p' value (i.e., $p' = 1$). In this case, the expected payoff is $5 - 11p$. Note, however, that $b < 0$ implies $9 - 20p < 0$ implies $p > 9/20$. So, your expected payoff is $5 - 11p < 5 - 99/20 = \$\,1/20$ (i.e., again, you get an expected payoff strictly less than $\$\,1/20$).

If, however, $b = 0$ (i.e., $p = 9/20$), then your expected payoff is $9p - 4 = \$\,1/20$ for every p' value, which is superior to all of the above. So, you want to choose $p = 9/20$ to maximize your expected payoff at $E(X_n) = \$\,1/20$.

Your expected payoff is the same regardless of which p' your opponent chooses, but the variance of payoffs is still a function of p'. Equation D.15 shows the conditional variance of the payoff to the nth game for general p'.

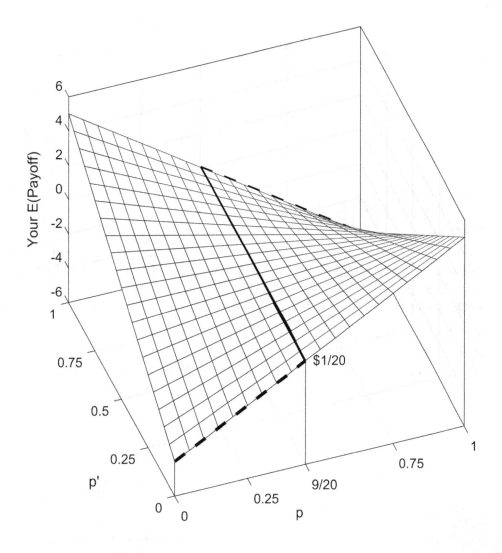

Figure D.11: Your Expected Payoff to a Coin Game

Note: Your expected payoff to the coin game in Question 4.57 is $E(X_n) = -20pp' + 9p + 9p' - 4 = b \cdot p' + a$, a linear function of p', where the coefficient is $b = (9 - 20p)$ and the intercept is $a = 9p-4$, as shown in Equation D.14. If you choose probability of a head $p < 9/20$, then the slope b is positive, and your opponent chooses the lowest possible p' (i.e., $p' = 0$) to hurt you the most (and he or she benefits the most). Your expected payoff is strictly less than $ 1/20 in this case (i.e., somewhere on the bold dashed line in the foreground). If you choose $p > 9/20$, then the slope b is negative, and your opponent chooses the highest possible p' (i.e., $p' = 1$) to hurt you the most. Again, your expected payoff is strictly less than $ 1/20 (i.e., somewhere on the bold dashed line in the background). If, however, you choose $p = 9/20$, then the slope b is zero, and your expected payoff is fixed at $ 1/20 for every p' (i.e., somewhere on the bold solid line level at $ 1/20 in the figure).

$$\left. V(X_n)\right|_{p=\frac{9}{20}} = \left(-6-\frac{1}{20}\right)^2 \cdot \frac{9}{20}\cdot p' + \left(5-\frac{1}{20}\right)^2 \cdot \left[\frac{9}{20}\cdot(1-p') + \frac{11}{20}\cdot p'\right]$$

$$+\left(-4-\frac{1}{20}\right)^2 \cdot \frac{11}{20}\cdot(1-p)$$

$$= 20\frac{19}{400} + 9.9\cdot p'. \tag{D.15}$$

Equation D.15 says that the variance of payoff, $V(X_n)$, increases in p' for each game. I think that risk aversion dictates that the opponent will choose $p' = 0$, so as to minimize the variability of his or her payoffs. (Any other p' changes the numbers in the remainder of my answer, but does not change the qualitative story.) Thus we obtain $\left. V(X_n)\right|_{p=\frac{9}{20},p'=0} = 20\frac{19}{400}$.

The question asks about repeated play. So, let $D(N) \equiv \sum_{n=1}^{N} X_n$ be the total dollar payoff to playing N games. Then we have that

$$E[D(N)] = E\left(\sum_{n=1}^{N} X_n\right) = \sum_{n=1}^{N} E(X_n) = \frac{N}{20}, \text{ and}$$

$$V[D(N)] = V\left(\sum_{n=1}^{N} X_n\right) = \sum_{n=1}^{N} V(X_n) = N\cdot 20\frac{19}{400}.$$

For large N, a standard central limit theorem result will yield that $D(N)$ is roughly normally distributed, centered on $N/20$, but with standard deviation $\sqrt{N\cdot 20\frac{19}{400}}$.

If you play 200 games, then $E[D(N)] = \$10$, and the standard deviation of your payoffs is $\$63.32$, rounding to pennies. The probability that you lose is $P[D(N) < 0] \approx P[(D(N)-10)/63.32 < -10/63.32] \approx N(-0.1579) \approx 43.7\%$, where $N(\cdot)$ is the cumulative standard normal function. (Note that X_n is skewed and very platykurtic, so $N = 200$ might not be large enough to yield a very accurate approximation.)

If you play 20,000 games, however, then $E[D(N)] = \$1,000$, and the standard deviation of your payoffs is $\$633.21$, rounding to pennies, which carries a roughly $N(-1.579) \approx 5.7\%$ chance of a loss.

If you play 2,000,000 games, then $E[D(N)] = \$100,000$, and the standard deviation of your payoffs is $\$6,332.06$, which carries virtually no chance of a loss (because $N(-15.79) \approx 0$).

So, unlike in Answer 4.56, repeated play is attractive here. Now you are like the owner of the casino that accepts only small bets, with a small edge in every game, and (almost) sure long-run profits.

Answer 4.58: You were asked to "write down the central limit theorem." In fact, this question is not well posed because many different central limit theorems (CLTs) exist. They differ in their assumptions (e.g., dependent data versus independent data or finite variances versus infinite variances, etc.) and in their dimensions (i.e, univariate versus multivariate).[37]

I suspect that the univariate Lindberg-Levy CLT (Feller, 1971, p. 259) is the single answer most likely to please. Let $X_1, X_2, \ldots$ be mutual independent random variables with a common distribution. Assume that $E(X_i) = 0$ and that $\text{var}(X_i) = 1$ for each i, then the distribution of the normalized sums $S_n = (X_1 + \cdots + X_n)/\sqrt{n}$ tends to the standard normal distribution as n tends to infinity. If we instead assume that $\text{var}(X_i) = \sigma$ for each i, then the normalized sums are given by $S_n = (X_1 + \cdots + X_n)/(\sigma/\sqrt{n})$, and their distribution also tends to the standard normal distribution as n tends to infinity.

Answer 4.59: This is a practical question; I often need to simulate correlated stock returns when simulating panel data for portfolio theory applications.

A certain amount of caution is required. The interviewer said that Z_1 and Z_2 are "uncorrelated" and "Gaussian." There are two possible interpretations, with slightly different answers. Let us take the simpler case first, with the strongest assumptions.

Case 1: I think that the interviewer meant that Z_1 and Z_2 are together *bivariate* normally distributed. In this case, Z_1 and Z_2 being uncorrelated implies that Z_1 and Z_2 are independent (Crack, 2020a). If we then define X_1 and X_2 as in Equations D.16 and D.17,

$$X_1 = \sigma_1 \cdot Z_1 + \mu_1 \tag{D.16}$$

$$X_2 = \sigma_2 \cdot \left[\rho \cdot Z_1 + \sqrt{(1 - \rho^2)} \cdot Z_2 \right] + \mu_2, \tag{D.17}$$

then $X_1 \sim N(\mu_1, \sigma_1^2)$, $X_2 \sim N(\mu_2, \sigma_2^2)$, and $\text{corr}(X_1, X_2) = \rho$ (DeGroot, 1989, p. 301), as requested. In this case, X_1 and X_2 are, like Z_1 and Z_2, bivariate normally distributed (Crack, 2020a), and their joint density function is given as follows for $-\infty < x_1, x_2 < \infty$ (DeGroot, 1989, p. 301):

$$f_{X_1, X_2}(x_1, x_2) =$$

$$\frac{1}{2\pi\sqrt{(1-\rho^2)}\sigma_1\sigma_2} e^{-\frac{1}{2(1-\rho^2)}\left[\left(\frac{x_1-\mu_1}{\sigma_1}\right)^2 - 2\rho\left(\frac{x_1-\mu_1}{\sigma_1}\right)\left(\frac{x_2-\mu_2}{\sigma_2}\right) + \left(\frac{x_2-\mu_2}{\sigma_2}\right)^2\right]}.$$

In the case where $\sigma_1 = \sigma_2 = 1$ and $\mu_1 = \mu_2 = 0$, X_1 and X_2 are, like Z_1 and Z_2, bivariate *standard* normally distributed. Note, however, that $\text{corr}(X_1, X_2) = \rho$ (so that $f_{X_1, X_2}(x_1, x_2)$ looks like a pinched bell in three dimensions), whereas

---

[37]See, for example, Feller (1971, pp. 258–265), Rao (1973, p. 128), White (2001), Crack and Ledoit (2010), and Crack (2018).

$\mathrm{corr}(Z_1, Z_2) = 0$ (so that $f_{Z_1,Z_2}(z_1, z_2)$ looks like a symmetric bell in three dimensions).

Case 2: It is possible, though unlikely, that this is a deeper question. If the interviewer meant that Z_1 and Z_2 are distributed *univariate* standard normal, then Z_1 and Z_2 being uncorrelated does *not* imply that Z_1 and Z_2 are independent. The key distinction here is that if two random variables are uncorrelated, then this means that they have no *linear* dependence, but they may still have *non-linear* dependence (Crack, 2020a).

In the case where Z_1 and Z_2 are distributed univariate standard normal and are uncorrelated, defining X_1 and X_2 as in Equations D.16 and D.17 still yields $\mathrm{corr}(X_1, X_2) = \rho$, as required (because Equations D.16 and D.17 are *linear* transformations). We still get that $X_1 \sim N(\mu_1, \sigma_1^2)$ (because X_1 is a linear transformation of Z_1). It is no longer true, however, that X_2 need be normally distributed, and it is no longer true that X_1 and X_2 need be bivariate normally distributed (Crack, 2020a). The problem is that only in the case where Z_1 and Z_2 are univariate normal and independent (or equivalently where Z_1 and Z_2 are distributed bivariate normally) does it follow that all possible linear combinations of Z_1 and Z_2 are normally distributed. Otherwise simple counterexamples can be built where linear combinations of Z_1 and Z_2 are not normally distributed and Z_1 and Z_2 are not bivariate normally distributed (see Crack, 2020a).

Answer 4.60:   Before defining the p-value, let us discuss statistical size. The statistical size (i.e., significance level) of a test is a pre-determined number. It is often a small number, like, say, 5%. This statistical size is the probability that you make a Type I error (i.e., the error you make when you reject the null hypothesis even though it is true).

The p-value associated with a particular realization of a statistical test is the post-determined statistical size at which the value of the realized test statistic exactly equals the critical value (or one of the critical values) for rejection of the null hypothesis given your estimated parameter value(s). Equivalently, at least in a univariate case, the estimated parameter value (that feeds into the test statistic) sits at one end of a 100-p% confidence interval for the population parameter value. It follows that for a pre-determined statistical size, any realized p-value at or less than that statistical size leads to a rejection of the null hypothesis.

Before you conduct your statistical test, the p-value, like the test statistic itself, is a random variable. If we have a continuous random variable test statistic, then, under the null hypothesis, the p-value is distributed uniformly on the interval $[0 \;\; 1]$.

Appendix E

Non-Quantitative Answers (Selected)

This appendix contains answers to selected questions in Chapter 5.

Answer 5.2.11: Why are they asking why they chose you to come to a final round interview? They are asking because the job is yours to lose! Put yourself in the interviewers' shoes. After much effort they have whittled many candidates down to a shortlist. The easiest way to cross names off the shortlist is to bring you all back and have you each explain why you are there. Anyone who says something stupid gets struck off the list. The last person left standing gets the job.

What are they trying to get at with this question? It comes back to the four points of the compass mentioned on p. 3: *skills, fit, effort,* and *acceptance.* After spending time with them in previous rounds, you must be able to reiterate why you are a good candidate: you have the **skills** that they seek; you **fit** into the culture in their organization; you are willing/able to put in the **effort** they require; you will **accept** a job if offered to you with reasonable terms.

What answers are they looking for? They want you to walk them through each of the above four points, tailoring your answer to what you have learned about them and what they have learned about you. They want you, but either they have some minor doubts remaining about you or they just can't choose between candidates. They are now giving you one final chance to kill your chances. Don't put a foot wrong!

Answer 5.2.26: A "tombstone" is of course an advertisement that lists (like the names on a tombstone) the underwriters associated with a public issue of a security. The particular placement of the underwriters' names on the tombstone carries with it implications for the perceived status of the underwriters on the deal.

A student came to see me. He told me that he was flying to Chicago the next day for a job interview with an investment bank. I did not recognize the name of the bank. He asked me what sort of non-quantitative questions he might face, so I pulled out my book and tried several on him. When I got to the tombstone question, I stopped and asked him if he knew the definition of a tombstone. I pulled out that

---

day's *Wall Street Journal* (WSJ) to see if there was a tombstone in the third section. The page at which I opened the WSJ contained a tombstone from the bank he was going to interview with the next day! I clipped it out and gave it to him, and he talked about it in his interview. It is worth keeping your eye on the tombstones in the WSJ (or online) in the weeks leading up to your interviews.

Answer 5.2.44: This is not necessarily a rejection. It may just be a test to see how you defend yourself. It is just the opposite way of asking you why you fit the job. A colleague of mine told me that he once started an interview with the statement "I don't think you are the right person for the job." He believed it, but he knew the candidate was talented and he was interviewing him just in case. My colleague thought the candidate would tell him why he was the right person, but instead the candidate just deflated like a burst balloon. The interview was a complete bust. If someone said that to me, I would answer "No! I fit because ..."

Answer 5.3.3: By 2015, yields on at least a dozen countries' government bonds had turned negative. Bond yields in these countries had already been low, because their governments were trying to boost economic growth. (In theory, low interest rates encourage borrowing to fund corporate investment, and low interest rates also discourage saving, so that individuals are more likely to spend money and boost economic activity.) Rates were pushed into negative territory both because of the central governments' original growth motivations and because of compounding economic forces.

By the end of 2015, roughly 5% of investment-grade bonds outstanding globally had negative yields, and by Q3 of 2019, this figure peaked at 29% (Mee, 2019), before falling back to about 20% by the end of 2019 (Ainger, 2019). The dollar bloc was a holdout, offering low but positive yields (Mee, 2019), but in late-March 2020, COVID-19 disruption pushed stock prices down dramatically. The accompanying flight to quality pushed yields on three-month U.S. Treasuries into negative territory (Bloomberg, 2020a), and soon afterwards yields on both three- and six-month U.S. Treasures turned negative (Bloomberg, 2020b). The U.S. Treasury yield curve, which had been inverted as recently as mid-February 2020, became upward sloping a week earlier (WGB, 2020). Negative U.S. Treasury yields reverted to positive territory over the following month, except for TIPS, whose yields became increasingly negative over the following few months (Bloomberg, 2020c).

Many of the countries with negative yields in 2015 had negative targets for key short-term rates (PIMCO, 2016), but they had not originally issued long-term bonds with negative yields. So, how can a low-yield bond become a negative-yield bond? It happens when investors, fearful of further deterioration in the local or global economy, rush to the quality of government bonds. This risk-off trade pushes bond prices up, even to the point where yields can become negative. This decline in yields can be further reinforced if some traders bet on yields becoming even more negative, and choose to buy bonds at negative yields hoping for capital gains as yields continue to fall. Many European governments did subsequently issue bonds with negative initial yields. For example, the U.K. issued bonds with negative yields for the first time in May 2020 (Ostroff, 2020).

Why buy negative-yield bonds? There are at least a half-dozen reasons:

- It could be a speculative bet that yields will become even more negative, as mentioned already.

- Of course, some investors (e.g., banks, for capital adequacy reasons) are required to hold government bonds. So, their demand exists regardless of yield.

- Note also that if a country experiences deflation that is worse than its negative bond yields, then investors in those negative-yield bonds still get a positive real yield.

- A foreign negative-yield bond may appear attractive once you hedge it into your domestic currency. For example, a U.S. investor buying a German 10-year bond in September 2019 with a -60 bps yield may pick up enough yield that the hedged German bond yield is comparable to, if not superior to, the U.S. 10-year Treasury yield (Mee, 2019). This yield pick-up is driven by the interest rate differential between the countries.

- Another reason to buy negative-yield bonds is that they may have negative betas. Investors may be prepared to hold negative-beta assets (even with negative expected returns) if they are powerful diversifiers. I certainly saw days in Q1 of 2020 when U.S. stock prices and U.S. bond prices were running full-tilt in opposite directions.

- Yet another reason to hold negative-yield bonds is that long-term bonds are in demand for use in liability-driven investing (LDI) in pension funds (Mee, 2019). Yield is at best a secondary consideration for a duration-matching strategy that uses bonds to match forecast liabilities.

What are the implications of negative government bond yields? Negative Treasury rates lead to low corporate rates. These low rates can squeeze profits for banks. With the profit incentive subdued, banks may lend less; this is an unintended outcome. To address this reduced profitability, banks may also charge higher fees for originating mortgages or other loans; this is another unintended outcome (CNBC, 2019).

Note, however, that negative short-term government interest rates do not automatically lead to negative interest rates at your bank, or negative yields on corporate bonds—because of the default risk premium and the term premium.[1]

---

[1]Nevertheless, UBS announced in August 2019 that it would charge a negative 75 bps interest rate for very large EUR deposits; something already being done by several competitors (Reuters, 2019). Also, in August 2019, a 10-year corporate bond (originally issued by Nestlé in November 2017 with a 1.25% yield and a 12-year maturity) became the first ever 10-year corporate bond to experience a negative yield (Molony, 2019). Nestlé had, however, previously experienced negative yields on shorter-maturity debt (Thompson and Moore, 2015). Part of the explanation is that Nestlé's debt is AA rated by multiple rating agencies, so investors rush to their debt when seeking safety, pushing prices up and yields down. Another part of the explanation is that term premiums in Europe have reduced substantially in recent years (Molony, 2019).

Suppose Sweden (read any country not the U.S.) pushes its short-term government interest rates into negative territory. This move may send Swedish institutional bond investors to U.S. Treasuries instead, in order to find safe bonds with a yield (a carry trade in currencies, presumably unhedged). This unexpected demand may drive up the price of U.S. Treasuries, driving down yields. This revealed demand means that non-U.S. institutions, especially banks, may view the USD as their new reserve currency.

What happens if the U.S. government pushes short-term rates negative, with flow-on effects on long-term U.S. rates (or if other countries' unusual demand for U.S. Treasuries pushes long-term U.S. rates negative)? What becomes the reserve currency then? Is it the GBP, EUR, AUD, or what? The global shifts in asset holding that accompany a change in effective reserve currencies will distort currency markets, and the consequences could have deep impacts on global trade (CNBC, 2019).

Note, finally, that in the 1930s and early 1940s, most coupon-bearing U.S. government bonds had negative nominal yields as they approached maturity. Sure enough, interest rates were low, and some of the above-mentioned economic factors were at play, along with tax considerations (Cecchetti, 1988). A bigger driver of these negative yields was, however, that these bonds had embedded options giving the holder the right to buy another Treasury security at an attractive price in the future. So, investors were happy to "overpay" for the bonds, relative to the promised coupons, giving the appearance of negative nominal yields (Cecchetti, 1988).[2]

Answer 5.3.15: This is an extension of previous questions asking at what level equity indices, or currencies, or interest rates or commodity prices are.

I think you have to state that nobody can give an exact number for a stock market index one year ahead. Sales and trading requires, however, a hearty personality and no lack of opinions. So, you have to provide an estimate.

I have to assume they mean the S&P 500. Obviously you need to know where it is today. You get to choose whether to provide an average sort of estimate (that is, growth in the next year will be similar to average of growth rates in the past), or provide a bullish or bearish estimate.

An average sort of estimate is obtained by taking today's level and adding something like 6–7% per annum for average historical annual growth in the index level (note that this forecast excludes dividend yield—which historically has been around 3% per annum—because the index levels do not include dividends) (Crack, 2020b,

---

[2]As an aside, I watched Fischer Black present his working paper "Interest Rates as Options" at Harvard in late 1993 (subsequently published after his death as Black [1995]). Black assumes that nominal short-term interest rates cannot be negative, because you have the option to hold cash, thereby earning a (superior) zero rate. Thus, we may think of nominal rates as the maximum of some "shadow rate" that can be negative, and the zero rate you earn in cash. I had, however, seen negative nominal Treasury rates in CRSP data from the 1930s and 1940s. I talked to Fischer Black about something else after the presentation, and then I subsequently wrote him a letter at Goldman Sachs in New York to ask him about these negative rates. We talked on the phone, and as he started to explain about the embedded options, I jumped to the above conclusion about "overpaying," which he said was correct. He kindly mailed me a copy of Cecchetti's paper.

Chapter 1).

Given volatility in equity index levels, however, it is important to know that we rarely get an average year in equities! For example, over the 91 years from 1928 to 2018 there was only one year where the total return on the S&P 500 was within 1% of the average annual return over that time period, and only 17 years where the return on the S&P 500 was within 5% of that average (Crack, 2020b, Chapter 1).

Instead of an average estimate, I think a more interesting answer might be to argue for either a bullish or a bearish outcome, and to have a really good justification ready. You might condition your forecast on growth rates in China, your outlook for interest rate changes, oil prices, employment, recent stock market behavior, etc.

Answer 5.3.20: Asking about market efficiency is very common in portfolio management interviews. Market efficiency means that prices (typically stock prices) reflect information to the extent that consistent positive trading profits cannot be made after accounting for transaction costs, taxes and risk aversion (each of which retards trading on news). There is a great deal of empirical evidence over the last 50 years to suggest that markets are largely efficient. Nevertheless, there exist many small deviations from efficiency, even in the larger markets, and prices that respond to news correctly *on average* (which is what most academic studies look at) leave much room for under- and over-reaction, and for trading opportunities.

Answer 5.3.25: This is basic macroeconomics, and you should be fully familiar with it. The two forms of macroeconomic policy are monetary policy and fiscal policy. Monetary policy tries to achieve the broad objectives of economic policy through control of the monetary system and by operating on the supply of money, the level and structure of interest rates, and other conditions affecting the supply of credit (Pearce [1984, p. 291]). With monetary policy, the Federal Reserve Bank ("the Fed") sell bonds and reduces the money supply—an "open market operation." This increases interest rates (the cost of money) and makes capital expenditures more costly. This in turn slows down growth in the economy and should fight the inflationary threat.

In addition to open market operations, the Fed implements monetary policy by managing the discount rate (the rate the Fed charges banks for loans), adjusting the Fed funds rate (the rate banks charge each other for loans of federal funds), managing reserve requirements for banks (the proportion of a bank's assets required to be held in Treasury securities), and operations in the government repo (i.e., repurchase) market.[3]

Fiscal policy refers to the use of taxation and government expenditure to regulate the aggregate level of economic activity (Pearce [1984, p. 160]). Increasing taxes and decreasing government spending should slow down growth in the economy and fight inflationary fears. Go to any standard macroeconomic text if you want more details

---

[3]A "repo" is a repurchase agreement. It is an agreement to repurchase a security in the future. You give up the security now in exchange for cash, agreeing to repurchase the security at a later date for a larger amount of cash. A repo is thus a collateralized loan. A reverse repo is the other side of the deal—you purchase securities now with an agreement to sell them later. Repos range in maturity from overnight ("O/N") to as long as five years; shorter-term repos are the most popular.

on fiscal or monetary policy.

Answer 5.3.31: The "Dow Jones Dogs strategy" buys the "Dow Jones Dogs" at the start of the year. These are the 10 Dow Jones Industrial Average (DJIA) stocks with the highest dividend yield. They are dogs because you get a relatively high dividend yield by having a low price relative to dividends. You are supposed to rebalance the portfolio every year. Historically this has been a profitable strategy. The CBOE introduced options on a Dow Jones Dogs index (the index had ticker symbol "MUT") in 1999, but saw no volume in them in 2009, and the index and options appear to have been delisted before 2014. Deutsche Bank offered an exchange-traded note (ETN) based on the return to the Dow Jones Dogs strategy (ticker symbol "DOD"), but it no longer exists. MUT and DOD moved very closely together when both existed. The ETN DODXF and ETF SDOG appear to have taken their places, with both dramatically underperforming the Dow 30 for the five years to August 2021.

Answer 5.4.3: Questions asking you to value a business are extremely common! They are mostly about finance skills, but as always, they want to hear you talk your way through it to see your personality (to see if you fit), and they want to confirm that you can think on your feet under pressure (another valuable skill).

What are they trying to get at with this question? Skills, skills, skills. Can you think on your feet and identify the important factors that feed into any business valuation? Are you aware of competing valuation techniques? Did you miss anything important?

What answers are they looking for? They do not necessarily need you to arrive at a numerical answer in this case, because some of the inputs cannot be estimated accurately until you do some research. So, I would focus on method, rather than numerical answers in this case. In other valuation questions they might supply enough data for a numerical answer, or they might sit you in front of EXCEL and ask you to build a spreadsheet.

I would announce that I will try two different techniques. My first approach involves market-determined prices for comparables: I know that NY sells licenses for street vendors via competitive bids. So, supply and demand means that the winning bids should give a rough estimate of a lower bound on the value. Winning bids are likely public, and should at least put me in the ballpark. Different locations (e.g., beside a major tourist hotspot, near to or distant from competing vendors) will carry different values. I would try to find something as comparable to the hot dog stand of interest as possible.

For my second approach I would look at a standard discounted cash flow (DCF) analysis (Crack, 2020b). I need to forecast cash flows and discount them back at an appropriate discount rate. So, I need to say what kinds of cash flows I will use and where I will get them, what sort of horizon I should use, and what an appropriate discount rate is.

I need unleveraged free cash flows (FCF) to capital. I would go out maybe 7-10 years and estimate a terminal value there using a perpetuity. FCF are given by operating cash flows (OCF) plus changes in net working capital (NWC) less capital expenditure (CAPEX) plus any sundry tax effects.

To get OCF I have to make an estimate of the foot traffic I will see, the typical transaction, the operating costs (fixed cost of the license, equipment rental, wages and variable costs of the product I sell), and depreciation (if I bought the stand). I would need to do some research on these: I could observe some vendors, check out wholesale costs of products, etc. NWC will be modelled in a spreadsheet, but given high turnover, I think it will be a small run-up at the start and then nothing much going on. CAPEX might be very low in this case if the stand is rented, or could be quite high initially if the stand is purchased outright.

The cost of equity could come from comparable publically traded small businesses in a similar line, but via the capital asset pricing model (CAPM). Something like Chipotle might be a good place to start. Remember to unlever the beta from the comparables and relever to your capital weighting (which is likely to be mostly debt I assume). I also need a market risk premium; standard numbers are 5%–7%.

I also need my cost of debt to find the WACC. I would ask some banking buddies what they would charge for a loan to someone starting a hot dog stand.

It's not enough to know the names of these concepts; you have to be prepared for the interviewer to drill more deeply on any one of the above-mentioned items.

Other competing techniques for firm valuation include the LBO method (not obviously better than DCF here), and the less-popular DDM method (but there are no obvious dividends to discount) (Crack, 2020b).

If they actually want a numerical answer, then I have to start making guestimates of all the above costs. Maybe a license is $10,000 per month, maybe the stand operates eight hours a day and I have one minimum wage employee working with me, maybe a stand costs $50,000 to build, or $1,000 per month to rent, maybe the typical transaction is $7 with costs of $1 and we can serve two people per minute for eight hours a day, etc. I think you'll need pencil and paper or a whiteboard or a spreadsheet to put this all together.

Answer 5.4.8: Given that fixed operating costs produce operating leverage, I expect that a 10% reduction in revenues will produce a more than 10% reduction in operating cash flows. Depending upon changes in net working capital, and CAPEX, etc., maybe this will produce a 10%–15% reduction in free cash flows, and a similar reduction in firm valuation, other things being equal.

If the discount rate reduces by one percentage point, however, and if the discount rate is in the 10% ballpark, then the simple gross return factor $(1+R)$ changes from, say, 1.10 to 1.09, which is only about a 1% relative change. If you compound this five or 10 times, it is still only a 5% or 10% relative change, respectively (to a first-order approximation). If we take a weighted average of these simple gross return discount rates, applied to the time series of free cash flows, this will yield maybe a 5% increase in firm value, other things being equal. Of course, this will depend upon the distribution of free cash flows through time.

In sum, I think a 10% reduction in revenues will have more than twice the impact on firm valuation (and in the opposite direction) that we would see with a one percentage point reduction in the discount rate.

Yes, you can almost certainly build a DCF model scenario where you prove me wrong, but I suspect my numbers will be about right for a typical firm.

Answer 5.4.21: The answer given by the interviewer was that if you are Avis or Hertz, cars are inventory. The same applies to an automobile manufacturer (or any of their distributors).

Answer 5.4.29: No. FCF does not include interest payments or repayment of principal because FCF is the cash flows generated by net assets and available to the owners of the company (both debt and equity holders). The tax benefit of interest payments is recognized in a lower after tax cost of debt in the WACC. Finally, financing costs are not cash outflows. They do not reduce cash available to owners. To the contrary, they *are* cash payments to owners and, therefore, have no net effect on cash flows available to owners (i.e., FCF).

Answer 5.5.3: My first answer is to hand the bomb to my boss and run! More seriously, if it is small, stick it in the fridge, pull the fridge to the floor (so the door does not just shoot off), and run and hit the fire alarm. If there is a vacant lot or river (or some other unpopulated region) outside, can you break a window and toss it out? Failing all of the above, put it against an external wall or window, and shove something heavy against it, like a flipped desk or two, to direct the blast outwards.

Answer 5.5.8: How many ping-pong balls can you fit in a jumbo jet? Why do they even ask these questions? Well, your reaction tells them about your skills. Not just quant skills, but your ability to perform under pressure. If you are unprepared for this sort of question, then it's a left-field shock. Some people freeze when shocked. Some people just get up and walk out; I've seen it happen! The interviewer wants to see how you perform under shock pressure.

After the initial shock is over, they want to see how you think about a quantitative problem of a sort that is typically not taught in college. That is, you cannot just do plain vanilla step-by-step algebra or calculus to solve it. It is a free-form problem requiring estimation and loose approximations; some rigid quants cannot solve this sort of problem. Do you have the skills to handle the shock pressure, maintain composure, and solve the left-field problem?

On one level, this is just a game. Beyond skills, they also want to know whether you play well with others. That's about fit or culture. Your reactions reveal your human nature. Your human nature reveals whether you fit or not. Also, if you make a clear concerted effort, then it signals an interest in making an effort more widely. Also, if you are willing to play along and work hard for the answer, that signals the attitude of someone who wants the job and is likely to accept it if offered it.

You need to be sure to answer clearly with step-by-step logical reasoning spoken out loud. If you close your mouth for 60 seconds and then declare the answer is 15 million, they have no idea how you got to the answer. They don't actually care about the numerical answer (assuming you are in the ballpark); they care only about the demonstrated reasoning process!

Whether its ping-pong balls in a 747, McDonald's in the U.S., barbers in Chicago, or pizzas eaten in the U.S., start by latching onto something you know about.

You have spent enough time on airplanes and you have seen enough ping-pong balls in your life that you should be able to figure this out. So, let's start with how many *people* fit inside a 747. (I would be speaking this out loud to the interviewer.) Well, it varies, but 500 sounds about right (and maybe 200 for a 737—a popular variation). Each person sits in a personal space about the size of a red British phone booth. OK, the seat is narrower, but there are aisles and overhead lockers etc., so it should be about right. A ping-pong ball is a bit bigger than one inch in diameter. A phone booth is about 36 inches wide, and let's say 75 inches high. Maybe it is 25 by 25 by 50 ping-pong balls in dimension. Although 25^2 is 625, I am going to round that to 600 for ease, and deduce that I get 30,000 ping-pong balls in a phone booth.

With 500 phone booths in the plane, five times three is 15 and I have to tag those six zeroes on the end of it. So, 15 million is my answer, but I might round it up to 20 million because those balls are not cubes, and they nestle in against each other more efficiently than do little cubes, and there is more vertical space on a 747 than other craft. Of course, there are other solution techniques, but they all involve approximations and some sort of estimation of relative volume.

Along the way I will ask the interviewer whether I include the cargo hold or not (maybe increase my answer by 50% in that case), etc. Ask if you are not sure of the assumptions. Maybe they have specific assumptions in mind.

Answer 5.5.9: As with the ping-pong balls question, there is no precise algebraic solution routine. You make several rough assumptions and hope the errors cancel. For example, the U.S. population is about 325,000,000 (mid-2021). Let's just call it 300,000,000. The average population of Bloomington, Indiana, is about 100,000 (it is lower when the students are gone and higher when the students are there). There are five McDonald's in Bloomington. I calculate $\frac{300,000,000}{100,000} \times 5 = 3,000 \times 5 = 15,000$. So, my estimate is 15,000 McDonald's outlets in the U.S.

Looking at online profiles of the company, and recent news stories, I estimate that of 38,500 McDonald's restaurants (mid-2021), roughly 14,000 of them are located in the U.S. So, my estimate is very close.

In general, you grab something you know, scale it up or down, and adjust for any biases. Let us try it again a different way. I think the prime candidates for eating at McDonald's are between five and 30 years old. If lifespan is uniformly distributed between zero and 75 years, then that is only one-third of the population (100,000,000). Half of these people are health nuts. That leaves 50,000,000 customers. Suppose they eat four meals per week. That works out to about 30,000,000 meals served per day in the U.S. If one outlet sells a burger every 20 seconds for 10 hours per day, that is 1,800 per day per outlet. Call it 2,000. 30,000,000 meals served per day at 2,000 per outlet implies about 15,000 outlets. Same as before.

As always, find something you know and scale it up or down. Be sure to know the population of the Earth, the U.S., the city you live in, and the city you interview in.

Answer 5.5.15: A representative of the bank that asked this question about Adolf Hitler subsequently denied that anyone at their bank would have asked this question, perhaps because of the Jewish roots of the firm. Knowing bankers at that firm, however, I am confident that they asked it, but then someone senior thought it made bad PR to acknowledge it. So, be prepared for similarly distasteful questions.

This question is mostly about fit (because your answer reveals your personality and your character). It is also a little about skills (e.g., how ethical, tactful, honest, direct, etc. are you?).

They purposefully picked a well-known and deeply-hated leader to bring your character to light. They want to know whether you know more about Hitler than just the well-known negatives. For example, Hitler unified a nation suffering hyper-inflation and WWI reparation problems. His scientists invented rocket engines and subsequently worked on the Apollo program that sent men to the moon. He spurred the building of the autobahns, etc. Hitler is, of course, pretty much universally hated for being deeply evil and unethical on so many different fronts (e.g., invading innocent countries, murdering millions of Jews, exploiting slave labor, etc.).

Hitler ultimately failed in pretty much all his grandiose endeavors because of allied (and even internal) opposition to his policies and foolish and reckless mismanagement of resources (e.g., invading Russia in winter, duh!).

It's all about fit, so whatever your view, be honest, or you risk ending up at a firm where you don't fit and where you won't prosper. My professional opinion is that Hitler's deeply evil/unethical behavior and reckless mismanagement of resources make him a worthless individual and unfit for any role in any organization—no constructive outcomes can possibly compensate for these negatives. On top of that, my father served as a young man in the British Army during WWII, manning an anti-aircraft battery in England. My mother's house in England was bombed only 10 days after their family moved out of the city to a safer village. Each of my parents was a witness to fear, death and destruction that scarred them for life. So, I think the son-of-a-bitch deserves to burn in hell for eternity, and I'd have no hesitation in saying so in an interview.

Are you, however, a cut throat mercenary who applauds Hitler's leadership skills? Do you just dispassionately view him as a case study we can learn from? Whatever your view, tell the truth, make it plain and hope that you fit.

Answer 5.5.16: The answer given by the interviewer was that you should threaten to kill yourself by hitting your head against the wall. The administrative nightmare that would follow would ruin the guard's upcoming weekend. He would have to give you a cigarette.

Answer 5.5.19: You have to figure that the coin is not fair. The probability of another head is essentially one. See Huff's book, "How to Lie with Statistics," for related arguments (Huff [1982, Chapter 3]).

In one of my other books, *Foundations for Scientific Investing* (Crack, 2020b), I describe an experiment I performed in an undergraduate classroom. A student rolled a pair of dice 36 times and we recorded on how many occasions a 7 or 11 occurred.

We then compared the outcome to a binomial table. Then it was my turn. I palmed the fair dice and swapped them for a loaded pair that always gives me a 7 or 11. As the odds stacked up against me, the students watched in amazement. Even when there was only one chance in a million that what they saw could be the result of rolling fair dice, there were still a few students in a class of over a 100 stubbornly clinging to the belief that the dice were fair. If I did the same in an MBA or PhD class, the wizened students would all see through it immediately, but some undergraduates are amazingly naive.

Answer 5.5.21: I have had several comments from readers on how to weigh a jet plane: Land it on an aircraft carrier and measure the displacement of the ship; land it on the ice (e.g., Arctic) and then crash into it with something big and see how far it moves; look at the size of the tire footprints and deduce it from the tire pressure. How about just looking in the manual?

Answer 5.5.27: I spent some time at NASA's web site. NASA says there are four forces on an airplane: thrust, drag, weight and lift. These forces move the airplane forward, backward, downward, and upward, respectively, and simultaneously. For example, level forward flight would require that lift balance weight, and that thrust more than compensate for drag.

NASA indicates that there is considerable debate/confusion over how lift is generated. They describe lift as a mechanical force that is generated when a solid object moves through a fluid and "turns" the fluid flow. The shape and "angle of attack" of an airplane's wing turn the fluid flow downwards, and, by Newton's Third Law of Motion (i.e., for every action there is an equal and opposite reaction) this provides upward lift.

NASA comments that wings are often shaped so that the wing, taken in cross section, has more surface area on the top surface than the bottom surface. The air flows more quickly over the top of the wing than the bottom. The variation in velocity of the fluid creates a pressure differential that produces lift (via Bernoulli's Principle). They state, however, that this wing shape is not necessary to create lift. Rather, it only contributes to it.

Answer 5.5.34: There are several possible responses that make sense. An obvious reason is safety: a round cover cannot fall down a round hole. Whereas if both hole and cover are either square or rectangular or oval, the cover can easily fall down the hole if lifted vertically and turned diagonally and dropped. Incidentally, I noticed in New Zealand that some of their manholes have rectangular covers. However, in this case, the covers are hinged and attached to a frame that is immovable—thus preventing the cover from falling.

Another reason for being round is that the (very heavy) covers may be rolled easily. Similarly, a (very heavy) round cover need not be manipulated before being returned to its hole—it may be replaced in any orientation. Finally, and with some sarcasm, manhole covers are round because the holes that they cover are round. It is easier to drill a round hole in the street than a square one. Have you ever tried drilling a *square* hole in anything?

References

Abramowitz, Milton and Irene A. Stegun, (Eds), 1972, *Handbook of Mathematical Functions and Formulas, Graphs and Mathematical Tables*, United States Department of Commerce, National Bureau of Standards, Applied Mathematics Series, 55 (December) Tenth Printing since 1964.

Ainger, John, 2019, "Bond World Is Backing Away From All That Negativity as 2019," Available at: https://www.bloomberg.com/graphics/negative-yield-bonds/ (dated December 23, 2019; downloaded July 29, 2020).

Akgiray, Vedat, 1989, "Conditional Heteroscedasticity in the Time Series of Stock Returns: Evidence and Forecasts," *The Journal of Business*, Vol. 62 No. 1, (January), pp. 55–80.

Alexander, David Richard, Mengjia Mo, and Alan Fraser Stent, 2012, "Arithmetic Brownian Motion and Real Options," *European Journal of Operational Research*, Vol. 219 No. 1, (May), pp. 114–122.

Armstrong, Zan and Martin Wattenberg, 2014, "Visualizing Statistical Mix Effects and Simpson's Paradox," *IEEE Transactions on Visualization and Computer Graphics*, Vol. 20 No. 12, (December), pp. 1032–1041.

Arnold, Tom, and Timothy Falcon Crack, 2004, "Using the WACC to Value Real Options," *Financial Analysts Journal*, Vol. 60 No. 6, (November/December), pp. 78–82.

Arnold, Tom, Timothy Falcon Crack, and Adam Schwartz, 2009, "Inferring Risk-Averse Probability Distributions from Options Prices Using Implied Binomial Trees: Additional Theory, Empirics, and Extensions." Working paper. Available at SSRN: http://ssrn.com/abstract=749904.

Arnold, Tom, Timothy Falcon Crack, and Adam Schwartz, 2010 "Inferring Risk-Averse Probability Distributions from Options Prices Using Implied Binomial Trees." A chapter in: G.N. Gregoriou and R. Pascalau (Eds.), Financial Econometrics Handbook. Chapman-Hall-CRC/Taylor and Francis: London, UK.

Anton, Howard, 1988, *Calculus with Analytical Geometry*, Third Edition, John Wiley and Sons: New York, NY.

Ayers, Frank Jr., 1962, *Matrices*, Schaum's Outline Series; McGraw-Hill: New York, NY.

Bachelier, Louis, 1900, "Théorie de la Spéculation," *Annales de l'Ecole Normale Supéieure*, Series 3, XVII, pp. 21–86, Gauthier-Villars: Paris. Note that an English translation by A. James Boness appears in Cootner (1964).

Ball, Clifford A. and Walter N. Torous, 1985, "On Jumps in Common Stock Prices and Their Impact on Call Option Pricing," *The Journal of Finance*, Vol. 40 No. 1, (March), pp. 155–173.

Barone-Adesi, G. and Robert Whaley, 1987, "Efficient Analytic Approximation of American Option Values," *The Journal of Finance*, Vol. 42 No. 2, (June), pp. 301–320.

Bates, David S., 1995, "Testing Option Pricing Models," Working Paper, The Wharton School, University of Pennsylvania.

Baxter, Martin and Andrew Rennie, 1998, *Financial Calculus*, Cambridge University Press: Cambridge, England.

Bera, Anil, Edward Bubnys, and Hun Park, 1988, "Conditional Heteroscedasticity in the Market Model and Efficient Estimates of Betas," *The Financial Review*, Vol. 23 No. 2, (May), pp. 201–214.

Bera, Anil and Matthew L. Higgins, 1993, "ARCH models: Properties, Estimation, and Testing," *Journal of Economic Surveys*, Vol. 7 No. 4, pp. 305–366.

Berndt, Ernst K., Bronwyn Hall, Robert Hall, and Jerry A. Hausman, 1974, "Estimation and Inference in Nonlinear Structural Models," *Annals of Economic and Social Measurement*, Vol. 3 No. 4, (October), pp. 653–665.

Bernoulli, Daniel, 1738, "Speciman Theoriae Novae de Mensura Sortis," *Papers of the Imperial Academy of Sciences in Petersburg*, Vol. V, pp. 175–192. Note that an English Translation appears in Bernoulli (1954).

Bernoulli, Daniel, 1954, "Exposition of a New Theory on the Measurement of Risk," *Econometrica*, Vol. 22 No. 1, (January), pp. 23–36 (Translated from the Latin by Louise Sommer).

Bickel P.J., E.A. Hammel, and J.W. O'Connell, 1975, "Sex Bias in Graduate Admissions: Data From Berkeley," *Science*, Vol. 187 No. 4175, (February 7), pp. 398–404.

Biger, Nahum and John Hull, 1983, "The Valuation of Currency Options," *Financial Management*, Vol. 12 No. 1, (Spring), pp. 24–28.

Binswanger, K. and P. Embrechts, 1994, "Longest Runs in Coin Tossing," *Insurance: Mathematics and Economics*, Vol. 15 No. 2–3, (December), pp. 139–149.

Black, Fischer, 1975, "Fact and Fantasy in the Use of Options," *The Financial Analysts Journal*, Vol. 31 No. 4, (July/August), pp. 36–41, 61–72.

Black, Fischer, 1976, "Studies of Stock Price Volatility Changes," *Proceedings of the 1976 Business Meeting of the Business and Economic Statistics Section of the American Statistical Association*, pp. 177–181.

Black, Fischer, 1989, "How We Came Up With the Option Formula," *The Journal of Portfolio Management*, Vol. 15 No. 2, (Winter), pp. 4–8.

Black, Fischer, 1993, "Beta and Return," *The Journal of Portfolio Management*, Vol. 20 No. 1, (Fall), pp. 8–18.

Black Fischer, 1995, "Interest Rates as Options," *The Journal of Finance*, Vol. 50 No. 5 , (December), pp. 1371–1376.

Black, Fischer and Myron S. Scholes, 1972, "The Valuation of Option Contracts and a Test of Market Efficiency," *The Journal of Finance*, Vol. 27 No. 2, (May), pp. 399–417.

Black, Fischer and Myron Scholes, 1973, "The Pricing of Options and Corporate Liabilities," *Journal of Political Economy*, Vol. 81 No. 3, (May/June), pp. 637–659.

Bloomberg, 2020a, "United States Rates & Bonds," downloaded from https://www.bloomberg.com/markets/rates-bonds/government-bonds/us on March 19, 2020 (EST).

Bloomberg, 2020b, "United States Rates & Bonds," downloaded from https://www.bloomberg.com/markets/rates-bonds/government-bonds/us on March 22, 2020 (EST).

Bloomberg, 2020c, "United States Rates & Bonds," downloaded from https://www.bloomberg.com/markets/rates-bonds/government-bonds/us on July 29, 2020 (EST).

Bollerslev, Tim, 1986, "Generalized Autoregressive Conditional Heteroskedasticity," *Journal of Econometrics*, Vol. 31 No. 3, (April), pp. 307–327.

Bollerslev, Tim, 1987, "A Conditionally Heteroskedastic Time Series Model for Speculative Prices and Rates of Return," *Review of Economics and Statistics*, Vol. 69 No. 3, (August), pp. 542–547.

Bollerslev, Tim, Ray Y. Chou, and Kenneth F. Kroner, 1992, "ARCH Modeling in Finance: A Review of the Theory and Empirical Evidence," *Journal of Econometrics*, Vol. 52 No. 1/2, (April/ May), pp. 5–59.

Boyce, William E. and Richard C. DiPrima, 1997, *Elementary Differential Equations and Boundary Value Problems*, Sixth Edition, John Wiley and Sons: New York, NY.

Boyle, Phelim P., 1977, "Options: A Monte Carlo Approach," *The Journal of Financial Economics*, Vol. 4 No. 3, (May), pp. 323–338.

Brealey, Richard A. and Stewart C. Myers, 1991, *Principles of Corporate Finance*, Fourth Edition, McGraw-Hill: New York, NY.

Brenner, Menachem and Marti G. Subrahmanyam, 1988, "A Simple Formula to Compute the Implied Standard Deviation," *The Financial Analysts Journal*, Vol. 44 No. 5, (September/October), pp. 80–83.

Brock, William A., David A. Hsieh, and Blake LeBaron, 1991, *Nonlinear Dynamics, Chaos, and Instability: Statistical Theory and Economic Evidence*, MIT Press: Cambridge, MA.

Bronshtein, I.N., K.A. Semendyayev, G. Musiol, H. Muehlig, 2004, *Handbook of Mathematics*, 4th Ed., Springer: Berlin.

Brown, Robert, 1828, "A Brief Account of Microscopical Observations Made in the Months of June, July, and August, 1827, on the Particles Contained in the Pollen of Plants; and on the General Existence of Active Molecules in Organic and Inorganic Bodies," *The London and Edinburgh Philosophical Magazine and Annals of Philosophy*, Vol. 4 No. 21, pp. 161–173.

Bull, G.A., 1948, "A Broken Stick," *The Mathematical Gazette*, Vol. 32 No. 299, (May), pp. 87–88.

Butler, Alexander W. and Timothy Falcon Crack, 2019, "A Rookie's Guide to the Academic Job Market in Finance: The Labor Market for Lemons," Working Paper, (August 7, 2019). Available at SSRN: https://ssrn.com/abstract=3433785.

Cecchetti, Stephen G., 1988, "The Case of the Negative Nominal Interest Rates: New Estimates of the Term Structure of Interest Rates During the Great Depression," *The Journal of Political Economy*, Vol. 96 No. 6, (December), pp. 1111–1141.

Chance, Don M., 1994, "Translating the Greek: The Real Meaning of Call Option Derivatives," *The Financial Analysts Journal*, Vol. 50 No. 4, (July/August), pp. 43–49.

Chesney, Marc and Louis Scott, 1989, "Pricing European Currency Options: A Comparison of the Modified Black-Scholes Model and a Random Variance Model," *The Journal of Financial and Quantitative Analysis*, Vol. 24 No. 3, (September), pp. 267–284.

Chincarini, Ludwig B., 2012, *The Crisis of Crowding: Quant Copycats, Ugly Models, and the New Crash Normal*, Bloomberg Press (Wiley): Hoboken, NJ.

Chordia, Tarun and Avanidhar Subrahmanyam, 1995, "Market Making, the Tick Size, and Payment-for-Order-Flow: Theory and Evidence," *Journal of Business*, Vol. 68 No. 4, (October), pp. 543–575.

Christensen, Peter Ove, and Bjarne Sørensen. 1994. "Duration, Convexity, and Time Value." *The Journal of Portfolio Management*, Vol. 20 No. 2, (Winter), pp. 51–60.

Christensen, Ronald and Jessica Utts, 1992, "Bayesian Resolution of the 'Exchange Paradox'," *The American Statistician*, Vol. 46 No. 4, (November), pp. 274–276.

CNBC, 2019, "What Would Negative Interest Rates Mean For Consumers And The Economy?," Available at https://www.youtube.com/watch?v=FiYTmTHFa9E (dated Nov 1, 2019; downloaded July 29, 2020).

Conze, Antoine and Viswanathan, 1991, "Path Dependent Options: The Case of Lookback Options," *The Journal of Finance*, Vol. 46 No. 5, (December), pp. 1893–1907.

Cootner, Paul H., (Ed.), 1964, *The Random Character of Stock Market Prices*, MIT Press: Cambridge, MA.

Cox, J. C., J. Ingersoll, and S. Ross, 1979, "Duration and the Measurement of Basis Risk," *The Journal of Business*, Vol. 52 No. 1, (January), pp. 51–61.

Cox, J. C. and S. Ross, 1976, "The Valuation of Options for Alternative Stochastic Processes," *The Journal of Financial Economics*, Vol. 3 No. 1/2, (January/March), pp. 145–166.

Cox, J. C., S. Ross, and M. Rubinstein, 1979, "Option Pricing: A Simplified Approach," *The Journal of Financial Economics*, Vol. 7 No. 3, (September), pp. 229–263.

Cox, J. C. and Mark Rubinstein, 1985, *Options Markets*, Prentice-Hall: Englewood Cliffs, NJ.

Crack, Timothy Falcon, 1997, *Derivatives Securities Pricing*, MBA Course Notes, Indiana University, Kelley School of Business, (Spring #II), 108pp.

Crack, Timothy Falcon, 1998, "Barrier Options: Density of Return and First Passage Time for a GBM," Notes, Indiana University, Kelley School of Business, (April 1), 20pp.

Crack, Timothy Falcon, 2004, *Basic Black-Scholes: Option Pricing and Trading*. See www.BasicBlackScholes.com, and the advertisement at the end of this book, for details.

Crack, Timothy Falcon, 2018, "A Note on Karl Pearson's 1900 Chi-Squared Test: Two Derivations of the Asymptotic Distribution, and Uses in Goodness of Fit and Contingency Tests of Independence, and a Comparison with the Exact Sample Variance Chi-Square Result," Working Paper, (November 14, 2018). Available at: https://ssrn.com/abstract=3284255

Crack, Timothy Falcon, 2020a, "What Everyone Should Know: About Univariate Normality and Bivariate Normality, and How They are Co-Related with Correlation and Independence," Working Paper, (July 28, 2020). Available at: https://ssrn.com/abstract=3292639

Crack, Timothy Falcon, 2020b, *Foundations for Scientific Investing: Capital Markets Intuition and Critical Thinking Skills*, Tenth Edition. See `http://www.Foundations ForScientificInvesting.com` and the advertisement at the end of this book for details.

Crack, Timothy Falcon, 2021, *Basic Black-Scholes: Option Pricing and Trading*. Revised Fifth Edition. See `www.BasicBlackScholes.com`, and the advertisement at the end of this book, for details.

Crack, Timothy Falcon and Olivier Ledoit, 1996, "Robust Structure Without Predictability: The 'Compass Rose' Pattern of the Stock Market," *The Journal of Finance*, Vol. 51 No. 2, (June), pp. 751–762.

Crack, Timothy Falcon and Olivier Ledoit, 2010, "Using Central Limit Theorems for Dependent Data: Addressing the Pedagogical Gaps" *The Journal of Financial Education*, Vol. 36 No. 1/2, (Spring/Summer), pp. 38–60. See also the typographically clearer working paper version available at: http://ssrn.com/abstract=587562

Crack, Timothy Falcon and Sanjay K. Nawalkha, 2000, "Interest Rate Sensitivities of Bond Risk Measures," *The Financial Analysts Journal*, Vol. 56 No. 1, (January/February), pp. 34–43.

Crack, Timothy Falcon and Sanjay K. Nawalkha, 2001, "Common Misunderstandings Concerning Duration and Convexity," *Journal of Applied Finance*, Vol. 1, (October), pp. 82–92.

DeGroot, Morris H., 1989, *Probability and Statistics*, Addison-Wesley: Reading, MA.

Derman, Emanuel, 2004, *My Life as a Quant: Reflections on Physics and Finance*, Wiley: Hoboken, NJ.

Derman, Emanuel and Iraj Kani, 1993, "The Ins and Outs of Barrier Options," *Goldman Sachs Quantitative Strategies Research Notes*, Goldman, Sachs, (June).

Derman, Emanuel and Iraj Kani, 1994a, "The Volatility Smile and its Implied Tree," *Goldman Sachs Quantitative Strategies Research Notes*, Goldman, Sachs, January, 26pp.

Derman, Emanuel and Iraj Kani, 1994b, "Riding on a Smile," *Risk*, Vol. 7 No. 2, (February), pp. 139–145.

Dixit, Avinash K. and Barry J. Nalebuff, 1991, *Thinking Strategically: The Competitive Edge in Business, Politics, and Everyday Life*, Norton: New York, NY.

Dupire, Bruno, 1994, "Pricing With a Smile," *Risk*, Vol. 7 No. 1, (January), pp. 18–20.

Edwards, Franklin R. and Cindy W. Ma, 1992, *Futures and Options*, McGraw-Hill: New York, NY.

Einstein, A., 1905, "Über die von der molekularkinetischen Theorie der Wärme geforderte Bewegung von in ruhenden Flüssigkeiten suspendierten Teilchen" (On the Molecular Kinetic Theory of the Heat-Generated Motion of Particles Suspended in Fluid), *Annalen der Physik*, Series 4, Vol. 17, pp. 549–560.

Engle, Robert F., 1982, "Autoregressive Conditional Heteroscedasticity with Estimates of the Variance of United Kingdom Inflation," *Econometrica*, Vol. 50 No. 4, (July), pp. 987–1007.

Engle, Robert F., 1993, "Statistical Models for Financial Volatility," *The Financial Analysts Journal*, Vol. 49 No. 1, (January/ February), pp. 72–78.

Euclid, 2008, *Euclid's Elements of Geometry*, J.L. Heiberg (Editor), Richard Fitzpatrick (Translator), Revised and Corrected Edition, Richard Fitzpatrick: Morrisville, U.S. Originally written about 300 BC.

Evans, Merran, Nicholas Hastings, and Brian Peacock, 1993, *Statistical Distributions*, Second Edition, John Wiley and Sons: New York, NY.

Fabozzi, Frank J. and T. Dessa Fabozzi, 1995, *The Handbook of Fixed Income Securities*, Irwin: New York, NY.

Fama, Eugene, F., 1965, "The Behavior of Stock Market Prices," *The Journal of Business*, Vol. 38 No. 1, (January), pp. 34–105.

Fama, Eugene F. and Kenneth R. French, 1988, "Permanent and Temporary Components of Stock Prices," *Journal of Political Economy*, Vol. 96 No. 2, (April), pp. 246–273.

Fama, Eugene F. and Kenneth R. French, 1992, "The Cross-Section of Expected Stock Returns," *The Journal of Finance*, Vol. 47 No. 2, (June), pp. 427–465.

Fama, Eugene F. and Kenneth R. French, 1993, "Common Risk Factors in the Returns on Stocks and Bonds," *Journal of Financial Economics*, Vol. 33 No. 1, (February), pp. 3–56.

Fama, Eugene F. and Kenneth R. French, 1996, "The CAPM is Wanted, Dead or Alive," *The Journal of Finance*, Vol. 51 No. 5, (December), pp. 1947–1958.

Farlow, Stanley J., 1993, *Partial Differential Equations for Scientists and Engineers*, Dover: New York, NY.

Feller, William, 1968, *An Introduction to Probability Theory and its Applications*, Volume I, Third Edition, John Wiley & Sons: New York, NY.

Feller, William, 1971, *An Introduction to Probability Theory and Its Applications*, Volume II, Second Edition, John Wiley & Sons: New York, NY.

Ferguson, Michael F. and Richard L. Shockley, 2003, "Equilibrium Anomalies," *The Journal of Finance*, Vol. 58 No. 6, (December), pp. 2549–2580.

Fisher, L. and R. Weil, 1971, "Coping with the Risk of Interest Rate Fluctuations: Returns to Bondholders from Naive and Optimal Strategies," *The Journal of Business*, Vol. 44 No. 4, (October), pp. 408–431.

Fleming, Jeff, 1998, "The Quality of Market Volatility Forecasts Implied by S&P100 Index Option Prices," *The Journal of Empirical Finance*, Vol. 5 No. 4, (October), pp. 317–345.

Fraser, Michael K., 1993, "What It Takes to Excel in Exotics," *Global Finance*, Vol. 7 No. 3, (March), pp. 44–49.

Fry, Ron, 2016, *101 Great Answers to the Toughest Interview Questions*, Seventh Edition, Career Press: Wayne, NJ.

Garman, Mark B. and Steven W. Kohlhagen, 1983, "Foreign Currency Option Values," *Journal of International Money and Finance*, Vol. 2 No. 3, (December), 231–237.

Geske, Robert, 1979, "A Note on an Analytic Valuation Formula for Unprotected American Call Options on Stocks with Known Dividends," *Journal of Financial Economics*, Vol. 7 No. 4, (December) pp. 375–380.

Gilbert, George T., 1991, "Positive Definite Matrices and Sylvester's Criterion," *The American Mathematical Monthly*, Vol. 98 No. 1, (January), pp. 44–46.

Girsanov, I.V., 1960, "On Transforming a Certain Class of Stochastic Processes by Absolutely Continuous Substitution Measures," *Theory of Probability and its Applications*, Vol. 5, pp. 285–301.

Gleick, James, 1987, *Chaos: Making a New Science*, Penguin: New York, NY.

Glosten, Lawrence R., and Paul R. Milgrom, 1985, "Bid, ask and transaction prices in a specialist market with heterogeneously informed traders," *Journal of Financial Economics*, Vol. 14 No. 1, pp. 71–100.

Gleick, James, 1993, *Genius: The Life and Science of Richard Feynman*, Vintage Books: New York, NY.

Goldman, B.M., H.B. Sosin, and M.A. Gatto, 1979, "Path Dependent Options: 'Buy at the Low, Sell at the High'," *The Journal of Finance*, Vol. 34 No. 5, (December), pp. 1111–1127.

Goldman, B.M., H.B. Sosin, and L.A. Shepp, 1979, "On Contingent Claims That Insure Ex-Post Optimal Stock Market Timing," *The Journal of Finance*, Vol. 34 No. 2, (May), pp. 401–414.

Grabbe, J. Orlin, 1983, "The Pricing of Put and Call Options on Foreign Exchange," *Journal of International Money and Finance*, Vol. 2 No. 3, (December), pp. 239–253.

Greene, William H., 1993, *Econometric Analysis*, Second Edition, MacMillan: New York, NY.

Hammer, Jerry A., 1989, "On Biases Reported in Studies of the Black-Scholes Option Pricing Model," *Journal of Economics and Business*, Vol. 41 No. 2, (May), pp. 153–169.

Harrison, J. Michael, 1985, *Brownian Motion and Stochastic Flow Systems*, John Wiley and Sons: New York, NY.

Harrison, J.M. and S.R. Pliska, 1981, "Martingales and Stochastic Integrals in the Theory of Continuous Trading," *Stochastic Processes and Their Applications*, Vol. 11, pp. 215–260.

Haug, Espen Gaarder, 2001, "The Options Genius," *Wilmott Magazine*, (July), pp. 1–4.

Haug, Espen Gaarder, 2007, *The Complete Guide to Option Pricing Formulas*, Second Edition, McGraw-Hill: New York, NY.

Haynsworth, Emilie V., 1968, "Determination of the Inertia of a Partitioned Hermitian Matrix," *Linear Algebra and its Applications*, Vol. 1 No. 1, (January), pp. 73–81.

Hendry, David F., 1986, "An Excursion into Conditional Varianceland," *Econometric Reviews*, Vol. 5 No. 1, pp. 63–69.

Heston, Steven L., 1993, "A Closed-Form Solution for Options with Stochastic Volatility with Applications to Bond and Currency Options," *The Review of Financial Studies*, Vol. 6 No. 2, pp. 327–343.

Holland, A.S.B., 1973, *Introduction to the Theory of Entire Functions*, Academic Press: New York, NY.

Huang, Chi-fu, 1992, *Theory of Financial Markets*, Unpublished book manuscript (incomplete), Department of Finance, Sloan School of Management, MIT, Cambridge, MA 02142.

Huff, Darrell, 1982, *How to Lie with Statistics*, Norton: New York, NY.

Hull, John C., 1997, *Options, Futures, and Other Derivatives*, Third Edition, Prentice-Hall: Englewood Cliffs, NJ.

Hull, John C., 1998, *Introduction to Futures and Options Markets*, Third Edition, Prentice-Hall: Englewood Cliffs, NJ.

Hull, John and Alan White, 1987, "The Pricing of Options on Assets with Stochastic Volatilities," *The Journal of Finance*, Vol. 42 No. 2, (June), pp. 281–300.

Hull, John and Alan White, 1993, "Efficient Procedures for Valuing European and American Path-Dependent Options," *The Journal of Derivatives*, Vol. 1, (Fall), pp. 21–31.

Hunter, William C. and David W. Stowe, 1992, "Path-Dependent Options: Valuation and Applications," *Economic Review (Federal Reserve Bank of Atlanta)*, Vol. 77 No. 4, (July/August), pp. 30–43.

Jarrow, Robert and Andrew Rudd, 1983, "Approximate Option Valuation for Arbitrary Stochastic Processes," *Journal of Financial Economics*, Vol. 10 No. 3, (November), pp. 347–369.

Jarrow, Robert and Stuart Turnbull, 1996, *Derivative Securities*, South-Western College Publishing: Cincinnati, OH.

Johannes, Michael and Suresh Sundaresan, 2003, "The Impact of Collateralization on Swap Rates," working Paper, Columbia Business School (July).

Jones, Frank J., 1991, "Yield Curve Strategies," *The Journal of Fixed Income*, Vol. 1 No. 2, (September), pp. 43–51.

Jordan, Lawrence A., 2002, *The Dirty Dozen: 12 Nasty Fighting Techniques for Any Self-Defense Situation*, Paladin Press: Boulder, CO, U.S.

Kahn, Ronald N. and Roland Lochoff, 1990, "Convexity and Exceptional Return," *The Journal of Portfolio Management*, Vol. 16 No. 2, (Winter), pp. 43–47

Kahneman, David and Amos Tversky, 1982, "The Psychology of Preferences," *Scientific American*, Vol. 246, pp. 160–173.

Kotz, Samuel and Norman L. Johnson (editors-in-chief), and Campbell B. Read (associate editor), 1982, *Encyclopedia of Statistical Sciences*, Vol. 6, John Wiley and Sons: New York, NY.

Krämer, Walter and Ralf Runde, 1997, "Chaos and the Compass Rose," *Economics Letters*, Vol. 54 No. 2, (February), pp. 113–118.

Krause, Robert (editor), 1998, *Global Equity and Derivative Market Risk*, Morgan Stanley Dean Witter Quantitative Strategies Group, Morgan Stanley and Co.: New York, NY.

Kritzman, Mark P., 1992a, "What Practitioners Need to Know About Utility," *The Financial Analysts Journal*, Vol. 48 No. 3, (May/June), pp. 17–20.

Kritzman, Mark P., 1992b, "What Practitioners Need to Know About Duration and Convexity," *The Financial Analysts Journal*, Vol. 48 No. 6, (November/December), pp. 17–20.

Kritzman, Mark P., 1993a, "What Practitioners Need to Know About Factor Methods," *The Financial Analysts Journal*, Vol. 49 No. 1, (January/February), pp. 12–15.

Kritzman, Mark P., 1993b, "What Practitioners Need to Know About the Term Structure of Interest Rates," *The Financial Analysts Journal*, Vol. 49 No. 4, (July/August), pp. 14–18.

Kritzman, Mark P., 1993c, "What Practitioners Need to Know About Hedging," *The Financial Analysts Journal*, Vol. 49 No. 5, (September/October), pp. 22–26.

Kritzman, Mark P., 2003, *The Portable Financial Analyst: What Practitioners Need to Know*, Second Edition, John Wiley and Sons: New York, NY.

Kuberek, Robert C., and Norman G. Pefley, 1983, "Hedging Corporate Debt with U.S. Treasury Bond Futures," *Journal of Futures Markets*, Vol. 3 No. 4, (Winter), pp. 345–353.

Kunitomo, Naoto and Masayuki Ikeda, 1992, "Pricing Options with Curved Boundaries," *Mathematical Finance*, Vol. 2 No. 4, (October), pp. 275–298.

Kwan, Clarence C. Y., 2010, "The Requirement of a Positive Definite Covariance Matrix of Security Returns for Mean-Variance Portfolio Analysis: A Pedagogic Illustration," *Spreadsheets in Education*, Vol. 4 No. 1 (Article 4), (June), 35pp.

Lacey, Nelson J. and Sanjay K. Nawalkha, 1993, "Convexity, Risk, and Returns," *The Journal of Fixed Income*, Vol. 3 No. 3, (December), pp. 72–79.

Latané, Henry A. and Richard J. Rendleman, Jr., 1976, "Standard Deviations of Stock Price Ratios Implied in Option Prices," *The Journal of Finance*, Vol. 31 No. 2, (May), pp. 369–381.

Lewis, William Dodge, Henry Seidel Canby, and Thomas Kite Brown (editors), 1942, *The Winston Dictionary*, The John C. Winston Company: Philadelphia. PA.

Lewis, Michael M., 1990, *Liar's Poker: Rising Through the Wreckage of Wall Street*, Penguin Books: New York, NY.

Litterman, Robert, and José Scheinkman, "Common Factors Affecting Bond Returns," *The Journal of Fixed Income*, Vol. 1 No. 1, (June), pp. 54–61.

Lo, Andrew W. and A. Craig MacKinlay, 1988, "Stock Market Prices Do Not Follow Random Walks: Evidence from a Simple Specification Test," *The Review of Financial Studies*, Vol. 1 No. 1, (Spring), pp. 41–66.

Lo, Andrew W. and Jiang Wang, 1995, "Implementing Option Pricing Models When Asset Returns are Predictable," *The Journal of Finance*, Vol. 50 No. 1, (March), pp. 87–129.

Lorenz, Edward N., 1963, "Deterministic Nonperiodic Flow," *Journal of the Atmospheric Sciences*, Vol. 20 No. 2, (March), pp. 130–140.

Lyons, N.I., and K. Hutcheson, 1996, "Generation of Ordered Multinomial Frequencies," *Applied Statistics*, Vol. 45 No. 3, pp. 387–393.

Macaulay, Frederick Robertson, 1938, *Some Theoretical Problems Suggested by the Movements of Interest Rates and Stock Prices in the United States Since 1856*, National Bureau of Economic Research: New York, NY.

MacMillan, L.W., 1986, "Analytic Approximation for the American Put Option," *Advances in Futures and Options Research*, Vol. 1 Part A, pp. 119–139.

Mee, Kristjan, 2019, "Six reasons why it can make sense to buy a bond with a negative yield," Available at: https://www.cazenovecapital.com/uk/charities/insights/market-news/six-reasons-why-it-can-make-sense-to-buy-a-bond-with-a-negative-yield/ (dated September 4, 2019; downloaded July 29, 2020)

Mehran, Jamshid and Ghassem Homaifar, 1993, "Duration and Convexity for Bonds with Embedded Options: The Case of Convertibles," *The Journal of Business Finance and Accounting*, Vol. 20 No. 1, (January), pp. 107–113.

Melino, Angelo and Stuart Turnbull, 1990, "Pricing Foreign Currency Options with Stochastic Volatility," *The Journal of Econometrics*, Vol. 45 No. 1/2, (July/August), pp. 239–265.

Merton, Robert C., 1973, "Rational Theory of Option Pricing," *Bell Journal of Economics and Management Science*, Vol. 4 No. 1, (Spring), pp. 141–183. Note that this appears as Chapter 8 in Merton (1992).

Merton, Robert C., 1976, "Option Pricing When Underlying Stock Returns Are Discontinuous," *The Journal of Financial Economics*, Vol. 3 No. 1, (January/March), pp. 125–144.

Merton, Robert C., 1992, *Continuous-Time Finance*, Blackwell: Cambridge, MA.

Meyerson, Mark D., 1996, "The x^x Spindle," *Mathematics Magazine*, Vol. 69 No. 3, (June), pp. 198–206.

Minton, Bernadette A., 1997, "An Empirical Examination of Valuation Models for Plain Vanilla U.S. Interest Rate Swaps," *The Journal of Financial Economics*, Vol. 44 No. 2, (May), pp. 251–277.

Molony, James, 2019, "The Death of Yields in Six Charts," 2019, Available at: https://www.schroders.com/fr/ch/wealth-management/insights/wirtschaft/the-death-of-yields-in-six-charts/ (dated October 15, 2019; downloaded July 30, 2020).

Mongan, John, Noah Suojanen, and Eric Giguère, 2012, *Programming Interviews Exposed: Secrets to Landing Your Next Job*, Third Edition, Wrox/John Wiley and Sons: New York, NY.

Mullins, David W., 1982, "Does the Capital Asset Pricing Model Work?," *Harvard Business Review*, Vol. 60 No. 1, (January/February), pp. 105–114.

Murphy, Gareth, 1994, "When Options Price Theory Meets the Volatility Smile," *Euromoney*, No. 299, (March), pp. 66–74.

Musiela, Marek and Marek Rutkowski, 1997, *Martingale Methods in Financial Modelling*, Springer-Verlag: Berlin.

Naik, Vasanttilak and Moon Lee, 1990, "General Equilibrium Pricing of Options on the Market Portfolio with Discontinuous Returns," *The Review of Financial Studies*, Vol. 3 No. 4, pp. 493–521.

Options Clearing Corporation, 1993, *Understanding Stock Options*, (September), The Options Clearing Corporation, 440 S. LaSalle St., Suite 2400, Chicago, IL 60605.

Ostroff, Caitlin, 2020, "U.K. Government Sells Bonds at Negative Yield for First Time," Available at: https://www.wsj.com/articles/u-k-government-sells-bonds-at-negative-yield-for-first-time-11589984194 (dated May 20, 2020; downloaded July 29, 2020).

Parkinson, Michael, 1977, "Option Pricing: The American Put," *The Journal of Business*, Vol. 50 No. 1, (January), pp. 21–39.

Pearce, David, W., 1984, *The Dictionary of Modern Economics*, The MIT Press: Cambridge, MA.

Peijnenburg, Jeanne, and David Atkinson, 2013, "Biased Coins: A Model for Higher-Order Probabilities," in *European Philosophy of Science: Philosophy of Science in Europe and the Viennese Heritage*, Galavotti, Maria Carla; Nemeth, Elisabeth; Stadler, Friedrich (Eds.).

Peterson, Richard L., Christopher K. Ma, and Robert J. Ritchey, 1992, "Dependence in Commodity Prices," *The Journal of Futures Markets*, Vol. 12 No. 4, (August), pp. 429–446.

PIMCO, 2016, "Investing in a Negative Interest Rate World," Available at: https://global.pimco.com/en-gbl/resources/education/investing-in-a-negative-interest-rate-world (dated 30 November, 2016; downloaded July 29, 2020).

Poitras, Geoffrey, 2013, "Partial Immunization Bounds And Non-Parallel Term Structure Shifts," *Annals of Financial Economics*, Vol. 8 No. 2, (December), pp. 1–27.

Poterba, James and Lawrence Summers, 1988, "Mean Reversion in Stock Returns: Evidence and Implications," *Journal of Financial Economics*, Vol. 22 No. 1, (October), pp. 27–60.

Press, William H., Saul A. Teukolsky, William T. Vetterling, and Brian P. Flannery, 1996, *Numerical Recipes in C: The Art of Scientific Computing*, Second Ed., Cambridge University Press: Cambridge, UK.

Protter, 2007, "The Work of Kyoshi Itô," *Notices of the American Mathematical Society*, Vol. 54 No. 6, (June/July 2007), pp. 744–745.

Raifaizen, Claude H., 1971, "A Simpler Proof of Heron's Formula," *Mathematics Magazine*, Vol. 44 No. 1, (January), pp. 27–28.

Rao, Calyampudi Radhakrishna, 1973, *Linear Statistical Inference and its Applications*, John Wiley & Sons: New York, NY.

Redington, F.M., 1952, "Review of the Principle of Life Office Valuation," *Journal of the Institute of Actuaries*, Vol. 78 No. 3, (December), pp. 286–340.

Reitano, Robert, 1992, "Non-Parallel Yield Curve Shifts and Immunization," *Journal of Portfolio Management*, Vol. 18 No. 3, (Spring), pp. 36–43.

Rendleman, Richard J., Jr. and Brit J. Bartter, 1979, "Two-State Option Pricing," *The Journal of Finance*, Vol. 34 No. 5, (December), pp. 1093–1110.

Reuters, 2019, "UBS plans to charge rich clients for Swiss cash deposits," Available at: https://www.reuters.com/article/us-ubs-group-negative/ubs-plans-to-charge-rich-clients-for-swiss-cash-deposits-idUSKCN1UQ26A (dated August 1, 2019; downloaded July 30, 2020)

Riquier, Andrea, 2019, "Mortgage industry should prepare for new interest-rate index, Fed working group says," Available at: https://www.marketwatch.com/story/mortgage-industry-should-prepare-for-new-interest-rate-index-fed-working-group-says-2019-07-11 (dated July 14, 2019; downloaded July 29, 2020).

Richardson, Matthew, 1993, "Temporary Components in Stock Prices: A Skeptic's View," *Journal of Business and Economic Statistics*, Vol. 11 No. 2, (April), pp. 199–207.

Ritchken, Peter, L. Sankarasubramanian, and Anand M. Vijh, 1993, "The Valuation of Path Dependent Contracts on the Average," *Management Science*, Vol. 39 No. 10, (October), pp. 1202–213.

Roll, R., 1977a, "A Critique of the Asset Pricing Theory's Tests: Part I: On Past and Potential Testability of the Theory," *The Journal of Financial Economics*, Vol. 4 No. 2, (March), pp. 129–176.

Roll, R., 1977b, "An Analytical Formula for Unprotected American Call Options on Stocks with Known Dividends," *The Journal of Financial Economics*, Vol. 5 No. 2, (November), pp. 251–258.

Rubinstein, M., 1994, "Implied Binomial Trees," *The Journal of Finance*, Vol. 49 No. 3, (July), pp. 771–818.

Rushton, S., 1949, "A Broken Stick," *The Mathematical Gazette*, Vol. 33 No. 306, (December), pp. 286–288.

Samuelson, P.A., 1963, "Risk and Uncertainty: A Fallacy of Large Numbers," *Scientia*, Vol 98, (April-May), pp. 108–113.

Samuelson, Paul A., 1965, "Rational Theory of Warrant Pricing," *Industrial Management Review*, Vol. 6 No. 2, (Spring), pp. 13–31.

Samuelson, Paul A., 1973, "Mathematics of Speculative Price," *SIAM Review*, Vol. 15 No. 1, (January), pp. 1–42.

Scott, Louis O., 1987, "Option Pricing when the Variance Changes Randomly: Theory, Estimation, and an Application," *The Journal of Financial and Quantitative Analysis*, Vol. 22 No. 4, (December), pp. 419–438.

Scott, Sir Robert Falcon, 2008, *Journals: Captain Scott's Last Expedition*, Ed. Max Jones, Oxford University Press: Oxford, U.K.

Sharpe, W.F., 1964, "Capital Asset Prices: A Theory of Market Equilibrium under Conditions of Risk," *The Journal of Finance*, Vol. 19 No. 3, (September), pp. 425–442.

Sharpe, William F., 1978, *Investments*, Prentice-Hall: Englewood Cliffs, NJ.

Shaw, William, Liz McCormick, Edward Bolingbroke, and Craig Torres, 2020, "Libor's Final Retirement Date May Get Delayed Until Mid-2023," Available here: https://www.bloomberg.com/news/articles/2020-11-30/three-month-dollar-libor-may-win-retirement-reprieve-to-mid-2023 (dated December 1, 2020; downloaded August 17, 2021).

Shiu, Elias S.W., 1990, "On Redington's Theory of Immunization," *Insurance: Mathematics and Economics*, Vol. 9 No. 2–3, (September), pp. 171–175.

Shreve, Steven E., 2004, *Stochastic Calculus for Finance II: Continuous-Time Models*, Springer: New York, NY.

Smith, Clifford W., Jr., 1976, "Option Pricing: A Review," *The Journal of Financial Economics*, Vol. 3 No. 1/2, (January/March), pp. 3–51.

Snyder, Gerard L., 1969, "Alternative Forms of Options," *The Financial Analysts Journal*, Vol. 25 No. 5, (September/October), pp. 93–101.

Spiegel, Murray R., 1956, *College Algebra*, Schaum's Outline Series; McGraw-Hill: New York, NY.

Spiegel, Murray R., 1968, *Mathematical Handbook*, Schaum's Outline Series; McGraw-Hill: New York, NY.

Spiegel, Murray R., 1975, *Probability and Statistics*, Schaum's Outline Series; McGraw-Hill: New York, NY.

Spiegel, Murray R., 1981, *Advanced Calculus*, Schaum's Outline Series; McGraw-Hill: New York, NY.

Sprenkle, Case M., 1961, "Warrant Prices as Indicators of Expectations and Preferences," *Yale Economic Essays*, Vol. 1 No. 2, (Fall), pp. 178–231. Note that this paper appears in Cootner (1964).

Stone, Brad, 2014, *The Everything Store: Jeff Bezos and the Age of Amazon*, Back Bay Books (Little, Brown & Co.): Boston, MA.

Strogatz, Steven, 2009, *The Calculus of Friendship: What a Teacher and a Student Learned about Life while Corresponding about Math*, Princeton University Press: Princeton, NJ.

Sullivan, Edward J. and Timothy M. Weithers, 1991, "Louis Bachelier: The Father of Modern Option Pricing Theory," *Journal of Economic Education*, Vol. 22 No. 2, (Spring), pp. 165–171.

Sullivan, Sara, 1993, "Risk reversals," *Euromoney Treasury Manager*, (December 3), p. 15.

Sundaresan, Suresh, 1997, *Fixed Income Markets and Their Derivatives*, South-Western College Publishing: Cincinnati, OH.

Swamy, K.N., 1973, "On Sylvester's Criterion for Positive-semidefinite Matrices," *IEEE Transactions on Automatic Control*, Vol. 18 No. 3, (June), pp. 306–306.

Thompson, Christopher and Elaine Moore, 2015, "Nestlé bond yields turn negative," Available at: https://www.ft.com/content/4b5c16a8-abcb-11e4-b05a-00144feab7de (dated February 4, 2015; downloaded July 30, 2020).

Thorp, Edward O., 1973, "Extensions of the Black-Scholes Option Model," *Proceedings of the 39th Session of the International Statistical Institute, Vienna*, appearing in *Bulletin of the International Statistical Institute*, Vol. 45 Book 2, pp. 522–529.

Thorp, Edward O., 2017, *A Man for All Markets: From Las Vegas to Wall Street, How I Beat the Dealer and the Market*, Random House: New York, N.Y.

Tian, Yisong, 1993, "A Modified Lattice Approach to Option Pricing," *The Journal of Futures Markets*, Vol. 13 No. 5, (August), pp. 563–577.

Trippi, Robert R., Edward A. Brill, and Richard B. Harriff, 1992, "Pricing Options on an Asset with Bernoulli Jump-Diffusion Returns," *The Financial Review*, Vol. 27 No. 1, (February), pp. 59–79.

Tversky, Amos and Daniel Kahneman, 1974, "Judgement under Uncertainty: Heuristics and Biases," *Science*, Vol. 185, (September 27), pp. 1124–1131.

Tversky, Amos and Daniel Kahneman, 1981, "The Framing of Decisions and the Psychology of Choice," *Science*, Vol. 211, (January 30), pp. 453–458.

Wallace, Anise, 1980, "Is Beta Dead?," *Institutional Investor*, Vol. 14 No. 7, (July), pp. 23–30.

WGB, 2020, "United States Yield Curve," Available at: http://www.worldgovernmentbonds.com/country/united-states/ (dated 16 Mar 2020; downloaded 16 Mar 2020).

Whaley, Robert, 1981, "On the Valuation of American Call Options on Stocks with Known Dividends," *The Journal of Financial Economics*, Vol. 9 No. 2, (June), pp. 207–211.

White, H., 2001, *Asymptotic Theory for Econometricians*, Revised 2nd Edition, Academic Press: San Diego, CA.

Wiggins, James B., 1987, "Option Values under Stochastic Volatility," *The Journal of Financial Economics*, Vol. 19 No. 2, (December), pp. 351–372.

Wilmott, Paul, 1998, *Derivatives: The Theory and Practice of Financial Engineering*, John Wiley and Sons: Chichester, England.

Wilmott, Paul, Jeff Dewynne, and Sam Howison, 1993, *Option Pricing: Mathematical Models and Computation*, Oxford Financial Press: Oxford, England.

Wilmott, Paul, Sam Howison, and Jeff Dewynne, 1997, *The Mathematics of Financial Derivatives: A Student Introduction*, Cambridge University Press: Cambridge, England.

Winkelbauer, Andreas, 2014, "Moments and Absolute Moments of the Normal Distribution," Working Paper arXiv:1209.4340v2, available at https://arxiv.org/abs/1209.4340v2, 4pp.

Xu, Xinzhong and Stephen J. Taylor, 1995, "Conditional Volatility and the Informational Efficiency of the PHLX Currency Options Market," *The Journal of Banking and Finance*, Vol. 19 No. 5, (August), pp. 803–821.

Zheng, Harry, 2007, "Macaulay Durations for Nonparallel Shifts," *Annals of Operations Research*, Vol. 151 No. 1, (April), pp. 179–191.

Zimmerman, Heinz and Wolfgang Hafner, 2007, "Amazing Discovery: Vincenz Bronzin's Option Pricing Models," The Journal of Banking and Finance, Vol. 31, pp. 532–546.

Story: I was telephone-interviewing a candidate for an active equity research job in London. His job would be the creation, testing, and implementation of strategies for beating the market. I asked him if he could draw upon his considerable experience in the markets to suggest to me a strategy he had heard of for beating the market. There was a very long pause (at least 20 seconds, which is a long time to hear nothing down a phone line), after which he answered simply "no." What did he think I was going to ask him about?!

Alphabets and Numerical Equivalences

Greek[a]				NATO Phonetic		Roman (Latin)[a]	
α	A	Alpha	1	A	Alpha	A	50; 500
β	B	Beta	2	B	Bravo	B	300
γ	Γ	Gamma	3	C	Charlie	C	100
δ	Δ	Delta	4	D	Delta	D	500
ϵ	E	Epsilon	5	E	Echo	E	250
ζ	Z	Zeta	7	F	Foxtrot	F	40
η	H	Eta	8	G	Golf	G	400
θ	Θ	Theta	0	H	Hotel	H	200
ι	I	Iota	10	I	India	I	1
κ	K	Kappa	20	J	Juliett	J	_[b]
λ	Λ	Lambda	30	K	Kilo	K	250
μ	M	Mu	40	L	Lima	L	50
ν	N	Nu	50	M	Mike	M	1,000
ξ	Ξ	Xi	60	N	November	N	90
o	O	Omicron	70	O	Oscar	O	11
π	Π	Pi	80	P	Papa	P	400
ρ	R	Rho	100	Q	Quebec	Q	90; 500
σ	Σ	Sigma	200	R	Romeo	R	80
τ	T	Tau	300	S	Sierra	S	7;70
υ	Υ	Upsilon	400	T	Tango	T	160
ϕ	Φ[c]	Phi	500	U	Uniform	U	_[d]
χ	X[c]	Chi	700	V	Victor	V	5
ψ	Ψ[c]	Psi	700	W	Whiskey	W	_[e]
ω	Ω	Omega	800	X	X-Ray	X	10
				Y	Yankee	Y	150
				Z	Zulu	Z	2,000

[a]Some information from Lewis et al. (1942, p1161). The book is out of print and the publisher defunct.

[b]Originally the same as I.

[c]The Greek letters Φ, X, and Ψ were not needed in the medieval Latin alphabet. However, the Romans used them as numerical symbols, writing D (or M), X, and L, respectively.

[d]Originally the same as V.

[e]Not used in medieval Latin.

Index

24 Essential Tips for Selling Print Replica eBooks on Amazon: How to Capture New Readers by Turning Your Physical Book into an eBook

Timothy Falcon Crack

PhD (MIT), MCom, PGDipCom, BSc (HONS 1ˢᵗ Class), IMC

This 54-page eBook gives more than two-dozen essential tips accumulated over several years of turning self-published physical print books into "print replica" eBooks sold on `www.Amazon.com`. A print replica eBook uses a simple pdf-formatted "text block" (i.e., the inside pages of a book, as distinct from its cover). Most software packages can output pdf files. So, there is no messing around with unfamiliar EPUB or MOBI formatting, HTML code, or reflowable eBooks (i.e., where the book reorganizes itself when the reader resizes the text). I assume that you have the content written and a cover image ready, and that you can handle marketing. My only goal is to guide you through the process of getting set up to sell "print replica" eBooks on `www.Amazon.com`. Although written as if you want to turn physical print books into eBooks, this is not a prerequisite. For example, there is no physical print edition of *this* eBook, but I followed the advice given here to set it up and sell it on Amazon. If you are not selling eBooks, then you are missing out on customers who prefer (or are tempted by) immediate delivery!

The latest edition is available at all reputable online booksellers.

`www.foundationsforscientificinvesting.com/books.htm`
`timcrack@alum.mit.edu`

Interviews With
Top University Teachers

How to Build Quality Teaching,

Inspire Your Students, and

Create More Time for Research

Timothy Falcon Crack

PhD (MIT), MCom, PGDipCom, BSc (HONS 1st Class), IMC

My goal is to help university teachers to build quality into their teaching. Quality teaching should inspire students and meet learning objectives, while exploiting teaching efficiencies that create more time for research. These outcomes should, in turn, improve job satisfaction and prospects for career success. To meet these goals, I conducted interviews with a select sample of outstanding university teachers in the U.S., U.K., Australia, Israel, and New Zealand. I interwove their advice with reflections upon my own 30-year award-winning university teaching career in the U.S. and in New Zealand. The advice is accompanied by a discussion of practical attitudes towards teaching and teaching motivation, and stories (and even some horror stories) that serve as parables. The majority of the advice is based on face-to-face instruction in the classroom, but much of it carries over to remote/online teaching. Much of the advice is "purely mechanical," in the sense that you don't need any special skills or abilities to implement it. Teachers can use this book to improve their job performance and job satisfaction, and to increase the likelihood of promotion and career success. Administrators can give this book to new university teachers to help build quality teaching from Day 1.

The latest editions are available at all reputable online booksellers.

http://www.KelleySchool.com
timcrack@alum.mit.edu

Pocket Heard on The Street

Timothy Falcon Crack

PhD (MIT), MCom, PGDipCom, BSc (HONS 1ˢᵗ Class), IMC

Two pocket-sized editions of finance job interview questions. Compared with the full-sized edition of *Heard on The Street*, these pocket editions are cheaper, physically smaller, and have fewer pages. They contain a careful selection of the best questions from the full-sized edition of *Heard on The Street*. The pocket editions are easy to put in your pocket or purse, and easy to read on the subway, bus, train, or plane! *Pocket Heard on The Street: Quantitative Questions from Finance Job Interviews* is a careful selection of the 75 best quantitative questions taken from the full-sized edition of *Heard on The Street*. Presented with detailed solutions. *Pocket Heard on The Street: Brain Teasers, Thinking Questions, and Non-Quantitative Questions from Finance Job Interviews* is a careful selection of 20 brain teasers, 30 thinking questions, and over 100 non-quantitative questions taken from the full-sized edition of *Heard on The Street*. The brain teasers, and more than half the thinking questions are presented with detailed solutions. Whereas the quantitative questions in the first pocket edition usually require math/stats, the brain teasers and "thinking questions" in the second pocket edition usually require little or no math. The thinking questions fall half-way between brain teasers and true quantitative questions.

The latest editions are available at all reputable online booksellers.

http://www.InvestmentBankingJobInterviews.com
timcrack@alum.mit.edu

Basic Black-Scholes:
Option Pricing and Trading

Timothy Falcon Crack
PhD (MIT), MCom, PGDipCom, BSc (HONS 1ˢᵗ Class), IMC

This book gives extremely clear explanations of Black-Scholes option pricing theory, and discusses direct applications of the theory to option trading. The presentation does not go far beyond basic Black-Scholes for three reasons: First, a novice need not go far beyond Black-Scholes to make money in the options markets; Second, all high-level option pricing theory is simply an extension of Black-Scholes; and Third, there already exist many books that look far beyond Black-Scholes without first laying the firm foundation given here. The trading advice does not go far beyond elementary call and put positions because more complex trades are simply combinations of these. The appendix includes Black-Scholes option pricing code for the HP17B, HP19B, and HP12C. This edition includes Bloomberg screens and expanded analysis of Black-Scholes interpretations. This edition is also accompanied by two downloadable spreadsheets. The first spreadsheet allows the user to forecast profits and transactions costs for option positions using simple models. The second spreadsheet allows the user to explore option sensitivities including the Greeks.

The latest edition is available at all reputable online booksellers.

http://www.BasicBlackScholes.com
timcrack@alum.mit.edu

Foundations for Scientific Investing:
Capital Markets Intuition and
Critical Thinking Skills

Timothy Falcon Crack

PhD (MIT), MCom, PGDipCom, BSc (HONS 1st Class), IMC

This book lays a firm foundation for thinking about and conducting investment. It does this by helping to build capital markets intuition and critical thinking skills.

This book is the product of 25+ years of investment research and experience (academic, personal, and professional), and 20+ painstaking years of destructive testing in university classrooms. Although the topic is applied investments, my integration of finance, economics, accounting, pure mathematics, statistics, numerical techniques, and spreadsheets (or programming) make this an ideal capstone course at the advanced undergraduate or masters/MBA level. I adopt a heavily scientific/quantitative focus, but most of the material should be accessible to a motivated practitioner or talented individual investor with only high school level mathematics.

Contents include literature reviews in advanced areas, unanswered research questions suitable for a master's or PhD thesis, an active alpha optimization exercise using actual stock market data, advanced TVM exercises, a review of retirement topics, an extensive discussion of dividends, P/E ratios, transaction costs, the CAPM, and value versus growth versus glamour, and a review of more than 100 years of stock market performance and more than 200 years of interest rates. Special attention is paid to difficult topics like the Roll critique, smart beta, factor-based investing, and Grinold-Kahn versus Black-Litterman models. Every investor needs capital markets intuition and critical thinking skills to conduct confident, deliberate, and skeptical investment. The overarching goal of this book is to help investors build these skills.

The latest edition is available at all reputable online booksellers.

http://www.FoundationsForScientificInvesting.com
timcrack@alum.mit.edu

Foundations for Scientific Investing:
Multiple-Choice, Short Answer, and
Long-Answer Test Questions

Timothy Falcon Crack

PhD (MIT), MCom, PGDipCom, BSc (HONS 1st Class), IMC

This book accompanies *Foundations for Scientific Investing*. It provides 600+ test questions (600+ multiple-choice, 125 short-answer questions, and the long-answer questions already appearing in *Foundations for Scientific Investing*). Suggested solutions to the multiple-choice and short-answer questions are given. These solutions are also available, free of charge, at the Web site for the book. If you have purchased the eBook version of this book (which uses DRM-PDF and is not able to be printed), it might be easiest to print out the Web-based solutions to consult while viewing the eBook questions. The multiple choice questions may also be useful as a test bank for instructors in any advanced investments class.

The latest edition is available at all reputable online booksellers.

http://www.FoundationsForScientificInvesting.com
timcrack@alum.mit.edu

How to Ace Your Business Finance Class: Essential Knowledge and Techniques to Master the Material and Ace Your Exams

Timothy Falcon Crack

PhD (MIT), MCom, PGDipCom, BSc (HONS 1st Class), IMC

This pocket-sized book is aimed at students in their first finance class at the undergraduate, MBA, or executive education level. I use 25 years of experience teaching this material to explain carefully the stumbling blocks that have consistently tripped up students year after year. This gives every student every opportunity to master the material. I also present safe strategies I have developed to help you solve numerical problems. Although these strategies take only an extra minute to implement, they frame each numerical problem so as to increase the likelihood that you detect and fix any errors, while reducing the likelihood that you make any errors in the first place. These techniques also increase the likelihood that you earn partial credit. Although this book is aimed primarily at students, the fact that I focus on essential knowledge and techniques also makes this book useful to instructors. The chapters of the book are as follows: Foundations, Financial Statements, TVM I (One Cash Flow), TVM II (Multiple Cash Flows), Inflation and Indices, Bonds and Interest Rates, Equities and Dividend Discount Models, Capital Budgeting I (Decision Rules), Capital Budgeting II (Cash Flows), Capital Budgeting III (Cost of Capital), Capital Budgeting IV (A Paradox), The CAPM and Interest Rates, Risk and Return, Market Efficiency, Capital Structure, and Dividends.

The latest edition is available at all reputable online booksellers.

www.foundationsforscientificinvesting.com/books.htm
timcrack@alum.mit.edu

PUBREF:2021.08.19.15:52.1,242,513.OU

CPSIA information can be obtained
at www.ICGtesting.com
Printed in the USA
LVHW061117140323
741587LV00014B/1294

9 781991 155412